Jesus as the Pierced One

McMaster Divinity College Press
**McMaster Biblical Studies Series,
Volume 4**

Jesus as the Pierced One
The Use of Zechariah 12:10 in John's Gospel and Revelation

BRET A. ROGERS

Foreword by Paul M. Hoskins

◆PICKWICK *Publications* · Eugene, Oregon

JESUS AS THE PIERCED ONE
The Use of Zechariah 12:10 in John's Gospel and Revelation

McMaster Biblical Studies Series, Volume 4
McMaster Divinity College Press

Copyright © 2020 Bret A. Rogers. All rights reserved. Except for brief quotations in critical publications or reviews, no part of this book may be reproduced in any manner without prior written permission from the publisher. Write: Permissions, Wipf and Stock Publishers, 199 W. 8th Ave., Suite 3, Eugene, OR 97401.

Pickwick Publications
An Imprint of Wipf and Stock Publishers
199 W. 8th Ave., Suite 3
Eugene, OR 97401

McMaster Divinity College Press
1280 Main Street West
Hamilton, Ontario, Canada
L8S 4K1

www.wipfandstock.com

PAPERBACK ISBN: 978-1-5326-9640-4
HARDCOVER ISBN: 978-1-5326-9641-1
EBOOK ISBN: 978-1-5326-9642-8

Cataloguing-in-Publication data:

Names: Rogers, Bret A., author. | Hoskins, Paul M., foreword.

Title: Jesus as the pierced one : the use of Zechariah 12:10 in John's gospel and Revelation / Bret A. Rogers; foreword by Paul M. Hoskins.

Description: Eugene, OR: Pickwick Publications, 2019. | McMaster Biblical Studies Series 4. | Includes bibliographical references and indexes.

Identifiers: ISBN 978-1-5326-9640-4 (paperback). | ISBN 978-1-5326-9641-1 (hardcover). | ISBN 978-1-5326-9642-8 (ebook).

Subjects: LCSH: Bible. John—Criticism, interpretation, etc. | Bible. Revelation—Criticism, interpretation, etc. | Bible. Zechariah—Criticism, interpretation, etc. | Christology.

Classification: BS2615.52 R63 2020 (paperback). | BS2615.52 (ebook).

Manufactured in the U.S.A.   06/03/20

To Rachel,
my beloved and faithful wife,
Luke, Levi, Anna, and Abigail,
who all helped me finish well

Contents

Foreword by Paul M. Hoskins / ix

Preface / xi

Abbreviations / xiii

1. Introduction / 1
2. Yahweh as the Pierced One: Zech 12:10 / 25
3. The Pierced One's First Redeeming Advent: John 19:37 / 78
4. The Pierced One's Second Redeeming Advent: Rev 1:7 / 121
5. Looking on the Pierced One Now: The Implications for John's Readers / 167
6. Conclusion / 218

Appendix 1: Comparative Analysis of Zech 12:10, 12a in John 19:37 and Rev 1:7 / 227

Appendix 2: Comparative Analysis of Early Greek Translations of Zech 12:10 / 229

Appendix 3: Proposed Identifications of the Pierced One / 230

Bibliography / 231

Index of Modern Authors / 259

Index of Ancient Sources / 265

Foreword

I HAVE HAD THE privilege of seeing this project develop from a seminar paper into a dissertation and now into a book. In this work, Bret Rogers defends a particular view of Zech 12:10, which has significant implications for John's use of this verse in John 19:37 and Rev 1:7. He shows that it is possible, and even likely, that Zech 12:10 refers to the piercing of God, and not merely the piercing of God's human representative. As Rogers argues in chapter 2, the Septuagint's odd translation of Zech 12:10 supports the idea that such a piercing would be hard to make sense of prior to the piercing of Jesus, who is God in the flesh (John 1:14). Rogers's work on Zech 12:10 and John 19:37 provides a helpful challenge to the many interpreters who opt to see in Zech 12:10 only the piercing of God's representative. In addition, a number of interpreters have worked out possible interpretations of the various elements of John 19:37's quotation of Zech 12:10 ("They will look on him whom they have pierced"). They have rarely, however, considered how John 19:37's quotation of Zech 12:10 could be related to John's allusion to the same verse in Rev 1:7. Even those who have noted and commented on the connection have not treated the significance of this commonality with the type of depth that one finds in Rogers's work. This is surprising, since scholars commonly note that the use of Zech 12:10 is one of the clear commonalities between the Gospel of John and Revelation.

Everyone who reads this work will emerge indebted to Rogers for his detailed, plausible interpretations of Zech 12:10, John 19:37, and Rev 1:7. He provides food for thought that will be helpful for all, even for those who remain unconvinced by his main points. John ties these

Foreword

verses together and Rogers attempts to interpret the connections between them. Along the way, he shows forth the marvelous richness of these verses, which are capable of being the focus of an entire book (like this one) and of several years of concentrated work (for Bret Rogers).

Paul M. Hoskins, Ph.D.
Southwestern Baptist Theological Seminary
Fort Worth, Texas

Preface

Before he fell asleep in the Lord, I remember talking with my Opa on the phone while he was in the hospital. John 1:18 was the text that afternoon: "No one has ever seen God; the only God, who is at the Father's side, he has made him known." "That's the key," he told me. "Once you see that Jesus is God, everything else in the Bible makes sense; it just falls into place. People have got to understand that." Having spent the last several years studying John's use of Zech 12:10, I could not agree more with my Opa's assertion. I only hope that what I have written in the following pages will help people to understand God's self-revelation in Jesus Christ and to see in his piercing the coming of God to save his elect before replacing all rebel kingdoms with his own. Until that Day of glory comes, let all thanksgiving abound to his name.

I am thankful the Lord provided Paul Hoskins to advise me through my doctoral studies, from which the current book sprang. Paul offered competent direction as a professor, constructive criticism as a reader, and consistent encouragement as a brother in Christ. He also prayed for me regularly. I am also thankful that Mark Taylor agreed to read my dissertation. He taught my first seminary class for the MDiv; it was fitting to have him see me through the last step for the PhD. Mark set the bar high for every professor thereafter in clear pedagogy and godly character. I am also thankful for George Klein. In terms of careful research and writing, no one has been more influential. I can still hear his counsel: "Writing is a lot like herding cattle; if you leave a gate open, they're going to go through it." George was a kind companion, knowing my weaknesses and supporting me still. I am also thankful to

Preface

Stanley Porter, David Fuller, and MDC Press for considering my work, offering careful feedback, and granting me the opportunity to publish with them.

The Lord also used Redeemer Church in Fort Worth. Members encouraged me. Some prayed for me. All of them welcomed eighty sermons through John's Gospel and twenty-three sermons through Zechariah. My fellow elders were always the first to hear me rant about quitting this project, and always the first to help me reevaluate my desires, admonish me in Christ, and counsel me away from pursuing my own comforts. The elders also helped shoulder the load when I devoted myself to writing. I thank the Lord for Bryan Walker, whose voluminous library was always nearby and served me well. I was never lacking in enough resources. Jonathan Watson ran this race before me, and his brotherly love helped me persevere when my confidence was waning.

The Lord also graced me with parents who cheered me on. More importantly, Allen and Kellie Rogers kept me looking on the pierced Jesus for strength, and mom gave me feedback on each chapter as they rolled out. My in-laws, David and Laurel Fort, persevered in prayer for me, and throughout their missionary endeavors were a continuous reminder that God's grace is sufficient. My children, Luke, Levi, Anna, and Abigail could not have been more patient with the work required to finish this project. I will never forget Luke's exhortation on the evening I truly wanted to give up: "It's just like mom always tells me, do your work unto the Lord, and work hard until it's done." Speaking of his mom, the Lord has given me such a wonderful gift in Rachel. She is an excellent wife, my partner in grace, and the sacrifices she made to see me finish are countless. When my soul felt dry and dead, she brought me Jesus. To him be blessing and glory and wisdom and thanksgiving, forever and ever.

Bret A. Rogers
Fort Worth, Texas
August 2017

Abbreviations

AB	Anchor Bible
ABD	Freedman, David Noel, ed. *The Anchor Bible Dictionary.* 6 vols. New York: Doubleday, 1992.
AnBib	Analecta Biblica
AOTC	Abingdon Old Testament Commentary
ArBib	The Aramaic Bible
ATDan	Acta Theologica Danica
ATR	*Anglican Theological Review*
AUSS	*Andrews University Seminary Studies*
BBR	*Bulletin for Biblical Research*
BDAG	Bauer, Walter, et al. *Greek-English Lexicon of the New Testament and Other Early Christian Literature.* 3rd ed. Chicago: University of Chicago Press, 2000.
BDB	Brown, Francis, et al. *Hebrew and English Lexicon of the Old Testament.* Oxford: Clarendon, 1907.
BECNT	Baker Exegetical Commentary on the New Testament
BETL	Bibliotheca ephemeridum theologicarum lovaniensium
BHK	*Biblia Hebraica.* Edited by Rudolph Kittel. Liepzig: Hinrichs, 1905–1906.
BHS	*Biblia Hebraica Stuttgartensia.* Edited by Karl Elliger and Wilhelm Rudolph. Stuttgart: Deutsche Bibelgesellschaft, 1983.
Bib	*Biblica*
BibAn	*Biblical Annuals*

Abbreviations

BJRL	*Bulletin of the John Rylands Library*
BNTC	Black's New Testament Commentary
BR	*Biblical Research*
BST	Bible Speaks Today
BZ	*Biblische Zeitschrift*
BZAW	Beihefte zur Zeitschrift für die alttestamentliche Wissenschaft
CAT	Commentaire de l'Ancien Testament
CBET	Contributions to Biblical Exegesis and Theology
CBQ	*Catholic Biblical Quarterly*
ConBNT	Coniectanea Neotestamentica
CTR	*Criswell Theological Review*
CurBS	*Currents in Research: Biblical Studies*
CurBR	*Currents in Biblical Research*
DJD	Discoveries in the Judaean Desert
DSS	Dead Sea Scrolls
EBC	Expositor's Bible Commentary
EBib	*Etudes bibliques*
ECNT	Exegetical Commentary on the New Testament
ESV	English Standard Version
ET	English Translation
ETL	*Ephemeridum theologicarum lovaniensium*
EvQ	*Evangelical Quarterly*
FB	Forschung zur Bibel
FOTL	Forms of the Old Testament Literature
GKC	*Gesenius' Hebrew Grammar*. Edited by Emil Kautzsch. Translated by Arther E. Cowley. 2nd ed. Oxford: Clarendon, 1910.
HALOT	Koehler, Ludwig, et al. *The Hebrew and Aramaic Lexicon of the Old Testament*. Translated and edited under the supervision of Mervyn E. J. Richardson. 4 vols. Leiden: Brill, 1994–1999.

Abbreviations

HAR	*Hebrew Annual Review*
HBS	Herders biblische Studien
HCSB	Holman Christian Standard Bible
HNTC	Harper's New Testament Commentary
HTKNT	Herders theologischer Kommentar zum Neuen Testament
HUCA	*Hebrew Union College Annual*
IBHS	Bruce K. Waltke and Michael O'Connor. *An Introduction to Biblical Hebrew Syntax*. Winona Lake, IN: Eisenbrauns, 1990.
IBS	*Irish Biblical Studies*
ICC	International Critical Commentary
IJST	*International Journal for Studies in Theology*
IVPNTC	IVP New Testament Commentary
JBL	*Journal of Biblical Literature*
JBT	Jarbuch für biblische Theologie
JETS	*Journal of the Evangelical Theological Society*
Joüon	Joüon, Paul. *A Grammar of Biblical Hebrew*. Translated and revised by T. Muraoka. 2 vols. Rome: Pontifical Biblical Institute, 1991.
JSNTSup	Journal for the Study of the New Testament Supplement Series
JSOT	Journal for the Study of the Old Testament
JSOTSup	Journal for the Study of the Old Testament Supplement Series
KHC	Kurzer Hand-Commentar
LBT	Library of Biblical Theology
LHBOTS	The Library of Hebrew Bible/Old Testament Studies
LNTS	The Library of New Testament Studies
LXX	*Septuaginta: Vetus Testamentum graecum auctoritate societatis litterarum gottingensis editum*
MT	Masoretic Text

Abbreviations

MwJT	*Midwestern Journal of Theology*
NAC	New American Commentary
NASB	New American Standard Bible
NCB	New Century Bible
NDBT	Alexander, T. Desmond, et al., eds. *New Dictionary of Biblical Theology: Exploring the Unity and Diversity of Scripture.* Downers Grove, IL: InterVarsity, 2000.
Neot	*Neotestamentica*
NET	New English Translation
NICNT	New International Commentary on the New Testament
NICOT	New International Commentary on the Old Testament
NIDOTTE	VanGemeren, Willem A., ed. *New International Dictionary of Old Testament Theology and Exegesis.* 5 vols. Grand Rapids: Zondervan, 1997.
NIGTC	New International Greek Testament Commentary
NIV	New International Version
NIVAC	NIV Application Commentary
NJB	New Jerusalem Bible
NovTSup	Novum Testamentum Supplment
NRSV	New Revised Standard Version
NSBT	New Studies in Biblical Theology
NT	New Testament
NTL	New Testament Library
OBO	Orbis biblicus et orientalis
OT	Old Testament
OTL	Old Testament Library
OtSt	*Oudtestamentische Studiën*
PNTC	Pillar New Testament Commentary
POuT	De Prediking van het Oude Testament
ProEccl	*Pro Ecclesia*
PRSt	*Perspectives in Religious Studies*
RB	*Revue Biblique*

Abbreviations

ResQ	*Restoration Quarterly*
RSR	*Recherches de science religieuse*
SB	Sources bibliques
SBB	Stuttgarter biblische Beiträge
SBJT	*Southern Baptist Journal of Theology*
SBLDS	Society of Biblical Literature Dissertation Series
SBLRBS	Society of Biblical Literature Resources for Biblical Study
SBLSymS	Society of Biblical Literature Symposium Series
ScEccl	*Sciences ecclésiastiques*
SCJ	*Stone-Campbell Journal*
SEBS	Scholars' Editions in Biblical Studies
SNTSMS	Society for New Testament Studies Monograph Series
SP	Sacra Pagina
SWJT	*Southwestern Journal of Theology*
TDNT	Kittel, Gerhard, and Gerhard Friedrich, eds. *Theological Dictionary of the New Testament*. Translated by Geoffrey W. Bromiley. 10 vols. Grand Rapids: Eerdmans, 1964–1976.
ThKNT	Theologischer Handkommentar zum Neuen Testament
TNTC	Tyndale New Testament Commentary
TOTC	Tyndale Old Testament Commentary
TrinJ	*Trinity Journal*
TS	*Theological Studies*
UF	*Ugarit-Forschungen*
VL	Vulgate
VT	*Vetus Testamentum*
VTSup	Supplements to Vetus Testamentum
WBC	Word Biblical Commentary
WMANT	Wissenschaftliche Monographien zum Alten und Neuen Testament
WTJ	*Westminster Theological Journal*

Abbreviations

WUNT	Wissenschaftliche Untersuchungen zum Neuen Testament
ZAW	*Zeitschrift für die alttestamentliche Wissenschaft*
ZBK	Zürcher Bibelkommentare
ZNW	*Zeitschrift für die neutestamentliche Wissenschaft und die Kunde der älteren Kirche*

1

Introduction

ZECHARIAH 12:10 STANDS AS an obscure prophecy for interpreters of Scripture, whether ancient or modern.¹ Beyond the diverse reception-history, text-critical problems, unusual grammar, and contextual ambiguities, the challenging question remains, "Who shall we say Zechariah's Pierced One is?" The Apostle John apparently finds resolution to Zechariah's prophecy in the person and mission of Jesus, referencing it once for Jesus' ignominious death (John 19:37) and again for Jesus' glorious return (Rev 1:7). Yet for all the mounting scholarship devoted to the NT writers' use of the OT,² including John's use of Zechariah in particular,³ no in-depth treatment exists for how John's

1. For the various difficulties involved with Zech 12:10, see Condamin, "Le Sens Messianique," 52–56; Sæbø, *Sacharja*, 96–103; Lacocque, *Zacharie*, 188–92; Devillers, "Le Transpercé," 87–104; Deissler, "Sach 12,10," 49–60; Mason, "Earlier Biblical Material," 234–40; Hübenthal, *Transformation*, 192–216; Bilić, *Jerusalem*, 328–58; Kubiś, *Zechariah in John*, 115–46. Kubiś (*Zechariah in John*, 146–71) offers the most extensive critical interaction with the earliest interpretations of Zech 12:10, including the ancient Greek, Syriac, and Targumic renderings.

2. Beginning with a groundbreaking work in the research of the NT writers' use of OT texts, some of the major works in NT studies by decade include the following: Dodd, *According to the Scriptures*; Lindars, *New Testament Apologetic*; Baker, *Two Testaments*; Carson and Williamson, eds., *It Is Written*; Beale, ed., *Right Doctrine*; Longenecker, *Biblical Exegesis*; Beale and Carson, eds., *Commentary*; Beale, *Handbook*.

3. See, e.g., Moo, *Old Testament*, 173–221; Black, "Slain Messiah," 97–114; Menken, "Quotations," 570–78; Duguid, "Messianic Themes," 265–80; Menken, *Old Testament Quotations*, 79–97, 187–203; Tuckett, *Zechariah and Its Influence*; Ham,

use of Zech 12:10 builds on an understanding of Jesus' divine identity in his eschatological mission, especially when considered in light of a joint study of John 19:37 and Rev 1:7.

THESIS

This study will examine how John's use of Zech 12:10 builds on an understanding of God's self-disclosure in Jesus' two-fold eschatological mission. John 19:37 will provide the initial insight to how God's self-disclosure in Jesus enables John to link the piercing of Jesus' side with the fulfillment of Zechariah's puzzling promise that people will somehow pierce Yahweh. Revelation 1:7 will then give further insight to how God's self-disclosure in Jesus enables John to maintain the eschatological elements of Zechariah's prophecy such that Jesus' piercing is both prerequisite for and fundamental to God's eschatological work. The purpose in bringing John 19:37 and Rev 1:7 into a single study is to demonstrate that God's self-revelation in Jesus appears to provide John the interpretive key that unlocks the mysterious promise of Zech 12:10. Considering the piercing of Jesus, whom John presents as God the Son incarnate, it becomes apparent how God receives the piercing as part and parcel to his eschatological work of salvation.

In order to pursue such a thesis, two major objectives stand in the way. First, it is necessary to investigate the identity of the Pierced One in Zech 12:10 and demonstrate the validity of understanding the Pierced One's identity as more than a human representative of Yahweh but as Yahweh himself. This first objective will also help gauge whether John imposes onto Zech 12:10 a meaning that was never present, or imports from Zech 12:10 a meaning that was justifiably always present yet hidden until God's final self-disclosure in Jesus Christ.

Second, I must investigate how the apostle John uses Zech 12:10 in the Fourth Gospel and Revelation in order to help his readers understand the Christological and eschatological significance of Jesus' crucifixion and return. Sound exegesis will demand giving adequate attention to the immediate contexts of John 19:37 and Rev 1:7 as well as to the broader narrative elements John employs for his theological

---

The Coming King; Jauhiainen, *Use of Zechariah*; Hübenthal, *Transformation*, 78–79, 165–77, 215–16; Kubiś, *Zechariah in John*, 171–218.

Introduction

presentation within each book. Also, a careful consideration of John's hermeneutical presuppositions will transpire in determining John's exegetical warrant for appropriating Zech 12:10 to explain Jesus' death and return the way he does. Inevitably, our study must also answer how and why John appropriates the same OT text for two separate events in Jesus' eschatological mission, his death and his return.

Pursuing the aforementioned thesis aligns with other contributions surrounding the NT writers' use of the OT, especially those related to the use of Zechariah.[4] Indeed, the following investigation into John's use of Zech 12:10 even finds precedent as far back as Justin Martyr (*Dial.* 32.2; cf. *1 Apol.* 52.11–12).[5] Nevertheless, the following study will contribute to the field of NT studies in at least four ways.

First, I will argue that identifying the Pierced One as Yahweh is a credible and defensible reading of Zech 12:10. Even the Jewish and Christian interpretations that, in my estimation, rightly understand Zech 12:10 along lines of future messianic hope inadequately explain the piercing of Yahweh, since they restrict the piercing to Yahweh's human messianic representative. Second, I will argue that John's use of Zech 12:10 to explain Jesus' identity and mission is credible, because Zechariah identifies Yahweh as the Pierced One and not merely with the Pierced One, a notion previous studies regularly overlook but which aligns well with John's development of God's self-disclosure in Jesus. Third, an in-depth study on the significance of the Pierced One's identity in Rev 1:7 is lacking, and the following study will fill that void. Fourth, by treating John 19:37 and Rev 1:7 as complementary elements within John's unified, eschatological narrative, the following study will be able to observe what previous research overlooks with respect to John's use of Zech 12:10, such as the eschatological nature of Jesus' death and the theological implications for the church's mission to the

---

4. See, e.g., Moo, *Old Testament*, 210–15; Black, "Slain Messiah," 81–85, 213–21; Menken, "Quotations," 570–78; Menken, "Textual Form," 494–511; Duguid, "Messianic Themes," 265–80; Devillers, "L'interprétation," 135–44; Hultberg, "Messianic Exegesis," 101–10; Tuckett, *Zechariah and Its Influence*, 111–21; Ham, *The Coming King*, 26–173; Jauhiainen, *Use of Zechariah*; Hübenthal, *Transformation*, 165–216; Kubiś, *Zechariah in John*, 27–480.

5. Skarsaune, *Proof from Prophecy*, 77–78, 154–56, 311.

nations before Jesus' return.[6] Such are the contributions the following study will pursue. Of course, none of them originated without the help of previous research on Zech 12:10 and John's use of it in John 19:37 and Rev 1:7. To this survey we now turn.

HISTORY OF RESEARCH

The survey of research will progress in three basic sections. The first section will survey the literature pertaining to the identity of the mysterious Pierced One in Zech 12:10 quite apart from its use by John and show where room exists for further refinement. Section two will lay out how interpreters have handled John's use of Zech 12:10 in John 19:37. The primary goal is to show that room for further work exists in explaining how and why John links Zechariah's Pierced One to Jesus' divine identity, especially in light of the cross, the climactic point of God's self-revelation in the Son. Lastly, section three will review literature on John's use of Zech 12:10 in Rev 1:7 and demonstrate that existing answers to how Zech 12:10 functions in Rev 1:7 and to how the prophecy contributes to John's theology throughout Revelation need development.

Survey of Literature on Zech 12:10

We begin, then, with research surrounding the identity of the Pierced One in Zech 12:10. While the diverse reception-history, text-critical problems, grammatically unusual constructions, and contextual ambiguities of Zech 12:10 could warrant a survey of its own, the following will only survey how interpreters answer the central interpretive question of Zech 12:10, "Who shall we say Zechariah's Pierced One

---

6. Previous studies seem to be more focused on identifying textual forms in John 19:37 and Rev 1:7 and clarifying their historical function. See, e.g., Menken, "Textual Form," 494–511; Schuchard, *Scripture within Scripture*, 141–49. These studies offer many helpful insights, but my aim is to offer a coherent treatment of all three texts together (i.e., Zech 12:10; John 19:37; Rev 1:7) along with their interconnected themes, especially in terms of John's theology. Highlighting a weakness in Schuchard's work, Evans concludes with a question I hope to answer: "It is good to know on which OT version the evangelist has depended, and it is equally helpful to observe how the evangelist has incorporated his quotations into his narrative, but how does knowing this significantly advance our understanding of Johannine theology?" Evans, "Scripture within Scripture," 824.

Introduction

is?" Answers to the latter question have included numerous referents over the centuries, but all of them fall into one of five major views.[7] Since more extensive interaction with the five views occurs in chapter 2, I will only summarize the five views here and show how my thesis corresponds to prior research.

Few argue for a past-collective identification of the Pierced One in Zech 12:10. The past-collective view identifies the Pierced One as a collective martyr whose death occurred prior to Zechariah's prophecy. That is, the singular reference to a Pierced One represents a larger body of people that actually suffers the piercing. Moreover, the past-collective view interprets the collective piercing as a past event to Zechariah's audience, such as the slaying of the Benjaminites in Judg 20:45–47.[8]

More popular is the present-collective identity of the Pierced One. The present-collective view makes a claim similar to the past-collective view by interpreting the Pierced One in a collective sense. However, these interpreters shift the occasion of the piercing from the past to the present, thereby associating the piercing with Zechariah's contemporaries, whether Jewish martyrs, prophetic figures, visionary disciples, or oppressed Judahites.[9]

The past-singular comes next in our five major views, since, to my knowledge, no collective interpretation for a time future to Zechariah exists. The past-singular view not only rejects a collective referent in the pronouns surrounding the Pierced One of Zech 12:10, but the past-singular view also includes identifications of the Pierced One associated with historical figures who died before the post-Exilic period in which Zechariah prophesied. Options usually include men like King Josiah (2 Chron 35:22–25), Gedaliah (2 Kgs 25:25; Jer 41:1–2), Uriah, son of

---

7. See the table in Appendix 3 for assistance. To my knowledge, no other work on Zech 12:10 organizes the research as I have done here into the five major categories.

8. Van Hoonacker, *Les Douze*, 682. See others mentioned in Chary, *Aggée-Zacharie*, 202.

9. See, e.g., Cohen, *Twelve Prophets*, 321; Lacocque, *Zacharie 9–14*, 191–92; Meyers and Meyers, *Zechariah 9–14*, 339; Mason, "Earlier Biblical Material," 165; Hanson, *Dawn of Apocalyptic*, 365–68; Troki, *Faith Strengthened*, 181–85; Kimḥi and M'Caul, *Prophecies of Zechariah*, 156–58; Floyd, *Minor Prophets*, 524–25.

Shemiah (Jer 26:20), and Zechariah, son of Jehoiada (2 Kgs 24:20–22; 2 Chron 24:20–22).[10]

Still others argue for a present-singular view. Interpreters in this fourth category also affirm the singular referent and believe that individuals serving in roles more relevant to Zechariah's audience are the most suitable candidates for the Pierced One. Contemporaries of Zechariah usually set forward as the Pierced One include Zerubbabel, Simon Maccabeus (1 Macc 16:11–17), Onias III (2 Macc 4:34), Joshua the high priest (*Ant.* 11.7.1), an unnamed prophet of Yahweh, or someone killed in the war of Zech 12:1–8.[11]

But the most prevalent singular view—and the most prevalent of all five major views categorized here—goes to the future-singular identification of the Pierced One. The future-singular view maintains a referent to a unique individual, but then interprets the prophet's words to be more future-oriented than any of the other views are willing to grant. Consistently, the conclusion is that the Pierced One of Zech 12:10 signifies a future messianic figure who stands as God's representative for Israel.[12]

Within the future-singular view, the works of Anthony R. Petterson, Niko Bilić, and Adam Kubiś provide the most extensive treatment of the identity of the Pierced One in Zech 12:10. My own thesis will attempt to build on their works and show where I believe further refinement exists for the identity of the Pierced One in Zech 12:10. For example, Petterson interacts with the exegetical details of Zech 12:10

---

10. Respectively, see the discussions in Mitchell, *Zechariah*, 330; Otzen, *Studien*, 173–74; Lévy, "Sacharja 12,10," 293–96; Meyers and Meyers, "Fortunes," 215–29.

11. Respectively, see the discussions in Lamarche, *Zacharie IX–XIV*, 120–21; Conrad, *Zechariah*, 183; Oesterley, *A History of Israel*, 269–71; Marti, *Das Dodekapropheton*, 447; Plöger, *Theokratie Und Eschatologie*, 105–8.

12. Some rabbinic traditions ascribe the piercing of Zech 12:10 to Messiah ben Ephraim, whom Gog will pierce in a final battle (*b. Sukk.* 52a). Similarly, see Targumic Tosefta in Mitchell, "Messiah," 223. See also Condamin, "Le Sens Messianique," 56; Lamarche, *Zacharie IX–XIV*, 120–30; Chary, *Aggée-Zecharie*, 204–6; Brandenburg, *Die Kleinen Propheten*, 110; Keil and Delitzsch, *Twelve Minor Prophets*, 388; McComiskey, "Zechariah," 1214; Selman, "Messianic Mysteries," 299; Kaiser, *Messiah in OT*, 223–26; Kohler, *Die Nachexilischen Propheten*, 206; Achtemeier, *Nahum–Malachi*, 161–63; Baldwin, *Zechariah*, 198; Cooke, "Unknown Martyr," 100; Boda, *Haggai, Zechariah*, 488; Duguid, "Messianic Themes," 275; Merrill, *Zechariah*, 320; Petterson, *Behold Your King*, 237–41.

Introduction

only in limited fashion, since his study has much broader aims. In my assessment, he has not advanced the discussions of prior commentators.

Bilić and Kubiś spend more time handling the exegetical minutiae of Zech 12:10. Nevertheless, several areas could use further attention. For instance, Bilić helpfully argues that the grammatical construction אֵת אֲשֶׁר functions the same way in Zech 12:10 and Jer 38:9, but I will build on his insight from additional OT passages that reflect the same grammatical construction, such as found in 1 Sam 16:3, 1 Sam 28:8, and Ezek 23:22. Also, Kubiś gives a footnote to the possibility of style having a potential bearing on the alternation of suffixes, but appears to dismiss the overall significance.[13] However, the following research will unveil several other passages that contain stylistic nuances similar to those found in Zech 12:10. Passages such as Isa 37:21–22, Isa 45:24, Zech 7:13, and Zech 9:9–10 should not only give further credence to the unique style found in Zech 12:10, but also lead to further precision regarding the same referent in the object of looking and the object of piercing than Kubiś seems willing to allow.[14] Finally, Kubiś and others have labored toward a plausible explanation for the LXX's odd rendering of Zech 12:10. However, previous studies have overlooked the way the LXX renders other OT passages wherein a human representative of Yahweh gets pierced. These findings seem to clarify why the LXX avoids the piercing of Yahweh in Zech 12:10, further confirming that

---

13. Kubiś, *Zechariah in John*, 119n16. Regarding the stylistic shift, he cites Merrill (*Zechariah*, 320). In addition to Merrill, one could add Boda (*Haggai, Zechariah*, 488). Both Merrill and Boda cite GKC (§144p), who provides several examples where this occurs between verbal forms (cf. Delcor, "Un problem," 193), and Kubiś lists these examples as Isa 22:19 and Lam 3:1. Beyond this footnote, Kubiś does not mention the stylistic nuance any further.

14. Kubiś appears to stand within the interpretive tradition that supposes the object of looking still differs from the object of piercing, even if a functional unity between the two objects is upheld. See, e.g., the translation of Zech 12:10 he favors most—"They shall look on me as far as the one they have pierced is concerned"—a translation he says "separates the person of God and the pierced one, but at the same time creates a certain link between these two figures." Kubiś, *Zechariah in John*, 121, 128. Similarly, see Merrill, *Zechariah*, 320; Boda, *Haggai, Zechariah*, 488; McComiskey, "Zechariah," 1214. However, Baldwin (*Zechariah*) asks an insightful question: "But how can two distinct people die in the death of only one?" (191). Unlike Kubiś and others, my proposal suggests no distinction between Yahweh and the Pierced One in the sense that the Pierced One himself belongs to the divine identity.

the Pierced One of the original prophecy is best understood as Yahweh. Readers will need to weigh the evidence for themselves, but in my judgment the combination of these insights further elucidates the identity of the Pierced One as Yahweh himself, even despite how subsequent manuscript traditions and translations handled the received text. Thus, were someone like the Apostle John to read Zech 12:10 centuries later as an explicit reference to the piercing of Yahweh, such a reading would be justified on the basis of the prophet's words alone.[15] These are but a few ways I intend to advance my thesis in light of previous work on the identity of the Pierced One in Zech 12:10. But before doing so, surveys of literature on John's use of Zech 12:10 in John 19:37 and in Rev 1:7 are still in order.

Survey of Literature on John's Use of Zech 12:10 in John 19:37

Regarding John's use of Zech 12:10 in John 19:37, many give minimal commentary beyond assertions that John wanted his readers to believe Jesus died to fulfill prophecy or to complete his Father's plan.[16] Other interpreters have rightly shown that John has more in mind. By citing Zech 12:10, John also identifies Jesus as God's promised, messianic

---

15. Among all the studies I have consulted, Kubiś comes closest to identifying the Pierced One as Yahweh directly, something my own thesis will attempt to solidify for the theological import behind its use in John 19:37. However, Kubiś is willing to make this assertion only from the perspective of John 19:37 and not from Zech 12:10 itself. Toward the close of his interpretation of Zech 12:10, Kubiś (*Zechariah in John*) argues that "the person killed must be different from YHWH, while not excluding the possibility that this person could be very closely connected with YHWH or almost inseparable. This was indeed the case with the Israelite kings, who in ancient Israel were understood as YHWH's agents on earth. This *functional identity* between YHWH and his royal agent or representative might explain the abrupt transition from the first person which refers to YHWH to the third person" (128). Then, regarding the use of Zech 12:10 in John 19:37, Kubiś concludes that "John embraces . . . the messianic interpretation of the oracle [i.e., the messianic interpretation of Zech 12:10 known to the Second Temple period], but he also reinterprets it in a totally new way: the pierced one is the Messiah who is the same as the one on whom they have looked, i.e. God. The pierced Messiah is God and the pierced God is the Messiah" (189).

16. Bultmann, *John*, 677; Barrett, *John*, 559; Hendriksen, *John*, 439; Tasker, *John*, 214; Morris, *John*, 727–28; Michaels, *John*, 976–78; Haenchen, *John*, 195, 201; Sanders and Mastin, *John*, 413–14; Milne, *John*, 285, 287; Maloney, *John*, 506; Borchert, *John 12–21*, 278–79; Brunner, *John*, 1127; Thompson, *John*, 405.

representative, who parallels the shepherd figure of Zech 13:7 or the Suffering Servant of Isa 53 and realizes God's saving purposes.[17] However, the majority of these interpretations unnecessarily diminish the stronger Christological point John reveals by applying Zech 12:10 to the piercing of Jesus. John's concern is not merely to disclose Jesus as God's human representative, but to disclose his divinity, to identify him with and as Yahweh, and to do so from an OT witness.

Martin J. J. Menken comes close to the same conclusion when he argues that the true onlookers in John 19:37 are those who see in the pierced Jesus the exalted Son of Man.[18] However, it remains unclear whether Menken includes the Son of Man within the divine identity of Yahweh. Moreover, he believes John's primary interest lies not so much in the identity of the Pierced One with Jesus as in the identity of those looking on the Pierced One with believers.

R. C. H. Lenski, Edwyn C. Hoskyns, J. J. O'Rourke, Klaus Wengst, and Craig S. Keener each take the piercing of Zech 12:10 as happening to Yahweh and then see John's appropriation as a deliberate identification of Jesus with Yahweh.[19] Yet none of these interpreters expound on their conclusion or integrate their conclusion into the high Christology saturating John's Gospel except for Lenski and O'Rourke, who, in one sentence, integrate their conclusion with what John affirms about Jesus being God's Son or what John affirms about "the Word" in John 1:1–14.[20]

---

17. Brown, *John XIII–XXI*, 954; Lindars, *John*, 590–91; Beasley-Murray, *John*, 355; Schnackenburg, *John*, 292–94; Carson, *John*, 627–28; Ridderbos, *John*, 622–23; Whitacre, *John*, 466–67; Lincoln, *John*, 482. That is not to neglect the fact that Brown, Lindars, Schnackenburg, and Carson do provide further treatment of the onlookers in John 19:37, which is also significant to understanding John's use of Zech 12:10. See chapter 5 below for more discussion surrounding the onlookers.

18. Menken, "Textual Form," 508, 511. Menken is later followed by Tuckett ("Zechariah 12:10 and the NT," 111–21).

19. Lenski, *John*, 1321; Hoskyns, *Fourth Gospel*, 535; O'Rourke, "Fulfillment Texts," 440–41; Wengst, *Das Johannesevangelium*, 267; Keener, *John*, 1:1156. Burge only recognizes the possible identification in parentheses: " . . . John reflects on Zechariah 12:10, where the prophet describes poignantly how Israel will look on the prophet (or God? or the Messiah?) and lament Israel's harmful lack of faith." Burge, *John*, 534.

20. Lenski, *John*, 1321; O'Rourke, "Fulfillment Texts," 441. After asserting that Zech 12:10 is speaking of Yahweh, Lenski concludes, "Jesus, as Jahweh or God's Son,

Likewise, Andreas Köstenberger argues that John's use of Zech 12:10 in John 19:37 solves the age-old mystery of how God could experience suffering from the hands of men. The mystery "can be understood more fully only in light of the incarnation and crucifixion of the Word-become-flesh, Jesus, who, as the God-man, was pierced for our transgressions as the messianic shepherd and the suffering servant . . . "[21] However, when it comes to explaining the "theological use" of Zech 12:10 in John 19:37, Köstenberger asserts that "John's appropriation of Zechariah 12:10 . . . operates on the basis of the hermeneutical axiom that Yahweh acts in the person of his authorized representative, the messianic shepherd, so that to strike and kill the shepherd, or to pierce him, is in a sense to pierce Yahweh himself."[22]

Two weaknesses surface in Köstenberger's approach. One, describing John's hermeneutical axiom as Yahweh acting in his authoritative representative is too narrow in the case of John 19:37. John seems intent to select Zech 12:10 over the more popular OT passages where a connection to Yahweh acting in his representative would be more straightforward (e.g., Isa 53; Ps 22). Moreover, because John now understands Jesus to share divinity with the Father, John's hermeneutical axiom—at least in the case of John 19:37—seems better described as Jesus is God.[23] Two, despite that Köstenberger affirms that Zech 12:10 refers to the piercing of Yahweh himself, he still applies the piercing to Yahweh's representative and relates it to the alternation of suffixes in

---

was thus pierced . . . '" and O'Rourke concludes, "John then would be interpreting the text in accordance with an analogy based on faith: Jesus was the Word who was God (cf. *Jn.* 1, 1–14)."

21. Köstenberger, "John," 504.

22. Köstenberger, "John," 505.

23. Similarly, in reference to the use of Isaiah in John 12:37–40, Carson concludes that John's appropriation of the OT texts depends partly on the governing Christology. Carson, "John and Johannine Epistles," 251. Also worthy of note is that Köstenberger's work on the Trinity in John's Gospel gives little attention to how John's use of Zech 12:10 in John 19:37 serves John's theological perspective, especially as it pertains to Yahweh achieving his mission to save his people in the person of Jesus. My conclusions will not contradict what Köstenberger develops, but could be used to strengthen his argument as it not only provides further evidence that Jesus should be identified with and as Yahweh, but also reveals that John's Christology stems from the OT and Jesus' reading of the OT. See Köstenberger and Swain, *Father, Son & Spirit*, 27–45, 111–34.

Introduction

the Hebrew text.²⁴ As mentioned above, a better explanation for the alternation of suffixes may exist.

Adam Kubiś, providing the most extensive treatment of the subject, also shows precedent in the literature for arguing that John identifies Jesus with and as Yahweh by citing Zech 12:10. He concludes,

> John embraces . . . the messianic interpretation of the oracle [i.e., the messianic interpretation of Zech 12:10 known to the Second Temple period], but he also reinterprets it in a totally new way: the pierced one is the Messiah who is the same as the one on whom they have looked, i.e. God. The pierced Messiah is God and the pierced God is the Messiah.²⁵

While I can agree with Kubiś's final conclusion, I actually believe he ends up minimizing the theological import of Zech 12:10, which does not need reinterpretation "in a totally new way" but elucidation in light of the self-revelation of God in Jesus Christ. In contrast to Kubiś, I am proposing that John is not reinterpreting Zech 12:10—that is, by adding a divine dimension to the merely human messianic dimension of the original—but citing Zech 12:10 because of the divine dimension that was always explicitly there in the original, however cryptic it must have seemed prior to Jesus' first advent.²⁶ Only through Jesus' earthly

---

24. Moreover, his commentary on John reveals that our conclusions from Zech 12:10 differ as he appears to qualify the piercing of Yahweh as "figuratively, with sorrow." See Köstenberger, *John*, 553.

25. Kubiś, *Zechariah in John*, 189.

26. Such a conclusion also sets the present study apart from the detailed study of Sandra Hübenthal, who works from the literary standpoint of intertextuality. Many of her interpretive questions revolve around how later readers of Zechariah transform and update earlier texts with new meaning. See Hübenthal, *Transformation*, 27–55. In the case of Zech 12:10, Hübenthal suggests the identity of the Pierced One was likely known when the original text was created but that knowledge was then lost, creating an openness (*Offenheit*) for future generations to fill by updating (*Aktualisierung*) the original text theologically with new meaning. Hübenthal, *Transformation*, 201. Not only have the emphases on the reader in literary approaches found warranted criticism by others—since it oftentimes assumes the NT writers were not concerned with the author's original intent—but Hübenthal also appears to dismiss how the historical meaning bound up with the author's intent is what constrains John to cite it the way he does regarding Jesus. See, e.g., Hübenthal, *Transformation*, 215–16. As a general critique of methodologies that diminish the importance of authorial intent, see, e.g., Hirsch, *Validity*, 1–67; Vanhoozer, *Is There a Meaning in*

ministry and the post-resurrection activity of the Spirit did John learn to read Zech 12:10 with this clarity; and such an understanding of Zech 12:10 is why John employed it for his purposes in John 19:37 and Rev 1:7, the latter of the two citations now deserving its own survey of literature.

Survey of Literature on John's Use of Zech 12:10 in Rev 1:7

When considering the literature on John's use of Zech 12:10 in Rev 1:7, the majority of interpreters admit that an allusion to Zech 12:10 exists. However, they regularly minimize the significance of the Pierced One's identity in relation to Jesus while focusing instead on the nature of the nations' mourning.[27] Their focus certainly stands justified, as the universal response of the nations further develops the motifs of Zechariah interwoven throughout John's Revelation, especially the additional allusion in Rev 1:7 to Zech 12:12–14.[28] Nevertheless, deserving equal attention is how the Pierced One in Zech 12:10 contributes to understanding Jesus' identity in Rev 1:7 as well as the significance of Jesus' eschatological mission through the book of Revelation. To my

---

This Text?, 37–97, 201–80. But for specific critiques of the intertextuality employed by Richard B. Hays and Steve Moyise, upon whom Hübenthal builds her methodology, see Beale, "Questions," 152–80; Litwak, "Echoes of Scripture?," 260–88. Beale's primary concern is that Moyise's approach of intertextuality aligns with postmodern reader-response theories that undermine authorial intent and dismiss how NT writers honor the original context/meaning of their OT quotations and allusions. Also important to observe, though, is that Moyise labels his work on Revelation "dialogical intertextuality" (versus "postmodern intertextuality"), he clarifies that readers cannot make texts mean whatever they like, and he denies the accusation of misappropriation of the OT by NT authors. Respectively, see the discussion in Moyise, "Intertextuality and Biblical Studies," 424; Moyise, "Authorial Intention," 36; Moyise, "Misappropriate," 17.

27. E.g., see Swete, *Apocalypse*, 9–10; Caird, *Revelation*, 18–19; Ladd, *Revelation*, 48–49; Ford, *Revelation*, 376; Morris, *Revelation*, 49–50; Aune, *Revelation*, 55–56; Mounce, *Revelation*, 50–51; Kistemaker, *Revelation*, 86; Prigent, *Apocalypse*, 122–23; Osborne, *Revelation*, 70; Smalley, *Revelation*, 37–38; Boxall, *Revelation*, 34; Blount, *Revelation*, 37–38. Patterson mentions no connection to Zech 12:10 in his comments on Rev 1:7. See Patterson, *Revelation*, 62–63.

28. See especially the arguments in Bauckham, *Climax*, 318–26; Hultberg, "Significance," 3–19. Cf. Beale, *Revelation*, 197–98. A portion of the research below will develop the significance of the mourning in relation to John's realized and consummated eschatology.

Introduction

knowledge, only a few interpreters interact with the identity and mission of Zechariah's Pierced One in this particular way from Rev 1:7.

As many do with John's use of Zech 12:10 in John 19:37, Randolf R. Rogers argues that in Rev 1:7 John only means to identify Jesus as the pierced Shepherd figure of Zechariah, but not necessarily as Yahweh.[29] Marko Jauhiainen looks at Zechariah's influence on Revelation as a whole. Regarding Rev 1:7, Jauhiainen concludes that John saw the coming of the Pierced One—who in Zech 12:10 is Yahweh—in terms of Jesus' coming.[30] However, like Rogers, Jauhiainen still maintains the distinction between Yahweh and his representative when interpreting Zech 12:10 and John's use of the prophecy in Rev 1:7, something I will argue can minimize the Christological point John intends to emphasize.[31]

G. K. Beale argues that John alludes to Zech 12:10 in order "to identify Jesus with the pierced God of Zechariah," even referring to Jesus as the messenger or associate mentioned in Zech 12:10.[32] However, unlike Rogers and Jauiainen, Beale clarifies that the significance of the allusion to Zech 12:10 is that Jesus must share divine status with God.[33] Beale follows Alan D. Hultberg's 1995 presentation on "The Significance of Zech 12:10 for the Theology of the Apocalypse." Hultberg's conclusion is that the broader contours of Zechariah, which meld the figures of Messiah and God, drive John's identification of the pierced Yahweh with Jesus.[34] Likewise, Sean M. McDonough's study on the *Dreizeitenformel*, "the one who is and who was and who is to come," in Rev 1:4 suggests that John fits within the early Christian tradition that viewed Yahweh's coming in the OT as Jesus' coming.[35] Drawing such a conclusion from Rev 1:4 then influences the way McDonough understands John's allusion to Zech 12:10 in Rev 1:7 as an equating of

---

29. Rogers, "Zechariah in Revelation," 69, 166.

30. Jauhiainen, *Use of Zechariah*, 143.

31. E.g., see Jauhiainen's comments in Jauhiainen, *Use of Zechariah*, 56, 75, 107, 113, 143.

32. Beale, *Revelation*, 196, 198n76; Beale and McDonough, "Revelation," 1090.

33. Beale, *John's Use*, 102–3.

34. Hultberg, "Significance," 20.

35. McDonough, *YHWH at Patmos*, 216–17.

Jesus' mission with that of Yahweh.[36] In a later study, Hans-Georg Gradl also links Rev 1:7 with the *Dreizeitenformel* of Rev 1:4 and concludes, "Prophetisch greift dies Apk 1,7 auf und expliziert das Kommen Gottes mit dem Kommen Christi."[37]

Based on these latter studies that recognize the Christological significance of John's appropriation of Zech 12:10 in Rev 1:7, ample precedent exists for pursuing the aforementioned thesis. In fact, the treatments of the Pierced One's identity in Rev 1:7 by Rogers, Jauiainen, Hultberg, Beale, McDonough, and Gradl are only cursory and leave room to develop the role Zech 12:10 plays in understanding Jesus' identity, his eschatological mission, and his revelation as a whole.

Moreover, by linking John's use of Zech 12:10 in John 19:37 more closely with John's use of Zech 12:10 in Rev 1:7, Revelation itself becomes part and parcel to understanding John's theology.[38] For example, John's use of Zech 12:10 in his Gospel does not suppress the narrative elements surrounding the prophecy of Zech 12:10, where expectation emerges for God's eschatological judgment against the nations. Rather, John's use of Zech 12:10 in Rev 1:7 helps readers see that John still upholds the eschatological thrust of the prophet's original words. Also, instead of advocating a position whereby John compromises the meaning of Zech 12:10 by universalizing the piercers, onlookers, and mourners, I will propose that John's appropriation adheres to the original meaning but applies it for the eschatological situation that rises with Jesus' two

---

36. From Rev 1:7, McDonough concludes, "We may also say that for John, the definition of who God is cannot be separated from Jesus Christ. God is defined as 'the one who is to come;' but this coming is in the person of Christ." McDonough, *YHWH at Patmos*, 217. A decade before McDonough's study, Bauckham drew the same conclusion: "This divine coming is nothing other than the 'coming' of Jesus Christ (cf. 1:7: ἔρχομαι), who in Revelation declares seven times 'I am coming' (ἔρχομαι: 2:5, 16; 3:11; 16:15; 22:6, 12, 22; cf. also 3:3)." Bauckham, *Climax*, 435.

37. Gradl, "Buch Und Brief," 421. My translation in context: "Prophetically, Rev 1:7 picks up [that the Christian minority should set their eyes on the one who is to come] and explains the coming of God in the coming of Christ."

38. One publication that seems to keep Revelation separate from John's theology is Köstenberger, *Theology*. Cf. Stevens, *Johannine Theology*; Erdmann, "Mission in John's Gospel and Letters," 207–26. However, others have included Revelation within the Johannine corpus. E.g., see Cook, "Glory Motif," 291–97; Rainbow, *Johannine Theology*, 42–51.

Introduction

advents.[39] These advances will also provide further insight to the nature of the nations' mourning in Rev 1:7, which appears to include dread more than it does repentance, a conclusion that challenges the growing acceptance of Richard Bauckham's argumentation.[40] Also, by juxtaposing John 19:37 with Rev 1:7, one gains deeper insight into John's theological vision of Jesus Christ and how his piercing affects those people living within the inter-advent age.

Conclusion to History of Research

In conclusion, the previous survey of literature reveals strong precedent for pursuing a thesis regarding the significance of Zechariah's Pierced One for Jesus' divine identity and eschatological mission in the writings of John. However, several observations prove that further refinement and development would benefit previous research. First, further grammatical and stylistic insights may not only help elucidate the Pierced One's identity in Zech 12:10 as Yahweh, but also prove that John's appropriation of Zech 12:10 to highlight Jesus' divinity is a justifiable one. Second, previous studies on John's use of Zech 12:10 in John 19:37 unnecessarily diminish John's stronger Christological point by viewing the Pierced One as Yahweh's human representative instead of as Yahweh himself. Third, related studies on John's use of Zech 12:10 in Rev 1:7 provide only a cursory treatment of the Pierced One in relation to Jesus' divine identity and eschatological mission. Furthermore, no in-depth study exists that develops the mission of the Pierced One in Zechariah, John's Gospel, and Revelation as a coherent whole, not to mention the effects such a divine-revelatory mission must have on people living between the Pierced One's first and second advents.

PRESUPPOSITIONS

Aiming to develop prior research along such theological lines betrays several underlying presuppositions guiding this study.[41] To begin, a

---

39. Cf. Beale and McDonough, "Revelation," 1090, who maintain that John "consistently develops the contextual ideas of his OT references."

40. See Bauckham, *Climax*, 218–26.

41. "Whether in biblical interpretation per se or in systematic theology, method concerns both the basic rational procedure for yielding and arranging results and,

proper understanding of the biblical authors' message stems first and principally from a charitable reading of their own writings,[42] which intend their readers to believe what they convey.[43] More specifically, John intends his readers to believe his eyewitness testimony to Jesus, including his access to both the historical events surrounding Jesus and their theological significance for the world.[44] Thus, the following approach embraces both the historical and the theological character of John's writings.[45]

---

importantly, the presuppositions and conceptual framework that one brings to the task." Stiver, "Method," 510. Cf. McKnight, "Presuppositions in New Testament Studies," 278–300.

42. In the words of Rosner, "Texts assume a certain kind of audience, someone who is best disposed to make sense of what is written, the person or group for whom the texts are intended." Rosner, "Biblical Theology," 5.

43. This charitable reading, or hermeneutic of love/trust, stands in contrast to what previous studies describe as a skeptical reading, or hermeneutic of suspicion. Rather than starting with the assumption that the true nature of things lies hidden behind John's theological embellishments or beneath layers added by a reconstructed Johannine community, I start with the assumption that John has written truthfully about what he witnessed in the Christ event, and that even the theological assertions he receives from the Spirit and ascribes to the Christ event never compromise its historicity or the true nature of things. Toward further justification for a hermeneutic of love/trust, see the arguments advanced by Stuhlmacher, *Hermeneutics of Consent*, 83–90; Thiselton, *New Horizons*, 604–11; Wright, *New Testament*, 1:64; Vanhoozer, *Is There a Meaning in This Text?*, 455–68; Jacobs, *Theology of Reading*, 9–35.

44. E.g., John 19:35; 20:30–31; 21:25; Rev 1:2; 22:6, 8; cf. 1 John 1:1–3. Also, while disagreeing with Bauckham's rejection of John, the son of Zebedee, being the author of the Fourth Gospel, Bauckham's conclusions regarding the historical and theological nature of the testimony present in all four Gospels lends further support to my approach. See Bauckham, *Jesus and the Eyewitnesses*, 472–508. For discussions advancing the historical and theological nature of all the NT documents, see Bockmuehl, *Seeing the Word*, 68–160.

45. In addition to history and theology, Köstenberger and Patterson add one more essential reality to a responsible hermeneutical method, namely, literature (i.e., canon, genre, language). Köstenberger and Patterson, *Biblical Interpretation*, 57–81, 693–710. I largely follow the same method here, but John's use of Zechariah sets the focus of my thesis primarily within the area of theology, since John's point in using Zechariah is theological in nature. For good reason, Köstenberger and Patterson include the NT writer's use of the OT in their section on theology. Köstenberger and Patterson, *Biblical Interpretation*, 703–8. Similar approaches to NT studies include Ridderbos, *Redemptive History*, 1–50; Schlatter, "Theology," 117–43; Marshall, *New Testament Theology*, 17–20; Bockmuehl, *Seeing the Word*, 101–19. In terms of the legitimacy of theological interpretation in relation to method, see Stiver, "Method,"

Introduction

Another underlying presupposition is that of canonical unity. Sufficient evidence exists to hold that the author of both the Fourth Gospel and Revelation is John, the son of Zebedee, the beloved disciple, and the Apostle of the Lord Jesus.[46] The internal coherency between the message of the Fourth Gospel and Revelation is not accidental, but belongs to the perspective of the same human author, who encounters Jesus in his earthly humility and heavenly glory, and who testifies to what he witnesses.[47] But the canonical unity extends even beyond John's Gospel and Revelation and also runs deeper than mere human

510–12. Contra Räisänen, *Beyond*, 160–62. Räisänen presents a false dichotomy between history and dogmatics, or exegesis and theology, and also gives an inadequate historical assessment of the two-fold nature of the NT documents. By being both historical and theological, these writings set their own parameters for interpretation.

46. Despite its formal anonymity, the external and internal evidence suggests the Fourth Gospel belongs to John the apostle and son of Zebedee. E.g., see the observations made by Köstenberger, *Theology*, 72–79; Carson, *John*, 68–81. Köstenberger also includes objections to the more recent proposal by Bauckham, *Testimony*, 33–92. Bauckham suggests that a John outside the Twelve wrote the Fourth Gospel. That the external evidence suggests the Apostle John also wrote Revelation, see, e.g., Beckwith, *Apocalypse*, 343–93. Additionally, when the internal evidence is weighed carefully, the results favor John the Apostle as the author of Revelation. Most significantly, see the arguments by Russell, "Possible Influence," 336–51; Feuillet, *The Apocalypse*, 95–108; Ozanne, "The Language of the Apocaplypse," 3–9; Poythress, "Testing," 350–69; Poythress, "Use of Conjunctions," 329–36; Osborne, *Revelation*, 2–6. For the linguistic similarities across the entire Johannine corpus, see Rainbow, *Johannine Theology*, 42–51. Theological similarities between the Fourth Gospel and Revelation are helpfully summarized in Keener, *John*, 1:133–38; Hoskins, *Revelation*, 16–21.

47. Some may still want to argue that the Fourth Gospel (and Revelation) originate with a Johannine "community," "school," or "sect" rather than identifying a single, common author. E.g., see Schüssler-Fiorenza, "Quest for the Johannine School," 402–27; Brown, *Community of the Beloved Disciple*; Smalley, "John's Revelation and John's Community," 549–71; de Jonge, "History of the Johannine Communities," 127–44. Even so, the conclusions of the following research still stand based on the existing coherency between the Fourth Gospel and Revelation in relation to Zech 12:10. However, one should still note the critiques in Bauckham, *Gospels for All Christians*, 9–48. Bauckham seriously questions the speculative mirror-reading behind such conclusions in the community hypotheses, and who questions whether the Gospels were addressed to such definable communities as portrayed by the aforementioned studies cited here. Cirafesi also notes the significance of Bauckham's critiques. Cirafesi, "Johannine Community Hypothesis," 173–93. Additionally, see the critiques of the "community hypothesis" in Klink III, *Sheep of the Fold*, 27–36, 107–51.

authorship. The unity also spans both Old and New Testaments. According to a charitable reading of both the prophet's and the apostle's claims, the essential message each has written ultimately stems from the same God.[48] God stands behind the OT storyline and the testimony of John, who celebrates Jesus as that storyline's fulfillment.[49] A proper method will be open to this inner-biblical unity and allow the salvation-historical framework of the canon to shape its exegetical conclusions instead of discarding such unity as an ahistorical imposition on

48. Zechariah characterizes his message in terms of divine revelation: the word of the Lord came to [Zechariah] (Zech 1:1, 7; 4:8; 6:9; 7:1, 4, 8; 8:1, 18); in other places, Zechariah delivers "the oracle [מַשָּׂא] of the word of the Lord" (Zech 9:1; 12:1); Zechariah introduces his message with "thus says the Lord [כֹּה־אָמַר יְהוָה]" (e.g., Zech 1:16, 17; 2:12; 3:7; 6:12; 7:9; 8:2; 11:4); and Zechariah equates his prophecy with hearing the voice of God (Zech 6:15; cf. 11:4). Then, in both his Gospel and Revelation, John characterizes his message in terms of divine revelation, as a message given by God or the Spirit. John's Gospel is the result of the Spirit bringing to John's remembrance what Jesus said and taught (John 2:17, 22; 7:39; 12:16; 14:26; 15:26–27; 16:4, 13–15; cf. 1 John 4:6), a message equivalent to God's word(s) (John 3:11–13, 32–34; 8:26, 28, 38, 47; 12:49–50). Likewise, Revelation is the result of what God gives John, even if through intermediaries (Rev 1:1; 22:6). Revelation is also the result of John being "in the Spirit" (Rev 1:10; 4:2; 17:3; 21:10), to such a degree of uniqueness that it places John in the category of prophet (Rev 22:8–9; cf. 22:6) and his words in the category of authoritative prophecy (Rev 22:10, 18–19). See also Jauhiainen, *Use of Zechariah*, 8. To affirm that divine inspiration stands behind the prophet's and apostle's words is not to jettison the importance of historical contexts, audiences, and available forms of communication, since the words of Scripture are "the product of a 'concursive' operation." Moo, "Problem of Sensus Plenior," 187–88.

49. If even the majority of the OT citations and verbal allusions listed in the indexes of NA27 and UBS4 show legitimate connections, then John demonstrates a working knowledge of the Law, the Prophets, and the Writings when explaining Jesus' identity and mission. Using this three-fold division of Scripture does not represent any commitment to a three-stage canonization process. Cf. Ellis, *OT in Early Christianity*, 3–50. Instead, the language represents early sources that appear to indicate a three-fold division of the books that were considered "canonical" by the first century (Sir 1:1–4; cf. Josephus, *Ag. Ap.* 1:38–42; Luke 24:44). For an extensive treatment, see Beckwith, *Canon*, 110–80. Spellman draws similar conclusions as Beckwith but then develops the implications of "canon-consciousness" among the biblical authors as well as among the believing community who interpret the biblical authors' message. Spellman, *Canon*, 87–94. Regardless, the point is that John's Gospel and Revelation of Jesus was only comprehensible when set within the framework of God dealing with and revealing himself to Israel in the Scriptures. As God's word to Israel, the OT centered on and revealed the significance of Jesus' identity and mission, something John learned from Jesus in his earthly ministry (John 5:39, 46; 13:18; 15:25; cf. Luke 24:44).

Introduction

the biblical text.⁵⁰ In fact, I hope to demonstrate that John's use of Zech 12:10 stands as one example validating the unity of the Testaments, the product of a single divine author.

METHODOLOGY

Nevertheless, demonstrating this inner-biblical unity must not come at the expense of drawing viable connections between Testaments, particularly between John/Revelation and Zechariah, or at the expense of demonstrating a later biblical author's hermeneutical warrant in making those connections.⁵¹ The following methodology attempts to address both concerns throughout the study.

Discerning Viable Connections

Drawing viable connections between Testaments is the first concern. The present study will primarily look at two types of Scriptural connections to Zechariah, a partial but direct quotation of Zech 12:10 in John 19:37, and an allusion to Zech 12:10, 12 (also intertwined with Dan 7:13) in Rev 1:7. G. K. Beale differentiates a quotation from an allusion as follows:

> A quotation is a direct citation of an OT passage that is easily recognizable by its clear and unique verbal parallelism . . . An allusion may simply be defined as a brief expression consciously intended by an author to be dependent on an OT passage. In contrast to a quotation of the OT, which is a direct

---

50. In this sense, my approach aligns best with those advocating a "canonical approach" to understanding the NT authors' use of the OT. E.g., Waltke, "Canonical Approach," 3–18; Packer, "Role of Hermeneutics," 349–50; Moo, "Problem of Sensus Plenior," 204–9; Carson, "Unity and Diversity," 77–86; "Current Issues," 27–32; "Systematic," 89–104; Dempster, *Dominion*, 15–43; Beale, *Handbook*, 95–102; Boda, *Return to Me*, 20–24. Regarding the historical justification for distinguishing the canonical writings from other ancient literature and how this relates to NT theology, see Balla, *Challenges*, 86–146.

51. Although I do want to heed Moisés Silva's wise caution: "the authority and validity of apostolic interpretation . . . do *not* depend on its conformity to modern exegetical method." Silva, "Text Form and Authority," 147–65. Contra Longenecker, *Biblical Exegesis*, 185–98.

reference, allusions are indirect references (the OT wording is not reproduced directly as in a quotation).[52]

The verbal parallels and introductory formula (e.g., "as it is written") usually make discerning an OT quotation fairly straightforward for interpreters. However, discerning allusions has proven more difficult, especially when the question of authorial intent persists.[53] For this study, I will build on the criteria developed by Jon Paulien in his work on discerning OT allusions in Revelation.[54]

For Paulien, one must consider both external and internal evidence to determine a direct allusion to an OT text. External evidence observes whether and how an author accessed the source text to which he alludes.[55] Internal evidence involves three criteria: (1) verbal paral-

---

52. Beale, *Handbook*, 29, 31. In light of the mounting literature on the NT use of the OT, especially a term like "allusion," it is important to notice that Beale includes authorial intent when defining an allusion. In doing so, Beale's approach stands apart from that of "intertextuality." Clay Ham summarizes the difference well: "Allusion . . . focuses on the relationship between the antecedent text and the author of the second text, that is, how the second text evokes the antecedent text. Intertextuality focuses on the relationship between the second text and its reader(s), that is, how the reader(s) may understand various connections between the second text and an antecedent text whether such a relationship between the two texts were intended or signaled by the author of the second text. Thus, allusion is concerned with the text and its author; intertextuality, with the text and its reader independent of its author." Ham, "Reading Zechariah," 87n13.

53. See especially Beale, "Questions," 152–80; Beale, "Response to Paulien," 23–34. Beale's primary contention is that when the NT authors use the OT, they do not distort the original intent of the OT writers even if later revelation enables them to expand/apply the OT text's significance for new audiences. More recently, Jauhiainen has argued that authorial intent becomes a moot point, as long as a "satisfactory explanation of how the allusion functions in its context" persists. Jauhiainen, *Use of Zechariah*, 32. However, see the arguments in Vanhoozer, *Is There a Meaning in This Text?*, 201–452.

54. Paulien, "Elusive Allusions," 37–53. Ian Paul highlights two weaknesses with Paulien's work: (1) Paulien "assumes too much about the relation between [authorial] intent and meaning" when differentiating an allusion from an echo; (2) Paulien's classification of allusions (i.e., certain allusions, probable allusions, possible allusions, uncertain allusions, non-allusions) "is based on the interpreter's confidence, rather than the text's (or even author's) attention." See Paul, "Revelation 12," 260–61. However, the following study will have no need to differentiate between allusions and echoes; and the spectrum of probable allusions only seems to increase subjectivity rather than provide solutions for it. So Jauhiainen, *Use of Zechariah*, 35.

55. Paulien, "Elusive Allusions," 41. Paulien's "external evidence" is similar to that

lels, when two or more words of significance exist between the OT and NT passages;⁵⁶ (2) thematic parallels, when the NT passage applies a similar OT idea or theme, even without the exact vocabulary;⁵⁷ and (3) structural parallels, when the NT author uses the same "language and themes in roughly the same order" as the OT text.⁵⁸ In addition to the three criteria Paulien lists for internal evidence, I would add a fourth, namely, the question of whether other NT authors reference the same OT text but with clearer evidence than the allusion at hand.⁵⁹ With Paulien, I would argue that an allusion need not satisfy all the criteria to be legitimate, but the more criteria the allusion satisfies, the greater the likelihood that the author intends his readers to make the connection to a particular OT passage.⁶⁰

Discerning Heremeneutical Warrant

In addition to discerning viable connections, the following study will put measures in place to discern the hermeneutical warrant driving the connections.⁶¹ The question of warrant stems from the tension one often feels when comparing the historical, contextual meaning of an OT verse with its appearance in a NT context. For instance, how can Matt 2:15 assert that Jesus fulfills the prophet's words when Hos

---

of Richard Hays's first criterion of seven, that of "availability." See Hays, *Echoes*, 29; Hays, *Conversion*, 34. Hays receives criticism for this first criterion in Porter, "Allusions and Echoes," 38. However, Beale rightly notes that while many of Porter's criticisms of Hays stand warranted, Porter's criticism of availability is overstated when authorial intent is at hand. Beale, *Handbook*, 34.

56. Paulien, "Elusive Allusions," 41–42.

57. Paulien, "Elusive Allusions," 42–43.

58. Paulien, "Elusive Allusions," 43.

59. Clearer evidence may include another NT author quoting—as opposed to merely alluding to—the same OT text in question (with or without an introductory formula), another NT author alluding to the same OT text in question but with more explicit development of the related idea or theme from that OT text, or even another NT author quoting from or alluding to the surrounding context of the OT text in question and developing the line of thought in similar fashions.

60. Paulien, "Elusive Allusions," 44, 46.

61. Here, I utilize part of Beale's ninefold approach to understanding the OT in the NT. Beale, *Handbook*, 41–54. However, I reverse step two (i.e., analyze NT context) with step three (i.e., analyze OT context) and combine steps seven and eight (i.e., analyze author's hermeneutic and analyze author's theological use, respectively).

Jesus as the Pierced One

11:1 refers to Israel coming out of Egypt? How can Rev 3:9 assert that self-professed Jews will bow before the church when Isaiah anticipates nations bowing before the Jews (Isa 45:14; 60:14)? Or, how can Peter conclude from Scripture to replace Judas when the Psalms he quotes speak about David's enemies (Acts 1:20)?

Such tension led Barnabas Lindars to suggest that the NT writers disregarded the original context of their OT references and "employed the OT in an ad hoc way."[62] Others like Richard Longenecker pointed to Jewish exegetical methods like pesher and "the atomistic manipulations of midrash."[63] For Longenecker, these non-contextual interpretations of the OT seemed acceptable during the apostolic era, even if such interpretations are more suspect today.[64] Others like Steve Moyise approach the tension from the standpoint of intertextuality, where questions about whether the NT writers respected the original OT context are minimized[65] in favor of determining meaning by the ongoing effects of the two contexts mutually interacting for the reader(s).[66]

---

62. Lindars, "Prolegomena," 143.

63. Longenecker, "Reflections," 4–8.

64. Moyise rightly objects, however, "If the NT authors used methods of exegesis that are now considered questionable, what does that do to the status of the conclusions reached by such methods? . . . If Paul (or Jesus?) used 'atomistic manipulations' to arrive at his conclusions, it is hard to see why such conclusions should continue to command respect." Moyise, "Context," 137. Likewise, see the critiques of Longenecker by Beale, "Right Doctrine," 387–404.

65. As Mark Boda observes, "Part of the attraction [of intertextuality] may lie in the fact that a reader-centered hermeneutic alleviates perceived instances of tension between the original intention of the Old Testament author and the ultimate intention of the New Testament reader, a problem that is often cited in studies of the New Testament appropriation of the Old." Boda, "Quotation and Allusion," 296.

66. For Moyise, "[Theories of intertextuality] make it clear that a quotation will always mean something different in its new setting because it has been 'relocated.' This being so, the question to ask is not whether a given quotation has been taken out of context but what is the effect of such a quotation on a reading of the text?" Moyise, "Context," 141. Again, Moyise asserts that "John was not seeking the original authorial intention of the OT authors, but seeking to discern the *trajectory* of interpretation that makes most sense of his present." Moyise, "Misappropriate," 20. In saying so, Moyise challenges the work of C. H. Dodd and his followers, who operate by the "axiom that a quotation is a pointer to its wider context [in the OT]." Moyise, "Intertextuality and Historical Approaches," 455. Nevertheless, he seems to nuance his research enough to include readings that result from Dodd's approach: " . . . scriptural quotations in the NT do not always evoke whole frameworks of meaning

Introduction

Differing from these approaches, G. K. Beale and others emphasize the importance of the OT author's original intent and attempt to demonstrate how beneficial it is to "distinguish between the enduring original meaning [of the OT passage] and how that meaning is responded to by subsequent writers, i.e., the 'significance' of that earlier meaning."[67] In other words, when using the OT, the NT writers are not forcing a meaning into the OT passage that was never present before. Instead, the NT writers draw from the meaning always present in the OT—a meaning sometimes extended and amplified by the OT itself—and then interpret its significance for their readers in light of the Christ event. Jon Paulien clarifies the matter even further:

> [The NT writers] were reading the OT from the perspective of where they understood themselves to be in the context of a divine plan for history. Given the belief that Jesus of Nazareth was the fulfillment of a divine plan announced in the context of Scripture as a whole, the NT writings are a reasonable and contextual reflection on that whole, as C. H. Dodd among others has pointed out. New Testament writers were offering an interpretation of the OT that they believed the OT writers would have given had they been alive to encounter Jesus.[68]

Publications such as the massive *Commentary on the New Testament Use of the Old Testament*, edited by G. K. Beale and D. A. Carson, have attempted to demonstrate how the NT writers interpreted the OT contextually and in a manner that complemented and built upon the OT author's original meaning.

The present study seeks to demonstrate the same. Thus, an important first step will be to ascertain the original meaning of Zech 12:10 as much as possible.[69] Chapter 2 will include analyzing the broad and

---

and it should not therefore be assumed as a presupposition." Moyise, "Scripture," 324. The clear inference is that sometimes scriptural quotations in the NT do evoke whole frameworks of meaning.

67. Beale, "Response to Paulien," 25. Beale leans heavily on the works of E. D. Hirsch and Kevin Vanhoozer, both of whom stress the importance of authorial intent for determining meaning.

68. Paulien, "Whirlwind," 20.

69. Boda also acknowledges the value of this first step for understanding the NT use of the OT. After stressing the importance of diachronic sensibilities alongside the

immediate context of Zech 12:10 to determine the original meaning for Zechariah's audience. Chapters 3 and 4 will then analyze the broad and immediate contexts of John 19:37 and Rev 1:7 where John appropriates Zech 12:10.[70] The primary goal of chapters 3 and 4 is not merely to determine source-texts or appropriation techniques—though both can serve the discussion—but more to determine John's hermeneutical axiom, the underlying theological assumption warranting him to use Zech 12:10 the way he does to explain Jesus' identity and mission.

PLAN FOR THE STUDY

The next chapter, then, will initiate our study by determining whether seeing the Pierced One as Yahweh is a justifiable interpretation of Zech 12:10. Chapter 3 will show how John uses Zech 12:10 in John 19:37 as a theological interpretation of Jesus' first redeeming advent. Chapter 4 will continue the analysis of John's use of Zech 12:10, but address questions related to Jesus' second redeeming advent in Rev 1:7. Chapter 5 will develop the theological significance of John applying the same OT passage to speak of two historically-separated advents within the development of Scripture's storyline. The final chapter will summarize the findings of chapters 1—5 and outline a few implications for hermeneutics, biblical theology, Christology, eschatology, missiology, and doxology.

---

synchronic, Boda outlines the initial steps of a "critical methodology for the study of quotation and allusion in the biblical texts." "In the diachronic phase," Boda writes, "the interpreter should identify inner-biblical connections (with attention to the lexical and structural similarities between the two texts), study the larger contexts of the two texts (antecedent and text under study) to understand their meaning, and then reflect on the way in which the antecedent is being used within the later text." Boda, "Quotations and Allusions," 297.

70. Beale suggests surveying "the use of the OT text in early and late Judaism that might be of relevance to the NT appropriation of the OT text." Beale, *Handbook*, 46–48. Comparisons between early renderings of Zech 12:10, such as the MT and Greek translations of LXX, Theodotion, Aquila, and Symmachus, will come interwoven throughout the study. Only a few Targumic traditions exist concerning Zech 12:10, while the Pseudepigrapha, Josephus, and Philo contribute nothing to the discussion. The DSS evidence is sparse for Zech 12:10 with only 4QXIIe supporting the reading וּקָרָֽד.

2

Yahweh as the Pierced One

Zech 12:10

How does the Apostle John use Zech 12:10 to build on an understanding of God's self-disclosure in Jesus' two-fold eschatological mission? As demonstrated in chapter 1, many interpreters understand John to connect Jesus with the Pierced One of Zech 12:10, because the Pierced One is Yahweh's messianic representative. The present study, however, seeks to demonstrate that John connects Jesus with the Pierced One, because John views the Pierced One as Yahweh himself. Therefore, an important first step is demonstrating the validity of identifying Zechariah's Pierced One as Yahweh.[1] The present chapter will focus on those elements of Zech 12:10 and its context that help illumine the identity of the Pierced One. Doing so will simultaneously gauge whether John imposes onto Zech 12:10 a meaning that was never present, or imports from Zech 12:10 a meaning that was justifiably

---

1. It will become evident that the following study accepts the single-authorship of Zechariah and often attributes content from chs. 1–8 and chs. 9–14 to the same prophet. Both halves of Zechariah seem to complement one another and maintain a unified message. However, that is not to suggest the following study depends on the single-authorship of Zechariah, nor to minimize the serious challenges others have proposed against it. The following studies in favor of single authorship have been helpful: Childs, *Introduction*, 482–85; Hill, "Linguistic Reexamination," 105–34; Ruffin, "Symbolism"; Moseman, "Unity of Zechariah"; Klein, *Zechariah*, 24–34; Wenzel, *Reading Zechariah*.

JESUS AS THE PIERCED ONE

always present, even if somewhat cryptic to the prophet's original audience.

The plan is to investigate several complexities with identifying the Pierced One, including a major textual difficulty, two grammatical difficulties, the use of דָּקַר ("to pierce") and its effect on translators of the LXX, and an evaluation of suggested personages in light of the passage's context, grammar, theology, and eschatological perspective. With each issue, the *Wirkungsgeschichte* of Zech 12:10 within early Judaism and Christianity will also merit attention.[2] However, before raising the first of these complex issues, a brief overview of the literary context for Zech 12:10 ensues.

LITERARY CONTEXT

Zechariah 12:10 falls within a much larger prophecy that exhorts the apathetic post-exilic community to live in the present with the hope and expectation that Yahweh will fulfill his promises to them as the new age irrupts.[3] In this sense, Zechariah reapplies to the post-exilic community what the pre-exilic prophets proclaimed to theirs (Zech 1:1–6; 7:7). In both cases, the people were to hope in what God would ultimately do for them in the end times, often referenced with phrases like בְּאַחֲרִית הַיָּמִים ("in the latter days"), or, in Zechariah's case, בַּיּוֹם הַהוּא ("in/on that day").[4] Indeed, in relation to the previous eleven

---

2. On the significance of *Wirkungsgeschichte* ("effective history") for biblical interpretation, see Bockmuehl, *Seeing the Word*, 66–68. Bockmuehl finds that the study of *Wirkungsgeschichte* aids NT studies, since "the meaning of a text is in practice deeply intertwined with its own tradition of hearing and heeding, interpretation and performance." Bockmuehl, *Seeing the Word*, 65. What Bockmuehl observes with respect to NT studies, I will also utilize for the study of Zech 12:10. In this case, I do not limit myself to asking how history *may* have produced Zech 12:10, as others have done. See, e.g., Otzen, *Studien*, 173–84. Otzen attempts to interpret the passage through cultic reconstruction. Rather, I extend the study of Zech 12:10 to include how history received and interpreted the message about the Pierced One.

3. Alongside Haggai (cf. Hag 1:1), Zechariah prophesies after the pre-exilic prophets had preached and then died (Zech 1:4–5). The term "irrupt" follows what Waltke considers the center of the OT's message: "the irruption (breaking in from without), not eruption (breaking out from within), of the kingship of the holy, merciful, and only God." See Waltke, *Old Testament Theology*, 143–69, esp. 144.

4. Zech 2:15 [ET 11]; 3:10; 9:16; 12:3, 4, 6, 8, 9, 11; 13:1, 2, 4; 14:4, 6, 8, 9, 13, 20, 21; cf. Isa 2:11, 17; Hos 2:18 [ET 16], 23 [ET 21]; Amos 9:11; Zeph 3:16. Notice also

chapters, Zech 12:10 falls within a context where a heightened repetition of the phrase "in/on that day" occurs. Of the book's twenty-two occurrences, the phrase "in/on that day" appears seventeen times in Zech 12:1—14:21, indicating that the events involving the Pierced One are eschatological in nature.[5] Moreover, if Yahweh's outpouring of "a spirit of grace and pleas for mercy" (רוּחַ חֵן וְתַחֲנוּנִים) in Zech 12:10 signals the same internal renewal by the Spirit that Isaiah, Ezekiel, and Joel anticipated coming with God's future messianic kingdom, then the eschatological nature of these events becomes all the more likely.[6] Within the scope of God's redeeming purposes, these events will transpire toward the end of history.

---

the heightened repetition of the phrase, "in that day," throughout Zech 12:1—14:21, where the message about the Pierced One occurs. The heightened repetition will inform the text's eschatological significance in determining the Pierced One's place within the scope of redemptive history (i.e., past, present, or future to the prophet's ministry).

5. For a study on why explicit expressions in the OT such as "latter days" do not merely refer to the indefinite future but refer to the eschatological time when God's purposes for his people in judgment and salvation will finally be carried out, see Beale, *NT Biblical Theology*, 92–112.

6. E.g., Isa 32:15; 44:3; 61:1; Ezek 11:19; 36:25–27; 39:29; Joel 2:28–32. The Hebrew in Zech 12:10 is ambiguous. The nouns in construct, רוּחַ חֵן, could simply be rendered "a spirit of grace" (so ESV, NIV, NET). If that is the sense here, then the human spirit is in view (cf. רוּחַ־אָדָם, "spirit of man," in Zech 12:1) that commiserates (cf. *HALOT*, s.v., "חֵן") over the Pierced One, and perhaps over what their sin did to him (cf. Zech 13:1). Nevertheless, Zech 4:6–7 anticipates a future work of Yahweh's Spirit (i.e., "by my Spirit [בְּרוּחִי]"), who will build the eschatological temple amid shouts of "grace, grace [חֵן חֵן] to it." Moreover, both Ezek 39:29 and Joel 3:1–2 (ET 2:28–29) speak similarly of Yahweh "pouring out" (שׁפך) his Spirit. If Yahweh's Spirit is in view, the construct may be rendered "the Spirit of grace" (so NASB). Petterson adds the following: " . . . given the background of Isaiah, Ezekiel and Joel, who all associate the sending of Yahweh's Spirit on the day his kingdom comes (e.g., Isa. 32:15; Ezek. 39:29; Joel 2:28–32), it is attractive to see God's Spirit at work here. In this case, 'grace and supplication' are produced in the people of God by the work of his Spirit." Petterson, *Zechariah*, 263. Regardless, Ezek 26:26–28 combines the gift of Yahweh's Spirit with the transformation of the human spirit. When Yahweh pours out his Spirit on people in future days, their human spirit will change and submit to Yahweh. Also linking the outpouring of Yahweh's Spirit in Joel to that of Zech 12:10 is Prior, *Joel*, 72–73. Such OT passages on the outpouring of God's Spirit are relevant, especially if one takes into account how the NT apostles understood their fulfillment in the new age inaugurated by Jesus' death and resurrection (e.g., John 3:3–10; 7:38–39; 14–16; Acts 2:1–21). Further discussion on the Spirit's eschatological work will transpire in chapters 3 and 5.

Similar to the first oracle stretching from Zech 9:1 to Zech 11:17, the second oracle initiated by Zech 12:1 further unveils the extent of Yahweh's saving promises.[7] By declaring that he "stretches out the heavens and establishes the earth and fashions the spirit of man within him" (Zech 12:1), Yahweh recalls his sovereignty over creation (cf. Gen 1:1; 2:7) and reinforces Israel's hope for a new creation[8] as Yahweh acts to establish his final rule on earth (Zech 14:6–9) and especially from a new Jerusalem (Zech 14:10–11, 21). In order to establish his presence and final rule from the new Jerusalem (Zech 9:9–13; 14:9, 20–21), Yahweh will form an abiding relationship with his restored people under a renewed covenant[9] and grant them military victory over their international oppressors (Zech 12:2–9).[10] The latter victory develops through Yahweh making Jerusalem an immovable city (Zech 12:2–3),[11] Yahweh

---

7. The word מַשָּׂא ("pronouncement" or "burden") in Zech 9:1 and Zech 12:1 initiates the two oracles that close out Zechariah, and perhaps make up two of the three that close out the Book of the Twelve (cf. Mal 1:1) where similar themes appear. A few examples consist of Yahweh as the great king (Zech 9:9–13; 14:9; cf. Mal 1:14), the prevalence of covenant (Zech 9:11; 13:9; cf. Mal 3:7), the final return of Yahweh (Zech 9:14–17; 12:1–9; 14:1–21; cf. Mal 4:1), and the salvation of the faithful remnant (Zech 13:9; cf. Mal 4:12–13). Devillers also mentions the connection with Mal 1:1, but only in passing. Devillers, "Le Transpercé," 88.

8. Cf. Klein, *Zechariah*, 350; Petterson, *Zechariah*, 259.

9. The abiding presence of Yahweh with his people appears in Zech 9:8, 16–17; 10:8–12; 13:9; 14:16, 20–21. The language of a renewed covenant occurs in Zech 9:11; 10:12; 13:9; 14:20 (cf. Exod 6:7; Lev 26:12; Isa 51:16; Jer 7:23; 24:7; 30:22; 31:33; 32:38; Ezek 36:28; 37:23).

10. Regarding the judgment of the nations, cf. also Zech 9:4–8, 14–15; 10:11; 14:1–5, 12–15.

11. Zechariah employs two metaphors. The first is that God will make Jerusalem "a cup of staggering" (Zech 12:2). At times, the "cup" (כּוֹס) is a metaphor for Yahweh's judgment (Ps 11:6; Jer 25:15; 49:12; Hab 2:16). God forces his enemies to gulp down his cup to the point of staggering in humiliating disillusionment (Ps 75:8; Isa 51:17; Jer 51:7). The difference in Zech 12:2 is that instead of כּוֹס Zechariah uses סַף, a much larger bowl/basin (*HALOT*, s.v. "סַף"). In this way, Zechariah signifies a greater future judgment. The surrounding oppressors may gather against God and his people, but God will force them to stagger with great judgment. The second metaphor is that God will make Jerusalem "a heavy stone for all the peoples" (Zech 12:3). Daniel 2:34–45 is helpful in that the prophet relates a stone to God's unshakable kingdom. Four worldly kingdoms get dashed to pieces by a stone that God raises up in the future and that eventually grows into a mountain (i.e., kingdom) filling the earth forever (Dan 2:44–45). Zechariah seems to employ the same imagery. The point of both metaphors is that all attempts by the nations to conquer God's people

fighting on behalf of his beloved people (Zech 12:4, 9), and Yahweh strengthening his people to defeat their enemies (Zech 12:5–8).[12]

At the same time, total salvation for the "house of David and the inhabitants of Jerusalem" will come not only by external victories granted over their enemy oppressors (Zech 12:2–9), but also by internal transformation of the covenant people themselves (Zech 12:10—13:1).[13] Essential to this internal transformation is Yahweh's gracious initiative (חֵן, "grace"; cf. Zech 4:7) that then leads the people to look upon the Pierced One and to experience heartfelt sorrow over the piercing they had collectively caused. Through the prophet, Yahweh declares the following words in Zech 12:10:

	Translation	MT
12:10a	Then I will pour out on the house of David and on the inhabitants of Jerusalem a spirit of grace and pleas for mercy.	וְשָׁפַכְתִּי עַל־בֵּית דָּוִיד וְעַל יוֹשֵׁב יְרוּשָׁלִַם רוּחַ חֵן וְתַחֲנוּנִים
12:10b	As a result, they will look upon me whom they have pierced;	וְהִבִּיטוּ אֵלַי אֵת אֲשֶׁר־דָּקָרוּ

are ultimately futile.

12. Some take the events of Zech 12:1–9 to refer to the capture of Jerusalem by Antiochus Epiphanes in 167 BCE. Others argue that it refers to the fall of Jerusalem by Rome in 70 CE. Both of those events are certainly future to Zechariah's prophecy. The difficulty is that neither of those events fit all the details of this prophecy, especially in the way it speaks of Yahweh's final defeat of all the rebellious nations and in the way that Zech 14:2–5 associates the same battle with Yahweh's climactic coming at the end of history (cf. Zech 14:6–9, 11). As will become clearer in chapters 3 and 4 below, these events surrounding Yahweh's final coming/appearing in Zechariah's prophecy seem best understood in light of both Jesus' first advent of humility and Jesus' second advent of glory. Cf. also the discussion in Petterson, *Zechariah*, 266–69, 299–301.

13. For example, the majority of Zech 9:1–17 deals with the external deliverance of the people, but their salvation does not happen apart from their inward transformation, even following sharp rebukes for their persistence in sin (e.g., Zech 10:7, 12). Likewise, and more explicitly, the second oracle reveals inward transformation in the midst of external victory (e.g., Zech 12:10–14; 13:1, 9; 14:16). T. E. McComiskey calls this latter emphasis a "spiritual renewal." See McComiskey, "Zechariah," 1214. The magnitude of the new spiritual work becomes intensified in the appearance of the verb שָׁפַךְ ("to pour out"), normally used when Yahweh pours out his wrath on Israel (Isa 42:25; Jer 6:11; 10:25; Ezek 7:8; 22:31; Hos 5:10) or the nations (Zeph 3:8). In the new work of which Zechariah and others speak, God will "pour out" his Spirit to transform the nation of Israel's spirit (Zech 12:10; cf. Ezek 39:29; Joel 2:28, 29).

| 12:10c | and they will mourn for him as one mourns for an only child, and grieve over him as one grieves over a firstborn. | וְסָפְדוּ עָלָיו כְּמִסְפֵּד עַל־הַיָּחִיד וְהָמֵר עָלָיו כְּהָמֵר עַל־הַבְּכוֹר |

With these words, the prophet communicates that Yahweh of Hosts will do much more than defeat rebel nations on behalf of his people (Zech 12:2–9). Indeed, Yahweh will also conquer every rebel pride that keeps Israel from rightly humbling themselves before him (Zech 12:10–14). That a formerly rebellious Israel is in view seems evident in that they committed a violent act of piercing (Zech 12:10), they mourn over their wretched deed (Zech 12:11), and they need their sin/uncleanness removed (Zech 13:1). This rebellious community receives "a spirit of grace and pleas for mercy," signaling Yahweh's work to change the recalcitrant nation[14] into a repentant nation, who are now largely aware of their need for Yahweh's mercy (Zech 12:12–14).[15] Because of Yahweh's gracious work toward his formerly rebellious people (Zech 12:10a), they will mourn with great sorrow and repentance as they look upon the one they pierced (Zech 12:10c–14).[16] Yet who is the mysterious Pierced One?

Already Zech 3:8 and Zech 6:12 anticipate a figure rather close to Yahweh, namely, עַבְדִּי צֶמַח ("my servant, the Branch"), who will consummate the typological patterns of priest and temple builder observed in Joshua and Zerubbabel respectively.[17] Another figure close

---

14. Klein, *Zechariah*, 364.

15. "Pleas for mercy" (תַּחֲנוּן) regularly occurs in contexts wherein the sinner desperately needs God's salvation, such that if God refused to act, then the sinner's soul would perish in Sheol (Ps 28:2), he would be cut off from God's sight (Ps 31:23 [ET 31:22]), the snares of death would swallow him whole (Ps 116:1), and the wrath of God would consume him altogether (Ps 143:1–2; cf. Ps 86:6; 140:7 [ET 140:6]). Psalm 130:1–4 serves as a fitting example: "O Lord, hear my voice! Let your ears be attentive to the voice of my pleas for mercy [תַּחֲנוּנָי]! If you, O LORD, should mark iniquities, O Lord, who could stand? But with you there is forgiveness, that you may be feared."

16. That mourning with repentant sorrow is in view is a common interpretation: Baldwin, *Zechariah*, 205; McComiskey, "Zechariah," 1214; Klein, *Zechariah*, 364; Petterson, *Zechariah*, 263.

17. According to Zech 3:6–9, the restored Joshua and his friends—most likely fellow priests (Zech 5:10–11, 14; cf. Ezra 2:36, 60; 8:29–30)—are a מוֹפֵת ("sign;" cf. Isa 8:18) pointing to the coming of a superior figure, the Branch. The vocabulary

to Yahweh also appears in Zech 9:9–11, who will eventually come as king; and through his humble and righteous reign, Zion will know a new covenant and the nations will experience peace. Then Zech 13:7 introduces yet another figure very close to Yahweh, namely, רֹעִי ("my shepherd") and עֲמִיתִי ("my companion"); and the way his demise directly effects the sheep seems to evoke how Yahweh earlier portrayed his relationship with Israel as that of a shepherd with his sheep.[18]

Any one of these figures—and perhaps all of them—may stand as suitable candidates for the Pierced One. However, is it also valid to identify the Pierced One as Yahweh, not just someone close with Yahweh? Asking such a question is justified by the thesis before us, but the question also seems justified by the sustained tension between Yahweh saving his people and Yahweh's king saving his people with some contexts making the two hardly distinguishable.[19]

---

employed suggests several characteristics about the Branch. He will serve as a king from David's line (צֶמַח, "Branch"; Zech 3:8; cf. Isa 4:2; Jer 23:5; 33:15; Ps 132:17; cf. Isa 11:1). He will establish a new covenant—taking the stone in Zech 3:9 as not only a stone upon which God's eyes are fixed (Zech 4:10; cf. idiom in 2 Sam 22:28; 2 Chr 20:12; Jer 16:17; 24:6), but also a stone likened to the tablets of the old covenant (e.g., Exod 24:12; 31:18; 34:1, 4; Deut 4:13) but surpassing it with the promise of the forgiveness of sins in a single day (Zech 3:9; cf. Jer 31:34). The Branch will also bring an abundant kingdom as anticipated elsewhere in Scripture (Zech 3:10; cf. Gen 49:10; 1 Kgs 4:25; Isa 25:6–8; Jer 31:10–12; Mic 4:1–4; Amos 9:11–14). The prophetic sign-act in Zech 6:9–14, where Joshua the high priest receives a royal crown, adds to our understanding of the Branch. He will be a priestly king—וְהָיָה כֹהֵן עַל־כִּסְאוֹ ("and he shall be a priest on his throne"). I understand the two persons at the end of Zech 6:13 (בֵּין שְׁנֵיהֶם, "between them both") as the Branch in his role as priest-king and Yahweh (cf. Ps 110:1, 5). As someone better and beyond Zerubbabel (Zech 6:13–14; cf. 4:6–10), the Branch will build the future temple of the Lord anticipated already in Zech 2:1–12 and by other prophets before him (cf. Isa 2:2–4; Jer 3:16–18; Ezek 40–48; Hag 2:7–9). The Branch will also bear royal honor (Zech 6:13), an answer to the lament of David's fallen line in Ps 89:44.

18. E.g., the Lord will protect them (Zech 9:15), he will save them as the flock of his people (Zech 9:16; 10:3), and he will whistle for them and gather them in (Zech 10:8). Moreover, like Ezek 34 and Jer 23, Zech 10:2 and Zech 11:4–17 suggest that only Yahweh, the true shepherd, can fill the void left by the worthless shepherds in Israel.

19. E.g., notice the similar vocabulary between Yahweh's coming in Zech 2:10—"Sing and rejoice, O daughter of Zion [וְשִׂמְחִי בַּת־צִיּוֹן], for behold, I come [בָא] and I will dwell in your midst"—and the king's coming in Zech 9:9—"Rejoice [גִּילִי] greatly, O daughter of Zion [בַּת־צִיּוֹן]! Shout aloud, O daughter of Jerusalem! Behold, your king is coming [יָבוֹא לָךְ] to you." Also, both the king and Yahweh bring salvation

Jesus as the Pierced One

In order to answer this question, I must address several obstacles that, when taken together, provide a complex problem in unveiling the Pierced One's identity. I will handle these obstacles in three steps: first, by analyzing one textual difficulty alongside two grammatical difficulties; second, by evaluating the use of דָּקַר ("to pierce") and especially its subsequent effect on the translators of the LXX; and third, by evaluating how personages other than Yahweh fall short of the message in Zech 12:10.

TEXTUAL AND GRAMMATICAL DIFFICULTIES

Several issues involving text-criticism, grammar, and syntax have produced noticeable differences among common English translations for Zech 12:10.[20] One major textual difficulty alongside two grammatical difficulties leave many careful scholars humbled in their attempts to understand the Pierced One of Zech 12:10.

The First-Person Reading of the MT

The first difficulty arises with whether one should accept the first-person reading of Zech 12:10b, אֵלַי ("to me"), presented by the MT. Instead of the first-person reading, some have opted for a third-person reading, אֵלָיו ("to him").[21] Several reasons appear to support the third-person

---

(Zech 8:7, 13; 9:9, 16), establish peace (Zech 8:12; 9:10), possess universal dominion (Zech 9:10, 14–15; 14:1–21), and even receive worship (Zech 14:9, 16, 17). Thus, the tension surrounds how they distinctly relate in the midst of incredible unity. Also, in reference to the shepherd-companion of Zech 13:7, some interpreters not only identify him with the Pierced One of Zech 12:10, but further assert that the shepherd must be God's equal. E.g., Keil and Delitzsch, *Twelve Minor Prophets*, 617; Baldwin, *Zechariah*, 198; Unger, *Zechariah*, 231; Klein, *Zechariah*, 386–87.

20. Comparing the ESV, NRSV, and NJB sufficiently demonstrates these challenges. The ESV maintains the peculiarities of the Hebrew: "so that, when they look on me [Yahweh], on him whom they have pierced, they shall mourn for him." The NRSV avoids Yahweh being pierced: "so that, when they look on *the one whom* they have pierced, they shall mourn for him." The NJB adjusts the meaning by changing the punctuation: "and they will look to me. They will mourn for the one whom they have pierced." For additional comparisons between English translations, see Kubiś, *Zechariah in John*, 119–25. The same challenges appear in differing German translations as well. See Deissler, "Sach 12,10," 50–52.

21. See, e.g., those listed in Lacocque, *Zacharie 9–14*, 189. Other textual emendations, such as those suggested in the apparatus of *BHS* and *BHK*, will merit further

reading. First, the third-person reading appears to remove the rather mysterious and offensive idea that God would suffer piercing. Second, the sudden shift from a first-person object to a third-person object within five words explaining closely related events disappears, allowing for a more straightforward interpretation. Instead of reading, "They will look to me ... and mourn for him," the sentence would maintain the third-person object throughout: "They will look to him ... and mourn for him."[22] Third, אֵלָיו ("to him") more closely resembles first-century translations such as John 19:37 (εἰς ὃν, "on whom") and Rev 1:7 (αὐτὸν, "him"). If one assumes that these first-century translations accurately reflect a Hebrew *Vorlage* other than the MT, the retroversion would not include the equivalent of אֵלַי (i.e., πρός με). Fourth, the variant אֵלָיו ("to him") exists elsewhere in numerous medieval manuscripts collected by Kennicott and de Rossi, a reception history that provides some warrant for the third-person suffix.[23] On internal and external grounds, therefore, some have found reason to select the third-person suffix over the first-person.

However, these arguments do not necessarily merit selecting the third-person over the first-person suffix. We shall deal with each in reverse order. First, according to Goshen-Gottstein, these collections of Kennicott and de Rossi do not ultimately "yield a single variant which is significantly, decisively, and undoubtedly connected with a pre-medieval tradition."[24] The collections show no conclusive evidence of predating the activity of the Masoretes and consist "mostly of

---

comment and critique below.

22. Furthermore, Barthélemy argues for the likelihood that the two occurrences of עָלָיו ("over him") following Zech 12:10b guided the copyist to pen אֵלָיו ("to him") in some manuscripts instead of אֵלַי ("to me"). Barthélemy, *Critique Textuelle de l'Ancien Testament*, 3:xlii.

23. For thirty-eight manuscripts that include אֵלָיו ("to him") as the preferred reading, see Kennicott, *Vetus Testamentum Hebraicum*, 2:300. De Rossi identifies seven manuscripts with אֵלָיו ("to him"). De Rossi, *Variae Lectiones Veteris Testamenti*, 3:217–20. Contra Jansma, "Inquiry," 118. Jansma counts thirteen in de Rossi. See also Sæbø, *Sacharja 9–14*, 97.

24. Goshen-Gottstein, "Hebrew Biblical Manuscripts," 77. A "pre-medieval tradition" describes those manuscripts that antedate 1100 CE. Therefore, antiquity also does not favor the collections of Kennicott and de Rossi in comparison to the MT. Likewise, see Tov, *Textual Criticism, 3rd Ed.*, 37–39.

secondary scribal changes, parallelisms, normalizations, harmonizations, or free associations."[25] Furthermore, one should not overlook the fact that Kennicott identifies eleven manuscripts that maintain אֵלַי ("to me") as the *Qere* and that de Rossi ultimately follows the MT.[26] Using Kennicott and de Rossi's collections solely for support not only ignores some of their own work, but also fails to see the uncertainty behind these respective traditions. In the end, these collections do not necessitate choosing אֵלָיו ("to him") over אֵלַי ("to me"); they only show that both variants remain viable.

Second, that the Apostle John quotes a portion of Zech 12:10b, using a translation representative of the third-person variant (e.g., εἰς ὅν in John 19:37), does not necessitate dismissing the reading found in the MT.[27] In many cases where NT authors quote more directly from the OT, the quoted texts will often undergo minor changes in order to befit the redemptive-historical situation and clarify a theological point for the recipients.[28] Furthermore, because the NT authors view Christ's first and second advents as fulfilling the OT's eschatological expectations, they often find warrant to change the language of a passage in order to connect the prophetic word more clearly with its historical realization, whether past, present, or future.[29] Thus, establishing a He-

25. Tov, *Textual Criticism*, 2nd Ed., 52.

26. See Kennicott, *Vetus Testamentum Hebraicum*, 2:100; De Rossi, *Variae Lectiones Veteris Testamenti*, 3:219. Conclusions regarding de Rossi were first observed in Sæbø, *Sacharja 9–14*, 97n4.

27. So also Orelli, *Minor Prophets*, 366.

28. E.g., notice how Matthew changes the feminine singular subject in וְקָרָאת ("and she will call") to the plural subject in καλέσουσιν ("they shall call") when he cites Isa 7:14 in Matt 1:23. This appropriation befits the confession, "Immanuel," made by those people whom the virgin-born Jesus saves from their sins (Matt 1:21). Regarding the apostles' "minor text modifications," see Moo, *Old Testament*, 363–97.

29. One clear example occurs with the use of Isa 28:16 in Rom 10:11 and 1 Pet 2:6. The apostles appear to follow the LXX (ἐπ' αὐτῷ, "upon him") over the Hebrew (no object), since it better identifies the cornerstone itself as the object of one's faith. For them, the Christ-event clarifies the ultimate aim of the prophetic word. Cf. also the differences in John's use of Isa 6:10 in John 12:40, or of Ps 69:4 (cf. Ps 35:19) in John 15:25, or of Exod 12:46 (cf. Num 9:12; Ps 34:20) in John 19:36. In other words, there is no need for John to follow the Hebrew so strictly with ὄψονται εἰς με ὅν ἐξεκέντησαν ("they will look on *me* whom they pierced"), since his double quotation in John 19:36–37 sufficiently associates the crucified Christ with Exodus's Passover lamb and Zechariah's Pierced One. Regarding John's typological interpretation of

brew *Vorlage* with the third-person suffix based on a NT citation alone is uncertain at best.

Third, replacing the MT with אֵלָיו ("to him") does not necessarily remove the difficulty of interpretation. Even though אֵלָיו ("to him") may evade the theological crux of piercing Yahweh, the text would still contain two third-person suffixes (i.e., אֵלָיו and עָלָיו) that could represent two different objects. The object of the people's looking (וְהִבִּיטוּ אֵלָיו, "they will look to him") could differ from the object of their mourning (וְסָפְדוּ עָלָיו, "they shall mourn for him"). Changing the MT to remove interpretive obstacles merely shifts the complex discussion away from Yahweh to another unknown martyr.[30] In this way, choosing a third-person suffix over the MT calls for equal labor in identifying the Pierced One, making both readings equal possibilities to this point.

Fourth, while keeping the first-person suffix would make Zech 12:10 the only place in the OT where Yahweh explicitly describes himself as pierced,[31] the following study will seek to answer how Yahweh may refer to himself in this way. Moreover, several positive arguments

---

Jesus as the Passover Lamb, see Hoskins, "Deliverance," 283–99. Likewise, John's conflation of OT texts in Rev 1:7 sufficiently identifies the returning Christ as Zechariah's Pierced One, who carries out his final mission as Daniel's Son of Man. The allusion in Rev 1:7 to portions of Zech 12:10–14 and Dan 7:13–14 will receive further treatment in chapter 4 below.

30. What is more, as this study will attempt to show below, the reading of the MT may ultimately provide more clarity to this scenario than that of the third-person variant. Accepting the third-person suffix in אֵלָיו merely provides readers with an unknown martyr. Maintaining the first-person suffix of the MT in אֵלַי supplies readers with a direct reference to the person of Yahweh himself: "Then I [i.e., Yahweh] will pour out on the house of David and on the inhabitants of Jerusalem a spirit of grace and pleas for mercy. As a result, they will look upon *me* [i.e., Yahweh] . . . " (Zech 12:10).

31. This does not deny that the OT bears witness to other figures directly related to Yahweh who also experience piercing. One clear example includes Yahweh's Suffering Servant in Isa 53:5, who is pierced (חלל, "to pierce") for the people's transgressions. Another example of a pierced messianic figure may include David, whose sufferings the Apostle John interprets as typological references to Christ. See, e.g., John 13:18 (Ps 41:9); 17:12 (Ps 41:9; cf. John 13:18); 19:24 (Ps 22:18); 19:36 (Ps 34:20); cf. Exod 12:46; Num 9:12); and especially John 15:25 (Ps 69:4) and John 19:28 (Ps 69:21). Further discussion on the Suffering Servant and the Davidic king as Yahweh's representatives continue below on pp. 61–63. Where I am saying Zech 12:10 is unique, and therefore dissimilar from a text like Isa 53, is in Zechariah's explicit claim that sees Yahweh himself as the one pierced.

exist for retaining אֵלַי ("to me") over the variant reading אֵלָיו ("to him"). To begin, extant versions support the first-person reading, including the LXX, *Peshîṭtâ* (Syriac), Targum, and Vulgate. As a translation of the Hebrew, the LXX[32] has καὶ ἐπιβλέψονται πρός με ("and they shall look toward me"), the *Peshîṭtâ* version has *wnḥwrwn lwty bmn ddqrw* ("and they shall look on me whom they pierced"), Targum Jonathan has וִיבְעוֹן מִן־קֳדָמַי ("they shall entreat from before me"), and the Vulgate has *et aspicient ad me quem confixerunt* ("and they look upon me whom they pierced").[33] Although these four versions differ at other places in Zech 12:10, all of them agree in their attestation of the first-person suffix as found in the MT.

Further, the reading found in the MT lays claim to be the *lectio difficilior*.[34] For the reasons already expressed above, it is easier to explain an emendation from the awkward אֵלַי to אֵלָיו than vice versa, especially if the latter makes Yahweh the object of the people's piercing. In applying the internal criteria of the *lectio difficilior* one should recognize the real possibility of facing equally difficult readings. However, that is not the case when comparing אֵלַי ("to me") with אֵלָיו ("to him").

---

32. By using "the LXX," I do not intend to suggest that "the Greek translation [of the OT] found in a given ancient manuscript or modern edition is a homogenous text produced in its entirety at one point in time." Jobes and Silva, *Septuagint*, 30. As Jobes and Silva note, "it is probably better to refer to the original translation of books other than the Pentateuch as the Old Greek (OG) so as to distinguish them from the original translation of the Pentateuch and from the later revisions and new translations." Yet, even Jobes and Silva acknowledge that "even the term *Old Greek* is not totally satisfactory." Therefore, following Jobes and Silva, "unless the context requires a distinction, we will . . . continue to use the term *Septuagint* [or, in my case, LXX] in its general sense . . . " Jobes and Silva, *Septuagint*, 32. See also Tov, *Textual Criticism, 3rd Ed.*, 128–29.

33. For the Aramaic texts, see the discussion in Mitchell, "Messiah," 221–41. Later Greek translations, such as Aquila, Theodotion, and Symmachus, also reflect the first-person suffix. See the thorough text-form analysis by Menken, "Textual Form," 494–504; Kubiś, *Zechariah in John*, 146–71. The transliteration from the Syriac in *Peshîṭtâ* comes from Menken, "Textual Form," 501. For a careful analysis and translation of the *Peshîṭtâ* version, see the excursus in Kubiś, *Zechariah in John*, 157–58.

34. The rule of *lectio difficilior* is that "the more difficult reading is to be preferred." Tov, *Textual Criticism, 3rd Ed.*, 275. Regarding the first-person reading as the more difficult one, see also Delcor, "Un Problèm," 192; Lamarche, *Zacharie IX–XIV*, 82; Sæbø, *Sacharja 9–14*, 100.

Finally, אֵלַי ("to me") remains a more reasonable and contextually appropriate reading when considered in light of the spiritual renewal mentioned in Zech 12:10a. The third-person reading אֵלָיו ("to him") is certainly plausible, if, for instance, one equates the Pierced One with a figure like Yahweh's kingly representative, whose coming the people must behold: "Behold [הִנֵּה]! Your king is coming" (Zech 9:9). However, in Zech 12:10a Yahweh gives the people "a spirit of grace and pleas for mercy [תַּחֲנוּן]," and in nearly every occurrence where a person/people express תַּחֲנוּן ("pleas for mercy"), Yahweh is the sole object of their faith (Pss 28:2, 6; 31:23 [ET 31:22]; 86:6; 116:1; 130:2; 140:7 [ET 140:6]; 143:1) or attention (Dan 9:3, 17, 18).

Also, additional aspects within Zechariah's redemptive portrait make Yahweh the most acceptable object of the people's actions.[35] These additional aspects become apparent in the pattern of spiritual renewal expressed elsewhere in Zech 9–14. As Yahweh is the object of the people's remembrance in Zech 10:9 (יִזְכְּרוּנִי, "they shall remember me") and the object of their call of dependence in Zech 13:9 (יִקְרָא בִשְׁמִי, "they will call upon my name"), so Yahweh is the object of the people's looking in Zech 12:10b (וְהִבִּיטוּ אֵלַי, "they will look to me"). The pattern of spiritual renewal, where Yahweh is not only acting for the people's redemption but simultaneously becoming the object of the people's faith, strengthens the contextual argument for the first-person reading. For all of the aforementioned reasons, therefore, I retain the

---

35 As I am doing here, others have tried to support the first-person suffix with such a contextual argument based only on the numerous first-person references to Yahweh throughout Zech 12. E.g., see Kohler, *Die Nachexilischen Propheten*, 199; Lamarche, *Zacharie IX–XIV*, 82; Chary, *Aggée-Zacharie*, 201; Lacocque, *Zacharie 9–14*, 189; Merrill, *Zechariah*, 319–21; Bilić, *Jerusalem*, 335–36. Kaiser does similarly, but relates each first-person reference to the Messiah. Kaiser, *Messiah in OT*, 225. However, additional contextual insights are necessary. Certainly, the first-person references throughout ch. 12 rightly acknowledge the centrality of Yahweh within the redemptive portrait, but the observation fails to realize that Yahweh is the subject of most of the verbs instead of the object as in Zech 12:10b. For the numerous first-person references to Yahweh throughout ch. 12, see Zech 12:2, 3, 4, 6, 9, 10. Thus, the same argumentation could still support the third-person suffix. When making a contextual argument for the first-person suffix, one must determine whether additional aspects within Zechariah's redemptive portrait make Yahweh the most acceptable object of the people's actions as well.

Jesus as the Pierced One

first-person reading of the MT, and proceed now to the two grammatical difficulties accordingly.

The Function of the Phrase אֶת אֲשֶׁר

The second difficulty for identifying the Pierced One in Zech 12:10b is grammatical. In particular, the phrase אֶת אֲשֶׁר determines whether and how the first-person suffix in אֵלַי (i.e., "me") relates to the verb דָּקָרוּ ("they pierced").[36] Will the people look to Yahweh whom they have pierced, or will they look to Yahweh concerning another they have pierced? Thus, the combination of אֶת, traditionally called the *nota accusativi*, with the relative particle, אֲשֶׁר, plays a significant role in determining the identity of the Pierced One. The traditional label of אֶת as *nota accusativi* simply refers to the chief (but not the only) function of the particle, namely, to mark the accusative or the direct object of a transitive verb.[37] If אֶת maintains its chief function in Zech 12:10b—and there is good reason to think that it does (see below)—then the relative particle, אֲשֶׁר, becomes the direct object of דָּקָרוּ; and the entire phrase, אֶת־אֲשֶׁר־דָּקָרוּ, functions as a relative clause modifying the object of the main verb in וְהִבִּיטוּ אֵלַי. The resulting translation would be, "and they will look on me [indirect object of וְהִבִּיטוּ] whom [direct object of דָּקָרוּ] they pierced," with Yahweh remaining the object of both the looking and the piercing. Yet before asserting that the phrase functions in this way, we must first evaluate the possibilities presented by others.

Among proposals honoring the phrase אֶת אֲשֶׁר present in the MT,[38] the history of interpretation varies. The LXX treats the phrase

---

36. The assumption here is that preposition אֶל functions with its most basic meaning, "towards" (cf. HALOT, s.v. "אֶל"; *IBHS* §11.2.2). Thus, the preposition moves the action in נבט ("to look") towards its object: "they will look to/on me" (cf. HALOT, s.v. "נבט"). The other occurrences of preposition אֶל following נבט with a specified object support this conclusion (Exod 3:6; Num 21:9; 1 Sam 16:7; 2 Kgs 3:14; Pss 34:5; 119:6; Isa 22:11; 51:1, 2, 6; 66:2; Jonah 2:5; Hab 1:13). So also Klein, *Zechariah*, 365–66.

37. See, e.g., Wilson, "Particle אֶת, II," 213–21. GKC §117a; *IBHS* §10.3.1; Bekins, "Information Structure," 45. However, Bekins labels אֶת as an "object preposition" instead of *nota accusativi*. Bekins, "Information Structure," 1n1.

38. Some view the grammatical peculiarity of אֵלַי אֶת אֲשֶׁר as a compelling reason to emend the MT. These scholars base their arguments on the assumption that the Hebrew (אֵלַי אֶת אֲשֶׁר) contains a "corrupt," "ungrammatical" construction

Yahweh as the Pierced One

in a causal sense, translating אֵת אֲשֶׁר with ἀνθ' ὧν ("because"). Targum Jonathan does likewise, but leaves its readers with a different scenario than that of the LXX. While the differences will merit further comment below, the causal reading from the Targum is obvious וְיִבְעוֹן מִן־קֳדָמַי עַל דְּאַטְלְטֵלוּ ("and they shall entreat me because they were

---

and is "unintelligible." The first two labels come from Oesterley, *A History of Israel*, 270. The latter appears in note 1 of GKC §138e. See also Sæbø, *Sacharja 9–14*, 100. Sæbø asserts that this text is "stricte dicta grammatisch unerträglich" ("*stricte dicta* grammatically unbearable"). Likewise, the apparatus of *BHS* suggests dropping the particle אֵת to produce the variant reading, אֶל־אֲשֶׁר (cf. note 1 in GKC §138e). *BHS* also suggests re-pointing אֱלַי to resemble the rare by-form אֱלֵי, rendering the phrase, אֱלֵי־אֲשֶׁר, while again dropping particle אֵת. The older *BHK* suggests another emendation, אֱלֵי מֵת ("to the dead one"). Kubis lists additional emendations proposed by later commentaries, but then dismisses each as conjecture based on external and internal textual criticism. Kubiś, *Zechariah in John*, 122–25. However, several factors prevent us from accepting these possible emendations. (1) The suggested pointing of preposition אֶל to read אֱלֵי never occurs in the MT outside the book of Job (Job 3:22; 5:26; 15:22; 29:19; cf. *HALOT*, s.v. "אֶל"). Jansma, "Inquiry," 118n56. (2) The readings offered by *BHS* and *BHK* find no clear support from the ancient versions. Cf. Kubiś, *Zechariah in John*, 123. (3) The readings suggested by *BHS* more likely represent a later gloss of the more difficult construction in the MT (i.e., אֵלַי אֵת אֲשֶׁר). Zeigler regards the aforementioned omission of the *nota accusativi* as a precursor to John 19:37 (ὄψονται εἰς ὃν ἐξεκέντησαν). Zeigler, *Duodecim Prophetae*, 8:319. In that sense, one could posit that the Apostle John either translated a Hebrew version missing the *nota accusativi*, or cited a Greek translation of the Hebrew that evidenced an omission of the *nota accusativi*. However, the external evidence favors keeping the *nota accusativi*. Moreover, it is equally plausible that John's gloss was intentional as he cites Zech 12:10b not from the standpoint of Yahweh, but from the standpoint of one of the onlookers. Cf. also Dahood, "Third Person Suffix," 63–64. Dahood also suggests that the pointing in the rare by-form, אֱלֵי, must assume a defectively-written אֱלוֹ (for אֵלָיו) prior to attributing the appearance of אֱלַי to a scribal error. (4) The variant readings mentioned in the apparatus of *BHS* and *BHK* require a textual omission of or change to the particle אֵת. Thus, both emendations question the integrity of the consonants in the MT, a text holding a historically privileged position among the ancient versions. Woude, "Pluriformity and Uniformity," 151–69; Tov, "History and Significance," 49–66 (esp. 62–66). Cf. also Condamin, "Le Sens Messianique," 53. Of course, exceptions to favoring the MT over other ancient versions still stand. See Tov, *Textual Criticism, 2nd Ed.*, 24–25, 298–99. Tov carefully notes how the unique socio-religious character of the MT "does not necessarily imply it contains the best text of the Bible." However, the research below suggests Zech 12:10b does not belong to those exceptions, as the same construction appears in other places in the MT, even where text-critical issues and anthropomorphic concerns do not cloud the context. Therefore, it seems more plausible to deal with the MT as it stands.

exiled").³⁹ The causal rendering of אֵת אֲשֶׁר also appears among several later interpreters.⁴⁰

Although the LXX and Targum independently render the phrase as one showing a causal relationship to אֵלַי ("to me"), a number of inconsistencies appear in the manner they each treat other texts of the OT. For example, of the 143 occurrences of אֵת אֲשֶׁר in the MT, the LXX never translates the phrase with ἀνθ' ὧν except in Zech 12:10.⁴¹ Even the LXX's other two instances of ἀνθ' ὧν within Zechariah provide little justification for its appearance in Zech 12:10 for אֵת אֲשֶׁר.⁴² Moreover, as others have proposed, choosing ἀνθ' ὧν may stem from the need to square the Hebrew phrase with a misreading of דָּקַר ("to pierce") for רָקַד ("to dance").⁴³ Yet even without surmising a misreading one

---

39. The Aramaic citation appears in Sperber, *Bible in Aramaic*, 3:495. The translation of the Aramaic comes from Cathcart and Gordon, *Targum*, 14:218. Italics were removed.

40. Kimḥi and M'Caul, *Prophecies of Zechariah*, 155. See also Troki, *Faith Strengthened*, 183–84. He takes אֵת אֲשֶׁר as equal to בַּעֲבוּר ("because") and argues that it does not mean "whom." Cf. Woude, *Zacharia*, 235–36. Even some English translations, such as the one by the Jewish Publication Society, illustrate this causal interpretation: "and they shall look unto Me because they have thrust him through."

41. The 143 occurrences of the *nota accusitivi* plus the relative particle אֲשֶׁר do not include Exod 29:33, Josh 1:15, Judg 6:31, 1 Kgs 11:34, Jer 41:2, Ezek 17:16, 20:11, or 20:21, since they exhibit a suffix attached to the *nota accusitivi*. The Greek construction, ἀνθ' ὧν, serves most often as a causal rendering of the Hebrew phrases, יַעַן אֲשֶׁר,תַּחַת אֲשֶׁר, and עַל אֲשֶׁר, or plain אֲשֶׁר—and rightly so. See *IBHS* §38.4a. See also Menken, "Textual Form," 500n18. Menken adds the simple יַעַן to his own list. However, the LXX never renders אֵת אֲשֶׁר in this causal sense, except in Zech 12:10b. For אֵת אֲשֶׁר, the LXX normally uses the relative adjective ὅσος and relative pronoun ὅς, whether alone, with ἄν, or with ἐάν.

42. The LXX understands the relative particle, אֲשֶׁר, in Zech 1:15 as initiating a causal clause, which not only makes sense within the context but also falls within the particle's semantic domain. Cf. *HALOT*, s.v. "אֲשֶׁר." Yet the LXX also transforms the purpose clause of Zech 13:4—initiated by לְמַעַן—into one that becomes causal with ἀνθ' ὧν, a transformation of לְמַעַן that occurs nowhere else when the LXX translates לְמַעַן. Cf. Bilić, *Jerusalem*, 50. Bilić notes this Greek phrase as a possible additional connection between chs. 12 and 13.

43. The LXX renders Zech 12:10b, καὶ ἐπιβλέψονται πρός με ἀνθ' ὧν κατωρχήσαντο καὶ κόψονται ἐπ' αὐτόν ("and they will look to me because they danced [presumably in mockery; cf. the VL's "insultaverunt" and the comments by Jerome in his letter to Pammachius], and they will mourn for him"). Also, in his commentary on the Minor Prophets, Jerome writes, "sin contrario ordine accipitur sc. dacaru, litteris commutates racadu ὠρχήσαντο, id est, saltaverunt, intelligitur" ("if, contrary to the received

Yahweh as the Pierced One

must still ask why the LXX has inconsistently treated דָּקַר in Zech 12:10 with the most obscure vocabulary, when elsewhere the LXX translates דָּקַר with vocabulary that conveys its meaning so accurately?[44] If such unambiguous vocabulary was available to the translators of the LXX, why opt for such obscure vocabulary in Zech 12:10 unless driven by a particular theological bias, namely, to evade the piercing of Yahweh?[45] Targum Jonathan also inconsistently translates דָּקַר as "to exile" in Zech 12:10, while in Judg 9:54, 1 Sam 31:4, and Isa 13:15, it retains the normal sense of "to kill."[46] Additionally, with respect to Targum Jonathan, one should not forget the strong possibility that this reading is a result of a later Jewish interpolation in response to the Christological exegesis of the early church.[47] For translation inconsistencies and/or theologi-

---

order—namely, דָּקַר—the letters were changed to רָקַד, then 'to dance' would be the meaning"), as cited in Jansma, "Inquiry," 118, with my translation. See also Menken, "Textual Form," 500n16. Menken gives several examples of deliberate letter transposition in early Judaism. Cf. Klauck, "Schriftzitate in Der Johannespassion," 156. Instead of a misreading of רָקַד for דָּקַר, one might also surmise that the translators of the LXX provided a proper reading of a poorly copied Hebrew *Vorlage*. However, a misreading seems to be the better guess of the two, since later recensions—whether Jewish (e.g., Aquila, Symmachus, or Theodotion) or Christian (e.g., Lucian)—correct the deficiencies of the LXX when it comes to דָּקַר in Zech 12:10, regardless if at least one of the recensions still distances Yahweh from the piercing (i.e., Aquila has σὺν ᾧ ἐξεκέντησαν, "*with* the one whom they have pierced"). For an overview of these aforementioned recensions, their nature, and their approximate dating, see Jobes and Silva, *Septuagint*, 46–56; Tov, *Textual Criticism, 3rd Ed.*, 141–47. Whether a misreading stands as the best proposal will receive further treatment below under the "The Use of דָּקַר and Its Effect on Translators of the LXX." See also the tables in Appendix 1 and Appendix 2 for a comparison between the MT, the LXX, and other ancient Greek translations.

44. E.g., ἀποκεντέω, "to pierce through" (Num 25:8; 1 Sam 31:4 [twice]); ἐκκεντέω, "to pierce" (Judg 9:54; 1 Chr 10:4; Jer 37:10); κατακεντέω, "to pierce/stab" (Jer 51:4); κεντέω, "to stab" (Lam 4:9). Hübenthal also highlights a related inconsistency over the LXX's translation of the same verb, דָּקַר, just a few verses later in Zech 13:3. Where the MT has וּדְקָרֻהוּ ("they shall pierce him through"), the LXX reads συμποδιοῦσιν αὐτὸν ("they shall tie his feet together" or "they shall bind him [hand and foot]"). Hübenthal, *Transformation*, 206. More to be said about Zech 13:3 below.

45. Further discussion regarding the potential theological bias will continue below under the section titled "The Use of דָּקַר and Its Effect on Translators of the LXX."

46. See Cathcart and Gordon, *Targum*, 14:218n28.

47. Regarding this theological move reflected in the Targumic literature, see Mitchell, "Messiah," 222–32. Mitchell argues for a pre-Christian interpretation and

Jesus as the Pierced One

cal bias, therefore, the causal interpretations employed by the LXX or Targum Jonathan do not gain my trust.[48]

Veering away from the causal interpretation of אֵת אֲשֶׁר, the proposals become numerous depending on the syntactical function one ascribes to particle אֵת.[49] Magne Sæbø views the phrase in apposition to the first-person suffix (י-).[50] However, Sæbø's proposal amounts to mere conjecture, since he sees the construction as evidence of a pre-Masoretic compositional process that combined two different forms.[51]

Other proposals lead to similar results as Sæbø, but without the guesswork attributed to a long unknown textual history. For example, some describe אֵת as a deictic particle, which directly "mark[s] an explanatory insertion" with respect to the Pierced One.[52] Providing even

---

dating of Targumic Tosefta and a post-Christian interpretation and dating of the standard text, Targum Jonathan. In agreement with Cathcart and Gordon (above), Mitchell bases his argument on (1) "marks of revision in the standard Targum," (2) "the early Christian use of Zech 12:10" alongside an "existing messianic interpretation in Israel," and (3) the likelihood that Tosefta's messianic reading would *not* have "arisen in the Christian period . . . after the death of Jesus of Nazereth." Mitchell, "Messiah," 230–31. In accordance with (1) above, see also the extensive treatment of Gordon, "Ephraimite Messiah," 184–95. Moreover, such messianic expectations mentioned in (2) of Mitchell's argument coincide with Rosenberg, "Slain Messiah," 259–61.

48. That the LXX and Targum—both of which happen to evade the literal piercing of Yahweh—may very well share a common source of exegetical traditions, see Dogniez, "Similarities," 89–102.

49. The numerous proposals become even more understandable in light of Muraoka's remarks: "No single particle has given rise to more widespread and also mutually more contradictory discussion than this so-called *nota accusativi*." Muraoka, *Emphatic Words*, 146.

50. Thus, Sæbø allows אֵת אֲשֶׁר to express a substantival idea rendered in English by "look to me, whom." Sæbø, *Sacharja 9–14*, 99–102. For Sæbø, the extensive textual history eventually combined two variations: (1) והביטו אלי and (2) והביטו את אשר-ד. Sæbø, *Sacharja 9–14*, 100.

51. Several in-depth treatments of particle אֵת have also mentioned the possibility of אֵת introducing a word or phrase in apposition to a nominal phrase. See Wilson, "Particle את, I," 149; Wilson, "Particle את, II," 221; MacDonald, "Particle את in Classical Hebrew," 269–70. However, none of these studies list Zech 12:10b in their examples. Moreover, the examples which are present in these studies differ significantly from the unique construction appearing in Zech 12:10b—where a pronominal suffix is attached to a preposition, followed by אֵת plus אֲשֶׁר and an attached verb—making the category of apposition a less likely candidate.

52. See Witt, "Zechariah 12–14," 46, 166n12. Witt obtains this category from

further specificity, others see particle אֵת functioning in a reflexive sense (i.e., "look on me, myself, whom"), or in an intensive sense (i.e., "look on me, the same one whom").[53] Based on recent studies in extra-biblical Hebrew, John Elwolde further suggests a "resumptive" use of אֵת, wherein the particle replaces the preceding preposition. Listing Zech 12:10 as an example, Elwolde's proposal suggests that אֵת אֲשֶׁר resumes the idea already expressed in אֵלַי (i.e., "look on me, *on whom*"). However, more recent studies have carefully questioned whether the particle אֵת carries such a non-accusative, emphatic function at all, as each of these aforementioned proposals sets forward in one degree or another.[54]

Moreover, eleven other places in the MT contain the same grammatical construction, where a pronominal suffix is attached to a

---

Fishbane, *Biblical Interpretation*, 48–51. Witt translates the text, "recognize me, whom." Witt, "Zechariah 12–14," 166.

53. These two proposals are listed by Kubiś, *Zechariah in John*, 120–21. For the reflexive sense, Kubiś follows Rudolf Meyer's category for particle אֵת functioning as a "Hervorhebungspartikel" (or "highlighting particle"). Kubiś references Meyer, *Hebräische Grammatik*, §105,1b–c; but see also Meyer, "Nota Accusativi," 213. For the intensive sense, Kubiś follows Saydon, "Meanings and Uses," 201–4; *IBHS* §10.3b. Wilson also lists twenty-five examples where אֵת may have the function of a reflexive or intensive pronoun. See Wilson, "Particle אֵת, I," 141. Significantly, however, Wilson then argues that while emphasis—in the sense of the reflexive and intensive proposals outlined here—may have been an original force of אֵת, "[the particle] came to be used merely as a sign 'to call attention to what was already direct and definite.'" Wilson bases his conclusion on (1) "the absence of any special emphasis from many words or expressions before which the particle אֵת is used"; (2) "the use of אֵת with a word in one place and its omission from the same word in a similar, if not parallel, construction"; and (3) "the absence of אֵת before words which the writer desired to make as emphatic as possible." Wilson, "Particle אֵת, I," 143, 144, 146. Thus, by using Wilson's study only as support for an emphatic use of particle אֵת, *IBHS* §10.3b, seems to overstate the point of Wilson's initial observations.

54. Hoftijzer, "Particle et in Classical Hebrew," 1–99; Muraoka, *Emphatic Words*, 146–58; Davies, "Particle 'et in Hebrew Inscriptions," 14–26; Rubin, "Studies," 173–86; Bekins, "Information Structure," 30–40. Even where rare, atypical examples seem to persist, in which אֵת does not serve its primary grammatical role in relation to the direct object or the accusative or an object clause, careful consideration should first be given to the use and non-use of אֵת in relation to the syntactical category being proposed. Regarding the "resumptive" proposal, Elwolde builds on the study by MacDonald, "Particle את in Classical Hebrew," 270–71. However, for developments in Mishnaic Hebrew versus that found in biblical Hebrew, see the study by Rubin, "Studies," 173–86.

Jesus as the Pierced One

preposition, followed by אֵת plus אֲשֶׁר and an attached verb.⁵⁵ However, in none of these places does אֵת אֲשֶׁר carry a non-accusative, emphatic syntactical function as the aforementioned proposals suggest for Zech 12:10b. That does not mean אֵת אֲשֶׁר in these eleven other places functions precisely like its appearance in Zech 12:10b, but only that in all eleven places the particle אֵת carries its primary grammatical role in relation to the accusative or the direct object of the verbal idea⁵⁶ and should contribute to understanding the usage in Zech 12:10b.⁵⁷ For example, 1 Sam 28:8 and Ezek 23:22 both exemplify places where אֵת אֲשֶׁר begins a relative clause directly related to the context's implied object. Furthermore, the construction's second occurrence within 1 Sam 16:3—the closest to Zech 12:10b of the eleven examples—at least illustrates how אֵת אֲשֶׁר can identify the personal object of the verbal idea following the preposition.⁵⁸ Such observations not only confirm the negative conclusions regarding the causal interpretation above, they also sharpen the syntactical function of אֵת אֲשֶׁר in Zech 12:10b, as אֵת is more likely carrying its primary role as *nota accusativi* and, as stated above, establishes a clause modifying the object of the main verb observed in the first-person suffix of אֵלַי. Additionally, these eleven examples also weaken another proposal by Michael Floyd that

---

55. Gen 49:1; Ruth 2:18; 3:4; 1 Sam 10:8; 15:16; 16:3 [twice]; 28:8; 2 Sam 19:38 [37 ET]; Isa 41:22; Ezek 23:22.

56. In the eleven examples alluded to already, the phrase אֵת אֲשֶׁר marks a relative clause functioning as the verbal object (Gen 49:1; Ruth 2:18; 3:4; 1 Sam 15:16; 16:3 [first occurrence]; Isa 41:22), describes the direct object of a verbal idea (2 Sam 19:38), and identifies the personal object of the verbal idea (1 Sam 16:3 [second occurrence]; 28:8; Ezek 23:22).

57. Lacocque argues that אֵת אֲשֶׁר appears in Zech 12:10, because of its dependence on Ezek 36:27 (אֵת אֲשֶׁר־בְּחֻקַּי). Lacocque, *Zacharie 9–14*, 190. Here Lacocque follows Delcor, "Un Problèm," 189–99. Delcor draws similar intertextual connections with Ezek 36. However, this suggestion fails to see that the construction in Ezek 36:27 is of a different type. Furthermore, simply because the same words appear does not mean there is an intentional intertextual correspondence. One must also determine how they function within their respective contexts.

58. First Samuel 16:3 states, "And you shall invite Jesse to the sacrifice, and I will show you what you shall do, and you shall anoint for me him whom I declare to you [וּמָשַׁחְתָּ לִי אֵת אֲשֶׁר־אֹמַר אֵלֶיךָ]." Cf. also *IBHS* §10.3.1a, which cites 1 Sam 16:3 as an example where the relative particle אֲשֶׁר is governed by אֵת: "and you shall on my behalf anoint *the one of whom* I will speak to you."

the phrase, אֶת אֲשֶׁר, is syntactically independent from the first-person suffix in אֵלַי.⁵⁹

Such a conclusion receives even further support from the work of Niko Bilić. Bilić insightfully recognizes one other occurrence that sharpens the syntactical function of אֶת אֲשֶׁר even further. He contends that Jer 38:9 also contains a comparable construction that provides the best clarification for Zech 12:10b.⁶⁰ These two texts appear below for comparative purposes.

Jer 38:9		אֲשֶׁר־הִשְׁלִיכוּ	אֵת	לְיִרְמְיָהוּ הַנָּבִיא	עָשׂוּ
Zech 12:10		אֲשֶׁר־דָּקָרוּ	אֵת	אֵלַי	וְהִבִּיטוּ
Jer 38:9	they did	to Jeremiah the prophet		*whom* they cast	
Zech 12:10	they will look	on me		*whom* they pierced	

Both constructions include an initial verbal form followed by a preposition—either לְ or אֶל—that marks the verb's direct object.⁶¹ The object is the unnamed, first-person suffix ־י in Zech 12:10b, while "Jeremiah the prophet" fills that spot in Jer 38:9. Each of these objects precedes אֶת אֲשֶׁר, while a second verbal form follows thereafter in the clause. It appears that in each case the author employs אֶת אֲשֶׁר to refer to its antecedent object. The only real differences between the two texts

---

59. Floyd, *Minor Prophets*, 524. Floyd argues that the phrase אֶת אֲשֶׁר is syntactically independent from the first-person suffix in אֵלַי, leaving the way open for a second object distinct from Yahweh: "look to me *regarding whomever*." However, the previous eleven examples make this a less likely option. Moreover, as will be established below, there is no need to leave room for a second object, which seems to be Floyd's primary motive in making the phrase syntactically independent. Menken also mentions this double object as a grammatical possibility, though he vies for another option that emphasizes the piercing of Yahweh. Menken, "Textual Form," 498–99.

60. Bilić, *Jerusalem*, 340–41. Bilić is not the first to point out the similarity between Zech 12:10b and Jer 38:8. See *BDB*, s.v. "אֵת"; Driver, *Minor Prophets*, 266; Keil and Delitzsch, *Twelve Minor Prophets*, 387. However, Bilić shows no interaction with Keil and Delitzsch or Driver in his discussion.

61. For the use of לְ to mark the accusative, see Joüon, §126k–l.

are the prepositions and their respective attached objects, one being a pronominal suffix while the other is a proper noun.

Nevertheless, at the level of syntax, the constructions function identically. First, both authors employ אֶת אֲשֶׁר to refer to its antecedent object.[62] The use forces the entire clause to modify "Jeremiah the prophet" in Jer 38:9 and "me" in Zech 12:10b without (need of) introducing a second object.[63] Second, the use of אֶת אֲשֶׁר following the preposition carries a particularizing force or adds definiteness that does not permit one to gloss over the object it modifies.[64] Jeremiah 38:9 makes this especially clear. The one against whom the people commit evil is also the man they threw into the cistern, "Jeremiah the prophet" (Jer 38:6–7). Likewise, the one to whom the people look in Zech 12:10b is also the one they pierce, "me," whose antecedent is none other than Yahweh himself.[65] Thus, our phrase appears to function in both texts as a relative clause that modifies the object of the main verb, with the particle אֶת playing its traditional role as *nota accusativi* and marking אֲשֶׁר as the direct object of דְּקָרוּ.[66]

62. For the words of Jer 38:9, לְיִרְמְיָהוּ הַנָּבִיא אֵת אֲשֶׁר־הִשְׁלִיכוּ אֶל־הַבּוֹר, we see no other way to translate the construction except as follows: "to Jeremiah the prophet [*the one*] *whom* they threw into the cistern." No change exists regarding the object the clause modifies.

63. A similar clause in Exod 33:12 may also support this conclusion, especially with the use of a three-place *hiphil* construction: וְאַתָּה לֹא הוֹדַעְתַּנִי אֵת אֲשֶׁר־תִּשְׁלַח עִמִּי ("but you have not let me know whom you will send with me"). Cf. *IBHS* §27.3b. The only difference between what occurs in Exod 33:12 and in Zech 12:10b is that the suffix is affixed to the verb instead of to a preposition following the verb.

64. When the object is a pronominal suffix not attached to the verb, see Wilson, "Particle את, II," 219. Wilson argues, "In every such case, inasmuch as the suffix cannot stand alone, the particle [אֵת] *must* be used." Cf. the examples in Joüon, §158l-m, where אֲשֶׁר "has the effect of a relative pronoun used absolutely." By saying the clause has a "particularizing force" we do not intend to make particle אֵת itself one of emphasis any more than what grammar and syntax allow. See the careful discussion on אֵת by Muraoka, *Emphatic Words*, 146–58. Rather, the entire construction has this force, especially following אֵלַי.

65. That this particularizing force directly identifies and associates Yahweh with the Pierced One is also recognized by McComiskey, "Zechariah," 1214; Meyers and Meyers, *Zechariah 9–14*, 337. Contra GKC §138.e, which the NRSV illustrates with a rather vague translation: "when they look on the one whom they have pierced."

66. Joüon, §157f, 158a. Joüon also observes that "sometimes, by a kind of anticipation, אֲשֶׁר is preceded by אֵת of the accusative or by the preposition which logically

Yahweh as the Pierced One

Therefore, having retained the more difficult reading of אֵלַי, and shown that the phrase אֵת אֲשֶׁר functions best as beginning a modifying clause to the object observed in the suffix -ִי, I conclude that Yahweh identifies himself as the object of the people's piercing in Zech 12:10b. Adam Kubiś lists the proposal I suggest here for אֵת אֲשֶׁר. He recognizes that particle אֵת may very well function as a *nota accusativi*, translating Zech 12:10b, "they shall look on me whom they have pierced."[67] However, Kubiś rejects this interpretation and argues still for another option, namely, that particle אֵת should "be understood as an accusative of limitation or of specification, separating God from the Pierced One while creating "a certain link between the two figures."[68] Thus, Kubiś

---

should follow it." Joüon, §158m.

67. Still, Kubiś presents two options: "the *nota accusativi* can be understood in two ways: (a) with two different objects—*they shall look on me* (indirect object: God) *the one whom* (direct object: the pierced one) *they have pierced*—the syntagma אֵת אֲשֶׁר is related to the main clause (with the verb וְהִבִּיטוּ) as a second direct object, or (b) with one common object for both clauses—*they shall look on me* (indirect object: God) *whom* (direct object: God) *they have pierced*—the syntagma אֵת אֲשֶׁר is related to the suffixed personal pronoun (אֵלַי)." Kubiś, *Zechariah in John*, 119–20. In Kubiś's sentence, syntagma are the elements in a linguistic chain of speech that occur sequentially. When viewed from a semantic perspective (see *IBHS* §§11.1.3a, 11.2e; HALOT, s.v. "נבט")—noting especially how נבט relates to preposition אֶל in similar idiomatic combinations (Exod 3:6; Num 21:9; 1 Sam 21:9; Isa 51:1, 2, 6; Jonah 2:5 [ET 4]; Hab 1:13), especially in combinations with a suffixed prepositional object (2 Kgs 3:14; Ps 34:6 [ET 5])—I am more inclined to choose option (b) from Kubiś's list. The verb-plus-preposition construction (i.e., "looking on/toward") makes Yahweh the central focus rather than the verbal construction itself. Also, Joüon observes that "the relative אֲשֶׁר can be determinate in respect of the meaning, hence *he who* 1Sm 16.3, *that which* Gen 9.24, *the fact that (how)* Josh 2.10" (Joüon, §125g). Listing the same Bible verses, Waltke and O'Conner observe that when governed by אֵת the relative particle אֲשֶׁר can function in the accusative as simply "whom" (*IBHS* §10.3.1a). Moreover, the discussion below related to the first- and third-person pronouns will further unveil why option (b) from Kubiś's list seems to be the better option.

68. Kubiś, *Zechariah in John*, 121. In so doing, Kubiś follows Meyers and Meyers, *Zechariah 9–14*, 307; Peterson, *Zechariah 9–14*, 108. For particle אֵת functioning as an accusative of limitation, see Joüon, §126g. Wilson labels this use of particle אֵת as the "accusative of specification" and lists it as a subcategory of adverbial accusatives. Wilson, "Particle את, II," 223. However, when comparing Zech 12:10b with the examples listed in Wilson's category of specification (i.e., Gen 17:11; Deut 1:22; Exod 1:14; Judg 21:22; Ruth 2:11; 1 Sam 12:7; 21:3; 2 Sam 16:17; 1 Kgs 8:15; 15:23; 1 Chr 21:6; Ps 78:8; Isa 66:14), enough difference prevails to convince me to choose a different syntactical function for אֵת.

renders Zech 12:10b, "they shall look on me as far as the one they have pierced is concerned."

While Kubiś provides a legitimate syntactical option, his primary motive for choosing the much rarer accusative of limitation is to avoid the theological problem of God being pierced and to avoid the grammatical problem of "two different pronouns referring to the same person (אֵלַי, עָלָיו)." Admittedly, the declaration that God suffers a piercing at the hands of mortals is striking, and certainly raises theological concerns.[69] However, the context constrains me to distinguish Yahweh as the only logical antecedent to the first-person reference; God himself remains central to the people's focus and serves as the object who endures their piercing.[70] Moreover, while Kubiś's concerns highlight one other grammatical difficulty in Zech 12:10b—namely, the sudden switch from a first- to third-person suffix—it is not a difficulty that requires two separate figures who are yet still linked; and to this explanation we now turn.

The Alternation of Suffixes

For the third difficulty, we encounter the *crux interpretum* of Zech 12:10b.[71] With a strange alternation between the first-person and third-person pronominal suffixes, the text proceeds to state that the people shall look אֵלַי ("on me") but mourn עָלָיו ("for him"). Where readers might have anticipated עָלַי ("for *me*"), in accordance with אֵלַי ("on me")

---

69. For orthodox Christianity, the primary theological concern is whether it is right to affirm that God, in his divine essence, can suffer at all or be acted upon by any force outside himself. Orthodox Christianity has historically denied such an affirmation, while affirming God's impassibility. For an introduction and summary of God's impassibility, see Dolezal, *All That Is in God*, 1–17, 19n20, 32–34. The present chapter certainly interprets Zech 12:10 to say that God will subject himself to a piercing, leaving the theological concern unanswered. However, chapter 3 will clarify how such an offensive reading of Zech 12:10 can square with the orthodox Christian understanding of God's impassibility. See especially the comments on p. 108n98.

70. As mentioned before, Yahweh is the subject of the first-person verbs in Zech 12:1–9 and the appropriate antecedent of the first-person reference here. So also McComiskey, "Zechariah," 1214; Boda, *Haggai, Zechariah*, 488.

71. So identified by Lacocque, *Zacharie 9–14*, 189; Woude, *Zacharia*, 235. See also Deissler, "Sach 12,10," 50–52. Deissler illustrates the difficulty by providing fourteen varying translations of Zech 12:10b from different interpreters.

of the previous clause, they encounter עָלָיו ("for him"). Such a sudden shift, and yet apparently deliberate juxtaposition of suffixes, entertains numerous interpretations that fall generally within three main views: the separate-figures view; the functional-identity view; and the single-figure view.[72]

Separate-figures View

The separate-figures view argues that the clause, וְסָפְדוּ עָלָיו ("and they shall mourn for him"), introduces a second object altogether, so that the people look to Yahweh, but mourn for another figure.[73] The separate-figures view distances Yahweh from the Pierced One for whom they mourn, even leading some to punctuate the latter clauses of Zech 12:10b as an altogether separate set of ideas.[74] Yahweh and the Pierced One are totally unrelated. The grammar certainly permits an additional object. Also, the existing alternation of suffixes could favor an additional object. Moreover, seeing two figures, Yahweh and a separate Pierced One(s), would seem to alleviate the theological difficulty wherein God undergoes what only mortals should suffer. Moreover, the context may support a human piercing instead of a divine one (see Zech 13:3, 7).[75]

---

72. Willi-Plein finds only "zwei Möglichkeiten des Textverständnisses" ("two ways of understanding the text"). Willi-Plein, *Sacharja*, 200. Still, it seems that what the following study categorizes as the "functional-identity view," Willi-Plein includes within her first way of understanding the text: "Sie blacken 'auch mich,' d. h. auf Gott, und trauern um einen andern (möglicherweise 'zusammen mit dem, den sie durchbohrt haben')" ("They look 'to me,' i.e. to God, and mourn regarding another [possibly 'in connection with the one, whom they have pierced']"). Willi-Plein, *Sacharja*, 200. However, enough difference exists between the "separate-figures" view and the "functional-identity" view, that we separate them here.

73. See, e.g., the interpretive translations found in Targumic Tosefta and *b. Sukk.* 52a. Although based on different premises, similar interpretations include those of Van Hoonacker, *Les Douze*, 683–84; Mitchell, *Zechariah*, 330–31; Cohen, *Twelve Prophets*, 321; Otzen, *Studien*, 175–83; Floyd, *Minor Prophets*, 524–25.

74. E.g., Van Hoonacker translates Zech 12:10b, "Et ils élèveront leurs regards vers moi. Celui qu'ils ont transpercé, ils se lamenteront sur lui." Van Hoonacker, *Les Douze*, 683. The New Jerusalem Bible reflects the same decision: "They will look to me. They will mourn for the one whom they have pierced." See also Condamin, "Le Sens Messianique," 54n2. Condamin finds similar examples in Cyril of Alexandria.

75. In Zech 13:3, 7, we find, "And if anyone again prophesies, his father and mother who bore him will say to him, 'You shall not live, for you speak lies in the name of Yahweh.' And his father and mother who bore him shall pierce him through

Jesus as the Pierced One

However, at least five weaknesses in the separate-figures view warrant its rejection. (1) To separate the pierced individual from the person of Yahweh misinterprets the clause אֵת אֲשֶׁר־דָּקָרוּ ("whom they pierced"), which directly modifies אֵלַי instead of introducing a new object.[76] As shown above, the clause introduced by אֵת אֲשֶׁר is not syntactically independent from אֵלַי. More accurately, it states something further about Yahweh: he is the one whom they pierced. (2) The alternation of suffixes does not require a change in objects. Other reasons may exist for the unique occurrence. As the single-figure view will show below, the change may very well reflect the course of events from God's perspective (employing "me") and then from the people's perspective (employing "him"). (3) Interpreters following Van Hoonacker have no textual and thus no grammatical warrant for punctuating the verse to reflect two entirely distinct and unrelated persons.[77] Van Hoonacker's syntactical decision rests primarily on unsubstantiated claims concerning the textual history of Zech 12:10b. Conversely, the grammar of the received text, corroborated by available concrete witnesses, strongly suggests otherwise: the clause אֵת אֲשֶׁר־דָּקָרוּ syntactically belongs to וְהִבִּיטוּ אֵלַי.[78] (4) The piercing of a false prophet in Zech 13:3 need not

---

[וּדְקָרֻהוּ] when he prophesies... Awake, O sword, against my shepherd, against the man who stands next to me."

76. That some shift the responsibility of "piercing" from the Israelites of Zech 12:10a to the Gentile nations attacking Jerusalem, forces them to introduce a second object. See Targumic Tosefta; *b. Sukk.* 52a; Cohen, *Twelve Prophets*, 321; Floyd, *Minor Prophets*, 524–25. Against this view, however, we need to add one more observation to the above comparison between Jer 38:9 and Zech 12:10. In both cases, the clause modifies its preceding object with a verb whose subjects are identical to the subjects of the initial transitive verb that demanded the object. Thus, in Jer 38:9, those who did evil to Jeremiah are the same subjects as those who cast him into the cistern. In Zech 12:10b, those who look to Yahweh are the same subjects the prophet says will have pierced him. We may also add that this construal within rabbinic circles is most likely in reaction to later Christian usage of the text for messianic purposes. Rosenberg, "Slain Messiah," 260n1. See also p. 41n47 above.

77. Van Hoonacker argues his case by changing וְסָפְדוּ ("and they will mourn") to יִסְפְּדוּ ("they will mourn"), as well as suggesting that scribes removed the original *wāw* attached to אֵת in order to keep others from misreading אֵלָיו וְאֵת for אֵת אֵלָיו. However, none of the ancient versions supports either reading.

78. Though few would place much weight on the accents of the Masoretes, it is worth stating in support of our argument that the MT highlights the noticeable break with an *ʾatnāḥ* at דְּקָרוּ, not at אֵלַי.

50

Yahweh as the Pierced One

discourage the piercing of Yahweh in Zech 12:10b. It could simply reinforce the kind of piercing in view with Yahweh.[79] Such a reading stretches one theologically, but Yahweh's involvement with a human piercing need not be a contextual stretch for Zech 12:10b.[80]

Functional-identity View

A second view, the functional-identity view, interprets the alternation of suffixes as an intentional way of showing that the people look to Yahweh, who is pierced in his appointed, human representative.[81] Unlike the separate-figures view, the functional-identity view keeps Yahweh and his representative closely related. In fact, the relationship between Yahweh and his appointed representative is so close that the piercing of his representative amounts to the piercing of Yahweh himself. Again, the grammar and syntax do not rule out the functional-identity view. Like the separate-figures view, the functional-identity view also alleviates some of the tension with Yahweh suffering the piercing by introducing two physically distinct persons. Yet, this second view maintains that Yahweh still undergoes the piercing, though only by way of a moral connection to his representative(s).[82] Additionally, this view gains con-

---

79. See the discussion on דָּקַר below. Others, like Merrill, even set forth reasons to believe that the author deliberately juxtaposed the piercing of Yahweh in Zech 12:10b with the piercing of the false prophets in Zech 13:3. Merrill, *Zechariah*, 320.

80. A fifth critique of the separate-figures view may also contribute, but I relegate it to a footnote for now since fuller treatment appears in later chapters: from the standpoint of the text's effective history, the broader Christian canon stands against the separate-figures view. The Apostle John reveals that in order to fulfill Zechariah's prophetic word, the soldiers pierced Jesus Christ, who, by John's own eyewitness testimony, is no one less than God enfleshed (John 1:1–18; 19:37).

81. Orelli, *Minor Prophets*, 366–67; Condamin, "Le Sens Messianique," 55–56; Lamarche, *Zacharie IX–XIV*, 83–84; Chary, *Aggée-Zecharie*, 206; Carson, *John*, 627–28; McComiskey, "Zechariah," 1215; Clark and Hatton, *Handbook*, 321–22; Köstenberger, *John*, 253–54; Klein, *Zechariah*, 368; Bilić, *Jerusalem*, 355–58; Petterson, *Behold Your King*, 238–39; Kubiś, *Zechariah in John*, 128.

82. See esp. Lamarche, *Zacharie IX–XIV*, 83; Lacocque, *Zacharie 9–14*, 190–92. Also, note that the idea of "representative" leaves room to interpret the one pierced in the sense of a collective martyr. See, e.g., Mason, "Earlier Biblical Material," 164–65; Meyers and Meyers, *Zechariah 9–14*, 336–38; Bilić, *Jerusalem*, 355–58.

Jesus as the Pierced One

textual support by strongly adhering to Yahweh's identification with the expected Davidic shepherd-king in the earlier narrative of Zechariah.[83]

While there is much to commend the functional-identity view, several weaknesses persist. (1) Interpreters often do not explain how one moves from Yahweh, whom the people pierce, to the fact that they pierce him in his human representative.[84] They simply assume that the piercing of Yahweh ultimately and actually refers to the piercing of his representative. On this point, Joyce Baldwin perceptively asks, "How can two distinct people die in the death of only one?"[85] (2) Interpreters who divide the effects of דָּקַר into moral and physical categories for Yahweh and the Pierced One respectively, fail to take seriously its use in the declaration, "they will look to me, whom they pierced."[86] This

---

83. Cf. Zech 9:9, 16; 10:3, 8; 13:7. See esp. Petterson, *Behold Your King*, 237–39. Moreover, in order to demonstrate the functional identity of Yahweh with his royal representative, Petterson cites Ps 2:7; 45:6; Isa 9:6; Jer 23:5–6 [cf. 33:16]; Ezek 34:11–16 [cf. 34:23–24]. As a result, the functional-identity view could also better cohere with the testimony of the broader Christian canon that identifies Jesus as the Davidic shepherd-king and God's agent of salvation. E.g., Matt 2:6 [cf. Mic 5:2]; 26:31 [cf. Zech 13:7]; John 10:11–18 [cf. Ezek 34:23–24; 37:24–28]; Heb 13:20; 1 Pet 5:4; Rev 7:17. For an extensive study of how the theme of God's shepherd-king develops from Zechariah into Matthew's Gospel, see Ham, *The Coming King*. Nevertheless, the functional-identity view inadequately accounts for the pointed Christological message the Apostle John conveys in his Gospel, namely, Jesus is Yahweh enfleshed (John 1:1–4, 14). Such an assertion must receive careful attention before it stands as a legitimate criticism, and that will come in due course. However, since the broader Christian canon stands within the text's effective history, it is worth adding here.

84. In other words, once those taking the second view accept the reading "to me," they do not explain the need for a representative. McComiskey illustrates this well. Shortly after affirming the concrete piercing of God, he states, "That the suffering described in this verse strikes one who is close to God . . . reminds us of the Servant of the Lord's being pierced (Isa 53:5) and suffering death on behalf of his people." McComiskey, "Zechariah," 1214–15. For similar examples, see Orelli, *Minor Prophets*, 367; Haily, *Minor Prophets*, 390; Carson, *John*, 627–28. Keil and Delitzsch provide a more convincing case on Christological grounds, but fail to attribute the piercing to Jesus as Yahweh. Instead, they attribute it to Jesus, "the Maleach Jehovah," in place of Yahweh. Keil and Delitzsch, *Twelve Minor Prophets*, 388. Along similar lines, Kohler refers to the Pierced One as a *Heilsmittler* ("mediator of salvation"). Kohler, *Die Nachexilischen Propheten*, 206.

85. Baldwin, *Zechariah*, 191.

86. Kubiś, however, remains unwilling to dismiss a real death conveyed by דָּקַר. Moreover, Kubiś demonstrates the grammatical plausibility of treating אֵת as an accusative of limitation: "look on me as far as the one they have pierced is concerned."

second criticism becomes more apparent with the treatment of the verb דָּקַר below. (3) The functional-identity view overlooks altogether, or too quickly dismisses,[87] an alternative explanation for the sudden shift in suffixes, namely, the sudden shift in suffixes is a feature that occurs in prophetic literature.[88] For example, in Isa 45:24 an abrupt transition between the first- and third-person suffixes occurs and Yahweh remains the referent in both cases: "They will say of me [לִי], 'Only in Yahweh are righteousness and strength.' Men will come to him [עָדָיו], and all who were angry at him will be put to shame." Both Isa 45:24 and Zech 12:10b show that the personal object of the alternating suffixes, Yahweh, has not changed but only the perspective from which the speaker describes him.[89]

However, the aforementioned observations have demonstrated the grammatical plausibility of treating אֵת as a *nota accusativi*, marking a relative clause modifying the object of the preposition, namely, "me" or Yahweh. Further, as will unfold shortly, a more plausible explanation for the alternation of suffixes exists.

87. Kubiś, *Zechariah in John*, 119n16. Regarding the stylistic shift, Kubiś cites Merrill and Boda, as well as a couple references they provide from Isa 22:19 and Lam 3:1. However, beyond a mere footnote, Kubiś does not mention the stylistic nuance any further.

88. See Boda, *Haggai, Zechariah*, 488. Boda follows Merrill, *Zechariah*, 320. Boda and Merrill both cite GKC §144p, who provides several examples where this occurs between verbal forms. Cf. Delcor, "Un Problèm," 193. However, we add Isa 45:24, since the abrupt transition occurs between first- and third-person suffixes, and Yahweh remains the referent in both cases.

89. Other examples in the prophetic literature exist where a shift occurs from the first- to third-person (or *vice versa*), but are dissimilar in that the shift happens between pronominal and/or verbal forms. For example, "because you have prayed to me [אֵלַי; first-person object = Yahweh] concerning Sennacherib king of Assyria, this is the word that the Lord [יְהוָה; third-person subject = Yahweh] has spoken concerning him" (Isa 37:21–22). Zechariah 10:10–11 stands as another example: "I will bring them [וַהֲשִׁיבוֹתִים; first-person subject = Yahweh] home from the land of Egypt, and gather them [אֲקַבְּצֵם; first-person subject = Yahweh] from Assyria, and I will bring them [אֲבִיאֵם; first-person subject = Yahweh] to the land of Gilead and to Lebanon, till there is no room for them. And he shall pass through [וְעָבַר; third-person subject = Yahweh] the sea of troubles and strike down the waves of the sea, and all the depths of the Nile shall be dried up." With respect to the shift in Zech 10:10–11, it is also significant that the LXX translates וְעָבַר בַּיָּם צָרָה ("and he shall pass through the sea of affliction") as διελεύσονται ἐν θαλάσσῃ στενῇ ("and they shall pass through the narrow sea"). As with Zech 12:10, there appears to be another attempt by the LXX to alleviate the theological difficulty of Yahweh passing through affliction and preferring instead to keep Ephraim—mentioned earlier in Zech 10:7—as the subject.

Jesus as the Pierced One

Single-figure View

These criticisms of the separate-figures view and the functional-identity view raise the need for still another view that more adequately explains the alternation of suffixes in Zech 12:10b. We believe the single-figure view meets that challenge. The single-figure view suggests that the clause וְסָפְדוּ עָלָיו ("and they shall mourn for him") preserves the object from the first-person suffix in אֵלַי throughout, so that the people look to Yahweh as the Pierced One and mourn for him.[90]

Several arguments buttress this interpretation. (1) As demonstrated above, the sudden shift from the first- to third-person exemplifies a stylistic feature characteristic of prophetic literature. Such a style becomes apparent elsewhere in Zechariah, even though the occurrence exists between first- and third-person verb forms instead of suffixes: "As he [i.e., Yahweh] called [כַּאֲשֶׁר־קָרָא], and they would not hear, so they called, and I [i.e., Yahweh] would not hear [אֶשְׁמָע]" (Zech 7:13). (2) The use and meaning of דָּקַר favors keeping Yahweh as the sole object to the people's actions.[91] This is unlike the arguments of some in the functional-identity view, who divide the action described by דָּקַר into moral and physical categories. When Yahweh remains the sole object of the people's piercing, no theoretical division of the verbal action is necessary. (3) The single-figure view does not shy away from affirming that Yahweh identifies himself with Zechariah's shepherd-king. In fact, the single-figure view complements the functional-identity view in that the shepherd-king represents Yahweh quite intimately.[92] However,

---

However, Klein, *Zechariah*, 305–7, shows good reason for maintaining Yahweh as the subject of עָבַר in Zech 10:11. This would strengthen the aforementioned suggestion that the LXX translates Zech 12:10 the way it does from theological bias. So also Baldwin, *Zechariah*, 190.

90. E.g., Calvin, *Twelve*, 15:364–65; Brandenburg, *Die Kleinen Propheten*, 109–10; Delcor, "Un Problèm," 192–94; Leupold, *Exposition of Zechariah*, 237–38; Merrill, *Zechariah*, 320.

91. See discussion on "The Use of דָּקַר" below.

92. E.g., the shepherd-king shares the same divine characteristics of Yahweh. Both the shepherd-king and Yahweh bring salvation (Zech 8:7, 13; 9:9, 16), establish peace (Zech 8:12; 9:10), and possess universal dominion (Zech 9:10, 14–15; 14:1–21). Moreover, Yahweh appears to identify himself with the shepherd in the notable switch from the shepherd's worth (שְׂכָרִי) to Yahweh's value (יְקַרְתִּי) in Zech 11:12–13. See this latter connection between Yahweh and the shepherd also made by

the single-figure view does so not from within the narrower context of Zech 12:10b, but by allowing the themes developed throughout the wider context of Zechariah to overlap and inform one another.[93] Thus, while the functional-identity view may still provide a legitimate reading at the wider contextual level, the single-figure view better serves the emphasis present within the narrower context of Zech 12:10.

Therefore, on grammatical, contextual, inner-biblical, and theological grounds, we believe the single-figure view most accurately describes the events declared in the prophetic word of Zech 12:10. All attention centers upon Yahweh, whether the people look, pierce, or mourn. Nevertheless, it would be a mistake to assume that all interpreters advocating the single-figure view uphold a monolithic understanding of the piercing of Yahweh. Hence, we now leave the textual and grammatical difficulties and evaluate the use of the verb דָּקַר, as well as its subsequent effect on the translators of the LXX, in order to support further the validity of identifying Zechariah's Pierced One as Yahweh.

THE USE OF דָּקַר AND ITS EFFECT ON TRANSLATORS OF THE LXX

Answering several semantic questions surrounding the use of דָּקַר will further sharpen the meaning of Zech 12:10b in relation to Yahweh.[94] To begin, what does the term דָּקַר denote when the different levels of context come into consideration?[95] The semantic range of דָּקַר is

---

Cooke, "Unknown Martyr," 100; Chary, *Aggée-Zecharie*, 206; Kim, "Jesus," 139–41; Duguid, "Messianic Themes," 275–80. See also the developments below under the "future-singular identification." Additionally, while I disagree with his treatment of the alternation of pronouns, the paper by Hultberg highlights how several overlapping themes stretching across Zechariah end up "melding the figures of Messiah and God." See Hultberg, "Significance," 20–23.

93. A possible fourth criticism will need to wait until proven in subsequent chapters, but the single-figure view also consists with the witness of the broader Christian canon, wherein the Apostle John twice appropriates Zech 12:10 to explain the fulfillment of the *missio Dei* in the God-man Jesus Christ (John 19:37; Rev 1:7).

94. Willi-Plein also notes the necessity of clarifying semantic questions regarding the verb דָּקַר. Willi-Plein, *Sacharja*, 200.

95. See chapter 6, "Determining Meaning," in Silva, *Biblical Words*, 136–69. In stressing the importance of context, Silva lists various levels of context that have bearing on the meaning of biblical words, including the immediate context (verbal *or* nonverbal), the whole chapter, the whole book, etc.

Jesus as the Pierced One

already quite limited with only eleven other occurrences of the verb in the MT.[96] Eight of these occurrences appear in contexts that unmistakably describe a literal piercing—whether by sword or spear—that ultimately leads to death.[97] In two other cases, only severe injury results from the verbal action, though death lingers nearby (Jer 37:10; 51:4). Lamentations 4:9 is the one other occurrence outside Zech 12:10, and the context of hunger suggests that a figurative use of דָּקַר is also possible.[98] Thus, unless the context of Zech 12:10 suggests a figurative piercing—like that found in Lam 4:9—then דָּקַר would best denote a literal piercing similar to the majority of cases elsewhere in the MT.

Of course, using דָּקַר in a literal sense would surely raise another question, namely, how can the immortal God experience a literal piercing at the hands of mere mortals? The question has led some interpreters to take דָּקַר in a figurative or metaphorical sense instead of the literal sense.[99] For example, John Calvin suggests that the people metaphorically wound God, piercing his heart by their sins and "obstinate contempt of his word."[100] However, the context seems to favor a literal

---

96. Num 25:8; Judg 9:54; 1 Sam 31:4 [twice]; 1 Kgs 4:9; 1 Chr 10:4; Isa 13:15; Jer 37:10; 51:4; Lam 4:9; Zech 13:3. Cf. *HALOT*, s.v. "דָּקַר."

97. E.g., in Num 25:8, Phinehas pierces two individuals through their bellies with a spear to relieve Israel from the plague. Elsewhere, kings Abimelech and Saul ask their armor bearer to pierce them with a sword to preserve royal dignity (Judg 9:54; 1 Sam 31:4 [twice]; 1 Chr 10:4). That Saul falls on his sword at the refusal of his armor bearer indicates that he meant the requested piercing to cause death. Isaiah 13:15 proves especially helpful in that the parallel clauses help clarify the lethal threat that דָּקַר poses: "All who are found will be thrust through [יִדָּקֵר]; all who are caught will fall by the sword."

98. Lamentations 4:9 implies that those who suffer a speedy death by the literal piercing (i.e., מְחַלְלֵי) of a sword are "happier" than those who suffer a prolonged death by the "piercing" (i.e., מְדֻקָּרִים) of the hunger caused by lack of produce in the land. Cf. Long, "דקר," 983.

99. E.g., Leupold, *Exposition of Zechariah*, 237; Smith, *Micah-Malachi*, 276; Boda, *Haggai, Zechariah*, 487–88. After proposing two options for the piercing of Yahweh—a figurative piercing or a substitutionary piercing (i.e., what I above called the functional-identity view of the suffixes)—Merrill opts for a figurative piercing. Merrill, *Zechariah*, 281–82.

100. Calvin, *John*, 18:242. He appears to be working from an assumption that metaphorically applies to God in the OT what becomes literally true after he appears in the flesh in the person of Jesus Christ in the NT. See this clarification in his comments on Zech 12:10 in Calvin, *Twelve*, 15:364–65.

piercing over a metaphorical piercing. Indeed, the immediate context of Zech 12:10b seems to indicate that a literal piercing has occurred. The people mourn for the one they have pierced and weep bitterly over him, as one weeps over a firstborn (Zech 12:10c). Such language often characterizes the response people have to the death of loved ones.[101] Also, the use of דָּקַר in a neighboring context, Zech 13:3, denotes a literal piercing of the false prophets and may support a literal piercing in Zech 12:10b.[102]

Moreover, as Klein argues, a "symbolic wound" in Zech 12:10b does not provide an answer for how the people are definitively cleansed from their sin in Zech 13:1.[103] Under the Mosaic covenant—a covenant still in effect after the exile—cleansing "for sin" and "for uncleanness" occurred only upon the actual and sacrificial death of another.[104] Zechariah 13:1 seems to anticipate a future cleansing for sin and for uncleanness, and then describes that future day of cleansing in the categories known to those still living under the old covenant.[105] Thus,

---

101. E.g., Gen 23:32; 50:10; 1 Sam 25:1; 2 Sam 1:12; 11:26; 1 Kgs 13:30; Jer 16:4. Significantly, the reference to mourning in 2 Sam 1:12 relates directly to the lethal piercing (דָּקַר) Saul suffers from his own sword in 1 Sam 31:4. Also, a great cry went up from Pharaoh and the Egyptians over the death of all the בְּכוֹר ("firstborn"), the same word used in Zech 12:10b.

102. Zechariah 13:3 says, "If anyone again prophesies, his father and mother who bore him shall say to him, 'You shall not live, for you speak lies in the name of the LORD.' And his father and mother who bore him shall pierce him through [וּדְקָרֻהוּ] when he prophesies." The instructions of Deut 13:1–12 concerning false prophets suggests that the piercing of the false prophets in Zech 13:3 should be understood as a literal piercing to cause death.

103. Klein, *Zechariah*, 366.

104. Zechariah 13:1 reads, "In that day a fountain will be opened for the house of David and for the inhabitants of Jerusalem, for sin [לְחַטַּאת] and for uncleanness [וּלְנִדָּה]." The expressions "for sin" and "for uncleanness" appear in contexts where an animal is sacrificed as a sin-offering for the purpose of atonement and/or cleansing before God (e.g., Lev 4:3, 14, 32–33; 12:6–8; 16:3, 5–6; Num 6:11, 14; Ezek 43:19–20, 22). Cf. HALOT, s.v. "חַטָּאת." Hence, the ESV also translates Zech 13:1, "On that day there shall be a fountain opened for the house of David and the inhabitants of Jerusalem, to cleanse them from sin and uncleanness." While not mentioning an opened fountain, Ezekiel uses the related imagery of God's people experiencing cleansing from their uncleanness and their idols through a sprinkling with clean water (Ezek 36:25–26, 33). See also Wright, "Unclean and Clean," 738. Wright highlights the figurative language of washing in the prophets.

105. Regarding the eschatological significance of the phrase בַּיּוֹם הַהוּא "in/on

JESUS AS THE PIERCED ONE

when read in light of the sacrificial context of Zech 13:1—as the events of Zech 12:10 and Zech 13:1 both relate to "that day"—it seems best to say that דָּקַר denotes a literal piercing in Zech 12:10b.[106] Those arguing for the functional-identity view of the alternation of suffixes (see above) normally maintain this literal piercing, but then argue that Yahweh undergoes the piercing insofar as Yahweh's representative undergoes the piercing. Such an explanation will merit further evaluation below, but if the grammar and syntax strongly suggest that Yahweh receives the action in דָּקַר (i.e., "to me, whom they pierced"), then how can another representative suffer what the text says that Yahweh suffers? I would suggest that if someone wants to maintain that Yahweh gets pierced in his representative—which I suggested still seems possible from the wider context of Zechariah—then perhaps it is better to assert that the representative is so closely connected with Yahweh that he somehow belongs to the divine identity.[107] The point is not to minimize the ex-

---

that day," which frames the events of both Zech 13:1 and Zech 12:10 (cf. Zech 12:9, 11) and thus relates both texts to the future, see the "Literary Context" above. Moreover, that Zech 13:1 envisions a future and cleansing sacrifice in conjunction with the piercing of Zech 12:10b, gains further support when linked with the promised covenant of Zech 9:11— גַּם־אַתְּ בְּדַם־בְּרִיתֵךְ שִׁלַּחְתִּי אֲסִירַיִךְ מִבּוֹר אֵין מַיִם בּוֹ ("as for you also, because of the blood of my [i.e., Yahweh's] covenant with you, I have set your prisoners free from the waterless pit"). Like the covenant made at Sinai, so would the new covenant be ratified with blood, signifying the death of another (Exod 24:8; cf. Heb 9:18, 20). Jesus applies such words to his own death (Matt 26:28; Mark 14:24; Luke 22:20; cf. 1 Cor 11:25; Heb 12:24), shortly after riding into Jerusalem to fulfill the role of Zechariah's humbly mounted shepherd-king (Zech 9:9; cf. Matt 21:5; John 12:15–16), whom John also views as the Pierced One (John 19:37). Thus, an inner-biblical precedent exists that connects Zechariah's Pierced One with the death of Zechariah's shepherd-king, whose spilt blood inaugurates a new covenant often associated with the cleansing from sin or forgiveness of sin (Jer 31:34; Ezek 36:26; cf. Zech 3:9).

106. The links between Zech 12:10 and Zech 13:1 are several: both happenings occur "on/in that day" (cf. 12:9); both speak of blessings on the "house of David and the inhabitants of Jerusalem"; and the cleansing in 13:1 seems to be in direct response to the plea for mercy in 12:10, both of which stand together elsewhere in the OT (e.g., 2 Chr 6:19–21; Ps 130:1–4; 143:1; Jer 31:9, 18–21). In terms of the literary structure, Butterworth also suggests that Zech 13:1 connects more closely with Zech 12 than with Zech 13:2–6. Butterworth, *Structure*, 198, 212, 216.

107. Such an assertion in the face of strict Jewish monotheism seems radical, but others have shown that it accurately represents all the biblical data, especially in light of the New Testament's testimony that Jesus is the revelation of God. See, e.g., Bauckham, *Jesus and the God of Israel*, 1–106. More surrounding this discussion will

traordinarily offensive and even mysterious claim that the narrower context appears to support, namely, that the people will literally pierce Yahweh—a conclusion made more explicit by the single-figure view above.

That a literal piercing of Yahweh is in view also seems evident from the way the LXX handles דָּקַר in Zech 12:10. Again, instead of ἐξεκέντησαν ("they have pierced"), the LXX reads κατωρχήσαντο ("they have danced").[108] As stated above, the translation of דָּקַר by the LXX in Zech 12:10 is inconsistent with the way the LXX translates דָּקַר elsewhere in the OT. For Zech 12:10 we find the most obscure vocabulary, while in every other instance except one the LXX translates דָּקַר with vocabulary that consistently conveys its meaning quite accurately. The one other instance where the LXX departs from the normal semantic domain of דָּקַר is Zech 13:3. If such unambiguous vocabulary was available to the translators of the LXX, and there is good evidence to suggest that there was,[109] why opt for such obscure vocabulary in Zech 12:10 and Zech 13:3 alone?

Some have suggested a simple misreading of דָּקַר ("to pierce") for רָקַד ("to dance"), as the outer radicals look very similar.[110] However, several observations make this proposal less likely. First, based on its

develop in chapter 3 below.

108. As a *hapax legomenon*, determining the meaning of κατορχέομαι is more difficult. LSJ, s.v. "κατορχέομαι," suggests three semantic fields, largely based on findings in classical literature: (1) to dance in triumph over one, to treat despitefully (e.g., Heroditus, *Hist.* 3.151; Philodemus, *Piet.* 52); (2) subdue or enchant by dancing (e.g., Lucianus, *Salt.* 22); (3) dance vehemently (e.g., Strabo, *Geogr.* 17.1.17). Of the three, the first field seems most befitting to Zech 12:10 and in the LXX. Still, translations of the LXX go two directions: (a) either the people look to God because they have treated God despitefully, i.e., they have danced in mockery against him (e.g., Kubiś, *Zechariah in John*, 148); or (b) the people look to God because they have danced triumphantly, presumably over the enemies that God defeats in Zech 12:9 (e.g., NETS). See p. 40n43 for comments on the VL and commentary by Jerome, as well as the discussion in Kubiś, *Zechariah in John*, 148.

109. See p. 41n44 for the vocabulary used elsewhere in the LXX for דָּקַר.

110. E.g., Muraoka, "New Index," 263. Regarding graphic similarity and letter transposition, especially that of ר/ד, see Tov, *Textual Criticism, 3rd Ed.*, 227–29; Tov, *Use*, 195–205. Menken even highlights the possibility of intentional letter transposition as a form of Jewish exegesis in relation to Zech 12:10. Menken, "Textual Form," 173. For a broader study, cf. Brooke, "Qumran," 85–100.

other nine occurrences in the MT, even the semantic domain of דָּקַר does not seem supportive of dancing so as to mock or despise as the LXX implies with its choice of κατορχέομαι ("to dance in triumph over") for רָקַד.[111] Second, דָּקַר also appears in Zech 13:3 and yet again receives an odd treatment with συμποδίζω ("to bind together"), when the semantics clearly imply more than a mere binding.[112] If the LXX treats דָּקַר in such an odd manner in both texts, then it seems more likely that an aversion to the literal force behind דָּקַר exists rather than a simple misreading, especially when the contexts in both cases suggests a literal piercing. Perhaps since both Zech 12:10 and Zech 13:3 include a most disturbing action against someone so dear—in Zech 13:3 the prophet's own parents pierce their son, and in Zech 12:10 God's own people pierce their covenant Lord—the LXX may be attempting to avoid the offensive language.[113]

Third, there is good reason to believe that a particular theological bias led the translators of the LXX to evade the literal piercing of Yahweh.[114] If a metaphorical piercing of Yahweh, or even the literal

111. Where the LXX maintains the meaning of רָקַד, it usually has ὀρχέομαι, "to dance" (1 Chr 15:29; Eccl 3:4; Isa 13:21), προσπαίζω, "to play" (Job 21:11), σκιρτάω, "to skip in exuberance" (Ps 114:4, 6), or ἐξάλλομαι, "to leap" (Joel 2:5). Cf. *HALOT*, s.v. "רָקַד"; Delcor, "Un Problèm," 194; Kubiś, *Zechariah in John*, 149–50. As Bynum adds, "Thus, if the LXX translator found the Hebrew verb, or mistakenly thought he read רָקַד in his *Vorlage*, his rendering of the same by the Greek κατορχέομαι would be a translation contradictory to all other LXX translations of the same verb רָקַד in the Scriptures." Bynum, *Fourth Gospel*, 104.

112. Even the LXX understands the parents to say of their prophet-son, οὐ ζήσῃ ὅτι ψευδῆ ἐλάλησας ἐπ᾽ ὀνόματι κυρίου ("You shall not live, because you have spoken lies in the name of the Lord"). However, see the use of συμποδίζω in Gen 22:9 LXX, where Abraham binds his son Isaac on the altar in order to sacrifice him. Such a use could certainly allude to the semantics of דָּקַר in Zech 13:3 but the evasion of the direct piercing still seems present.

113. In regards to the theological exegesis characterizing the LXX, Tov explains, "Theological exegesis relates to the description of God and his acts, the Messiah, Zion, the exile, as well as various ideas, such as that of repentance. Such exegesis may be expressed through theologically motivated choices of translation equivalents, in changes in words and verses . . . or in expansions or omissions of ideas considered offensive." Tov, *Textual Criticism*, 3rd Ed., 120.

114. By attributing the decision to a theological bias, I am not suggesting a widespread, homogenous theological approach among all the translators of the LXX. I am limiting my inferences to "the particular book from which they were drawn," to use the words of Jobes and Silva, *Septuagint*, 94. Moreover, as Jan Joosten remarks,

Yahweh as the Pierced One

piercing of a human representative on behalf of Yahweh, was such a straightforward understanding of Zech 12:10, then why does the LXX render דָּקַר the way that it does, and do so only within Zech 12–13?[115] I would suggest that the shock of Yahweh undergoing a literal piercing seems to have had a troubling effect on the translators of the LXX such that they refused to let such a piercing fall directly on Yahweh.[116] Warrant for such a suggestion gains further support from the way the LXX preserves the mortal wounding of Yahweh's representative in three additional OT contexts where the semantics overlap with that of דָּקַר, namely, Isa 53:5, Ps 22:16, and Zech 13:7.

"The theological interpretation should not be the first one we reach for [among other explanations], but the last one, to be applied only when more down-to-earth explanations fail. This call for prudence should certainly be headed . . . However, the call for prudence should not be taken to imply that no theological modifications are to be found in the Septuagint." Joosten, "To See God," 298.

115. The suggestion that the LXX represents a Hebrew *Vorlage* differing from the MT was addressed above on p. 40n43 and p. 60n111. Moreover, see the arguments against a differing Hebrew *Vorlage* in Delcor, "Un Problèm," 194; Kubiś, *Zechariah in John*, 149–50. Furthermore, while the Hebrew manuscripts among the DSS provide little for Zech 12:10, evidence from one fragment confirms the presence of דְּקָרוּ. Fragment 4QXIIe contains two letters at the end of a phrase in Zech 12:10, namely, רו, and seems indicative of a Hebrew text like that of the MT. Bynum, *Fourth Gospel*, 144–45; Fuller, "4QXIIe," 264.

116. Likewise, Kubiś, *Zechariah in John*, 150–51, highlights the possibility of "a deliberate interpretation" in addition to circumventing the "scandalous anthropomorphism," but he asserts too much regarding the LXX translator's attentiveness to semantics and context when he translates דָּקַר from Zech 13:3. Nowhere else does the LXX render דָּקַר with συμποδίζω. Moreover, wherever συμποδίζω occurs in the LXX, it consistently conveys the idea of restraint or binding as consists in the Hebrew and never falls within the semantic range of piercing or wounding (Gen 22:9 [עקד]; Pss 18:40 [כרע]; 19:9 [כרע]; 77:31 [כרע]; Hos 11:3 [רגל]; Dan 3:20, 22 [כפת]). In addition to Kubiś, Bynum draws a similar conclusion as stated above, even while granting the most charitable reading to the LXX: "the reading κατωρχήσαντο is best explained as an intentional evasive rendering due to an exegetical and theological agenda of the translator, most likely to avoid the anthropomorphism of God being pierced." Bynum, *Fourth Gospel*, 108. From his assessment of John's citation of Zech 12:10 in the Fourth Gospel, Schuchard also comments, " . . . John apparently finds the OG itself unsatisfactory because it seems to consciously avoid any suggestion that God himself might be 'pierced.' This, however, is exactly what John is intent on asserting." Schuchard, *Scripture within Scripture*, 149.

Jesus as the Pierced One

Consider the piercing[117] of Yahweh's representative in Isa 53:5, the Suffering Servant.[118] Where Isa 53:5 in the MT reads, וְהוּא מְחֹלָל מִפְּשָׁעֵנוּ ("but he was pierced for our transgressions"), the LXX has, αὐτὸς δὲ ἐτραυματίσθη διὰ τὰς ἀνομίας ἡμῶν ("but he was wounded on account of our sins"). While the verb τραυματίζω ("to wound") still seems softer than the Hebrew חָלַל ("to pierce"), the LXX regularly uses τραυματίζω in contexts where people suffer lethal wounds.[119] Thus, the LXX preserves the piercing of Yahweh's representative in Isa 53:5.

There is also David, who, as Israel's anointed king, stands as God's representative and sometimes in inseparable fashion.[120] In Ps 22, David suffers immensely, even to the point of feeling forsaken by God (Ps 22:1–2). Within this context comes Ps 22:17,[121] which, at a text-critical level, stands as a notoriously difficult verse, especially where the MT reads כָּאֲרִי יָדַי וְרַגְלָי (literally, "like a lion my hands and my feet"). The LXX translates the Hebrew as, ὤρυξαν χεῖράς μου καὶ πόδας ("they have dug/gouged/pierced my hands and feet"), which is then followed by

---

117. While the verb in Isa 53:5 is חָלַל instead of דָּקַר, both verbs appear together in Jer 51:4 and Lam 4:9 with parallel meaning, justifying a comparison with how the LXX handles the piercing of Yahweh's representative in Isa 53:5.

118. What makes the Servant such a suitable example to compare with Zechariah's Pierced One is not only his apparent redemptive suffering (Isa 53:5–12; cf. Zech 13:1), but also his inclusion within the divine identity of Yahweh himself. See, e.g., Bauckham, *Jesus and the God of Israel*, 32–59. Bauckham aptly demonstrates this latter point of comparison by showing that Isa 40–55 characterizes the Servant with the same language used to describe Yahweh's person and redemptive acts. One might also consider how Isaiah ascribes to the Suffering Servant in Isa 52:13 the same language applied to Yahweh and his temple mount, namely, their being high and lifted up (e.g., Isa 2:2, 11, 17; 5:16; 12:4; 30:18).

119. E.g., the lethal wound occurs as the result of an archer's shot (1 Sam 31:3) or a soldier's sword (Jer 8:23; Ezek 28:23; 30:4; 32:28; 35:8).

120. E.g., Pss 2:1–9; 69:6–8; 72:8–11, 15, 17–19; 110:1–7; 118:10–27. See also the relationship between Yahweh and his anointed, Davidic king in 2 Sam 7:14, where God relates to the king as father, Isa 9:6, where the royal Davidide would be called אֵל גִּבּוֹר ("Mighty God"), and Ezek 34:23–24, where the roles of God and his shepherd-king overlap (cf. Ezek 34:11–16; 37:24–25). Along similar lines, Petterson adds to the discussion Ps 45:6, where the people address the king as אֱלֹהִים ("Elohim"), and Jer 23:5–6, where the king's name will be יְהוָה צִדְקֵנוּ ("Yahweh is our righteousness"). Petterson, *Behold Your King*, 238.

121. Psalm 22:17 in the MT is Ps 21:17 in the LXX and is Ps 22:16 in most English translations.

the Vulgate and several English versions, usually translated "they have pierced my hands and feet."[122]

For some time, many scholars have rejected the LXX's translation and sought to make sense of the MT, sometimes offering possible textual emendations.[123] However, recent manuscript evidence from the DSS has shown that the LXX may have been translating from a Hebrew *Vorlage* that differed from the MT. Column eleven of the 5/6ḤevPsalms Scroll appears to reflect the translation given by the LXX. Instead of כָּאֲרִי ("like a lion"), as in the MT, 5/6ḤevPsalms has כארו, presupposing the verb כרה ("to dig"), and in this way supporting the LXX's understanding that the predator-like wicked pierce God's kingly representative.[124] Nevertheless, regardless of whether one accepts the variant of 5/6ḤevPsalms, the point still stands that the LXX seems more willing to let violence fall on Yahweh's representative than on Yahweh himself. If the LXX accurately represents an earlier Hebrew *Vorlage* for Ps 22:17, then the translators preserved the literal violence to Yahweh's representative. If the MT for Ps 22:17 is the best reading, then the LXX still seemed content to interpret the text in a manner that allowed violence to fall on Yahweh's representative.

That leaves one further example, Zech 13:7. The MT reads, חֶרֶב עוּרִי עַל־רֹעִי וְעַל־גֶּבֶר עֲמִיתִי . . . הַךְ אֶת־הָרֹעֶה וּתְפוּצֶיןָ הַצֹּאן ("Awake, O sword, against my shepherd, [and/namely] against the man, my companion . . . Strike the shepherd that the sheep may be scattered").[125] The shepherd appears to represent Yahweh[126] and to stand in close relationship

---

122. Psalm 21:17 in the VL reads, "circumdederunt me venatores concilium pessimorum vallavit me vinxerunt manus meas et pedes meos" ("for many dogs have encompassed me: the council of the malignant has besieged me. They have pierced/dug my hands and feet"). Among the English translations are RSV, NASB, NIV, ESV, and HCSB.

123. E.g., see those listed in Gren, "Psalm 22:16," 291–94; VanGemeren, *Psalms*, 246.

124. See especially VanderKam and Flint, *Meaning*, 124–25; Gren, "Psalm 22:16," 288–95.

125. The verb דָּקַר appears in relation to חֶרֶב, ("a sword," Judg 9:54; 1 Sam 31:4; 1 Chr 10:4; Isa 13:15), justifying a comparison with the LXX's treatment Yahweh's shepherd in Zech 13:7.

126. The shepherd is רֹעִי ("*my* shepherd"), much like the Suffering Servant in Isaiah is עַבְדִּי ("*my* servant," Isa 52:13; 53:11), and the Davidic king in Psalms is בְּנִי

Jesus as the Pierced One

to Yahweh.[127] Nevertheless, even at Yahweh's command, the sword must strike the shepherd, a violent act the LXX appears to preserve: ῥομφαία ἐξεγέρθητι ἐπὶ τοὺς ποιμένας μου καὶ ἐπ' ἄνδρα πολίτην μου . . . πατάξατε τοὺς ποιμένας καὶ ἐκσπάσατε τὰ πρόβατα ("O sword, awake against my shepherds, and against the man, my compatriot . . . Smite the shepherds, and draw out the sheep"). Granted, the LXX envisions a broader group facing the sword, changing the singular רֹעִי ("my shepherd") to the plural ποιμένας μου ("my shepherds"). In this way, the LXX likely understands the sword to strike the shepherd(s) who are not representing Yahweh as they ought. Nevertheless, regardless of the positive or negative representation, the LXX still appears to include Yahweh's compatriot among those slain by the sword, again preserving the literal piercing when Yahweh's representative is in view.

Thus, when Scripture elsewhere promises that a literal piercing will happen to Yahweh's representative and not directly to Yahweh, the LXX translates the piercing in a less obscure manner. Such a pattern suggests that the translators of the LXX understood the piercing of Zech 12:10 not merely to apply to Yahweh's representative but to Yahweh himself, which is why they sidestepped it. Also, fragment 4QXIIe supports the presence of דְּקָרוּ in the MT,[128] there is evidence in the neighboring text of Zech 13:3 that the LXX understood the implications of applying דָּקַר in its literal sense to Yahweh, and the easiest move for the translator would be to render the passage in a way that avoids the piercing of Yahweh altogether.[129] Moreover, suggesting that a theological bias led the LXX translators to sidestep the scandalous piercing of Yahweh seems

---

("*my* son," Ps 2:7) or מְשִׁיחִי ("*my* anointed," Ps 132:17).

127. Lev 5:21 [ET 6:2]; 18:20; *HALOT*, s.v., "עָמִית." Cf. the discussion in Baldwin, *Zechariah*, 198; Klein, *Zechariah*, 386–87; Ulrich, "Two Offices," 260–62.

128. Again, see Bynum, *Fourth Gospel*, 144–45; Fuller, "4QXIIe," 264.

129. As mentioned above, NETS suggests that the people of Zech 12:10 look to God because they have danced triumphantly over their enemies (cf. Zech 12:9), as opposed to dancing in mockery against God. Such an English rendering of the LXX's κατωρχήσαντο may better represent how the early translators sidestepped the piercing of God—perhaps even through deliberate letter transposition—while simultaneously maintaining a reading that squared with the context of Zech 12:9. While this reading of κατωρχήσαντο may stand closer to what the translators of the LXX intended to convey, it still serves as another example of how the LXX avoids the piercing of Yahweh.

Yahweh as the Pierced One

reminiscent of other instances where the LXX translators attempt to preserve God's transcendence at the expense of his humility or nearness.[130] Indeed, Zech 10:11 is one example where the LXX changes the third-person, singular verb to a third-person, plural verb, perhaps as a way to avoid Yahweh passing through trouble.[131] Thus, instead of a different *Vorlage*, or a misreading, it seems more likely that some negative disposition or theological apprehension to the literal piercing of Yahweh exists. If so, then the effect that Zech 12:10 had on translators of the LXX lends further support to דָּקַר carrying the meaning of a literal piercing, a literal piercing the translators intentionally evaded.[132]

---

130. In the past, some interpreters would refer to these instances as anti-anthropomorphisms. See, e.g., Fritsch, *Anti-Anthropomorphisms*. However, others have criticized the extent to which such interpretive decisions actually occur in the LXX. E.g., Orlinsky, "Treatment," 193–200; Wittstruck, "So-Called," 29–34. Nevertheless, with such criticisms in mind Tov observes, "As a rule, the translators did not flinch from rendering verses or words literally that may be considered to be anthropomorphic or anthropopathic, that is, portraying God's appearance and feelings according to those of human beings. However, sometimes they avoided literal renderings." See Tov, *Textual Criticism, 3rd Ed.*, 121. Tov makes this observation before citing Isa 6:1 as an example. In a separate study, Tov observes examples wherein the LXX appears to give anti-anthropomorphic renderings of Num 12:8, Exod 4:24, Exod 24:10, and Josh 9:14. See Tov, "Exegesis," 267–68. Along similar lines, Joosten notes several cases when the LXX introduces the notion of seeing God "into a number of contexts where the Hebrew text doesn't have it," but he still highlights several places where the LXX has "the tendency to 'edit out' the notion of seeing God" (e.g., Exod 3:6; 24:10, 11; Num 12:8), which he attributes to a multiplicity of factors related to the translators' Palestinian or Alexandrian milieu. Joosten, "To See God," 299.

131. Zechariah 10:11 of the MT reads, וְעָבַר בַּיָּם צָרָה ("and he [i.e., Yahweh] shall pass through the sea of troubles"), while the LXX has, καὶ διελεύσονται ἐν θαλάσσῃ στενῇ ("and *they* shall pass through a narrow sea"). The LXX changes the third-person, singular verb to a third-person, plural. Some have understood the third-person, singular verb in the MT to refer back to Ephraim in Zech 10:7—seeing the collective noun (אֶפְרַיִם) to require a singular verb—while others view the MT as an inferior reading to the LXX altogether. However, Klein carefully shows that the more contextually appropriate reading understands Yahweh as the subject of the third-person, singular verb, עבר. Klein, *Zechariah*, 305–8.

132. Delcor's proposal that the LXX's use of κατορχέομαι intentionally enlarges the meaning of דָּקַר by including the semantics of an interchangeable term, חָלַל ("to be defiled, to profane, *to pierce*"; cf. Jer 51:4), does not take away from my suggested theological bias. Delcor proposes that if the semantics of דָּקַר overlaps enough with חָלַל—which can mean "to profane" in contexts like Ezek 36:23—then perhaps the LXX translators insinuate that the people become remorseful over the way they have pierced Yahweh with their dance of profanation before idols. See Delcor, "Un

Jesus as the Pierced One

To this point, then, I have attempted to argue that Yahweh is the object of the people's piercing and that דָּקַר refers to a literal piercing, letting the obvious tension linger over how Yahweh could possibly endure a literal piercing. However, the tension awaits a future explanation, which will come only with the progress of revelation. That is to say, explaining how Yahweh will endure a literal piercing from Zech 12:10 is not required for asserting that Yahweh will endure a literal piercing. The promise of Zech 12:10 still stands for his hearers, even if mysterious to them. They were to trust that what God promised them in the present would receive fuller explanation as God's purposes in redemptive history drew to their completion.

This leads to one further observation bound up with the verb דָּקַר and its surrounding context. Though some have argued that the piercing occurred in the past,[133] and others have searched for a piercing within the timeframe of Zechariah's ministry,[134] the grammar, syntax, and context suggest that this prophetic word looks to the distant future. As noted above in setting the literary context, the prophet repeatedly sets these events "in that day," the eschatological day of God's redemption. Furthermore, vv. 3, 8, and 9 of Zech 12 include the verbal form, וְהָיָה ("it shall come to pass"), which, as Klein argues, "unambiguously indicates a future setting for the immediate context."[135] The repeated sequence of imperfect verbs followed by perfect verbs with *wāw* consecutives also buttresses the argument for a fulfillment that lies in the

---

Problèm," 196; Kubiś, *Zechariah in John*, 151–52. Idolatry is certainly present in the context (e.g., Zech 13:2), but as stated above, the context also suggests that דָּקַר carries its literal and not figurative sense of piercing. Yet, even if Delcor's proposal is correct, it still forces us to ask why the LXX does not translate דָּקַר in a more straightforward manner as it does everywhere else outside of Zech 12–13.

133. Mitchell, *Zechariah*, 330. Mitchell sets the piercing in the past: "This means that the one pierced is not the Messiah, whose advent, all will agree, was still future when these words were written, but some one [sic] who had at the time already suffered martyrdom."

134. Driver, *Minor Prophets*, 265. Driver makes the piercing a present event, arguing that "the context point[s] plainly to some historical event in the prophet's own time, for which the people would eventually feel the sorrow here describes (vv. 10b–14)."

135. Klein, *Zechariah*, 353. Moreover, as stated in GKC §112y, "very frequently the announcement of a future event is attached by means of וְהָיָה."

future.[136] While the perfect verb דְקָרוּ lacks the *wāw* consecutive, it does not break the sequence in Zech 12:10, since it stands within a modifying clause and communicates the resulting state of the people's action at a time future to the message spoken by the prophet.[137] That is to say, the people will have already pierced Yahweh when their promised looking to him and mourning for him come to fruition. Thus, while the tension of Yahweh's literal piercing remains for his readers, it is apparently not a tension without future resolution.

THE IDENTITY OF THE PIERCED ONE

Having treated the textual and grammatical difficulties and answered several questions surrounding the use of דָּקַר, our study embarks on its final section concerning the identity of the Pierced One in Zech 12:10b. Again, the aim is to demonstrate the validity of identifying Zechariah's Pierced One as Yahweh, and to this point in our study the contextual, grammatical, lexical, and theological evidence favors the divine identity. However, except for the criticism dealt to the metaphorical interpretation of the piercing of Yahweh, there has been little explanation for why the personages set forth by others ultimately fall short of the message in Zech 12:10. The lens of our research has focused more narrowly on the details of Zech 12:10b, but it is now time to zoom out and see the bigger picture. By combining the answers concerning the use of דָּקַר with the conclusions regarding the textual and grammatical difficulties, a proper identification of the Pierced One should cohere with at least five criteria.

1. אֵלַי ("on me") of the MT is the best reading, and the context shows that the first-person suffix (־י) refers to Yahweh.
2. The phrase אֵת אֲשֶׁר ("whom") modifies the first-person suffix in אֵלַי ("on me"), making Yahweh the object of דְקָרוּ ("they pierced").

---

136. See GKC §112d, p. Also, note how the sequence follows the eschatological phrase בַּיּוֹם הַהוּא on three occasions in close proximity to Zech 12:10, in vv. 6, 8, and 11.

137. *IBHS* §30.3b, 30.5.3b.

3. The alternation from a first-person suffix in אֵלַי ("on me") to a third-person suffix in עָלָיו ("on him") preserves Yahweh as the object of וְסָפְדוּ ("they will mourn").

4. The lexical evidence, the contextual layers, and the treatment by the LXX, suggests that the verb, דָּקַר ("to pierce"), conveys a literal piercing of Yahweh.

5. The communicated events in Zech 12:10 are eschatological, pointing to a future day when Yahweh will somehow subject himself to the literal piercing.[138]

With these criteria in mind, we will now assess the suggested persons normally identified as Zechariah's Pierced One by various interpreters. In order to streamline the assessment and minimize redundancy, this study categorizes the prior identifications of the Pierced One into five main groups. Two belong to the collective interpretation, which I refer to as the past- and present-collective identification; and three belong to the singular interpretation, which I refer to as the past-, present-, and future-singular identification.[139]

---

138. While I am postponing such connections for later chapters, adding a sixth criterion merits consideration here, at least from the perspective of the text's effective history. That is, the Pierced One's identity must cohere with the broader witness of the Christian canon. At least four assumptions stand behind this criterion. One, the function of the Christian canon in exegesis presupposes a deep unity between the Testaments. Two, the OT informs how one understands the NT. Three, the teachings of Jesus and the apostles in the NT inform how one should understand the message of the OT and set parameters for the interpretations one may draw from the text of the OT. In other words, believing the NT message that the Christ is Jesus has bearing on whether or not one finds in the Scriptures of Israel what Jesus apparently thinks people ought to have found there before (Luke 24:13–35, 44–49; John 3:1–10; 5:37–46). Four, the apostles respect the contexts of the OT passages they appropriate. See the discussions in Dodd, *According to the Scriptures*, 64–67, 126; Marshall, "Assessment," 1–21; Moo, *Old Testament*, 351–93; Hays, "Gospels," 402–18; Waltke, *Old Testament Theology*, 29–55. While I will only proceed with the five criteria listed above, I must admit at least some personal constraint by this sixth observation, and it would not demonstrate transparency to withhold it from the reader.

139. See the table in Appendix 3 for assistance. To my knowledge, no other work on Zech 12:10 organizes the research as I have done here into the five major categories.

Yahweh as the Pierced One

Past-collective Identification

Few argue for a past-collective identification of the Pierced One in Zech 12:10.[140] The past-collective view identifies the Pierced One in the sense of a collective martyr whose death occurred prior to Zechariah's prophecy. That is, the singular reference to a Pierced One actually represents a larger body of people who actually suffers the piercing.[141] Moreover, the past-collective view interprets this collective piercing as a past event to Zechariah's audience, such as the slaying of the Benjaminites in Judg 20:45–47.[142] However, the past-collective interpretation falls short in that it fails to interpret the text in accordance with the emphatic eschatological context.[143] It also places the physical suffering upon a body of people and not upon Yahweh, a reading that stems from seeing the clause אֵת אֲשֶׁר־דָּקָרוּ as syntactically disconnected from וְהִבִּיטוּ אֵלַי. Furthermore, the remainder of the canonical witness signals no correspondence, even at typological levels, with the war between Israel and Benjamin or the mourning thereafter.[144]

Present-collective Identification

More popular is the present-collective identification of the Pierced One. The present-collective view also interprets the Pierced One in a collective sense, but it differs from the past-collective view by shifting the piercing from a past event to a present event. In other words,

---

140. Van Hoonacker, *Les Douze*, 682. See others mentioned in Chary, *Aggée-Zecharie*, 202.

141. Using the singular in a collective sense is certainly not foreign to the OT (cf. *IBHS* §7.2.1d). Two common examples of the collective use of a singular term, which also have significant theological repercussions, are בֵּן in Hos 11:1 (cf. Exod 4:22–23; Matt 2:15) and זֶרַע in Gen 12:7 (cf. Gal 3:16). However, what differentiates these two examples from the one proposed by Van Hoonacker concerning the Pierced One is that the broader canonical witness teaches us to interpret them in this collective sense. Such an inner-biblical interpretation is never the case with Zech 12:10b.

142. Van Hoonacker, *Les Douze*, 682.

143. See the "Literary Context" above, regarding the eschatological nature of Zech 12:10.

144. Van Hoonacker attempts to make contextual connections between Hadadrimmon of Zech 12:11 and Rimmon of Judg 20–21. However, Judg 21:2 specifies that Israel's mourning took place at Bethel, not Rimmon; and Zech 12:11 compares the mourning to that in the plain of Megiddo.

Jesus as the Pierced One

present-collective interpreters associate the piercing with some of Zechariah's contemporaries, whether Jewish martyrs, prophetic figures, visionary disciples, or oppressed Judahites.[145]

However, the present-collective identification also fails to interpret the piercing in light of the eschatological framework signaled by the literary context of Zech 12–13. Moreover, the singular referent in the subsequent mourning and bitterness—i.e., the mourning as over an only child or over a firstborn and the bitterness "over him" (עָלָיו)—suggests an individual is in view as opposed to a number of people.[146]

---

145. Some rabbinic traditions fit within this group, such as Kimḥi and M'Caul, *Prophecies of Zechariah*, 156–58; Cohen, *Twelve Prophets*, 321; Troki, *Faith Strengthened*, 181–85, as does Floyd, *Minor Prophets*, 524–25. Because they shift the responsibility of the piercing from the Jews to the Gentile nations of Zech 12:1–9, these interpreters change the object of the piercing from Yahweh to "those Jews who fell in defence [sic] of their city." Cohen, *Twelve Prophets*, 321. Lacocque argues for a collective martyrdom, which he sees fulfilled in a royal and messianic sense by the oppressed Judahites of Zech 12:1–9. Lacocque, *Zacharie 9–14*, 191–92. Meyers and Meyers preserve the Jews as the subjects of דְּקָרוּ, but see the Pierced One representing a group of prophetic figures both contemporary to Zechariah's audience and representative of all prophetic figures up until Zechariah's day. Meyers and Meyers, *Zechariah 9–14*, 339. See also Mason, "Earlier Biblical Material," 165. Mason interprets עָלָיו as a reference to "the prophet and/or his circle." Mason argues on the assumption that the true prophet "felt himself to stand [closely] to Yahweh," and "related to him as his representative or mouthpiece, so that harm to the prophet was injury to Yahweh himself (cf. Jer 26:19)." Cf. Hanson, *Dawn of Apocalyptic*, 365–68. Hanson identifies the Pierced One as the visionary disciples of Second Isaiah.

146. Rabbinic interpreters will suggest that the Gentile nations are the subject behind דְּקָרוּ and that the Jews are the collective referent who suffer piercing. E.g., Cohen notes that most Jewish commentators assume that "the slain in battle [i.e., the pierced ones] are those [Jews] whom the heathens *have thrust through*" (italics original). Cohen, *Twelve Prophets*, 321. Isaac ben Abraham of Troki (1533–1594), whose work in Jewish apologetics still plays an influential role in contemporary Jewish circles, interprets this passage similarly. See his exposition of Zech 12:10 in Troki, *Faith Strengthened*, 181–85. Cf. Kimḥi and M'Caul, *Prophecies of Zechariah*, 156–58. However, even this collective reference to the nations also falls short of the context, since nothing within Zech 12:10 suggests, or even requires, a change in subject *from* the house of David and the inhabitants of Jerusalem who "look" *to* other Gentile nations who "pierce." If the subject remains Israel instead of the nations, then the need for an object other than Yahweh disappears. Floyd counters by suggesting that the relative particle, אֲשֶׁר, could be indeterminate, including all the Jews and Gentiles pierced in the battle of Zech 12:9. According to Floyd, Jerusalem looks to Yahweh regarding whomever the nations or the Jews pierced in battle, and then they mourn for each casualty. Floyd, *Minor Prophets*, 524–25, 527–28. However, see the critiques of Floyd on p. 45n59 and p. 50n76. Moreover, the mourning over a lone individual in

Additionally, present-collective interpreters do not maintain Yahweh as the object of the verbs throughout Zech 12:10b, so that Yahweh is the object of the people's looking, piercing, and mourning.[147]

Past- and Present-singular Identification

The past-singular identification comes next in the five major views, since, to my knowledge, no collective interpretation for a time future to Zechariah exists. Because similar critiques will apply to the past- and present-singular identification, I will handle the past- and present-singular views together.

The past-singular identification rejects a collective referent in the pronouns surrounding the Pierced One, and then postulates historical figures that died before the post-exilic period in which Zechariah prophesied. Options usually include men like King Josiah (2 Chr 35:22–25),[148] Gedaliah (2 Kgs 25:25; Jer 41:1, 2),[149] Uriah the son of Shemaiah (Jer 26:20),[150] and Zechariah the son of Jehoiada (2 Chr 24:20–22).[151] Still others argue for a present-singular identification, wherein they maintain the singular referent but believe that individuals contemporary to Zechariah's audience are the most suitable candidates, such as Zerubbabel,[152] Joshua the high priest,[153] or someone killed in the war of

---

Zech 12:10 points away from Floyd's suggestion of mourning over many casualties.

147. Meyers and Meyers may go so far as to assert that the Davidides and leaders look to Yahweh "and at the same time to the stabbed one," but they then separate Yahweh from the stabbed one by making prophetic figures—and thereby true prophecy in general—the collective referent behind אֲשֶׁר and עָלָיו. Yet by making these prophetic figures the objects of the people's piercing and mourning, they remove the literal piercing from Yahweh, which I have argued throughout is the more defensible reading contextually and syntactically. Cf. also the critique of Meyers and Meyers by Klein, *Zechariah*, 367–68.

148. See Otzen, *Studien*, 173–74. Otzen cites the view of Grützmacher.

149. Cf. Meyers and Meyers, "Fortunes," 215–19.

150. Though Mitchell dismisses Uriah the son of Shemaiah as a remote option, he still mentions how others propose the option. See Mitchell, *Zechariah*, 330.

151. Lévy, "Sacharja 12,10," 293–96.

152. Conrad, *Zechariah*, 183.

153. Plöger, *Theokratie Und Eschatologie*, 105–6. Plöger suggests the connection to the death of Joshua the high priest (see Josephus, *Ant*. 11.7.1) as the potential context shaping the distress to accompany the events of Zech 12:1–9.

Zech 12:1–8.[154] Those who attribute the composition of Zech 9–14 to a period well beyond Zechariah's time propose figures contemporary to the Maccabean era, such as Onias III (2 Macc 4:34),[155] Judas Maccabeus (1 Macc 9:17–21),[156] or Simon Maccabeus (1 Macc 16:11–17).[157]

However, the criticisms raised against a Maccabean dating to the composition of Zech 9–14 questions whether these Maccabean figures are accurate identifications of the Pierced One,[158] and each Maccabean figure suffers the same following criticisms that the other figures in the past- and present-singular identifications do. To begin, all of the suggestions inadequately explain the piercing of Yahweh. Even if one embraces the functional-identity perspective of the suffixes as outlined above, none of the figures listed by the past- or present-singular identification share the same kind of inseparable relationship with Yahweh that we see in other representatives like the Suffering Servant or King David.[159] Also, like the collective identifications above, both the past- and present-singular identifications continue minimizing the eschatological setting for the events described in Zech 12:10.[160] Furthermore,

154. Floyd, *Minor Prophets*, 524–25.

155. Marti, *Das Dodekapropheton*, 447; Oesterley, *A History of Israel*, 269–71.

156. "Suivant saint Ephrem, ce passage, pris au sens littéral, se rapporte à la mort de Judas Macchabée et au deuil qui suivit" ("According to St. Ephrem, this passage, taken literally, refers to the death of Judas Maccabeus and mourning that followed"). Condamin, "Le Sens Messianique," 53.

157. Duhm, *Zwölf Propheten*, 107–8.

158. For a discussion on the dating of Zech 9–14, as well as the criticisms raised against the Maccabean dating, see Baldwin, *Zechariah*, 66–69; Hill, "Linguistic Re-examination," 105–34; Meyers and Meyers, *Zechariah 9–14*, 52–55; Hill, *Zechariah*, 108–9.

159. For further comments regarding the relationship that Yahweh shares with the Suffering Servant and King David, see the "functional-identity" view of the suffixes above on pp. 51–53. Of the figures listed above by the past- and present-singular identification, Zerubbabel comes closest to standing as Yahweh's representative, especially if one grants that he serves as a type, whose historical role as royal temple-builder (Zech 4:6–10; cf. Hag 2:23) points to and would be surpassed by the eschatological role of the "Branch" in Zech 3:8 and Zech 6:12. However, with no historical record of Israel piercing Zerubbabel and then looking to Yahweh with great mourning, identifying the Pierced One as Zerubbabel remains difficult to confirm. Moreover, it hardly seems thinkable that the sacrifice of Zerubbabel would open the fountain of cleansing in Zech 13:1.

160. Again, see the "Literary Context" above for the eschatological nature of

the figures in the past- and present-singular identification do not befit the wider context of Zech 12–13. For instance, of the deaths we know about, for none of them does Israel look to God and mourn as the result of Yahweh pouring out "a spirit of grace and pleas for mercy," as specified in Zech 12:10a.[161] Nor is the piercing of any of these individuals of such significance that Yahweh opens a fount for cleansing Israel's sin and uncleanness, such as Zech 13:1 seems to indicate.[162] For these reasons, I find the past- and present-singular views unconvincing and prefer still a fifth view.[163]

Future-singular Identification

The most prevalent singular view—and the most prevalent of all five major views categorized here—goes to the future-singular identification of the Pierced One. The future-singular view maintains a referent to a unique individual but then locates that individual, and the events surrounding him, in a day future to Zechariah's ministry. Consistently,

---

Zech 12:10. Certainly, prophets would often use historical persons as types that anticipated greater fulfillment in the antitype (e.g., a new David in Jer 23:5; Ezek 34:23; 37:24–28). For an excellent survey and current discussion of typology, see Hoskins, *Jesus as Fulfillment*, 18–32. Among the personages listed above, perhaps Josiah—as a king in Judah who was pierced by an arrow in battle—would come closest to serving as a potential type (2 Chr 35:22–25). Yet the literal piercing of Yahweh by his own covenant people—instead of by the nations as in Josiah's case (2 Chr 35:20, 23)—seems to break down the historical correspondence that would qualify Josiah as the identity behind the Pierced One.

161. Such a critique even applies to the extensive mourning (i.e., "all Judah and Jerusalem") over the death of King Josiah in 2 Chr 25:24–25. The critique especially applies where the mourning of Israel receives little to no attention in relation to figures like Gedaliah (see 2 Kgs 25:25–26; Jer 41:1–18), Uriah the son of Shemiah (see Jer 26:20–23), or Zechariah the son of Jehoiada (see 2 Chr 24:20–22). Josephus only describes how horrible was the death of Joshua the high priest, and then moves on to the retaliation of Bagoses (see Josephus, *Ant.* 11.7.1). We know nothing of Zerubbabel's death.

162. See "The Use of דָּקַר and Its Effect on Translators of the LXX" on pp. 55–67 (esp. pp. 57n104 and 57n105).

163. One further criticism of the past- and present-singular views is worth considering, namely, none of these figures coheres with the testimony of the broader Christian canon, which finds the fulfillment of Zech 12:10 in the person of Jesus. However, a full articulation must wait until chapters 3 and 4 below on John 19:37 and Rev 1:7, respectively.

the conclusion is that the Pierced One of Zech 12:10 signifies a future messianic figure, who stands as God's representative for Israel, such as Messiah ben Ephraim,[164] Isaiah's Suffering Servant,[165] and/or Zechariah's shepherd-king.[166]

Because the future-singular identification acknowledges the eschatological aspects of Zech 12:1—13:1, it shares more in common with the findings of this chapter than with the past- and present-singular identifications. Also, a number of interpreters who maintain a future-singular identification of the Pierced One also maintain the functional-identity view of the suffixes, thus suggesting that Yahweh suffers piercing insofar as his close, human representative suffers piercing. Their point simply becomes sharper in that Yahweh's close, human representative is also the expected messiah. As mentioned above, such a view may very well complement my interpretation of Zech 12:10, but it does so at the wider contextual level. That is to say, Zechariah elsewhere points to the messiah using significant figures—e.g., the branch,

---

164. Some rabbinic traditions ascribe the piercing of Zech 12:10 to Messiah ben Ephraim, whom Gog will pierce in a final battle (*b. Sukk.* 52a). Similarly, see Targumic Tosefta in Mitchell, "Messiah," 223. Additional "ancient and medieval Jewish exegetical tradition" identifying the Pierced One with Messiah ben Ephraim appears in Kubiś, *Zechariah in John*, 139n113.

165. E.g., Condamin, "Le Sens Messianique," 54–55; Lamarche, *Zacharie IX–XIV*, 120–30; Chary, *Aggée-Zacharie*, 204–6; Meyer, "Metaphors," 80–81; Rosenberg, "Slain Messiah," 260; Mitchell, *Psalter*, 208–9; Deissler, "Sach 12,10," 57, 59; Webb, *Zechariah*, 169–70; Petterson, *Behold Your King*, 240–42. However, some have argued for more differences than similarities between the Suffering Servant and the Pierced One. Cf. Baldwin, *Zechariah*, 198; Mason, "Earlier Biblical Material," 164; Boda, *Haggai, Zechariah*, 488.

166. E.g., Cooke, "Unknown Martyr," 100; Lamarche, *Zacharie IX–XIV*, 108–10, 119–25; Merrill, *Zechariah*, 320; Selman, "Messianic Mysteries," 299; Duguid, "Messianic Themes," 275; McComiskey, "Zechariah," 1214; Ulrich, "Two Offices," 261; Kubiś, *Zechariah in John*, 145. Some of these interpreters—e.g., Lamarche, McComiskey, and Kubiś—argue that Zechariah's Pierced One is both Zechariah's shepherd-king and Isaiah's Suffering Servant. For the pre-Christian influence that the Suffering Servant of Isa 53 had on Zech 12:10 and Zech 13:7, see Hengel, "Isaiah 53," 85–90. Others mention a connection to the messiah of Zechariah's message or to Yahweh's servant in general, but leave the connections somewhat general. See, e.g., Justin, *Dial.* 32.2; cf. *1 Apol.* 52.11–12; Kohler, *Die Nachexilischen Propheten*, 206; Keil and Delitzsch, *Twelve Minor Prophets*, 388; Brandenburg, *Die Kleinen Propheten*, 110.

Yahweh as the Pierced One

the king, and the shepherd[167]—who so share in Yahweh's character, and so actualize Yahweh's saving purposes, that the figures of messiah and Yahweh progressively meld.[168] Thus, the Christian messianic interpretation within the future-singular position could merit strong consideration alongside my thesis that Yahweh is the Pierced One.[169]

Even still, at the narrower contextual level, Zech 12:10b seems to envision more than the future literal piercing of a human, messianic representative of Yahweh. The prophet seems to envision the future

---

167. See the "Literary Context" of the present chapter, where the roles of the branch, king, and shepherd were outlined briefly.

168. Here I am borrowing language from Hultberg's presentation, when he observed that a major theme in Zechariah is "the coming of God in his viceroy and the consequent melding of the figures of Messiah and God." Hultberg, "Significance," 20. See also p. 54n92 regarding the similarities between Yahweh and the shepherd-king in Zechariah. Regarding the branch, he too will possess royal honor and establish peace (Zech 6:13; cf. Jer 23:5–6), just as the shepherd-king and Yahweh both possess royal honor and establish peace (Zech 8:12; 9:10, 14–15; 14:1–21). Furthermore, see Lamarche, *Zacharie IX–XIV*, 105–23, who argues that the literary structure of Zech 9–14 reveals that Yahweh's redemptive agents in 9:9–10 (the king), 12:10—13:1 (the pierced servant), and 13:7–9 (the shepherd; cf. 11:4–14) are various aspects of the same messianic deliverer for Israel. The literary connections within Lamarche's sweeping chiasm may not be enough to warrant all three representing the same individual. See the fair critiques by Baldwin, *Zechariah*, 79; Klein, *Zechariah*, 46. Nevertheless, see the same connections developed by Cook, "Metamorphosis," 453–66; Hultberg, "Significance," 15, 20–22. Both Cook and Hultberg move beyond mere literary connections. Moreover, one should also give due attention to the witness of the broader Christian canon, wherein the apostles identify Jesus as Israel's messiah using all three contexts from Zechariah (e.g., Matt 21:5; 24:30; 26:15, 28, 31; 27:9–10; John 12:15; 19:37). Regarding this connection in the Fourth Gospel see also Bruce, "Zechariah and Passion Narrative," 351; Pryor, *John*, 81; Carson, *John*, 627–28. For Matthew's Gospel, see Ham, *The Coming King*, 96, 107–26.

169. Along these lines, Zech 12:8 falls within the same eschatological context of the Pierced One and adds that the house of David shall be like God, like the angel of the Lord. While some have understood this statement ontologically (i.e., the house of David will gain divine status), Petterson, referring to Exod 13:21 and 2 Sam 14:17–20, seems closer to the point when he understands the statement functionally (i.e., the house of David will lead like Yahweh). Petterson, *Behold Your King*, 219; Petterson, *Zechariah*, 264. Still, the ambiguous relationship that exists between Yahweh and the king—the king, in this case, being signified by the house of David—eventually becomes even closer in Zech 12:10 for Petterson. Also referring to Zech 12:7–8, Ulrich says that "it will be as if Yahweh himself were incarnate on David's throne." Ulrich says this just before linking the Yahweh/me/him ambiguity in Zech 12:10 to the shepherd/companion in Zech 13:7. Ulrich, "Two Offices," 262.

literal piercing of Yahweh himself, and some messianic interpretations within the future-singular position, especially those interpretations supported by the Targums and rabbinic literature, fall short by jettisoning the literal piercing of Yahweh altogether.[170] Any messianic interpretation of Zech 12:10 that denies or evades the literal piercing of Yahweh ultimately seems inadequate. Part and parcel to the messianic development in the book of Zechariah is that Yahweh reveals himself as, and not simply with, the Pierced One, however mysterious and offensive it must have rung in the ears of Zechariah's audience.

CONCLUSION

Therefore, according to our study of Zech 12:10, identifying the Pierced One as Yahweh and not merely with Yahweh seems to be a valid interpretation. In fact, numerous observations buttress such a divine identification of the Pierced One. First, the most historically viable and contextually supported reading is that of the MT, אֵלַי, with Yahweh standing as the object of the preposition and focus of the verbal action in וְהִבִּיטוּ. Second, the clause אֵת אֲשֶׁר־דָּקָרוּ modifies the first-person suffix in אֵלַי, also making Yahweh the object of דְּקָרוּ. Third, taking the alternation of suffixes as a stylistic feature highlighting the same object from differing perspectives, Yahweh remains the central object throughout the entire text, whether the people look, pierce, or mourn.

---

170. See above as well as the discussion over the Targum's interpretation of Zech 12:10 by Kubiś, *Zechariah in John*, 162–69. Kubiś shows how the Targum's replacement of the piercing with the idea of exile is contextually incompatible with Zech 12:1–13:1. Kubiś also shows that the marginal note in *Codex Reuchlinianus*—which provides the same interpretation as *b. Sukkah* 52a in the rabbinic literature—identifies the Pierced One with Messiah ben Ephraim/Joseph, which would be a more contextually appropriate reading. Even so, the messianic references in Zechariah reflect linkages more so with the line of David (and thus Judah) than to Ephraim (e.g., Zech 3:8 ["the branch" // Jer 23:5; 33:15; cf. Isa 11:1]; Zech 3:10 ["under his vine and under his fig tree" // Gen 49:10–11; 1 Kgs 4:25]; Zech 9:9 [Zion's king // Ps 2; Isa 9:6–7]; Zech 9:10 ["river to ends of the earth" // Ps 72]; Zech 12:7, 8 ["house of David"]; Zech 13:7 ["my shepherd" // Ezek 34:23; 37:24]). Moreover, nowhere in Scripture does the Lord possess such a close relationship with Ephraim as he shares with his anointed King David, and which he also shares with the branch, king, and shepherd in Zechariah. Yet even more significant for the argument before us is that the piercing of Ephraim is not the actual piercing of Yahweh, as John seems to suggest is the case with Jesus Christ. See chapter 3 below.

Yahweh as the Pierced One

Fourth, the wider context and the seeming aversion by the LXX to Yahweh's piercing, both suggest that the use of the verb דָּקַר conveys a literal piercing of Yahweh. Fifth, the wider context of Zech 12:10 suggests that Zechariah's audience should have understood the piercing—along with the corporate looking and mourning—to accompany the eschatological days of God's redeeming mission. Interpreting Zech 12:10 to say that the immortal Yahweh actually suffers piercing at the hands of mortals certainly presents a *sui generis* problem. However, the Apostle John seems ready to provide a *sui generis* solution by building on God's self-disclosure in the two-fold eschatological mission of Jesus Christ. That subject will occupy the next two chapters on John's use of Zech 12:10 in John 19:37 and Rev 1:7.

3

The Pierced One's First Redeeming Advent

John 19:37

Having demonstrated the validity of identifying the Pierced One as Yahweh, we now stand in a better position to determine how the Apostle John uses Zech 12:10 to build on an understanding of God's self-disclosure in Jesus' two-fold eschatological mission. Also, if we find that John connects Jesus with the Pierced One because he includes Jesus within the divine identity,[1] then we are in a much better position to say that John is not imposing onto Zech 12:10 a meaning that was never present, even if somewhat cryptic to the prophet's original audience. Rather, John seems to answer the *sui generis* problem, God is pierced, with the *sui generis* answer, Jesus is God.

---

1. As Vanhoozer observes, "'identity' . . . is susceptible of several meanings: numeric oneness, ontological sameness or permanence in time, and the personal identity of self-continuity." Vanhoozer, "Trinity," 47. With Vanhoozer, Bauckham, Köstenberger, Swain, and others, it is this last sense that captures what I mean by including Jesus within the "divine identity." Vanhoozer, "Trinity," 47–71; Bauckham, *Jesus and the God of Israel*, 6–7; Köstenberger and Swain, *Father, Son & Spirit*, 34–39. In the Scripture, God is not conceived of merely along metaphysical lines of ontology (i.e., what divinity is), but along personal lines of identity (i.e., who God is). By ascribing to Jesus characteristics that the OT reveals as belonging exclusively to God, the apostles argue that Jesus, as Son, is intrinsic to who God is. See especially, Bauckham, *Jesus and the God of Israel*, 18–31; Köstenberger and Swain, *Father, Son & Spirit*, 27–44, 111–33; Wellum, "Lord and Son," 26–27. The research below will seek to demonstrate that John is doing the same with his use of Zech 12:10.

The Pierced One's First Redeeming Advent

Available to John were other, less ambiguous OT passages that foretell the piercing of God's messianic representative. However, John selects the more ambiguous OT passage, that is, Zech 12:10, which does not clearly point to the piercing of God's representative but to the piercing of God himself. Thus, John 19:37 provides the initial insight to how God's self-disclosure in Jesus' first redeeming advent enables John to link the piercing of Jesus' side with the piercing of God. By linking Jesus' piercing with Zech 12:10, John simultaneously affords his readers a biblical-theological framework in which to comprehend Jesus' divine identity and mission. The plan for chapter 3, then, is not to focus on identifying which textual form stands behind John's OT quotation. Other studies already provide adequate treatment of the potential textual forms behind John 19:37 and their historical function.[2] The growing consensus is that John, in contrast to the LXX, creates his own quotation of Zech 12:10 to represent his Hebrew *Vorlage* more accurately.[3] Building on these previous studies, the plan is to focus on John's biblical-theological development of Zech 12:10 in John 19:37.

Four steps will contribute to this development. Step one, we must first establish that John is quoting from Zech 12:10. Step two, we must understand the quotation within the broader narrative framework of

---

2. E.g., Moo, *Old Testament*, 210–15, 353; Menken, "Textual Form," 494–511; Hübenthal, *Transformation*, 192–213; Bynum, *Fourth Gospel*, 139–68; Kubiś, *Zechariah in John*, 171–81.

3. Freed, *Old Testament Quotations*, 125; Morris, *John*, 823; Moo, *Old Testament*, 368n2; Menken, "Textual Form," 504; Jauhiainen, *Use of Zechariah*, 103; Michaels, *John*, 976; Kubiś, *Zechariah in John*, 180; Bynum, *Fourth Gospel*, 168. Bynum qualifies that John's quotation is "a reliable witness to a text form in Greek [which he believes is the Greek Minor Prophets Scroll 8ḤevXIIgr, or "R"], and its corresponding Hebrew *Vorlage* [which he believes closely resembles the MT]." Bynum, *Fourth Gospel*, 53–56, 168. Bynum also concludes his lengthy study, showing that the author of the Fourth Gospel "was sympathetic to the concern of his era for biblical accuracy, for fidelity to the proto-MT, and for the correctness of the LXX." Bynum, *Fourth Gospel*, 171. Cf. Schuchard, *Scripture within Scripture*, 149. Schuchard argues throughout his study that John is solely dependent on the Old Greek except when it comes to citing Zech 12:10 in John 19:37, where John appears to use a corrected version of the Old Greek. Schuchard, *Scripture within Scripture*, 145–49. Bynum's caution brings balance, after comparing and contrasting several of John's OT citations: "It is important to affirm the definite influence of the LXX upon John's citations, but it is equally important to have an adequate view of John's relationship to the Hebrew text in its pluriform possibilities" Bynum, *Fourth Gospel*, 119.

Jesus as the Pierced One

John's Gospel. Step three, we must then seek to understand the warrant John has for applying Zech 12:10 to the piercing of Jesus in particular. Step four, answering the question of warrant will lead to several observations regarding the biblical-theological significance that Zech 12:10 contributes to John's presentation of Jesus' identity and mission.

STEP ONE: ESTABLISHING THE QUOTATION

While he occasionally identifies the prophet behind an OT citation,[4] John excludes any direct reference to a particular prophet in John 19:37. Nevertheless, sufficient evidence exists that John is quoting a portion from Zech 12:10.[5] First, while the vocabulary in John's quotation differs from the LXX,[6] only Zech 12:10 contains the same elements John 19:37 mentions: a people look on Yahweh/God whom they themselves were complicit in piercing.[7] Second, elsewhere in his Gospel John develops unique themes analogous to chs. 9–14 of Zechariah's prophecy.[8] Third, John also alludes to Zech 12:10 in Rev 1:7, the latter containing even further connections to the wider context of Zech 12:10.[9] Fourth, other early Greek translations of Zech 12:10 show similarities with

---

4. E.g., John 1:23 ["as the prophet Isaiah said"]; 1:45 ["we have found him of whom Moses in the Law ... wrote"]; 5:46 ["for if you believed Moses, you would believe me; for he wrote of me"]; 12:38–41 ["so that the word spoken by the prophet Isaiah might be fulfilled"].

5. Contra Reim, *Studien*, 53–56. Reim argues that John's quotation stems from the Synoptics.

6. A parallel reading of the MT, LXX, and GNT appears in the table of Appendix 1.

7. Anticipating further discussion below, John's inclusion of Jesus in the divine identity suggests the closest parallel to Zech 12:10. Moreover, John's use of the relative pronoun ὅν ("him whom") instead of the personal pronoun με ("me"), aligns with early practices in Jewish interpretation of Scripture "to adapt the OT verse to its new context without altering its meaning." Moo, *Old Testament*, 374. To look directly upon the pierced Jesus ("him") was to look on the pierced God, the Son who reveals the Father ("me").

8. See especially Kubiś, *Zechariah in John*, 27–114.

9. Further discussion on Rev 1:7 appears below. Even if one does not accept that John stands behind both John 19:37 and Rev 1:7, the allusion to Zech 12:10 in Rev 1:7 still stands as an example of where another NT author references the same OT text with additional, clarifying evidence. See "Methodology" above, which explains the latter point.

The Pierced One's First Redeeming Advent

John's translation of Zech 12:10.[10] Thus, the intentional connection to Zech 12:10 seems evident. But how then does John use Zech 12:10 to build on an understanding of God's self-disclosure in Jesus' two-fold eschatological mission? Answering that question from the perspective of John 19:37 requires another step.

STEP TWO: THE QUOTATION OF ZECH 12:10 IN THE NARRATIVE OF JOHN'S GOSPEL

We must understand John's quotation of Zech 12:10 within his Gospel's broader narrative framework.[11] While numerous proposals for the structure of John's Gospel exist, several studies show overlapping agreement that John's Gospel unfolds in two major units pivoting around the transitional material in chs. 11 and 12.[12] The first major

---

10. As noted in chapter 2, the LXX misconstrues the Hebrew with ἀνθ' ὧν κατωρχήσαντο ("because they danced"). However, other Greek translations such as Aquila and Theodotion use similar vocabulary as John (i.e., ἐξεκέντησαν). Lucian also has the exact rendering as John (i.e., εἰς ὃν ἐξεκέντησαν). However, the possibility exists that the third-century Lucian was influenced by the text of John. Cf. Delcor, "Un Problèm," 192. Symmachus only comes close to John's vocabulary with the cognate verb form, ἐπεξεκέντησαν. Cf. Menken, "Textual Form," 500–501. A parallel reading of Aquila, Theodotion, Symmachus, Lucian, and John 19:37 appears in Appendix 2 below.

11. As D. Moody Smith, Jr. observed, "The exegesis of any text must take account of its position and role in the document of which it is a part." Smith, Jr., *Composition*, 11. Objections to the literary unity of John's Gospel have received sufficient treatment by Mlakuzhyil, *Structure*, 35–50.

12. The overlapping agreement comes despite methodological dissimilarities among these studies. E.g., using the development of the Jewish feasts, Donatien Mollat divides John's Gospel into two main sections following the Gospel's prologue: "Le Ministère de Jésus" (1:19—12:50) and "L'Heure de Jésus: La Pâque de L'Agneau de Dieu" (13:1—20:31). Mollat, "L'Évangile Selon Saint Jean," 35–40. Based on what he calls "stages of living and believing," Brodie divides John's Gospel into Books One, "The Years of Jesus' Life" (chs. 1-12) and Book Two, "The Central Passover Mystery" (chs. 13-21). Brodie, *John*, xi, 42–45. Similarly, after establishing twelve literary criteria, four structural schemes, and twelve dramatic devices, George Mlakuzhyil's major study concludes that John's Gospel contains four major sections, the two central divisions being "Jesus' Signs" (John 2:1—12:50) and "Jesus' Hour" (John 13:1—20:29). Mlakuzhyil, *Structure*, 329–428. Yet Mlakuzhyil further considers the close of "Jesus' Signs" in John 11:1—12:50 to serve as the opening of "Jesus' Hour" simultaneously, and, therefore, he labels it "the bridge-section." Mlakuzhyil, *Structure*, 415–16, 461–67. Andreas Köstenberger observes widespread agreement over a four-fold division of John's Gospel. Aside from the Prologue (John 1:1–18)

JESUS AS THE PIERCED ONE

unit, extending from John 2:1 to John 12:50, contains unique signs that Jesus performs that bear witness to the fact that God the Father has sent his Son, the Messiah or Christ (e.g., John 4:34; 5:20, 36; 9:3; 10:25). Not only did the signs consist of works that God the Father performed through his sent Son,[13] but the signs carry redemptive-historical continuity with how the Scriptures expected God to save the world in the final kingdom of his Messiah.[14] In fact, John's direct appeal to Scripture in the first major unit serves to highlight that Jesus' signs or works are in accordance with "what is written."[15] Thus, the signs appear to

---

and Epilogue (John 21:1–25), the two major units consist of what he calls "Act I: Sēmeio-Drama" (John 1:19—12:50) and "Act II: Cruci-Drama" (John 13:1—20:29), with John 11–12 serving as a transition between the two acts. Köstenberger, *Theology*, 168–70. D. A. Carson downplays a strict binary division of John's Gospel and couples ch. 12 with ch. 11 as a "transition" between "Jesus' Self-Disclosure in Word and Deed" (John 1:19—10:42) and "Jesus' Self-Disclosure in His Cross and Exaltation" (John 13:1—20:31). Carson, *John*, 103–6. So also Ridderbos, *John*, 381–83; Burridge, *Four Gospels*, 139–40; Keener, *John*, 1:xvii–xviii. Evans also explains how ch. 12 links the book of signs with John's passion narrative, but does so from the standpoint of John's differing quotation formulas. Evans, "Quotation Formulas," 81.

13. E.g., John 5:17–19, 36; 9:32–33; 10:32–33, 37–38; 11:40–42; 14:11.

14. Thus, e.g., taking just the six commonly acknowledged signs in John's Gospel, the miracle at Cana demonstrates that Jesus brings the sweet wine of God's final kingdom (John 2:1–11; cf. Gen 49:10–11; Isa 25:6–8; Jer 31:10–14; Amos 9:11–14); the healing of the official's son, the healing of the invalid man, and the healing of the blind man, demonstrate that Jesus is powerful to realize the OT hopes that the lame would leap like the dear, the blind would see, and that the earth would finally rest from sickness and sin (John 4:46—5:17; 9:1–41; cf. healing, Isa 35:5–6; 61:1; rest, Gen 2:1–3; Exod 20:8–11; Deut 5:12–15; Ps 95:7–11 [cf. Heb 3:7—4:10]); the feeding of the five thousand before calming the seas demonstrates that Jesus not only possesses Yahweh's might to silence creation's turmoil as in the Red Sea crossing, but also, typologically speaking, he is the superior 'bread' that gives eternal life to his citizens (John 6:1–59; cf. Exod 16–17; Neh 9:15, 20; Ps 107:23–32); and the raising of Lazarus from death to life demonstrates that Jesus, as the resurrection and the life, is the answer to the veil of death cast over the nations (John 11:1–53; cf. Isa 25:7; Hos 13:14). See also Schreiner, *Theology*, 67. While I do not identify the temple clearing in John 2:12–22 as one of John's "signs," some do. E.g., see Köstenberger, "Seventh Sign," 87–103. Even still, the temple clearing would also show the same continuity with the messianic expectations in Scripture. The temple clearing and establishment of a superior temple demonstrates that Jesus cleanses God's people from their corruption to bring the anticipated day of true worship (John 2:12–22; cf. Ps 69:9; Mal 3:1, 3; Zech 13:1–7; 14:21).

15. These are most clearly identified in the places where John includes an introductory formula with γράφω (John 2:17; 6:31, 45; 10:34; 12:14), and in one place

serve a two-fold function in identifying Jesus: the signs reveal Jesus' filial identity with God the Father—more on the significance of this development appears below—and the signs connect the Son of the Father to the expected Christ of Scripture. Both functions of the signs support John's introductory goal of bearing witness to Jesus as the only Son from the Father (John 1:14), as well as the larger purpose of John's Gospel: to persuade others to believe that Jesus is the Christ, the Son of God (John 20:30–31). However, the first major unit ends on the tragic note of Israel's and the world's unbelief despite Jesus' revelatory signs (John 12:37–50).

The second major unit, extending from John 13:1 to John 20:31, discloses that God glorifies his Son through the ignominy of a cross before raising him from the dead. Even throughout the discourse of John 14–16, where Jesus prepares the disciples for his return to the Father and the future gift of the Spirit, Jesus keeps his glorification through death a major theme and even uses his determined suffering to equip the disciples for their difficult mission.[16] Yet John's presentation of Jesus' suffering and death in the face of Israel's and the world's unbelief never leaves the reader despairing. Despite the world's unbelief, God's purpose in sending his Son remains unhindered. The appointed "hour" of Jesus' passion and death actually serves the fulfillment of God's plans for his Son and Messiah.[17]

Indeed, whereas nonexistent throughout most of the Gospel's first major unit, an explicit element of prophetic fulfillment enters the picture as the narrative transitions from ch. 12 into the Gospel's

---

with ἡ γραφή (John 7:38). That is not to suggest that John's only appeal to Scripture is when he explicitly asserts that Jesus' signs/works are in accordance with what is written. As others have observed, John uses the OT in numerous ways, including quotations, verbal allusions, thematic parallels, replacement motifs, and typology. E.g., see the survey by Carson, "John and Johannine Epistles," 245–56.

16. John 14:30–31; 15:12–13, 20, 25; 16:16, 20, 33.

17. John 13:1–3, 18–19, 21, 38; 14:29; 16:22; 17:1–5, 12; 18:9, 32; 19:11, 28. These references in the Gospel's second major unit to the Father's and Jesus' sovereign control over the events leading up to Jesus' crucifixion as well as the crucifixion itself complement the ordained 'hour' for Jesus' death so heavily emphasized in the Gospel's first major unit (John 2:4; 4:23; 7:30; 8:20; 12:23, 27; cf. 13:1; 17:1). For further study on the sovereignty of God over Jesus' crucifixion at the hands of accountable men in John's Gospel, see Carson, *Divine Sovereignty*, 128–62, 201–22.

second major unit.[18] In John 12:38, 13:18, 15:25, 17:12 (the OT quotation only implied), 19:24, and 19:36, the use of ἵνα plus πληρόω makes up an unique formula that John suddenly and consistently employs to introduce several OT passages in relation to Jesus and his passion.[19] As others have demonstrated, when πληρόω introduces an OT passage, the term "naturally signals the realization of a predictive notion in the OT references it introduces."[20] Thus, even the people's rejection and Jesus' sufferings explicitly "fulfill" the Scriptures as the Gospel's second major unit draws to a close. Everything encompassed in the Christ-event—even the world's unbelief so emphasized by ch. 12—serves to bring Scripture, and God's covenant-promises communicated therein, to its intended goal, consummation, and completion.[21] As John's narrative

---

18. Of course, this explicit element of prophetic fulfillment, noted by the use of πληρόω, does not intend to ignore much broader developments of OT themes spanning the entire Gospel, many of which seem to point to a 'typological' fulfillment comparable to those passages citing the OT with the explicit 'fulfillment' formula (e.g., John 13:18; 19:24, 28; 19:36). See, e.g., Hoskins, *Jesus as Fulfillment*, 18–36, 108–93; Hoskins, *Death of Christ*, 38–44, 85–115; Hoskins, "Deliverance," 285–99; Schmidt, "Typology," 53–55, 57–64.

19. On two occasions, πάλιν joins two quotations to the formula (John 12:39; 19:36). On one occasion, in John 19:28, John uses ἵνα plus τελειόω, but the meaning appears to be the same. However, note the possible distinction made by Moule, "Fulfillment-Words," 318–19.

20. Schmidt, "Typology," 57. Schmidt's words about πληρόω are part of a larger discussion that demonstrates the predictive element within both direct prophecy and typological prophecy. Still, his words about πληρόω summarize what previous studies have found. See, e.g., BDAG, s.v. "πληρόω"; Delling, "πληρόω," 295–97; Moule, "Fulfillment-Words," 293–320; Moo, *Old Testament*, 383–86; Moo, "Problem of Sensus Plenior," 191–92. Likewise, Beauchamp speaks of how fulfillment formulas in the NT do one of the following: realize a prediction, uphold a promise, or carry out a process. Beauchamp, "Lecture Christique," 105–15. John's quotation functions in both the first and third ways. Moreover, on two further occasions John employs πληρόω to signal the realization of a predictive notion in Jesus' own words about his betrayal and death (John 18:9, 32; cf. 17:12; 12:32–33). Not only does this seem to place Jesus' words on the same level as God's words in the OT, since they too effect the future, but their realization in Jesus' passion parallels how John understands certain OT passages to be 'fulfilled' in Jesus.

21. Moule, "Fulfillment-Words," 294, 300. Cf. also Kraus, "Johannes," 3; Manns, "Zacharie 12,10," 302. Both Kraus and Manns observe the change in fulfillment formulas between the book of signs (John 2:1—12:50) and the passion narrative (John 13:1—20:31). Likewise, after developing a panorama of John's familiarity with the acts of God throughout Scripture, Paul A. Rainbow concludes thus: "Far from

draws nearer to the cross, the fulfillment motif becomes more explicit than ever and not only legitimates Jesus' cross-mission, but also sees in that very mission all of Scriptures' hopes realized and perfected.[22]

John's use of Zech 12:10 in relation to Jesus' piercing falls within the explicit fulfillment framework of his Gospel's second major unit. Indeed, being the last OT quotation appearing in John's account of the passion, Zech 12:10 appears to draw the explicit fulfillment framework to a close in relation to Jesus' piercing. The explicit fulfillment framework beginning in John 12:38–40, where unbelief blinded the people to the glory of God revealed in Jesus' signs, now draws to a close in John 19:37 with Jesus being pierced in fulfillment of Zech 12:10. Unbelief does not possess the ultimate word, therefore, but God's will revealed in Scripture does. God's will in Scripture now finds its climax in the Christ event.

Still persistent in their unbelief, the Jews request the Romans to break the legs of the crucified men, so that their hanging bodies would not defile the Sabbath (John 19:31; cf. Deut 21:23). After breaking the legs of the two thieves, the soldiers find it needless to break Jesus' legs since he is already dead (John 19:32–33). Nevertheless, one soldier thrusts his spear into Jesus' side, causing blood and water to pour out from his body (John 19:34). What John beheld firsthand serves as proclamation to his readers, that they might believe (John 19:35; cf. 20:31). John's editorial comment in v. 36 then introduces his understanding of the events that he has witnessed, a rationale that stems directly from the Scriptures.[23] In other words, the explanatory γὰρ following v. 35 means

---

ignoring, minimizing or sidelining the biblical record, John's proclamation of Jesus Christ presents [Jesus] as the goal of salvation-history . . . Divine revelation culminated in God's agent, Jesus Christ." Rainbow, *Johannine Theology*, 89.

22. Regarding the legitimization of Jesus' mission, see Köstenberger, "John," 416. See also Evans, "Old Testament in the Gospels," 587; Evans, "Quotation Formulas," 83. Bynum states similarly, " . . . the change in introductory formula indicates that a change in perception and perspective is now taking place between what Jesus continued to do that had already been written, compared to what was now coming to a new and unique depth of development and fulfillment in the events recorded in the passion narrative." Bynum, "Quotations," 54.

23. See also Carson, "John and Johannine Epistles," 248. Carson finds that John's audience needed "to be provided with a rationale, a biblical rationale, for the substantial rejection of Jesus by his fellow Jews."

that John cares not merely for his readers believing the events he has witnessed, but that his readers firmly believe what the Scriptures teach concerning those events.[24] In doing so, John bears witness to more than the perceptible facts surrounding Jesus' death, such as the non-broken legs, the actual piercing, and the blood and water pouring out; he also bears witness to the invisible meaning of these facts,[25] a meaning that is apparently inherent to prior revelation in Scripture. Therefore, the apostle goes on to assert the following in John 19:36–37:

	GNT	Translation
19:36a	ἐγένετο γὰρ ταῦτα ἵνα ἡ γραφὴ πληρωθῇ	For these things occurred, in order that the Scripture would be fulfilled,
19:36b	ὀστοῦν οὐ συντριβήσεται αὐτοῦ	"Not a bone of his will be broken";
19:37a	καὶ πάλιν ἑτέρα γραφὴ λέγει	and again another Scripture says,
19:37b	ὄψονται εἰς ὃν ἐξεκέντησαν	"They will look on him whom they have pierced."

Like the rest of his OT quotations from John 12:38 onward, John includes the explicit fulfillment formula in John 19:36–37. Although John 19:37 by itself lacks the explicit fulfillment formula, one should make no exception. Like his pair of quotations from Isaiah in John 12:38–39, John includes πάλιν to introduce the second of two quotations in 19:36–37. As a linking adverb, πάλιν extends the fulfillment motif in both John 12:38–39 and John 19:36–37 to the latter quotation in each pair.[26] That John uses the plural ταῦτα in John 19:36, also lends

---

24. Cf. Menken, "Not a Bone," 156; Black, "Messianic Use," 111–13.

25. See Kubiś, *Zechariah in John*, 181–82. Kubiś argues, "The *interpretive* or *hermeneutical* function of the scriptural quotations in vv. 36–37 is corroborated by the very nature of the eyewitness' testimony referred to in v. 35: it is not simply the witnessing of a visible, perceptible *fact* (factual or phenomenal aspect), but also a witness to an invisible *meaning* of this fact."

26. See this usage in BDAG, s.v. "πάλιν." Likewise, see the discussions in Schuchard, *Scripture within Scripture*, 141–42; Obermann, *Erfüllung*, 317–18; Kubiś, *Zechariah in John*, 184–86; Schmidt, "Typology," 63–64; Bynum, "Quotations," 65. Cf. also Carson, "John and Johannine Epistles," 248; Hengel, "Die Schriftauslegung," 281; Evans, *Word and Glory*, 176. Each of these interpreters largely assume the fulfillment formula applies to both citations in John 19:36–37.

The Pierced One's First Redeeming Advent

credibility to extending the fulfillment formula to the quotation of John 19:37.[27] Jesus' piercing, then, does not merely correspond with what the Scripture says; Jesus' piercing somehow signals the realization of the predictive notion in the prophet's words, "they will look on him whom they pierced."

Yet how does John see in Jesus' piercing a realization of the predictive notion in Zech 12:10? If part of the predictive notion in Zech 12:10 is the piercing of God, as chapter 2 attempted to demonstrate, then what leads John to the conclusion that God is pierced when Jesus is pierced? We must take another step to find out.

STEP THREE: THE WARRANT IN THE DIVINE GLORY JOHN WITNESSES THROUGH JESUS[28]

What warrant does John have for applying Zech 12:10 to the piercing of Jesus in particular? In his study on the use of the OT in the Gospel Passion narratives, Douglas J. Moo made an important distinction between the surface-level exegetical methods whereby authors would apply specific OT texts to a new situation and the deeper theological convictions driving such an application.[29] The former Moo called "appropriation techniques," and the latter he called "hermeneutical axioms."[30] The question posed in step one seeks to discover the hermeneutical axiom driving John's appropriation of Zech 12:10 for Jesus' piercing. That is, what is it for John that "legitimizes" the transfer of

---

27. Contra Keener, *John*, 1:1156. Keener finds the second appeal to Scripture different than the first in John 19:36–37.

28. These observations do not presuppose that John's interpretation of the OT becomes warranted only upon satisfying modern historical-critical canons that remain indifferent to divine revelation and the unity of the Testaments. Cf. Silva, "Text Form and Authority," 147–65; Linnemann, *Historical Criticism*, 83–159. Rather, they presuppose that John's appropriation of the OT accords with and continues the coherency of God's revelation to his covenant people throughout all biblical history for their salvation. See "Methodology" in chapter 1 above, as well as Goldsworthy, "Relationship," 81–89.

29. Moo, *Old Testament*, 25–78. Cf. Moo, "Problem of Sensus Plenior," 194.

30. Moo, *Old Testament*, 9, 374, 381. Likewise, see the discussion on the hermeneutical and theological presuppositions of the New Testament authors in Bock, "Scripture Citing Scripture," 261–64; Beale, *Handbook*, 95–102.

language from Zech 12:10 to the person of Jesus and the circumstances surrounding his piercing?[31]

Andreas Köstenberger represents many interpreters who have suggested or implied from John 19:37 that John's basic hermeneutical axiom is that "Yahweh acts in the person of his authorized representative, the messianic shepherd, so that to strike and kill the shepherd, or to pierce him, is in a sense to pierce Yahweh himself."[32] Such an assertion has great merit, especially in light of the way John appropriates other OT passages in relation to Jesus.[33] For instance, the Son of Man, the Suffering Servant, the Davidic king of Israel, and the (Good) Shepherd are all messianic figures from the OT who represent Yahweh in an eschatological mission to save his people; and John identifies Jesus with each aforementioned figure in his mission to the cross.[34]

However, a pair of observations contributes a further nuance to John's hermeneutical axiom in the case of John 19:37. To begin, despite the fact that Köstenberger and others affirm that Zech 12:10 refers to the piercing of Yahweh himself, they still apply the piercing to Yahweh's representative and relate their conclusion to the alternation of suffixes in the Hebrew text.[35] As argued in chapter 2, a stylistic explanation

---

31. Moo, *Old Testament*, 381. The original quotation states, "Specifically, it must be asked how Jesus and the evangelists 'legitimized' the transfer of language from various OT passages to the circumstances of Jesus' passion."

32. Köstenberger, "John," 505.

33. Also worthy of note is that Köstenberger and Swain's very helpful contribution on the Trinity in John's Gospel still gives little attention to how John's use of Zech 12:10 in John 19:37 serves John's theological perspective, especially as it pertains to Yahweh achieving his mission to save his people in the person of Jesus. My conclusions will not contradict what Köstenberger and Swain develop, but could be used to strengthen their argument as it not only provides further evidence that Jesus should be identified with and as Yahweh, but also reveals that John's Christology stems from the OT and Jesus' reading of the OT. See Köstenberger and Swain, *Father, Son & Spirit*, 77.

34. E.g., the Son of Man (John 3:13–14; 5:27–29 [Dan 7:13; cf. Dan 12:2]; 8:28; 12:23, 34; 13:31); the Suffering Servant (John 12:38 [Isa 53:1]); the Davidic king of Israel (John 1:49; 2:17 [Ps 69:9]; 12:13–15 [Zech 9:9]; 13:18 [Ps 41:9]; 15:25 [Ps 69:4; cf. Ps 35:19]; 19:24 [Ps 22:18]); the Good Shepherd (John 10:11–18, 25–29 [Ezek 34; Jer 23:1–6; Zech 9–11]; 16:32 [cf. Zech 13:7]).

35. Moreover, his commentary on John reveals that our conclusions from Zech 12:10 differ as he appears to qualify the piercing of Yahweh as "figuratively, with sorrow." See Köstenberger, *John*, 553.

The Pierced One's First Redeeming Advent

may better account for the alternation of suffixes, even though a representative (i.e., functional-identity) view remains compatible from a wider contextual reading of Zech 12:10.

Furthermore, John seems intent to select Zech 12:10 over the more popular OT passages where a connection to Yahweh acting in his representative would be more straightforward. In fact, John has already alluded to the Suffering Servant and the Righteous Sufferer in the Psalms by quoting Isa 53:1 in John 12:38 and also Ps 22:18 in John 19:24. Both the Suffering Servant and the Righteous Sufferer are OT figures that unambiguously undergo piercing as Yahweh's representative.[36] While John's use of Zech 12:10 could present yet another OT example where Yahweh's representative undergoes piercing, John could also be importing still a further theological point that the other OT passages do not make as explicit, namely, the expectation that Yahweh himself actually suffers piercing. If such theological import exists in Zech 12:10, as chapter 2 sought to demonstrate, then perhaps John's hermeneutical axiom also includes his conviction that the Christ is himself Yahweh.[37] Stated differently, John appears to interpret the OT convinced that Yahweh's eschatological self-revelation culminated in the person of Jesus, the Christ.

Such a conviction certainly befits John's overarching testimony concerning Jesus' identity as the divine Messiah, that is, Son of God and Christ (John 20:31).[38] The prologue of his Gospel introduces the

---

36. While John's quotation is only from Isa 53:1, there is good reason to believe that he also had the context of Isa 53:5 in mind, which begins as follows in reference to the Suffering Servant: "but he was pierced for our transgressions." Also, if one grants the aforementioned observation that the LXX and 5/6ḤevPsalms Scroll supports the translation, "they have pierced my hands and feet" from Ps 22:16, then John is using Ps 22:18 to compare Jesus to the Righteous Sufferer, David, who also experienced piercing as Yahweh's representative. Here, of course, I am accepting Dodd's seminal thesis that the NT apostles remained faithful to the respective contexts of their OT quotations: Dodd, *According to the Scriptures*, 11–27, 111–38.

37. Similarly, in reference to the use of Isaiah in John 12:37–40, Carson concludes that John's appropriation of the OT texts depends partly on the governing Christology. Carson, "John and Johannine Epistles," 251. Regarding John's Christological use and interpretation of Scripture, see Miller, "'They Saw His Glory,'" 127–51.

38. The designation, "Son of God," in relation to Jesus can take on several different meanings throughout Scripture. Jesus can be "Son of God" by virtue of being the new Adam (Luke 3:38; cf. 1 John 3:8), the ultimate Israel (Exod 4:22–23; Hos 11:1;

89

reader to the Word, who is also the unique one from the Father and then explicitly named "Jesus" (John 1:1, 14, 17).[39] Showing consistency with the rest of the NT in general, John employs the articular ὁ θεός to refer to God the Father in his assertions concerning the Word.[40] The Word not only existed with God (πρὸς τὸν θεόν) in the beginning—showing personal distinction between the Word and God the Father—but even what God the Father was, that the Word was too (θεὸς ἦν ὁ λόγος)[41]— showing an identity of being, a unity in divine essence (John 1:1).[42]

Matt 2:15), the promised Davidic King (2 Sam 7:13–14; Isa 9:6; Luke 1:32–33; John 1:41), and the Messiah (Ps 2:7; Acts 13:33; Heb 1:5; 5:5). John's Gospel stresses an additional nuance, namely, Jesus is "Son of God" by virtue of his eternal relationship with the Father, being distinct in person from and yet one in essence with the Father. Hence, not just Messiah but divine Messiah, not just Christ but Son of God. For a brief treatment of the subject, see Carson, *Son of God*, 13–42.

39. While the name 'Jesus' does not appear until John 1:17, and as a replacement of (cf. ἀντί in John 1:16) the grace that was given earlier through Moses, the context suggests that the preexistent λόγος points to Jesus. The ὅτι clause in v. 17 modifies the assertion about "his fullness" (τοῦ πληρώματος αὐτοῦ) in v. 16, which, as another ὅτι clause, modifies the assertion about "the unique Son from the Father" (μονογενοῦς παρὰ πατρός) in v. 14, who is also identified as the Word who became flesh (ὁ λόγος σὰρξ ἐγένετο). Moreover, the overall thrust of John's Gospel is that of the Father sending the Son, who is Jesus, from above to below (e.g., John 3:16–17; 5:30; 17:3), which presupposes the relationship that John is seeking to develop in his prologue between the Word and God the Father (cf. John 17:5, 24). Likewise, see Hengel, Martin, "Prologue," 271; Köstenberger and Swain, *Father, Son & Spirit*, 113.

40. See especially the discussion in Rainbow, *Johannine Theology*, 95–96.

41. On the textual integrity of John's prologue, especially in relation to the ascription of θεός to Jesus in John 1:1 and John 1:18, see Wright, "Jesus," 229–66.

42. For the grammar of John 1:1c (καὶ θεὸς ἦν ὁ λόγος), including a careful discussion of the abuse of Colwell's Rule, see Wallace, *Grammar*, 257–70. Wallace carefully exposes that rejecting the translation of John 1:1c, "and the Word was *a* god," cannot be based on an appeal to Colwell's Rule as it has been so often misunderstood. Then, after clarifying and refining Colwell's Rule, Wallace applies his findings to John 1:1c. According to his study, the predicate θεός in John 1:1c cannot be indefinite or definite. Rather, on both grammatical and theological grounds θεός must be qualitative. To quote Wallace at length, "[That θεός is qualitative] is true both grammatically (for the largest proportion of pre-verbal anarthrous predicate nominatives fall into this category) and theologically (both the theology of the Fourth Gospel and of the NT as a whole). There is a balance between the Word's deity, which was already present in the beginning (ἐν ἀρχῇ . . . θεὸς ἦν [1:1]), and his humanity, which was added later (σὰρξ ἐγένετο [1:14]). The grammatical structure of these two statements mirrors each other; both emphasize the nature of the Word, rather than his identity. But θεός was his nature from eternity (hence, εἰμί is used), while σάρξ was added at the

The Pierced One's First Redeeming Advent

Similarly, while "no one has ever seen God [θεὸν]"—presumably in any unqualified sense (cf. Num 12:8; Isa 6:5)[43]—"the one-of-a-kind [Son], God [in his own right] [μονογενὴς θεὸς], who is in the Father's bosom, he has explained him" (John 1:18).[44] As with the Word in John 1:1, the "only God" in John 1:18 not only possesses what is divine (θεὸς), but he is also distinct in person (μονογενὴς) from the Father. According to John, this qualifies the Word to reveal God the Father. Hence, when the Word adds humanity to what he had always been before—that is, distinct from the Father in person yet one with the Father in being—John witnesses glory in the Word's mission "as of an only Son (μονογενοῦς) from the Father" (John 1:14).[45] Intrinsic to the

incarnation (hence, γίνομαι is used). Such an option does not at all impugn the deity of Christ. Rather, it stresses that, although the person of Christ is not the person of the Father, their essence is identical . . . The idea of a qualitative θεὸς here is that the Word had all the attributes and qualities that 'the God' (of 1:1b) had. In other words, he shared the essence of the Father, though they differed in person." Wallace, *Grammar*, 269.

43. So Carson, *John*, 134. Ridderbos uses "unveiled presence." Ridderbos, *John*, 59. Rainbow explains that no one has beheld "what God is in naked reality." Rainbow, *Johannine Theology*, 97.

44. Some have argued, historically on etymological grounds but more recently on theological grounds as well, that μονογενὴς carries the connotation of generation or begottenness, and thus John 1:14 and John 1:18 refer to the Son's eternal generation. E.g., Dahms, "Monogenēs," 222–32; Rainbow, *Johannine Theology*, 103–5. However, others have given sufficient reason to doubt that such a connotation is inherent to John's use of μονογενὴς in John 1:14 and John 1:18 (cf. John 3:16, 18; 1 John 4:9), even though the theological notion may still exist elsewhere in John's Gospel (e.g., John 5:26). E.g., see the discussion and survey of literature in Keener, *John*, 1:412–16; Köstenberger, *John*, 42–45; Köstenberger and Swain, *Father, Son & Spirit*, 76–79; Carson, *Son of God*, 80–84. Instead, based on its usage in the OT and Second Temple literature, μονογενὴς is better understood as "one-of-a-kind" (cf. BDAG, s.v., "μονογενὴς"). With regard to John 1:18 in particular, I have followed Köstenberger and Swain in understanding μονογενὴς to function as "a substantive in its own right as in 1:14" (i.e., "one-of-a-kind [Son], God [in his own right]"), instead of translating it attributively (i.e., "one-of-a-kind God"). Köstenberger follows Hofius, "Joh 1,18," 163–71.

45. That he is "from" (παρὰ) God the Father seems to be more of an assertion about the Word/Son's sent-ness in mission than his eternal generation (cf. παρὰ in John 6:46; 7:29; 9:30; 15:26a; 16:27, 28). That is not to say that the Word was not the Son prior to his incarnation, but that the Word already shared filial relationship to the Father before his being sent. Hence John can also say that the Father sent no one other than the Son (John 3:17; cf. Heb 1:2–3; Col 1:15–19). As others rightly have pointed out, John's use of λόγος ("Word") to open a Gospel about the Son sent from

Word's filial identity with the Father is the revelation of a unique glory full of grace and truth that is now discernable to John in Jesus,[46] the Word-made-flesh, including what is discernable in the propositions Jesus made about his unity with the Father (e.g., John 5:18; 10:30; 14:9).[47] In this way, John benefits from privileged access to God the Father's self-revelation in the Word/Son/Jesus; and from the very outset, John's Gospel develops the glory he witnessed in Jesus as divine Son from the Father.[48]

Certainly, John's interests also lie in revealing Jesus as the Messiah/Christ, but never to the neglect that the Christ is also the divine Son of God (John 1:1–18; 20:31). Yet what could possibly compel John,

---

the Father has its origins in the self-revealing "word" of God in the OT, which now finds its climax in the sent Son. As the Word or Son, Jesus is God's self-revelation. E.g., see Carson, *John*, 115–16; Köstenberger, *Theology*, 338–41.

46. Likewise, Köstenberger and Swain assert, "The logic of John's argument here is that the invisibility of God necessitates revelation. This revelation was accomplished by the *monogenēs theos* (cf. 1:14), that is, Jesus Christ (1:17)." Köstenberger and Swain, *Father, Son & Spirit*, 50. Cf. Stibbe, "Father's Story," 175–76.

47. Some have argued that the Gospels portray the historical Jesus inaccurately, since the Jesus of the Christian faith as represented by the four Gospel traditions cloaks him in the theological agendas attributed to anonymous communities separated from the eyewitness accounts by an extensive period of time. However, Bauckham finds such assumptions misguided, and he argues that the Gospels represent trustworthy historiography based on the authoritative testimony of real eyewitnesses that remained the primary sources for each Gospel writer's account. Long periods of time filled with the succession of oral traditions did not delay the Gospels' composition. Instead, their final form is "much closer to the form in which the eyewitnesses" testified. Bauckham, *Jesus and the Eyewitnesses*, 6. Accepted and studied on this appropriate and more natural basis, the Gospels not only provide reliable history concerning Jesus, but also grant theological access to the meaning of his life and mission. Bauckham, *Jesus and the Eyewitnesses*, 508. While I disagree with Bauckham's conclusion that John the son of Zebedee did not author the Fourth Gospel, I do believe that John's testimony concerning Jesus is based on eyewitness testimony and historically accurate. Thus, while we only have access to Jesus' words through John, John's testimony accurately represented Jesus.

48. Cf. Swain and Allen, "Obedience," 113–34. Commenting on Thomas Aquinas' understanding of John's prologue, Swain and Allen write, "In other words, the 'order' of the Fourth Evangelist's contemplative teaching is to reveal to us the *nature* of the divine Word in order that we may appreciate both the character and the consequence of his *action*. Because the Word is the Father's perfect self-communication (Jn 1:1), dwelling in eternal repose at the Father's side (Jn 1:18), his mission can result in the perfect revelation of the unseen God (Jn 1:18), and not simply the witness to a greater light (cf. Jn 1:6–8)." Swain and Allen, "Obedience," 118.

a monotheistic Jew,[49] to include Jesus in the divine identity and assert that Jesus fulfills what was previously stated about Yahweh? As John's Gospel develops, at least three key factors shape John's conviction that Jesus is God, and, therefore, serve his hermeneutical axiom in appropriating Zech 12:10.

Jesus' Words and Works

An initial factor is that John witnesses the glory of God in and through Jesus' words and works.[50] John regularly casts Jesus' ministry in terms of his sent-ness.[51] God the Father sends and entrusts Jesus the Son with a unique mission, a mission the Son always knows without mediation and accomplishes unwaveringly (John 5:19–20; 8:29). As Jesus obeys the Father in all that he says and does, he reveals the one who sent him. Moreover, because of his eternal filial identity with God, all that Jesus the Son says and does directly reveals who God is and what God is like.

In terms of Jesus' words, Jesus always speaks God's truth and thereby reveals the loving character of the Father and his saving

---

49. Internal evidence suggests that John the son of Zebedee was a Jew: (1) he was a resident of Galilee, who was in the fishing business with his father (Matt 4:21; Mark 1:14, 20); (2) the status of his family was significant enough for him to be known to the high priest in Jerusalem (John 18:15–16; cf. 13:23; 19:26, 27; 20:2–4, 8); (3) he is deeply acquainted with the OT Scriptures and alludes to them very often; (4) as one of the disciples, he is later concerned with the kingdom being restored to Israel (Acts 1:6, 13); and (5) he becomes a pillar in the Jerusalem church, whose primary mission was to the circumcised (Gal 2:9). Cf. Carson, Moo, and Morris, *Introduction*, 236.

50. Cf. also Rainbow, *Johannine Theology*, 192–93. For Rainbow, Jesus' works include speaking words and doing deeds. That seems justified by the way John pairs Jesus' words and works in John 14:10.

51. E.g., John 3:34; 4:38; 5:23–24, 36–38; 6:29, 38–39, 44, 57; 7:16, 18, 28–29; 8:16, 18, 26, 29, 42; 9:4; 10:36; 11:42; 12:44–45, 49; 13:20; 14:24; 15:21; 16:5; 17:3, 8, 18, 21, 23, 25; 20:21. See also the study by Köstenberger, *Missions*, 96–120.

Jesus as the Pierced One

initiative in his Son.[52] More pointedly, Jesus speaks only God's words.[53] He bears witness to what he has beheld "from above," or "in the Father's bosom," a unique privilege unknown to a mere prophet or even an angelic mediator.[54] By having the Spirit "without measure," Jesus also utters the words of God always, such that to hear his words is to hear the Father,[55] and to receive his words attests not merely that Jesus is true but that God himself is true (John 3:33). More than that, because of his unity with the Father, inherent to Jesus' words is the power to give life to the dead in the present or the future, something the OT reserves for Yahweh.[56] John's presentation also suggests that Jesus' words carry the

---

52. Abiding in Jesus' words is equivalent to knowing the truth (John 8:31–32). Jesus speaks only the truth that he has heard from God (John 8:40). Jesus' purpose in coming, or being sent by the Father, was to bear witness to the truth (John 18:37). To be clear, John regularly presents "truth" (ἀλήθεια) in relation to Jesus' person. So, e.g., as "the way, the truth, and the life," Jesus makes himself the exclusive point of access to the Father (John 14:6–7; cf. 3:33). In John 1:14, "the Word became flesh and dwelt among us, and we have seen his glory, as the one-of-a-kind Son from the Father, full of grace and truth" (cf. John 1:17). Or, again in John 1:17, "the law was given through Moses; grace and truth came through Jesus Christ." The point isn't that God's truth didn't exist before Jesus' coming, but that we see God's truth now bound up in the person of Jesus, the Word made flesh. Thus, by "truth" John means to say more than that Jesus made truth claims in a logical or philosophical sense. The point is what his words directly reveal about God the Father and his work to save through his Son. Hence, knowing such "truth" is what liberates from sin, because such truth binds you to Jesus and his Father (John 8:32–34; cf. 14:6–11).

53. John 12:49–50; 14:10, 24; 17:8; cf. 5:19–20.

54. John 3:32; 8:38; cf. 1:18; 3:11–12; 16:28.

55. John 3:34; 5:24; 7:16; 8:26, 28. Notice also the links in John 5:37–38, where hearing God's voice, having God's word abiding in you, and believing the sent Son's testimony are equivalent. In John 8:47, Jesus chides the Jews for not being able to hear God's words, because they are not 'of God' (ὅτι ἐκ τοῦ θεοῦ οὐκ ἐστε), a phrase reminiscent of the new birth in John 1:13 (ἐκ θεοῦ ἐγεννήθησαν). Indirectly, then, Jesus implies that the words the Jews have been hearing from him are no less than God's words.

56. For someone not to obey the Son means they do not possess eternal life in the present age (John 3:36; cf. 6:68; 8:51). Jesus' words spare the life of the official's son, raise an invalid man, and summon the dead Lazarus out of the tomb (John 4:50; 5:8–9; 11:43). Jesus' words are spirit and life (John 6:63). Like God the Father's words, Jesus' words also waken the dead in the present age and will summon people out of their tombs at the final resurrection (John 5:25, 28–29). Examples in the OT where God's word brings life to his people abound (e.g., Deut 8:3; 32:47; Ps 119:25, 107; Ezek 37:3–14).

same history-shaping character of God's word in OT revelation.[57] Even some of the responses to Jesus' words further suggest that Jesus' assertions bore an authority and power reserved for God alone.[58] According to John's testimony, therefore, Jesus' words reveal God directly. What his ears witness is not the word of God mediated through another sent prophet from below (cf. John 1:6; 3:31), but the word of God spoken by God, the sent Son from above.

In terms of Jesus' works, they too carry a unique character: they are works that "no one else did" (John 15:24). Not only did Jesus receive the works that the Scriptures exclusively reserved for God's coming Messiah,[59] but he performed them as God's eternal, one-of-a-kind Son now clothed with humanity. In fact, according to Jesus' own testimony, his works reveal that God the Father is in him and that he is in the Father (John 10:38; 14:10–11). That is, there exists such a unity between the Father and the Son that to witness Jesus' works—at least from the perspective of faith, even incomplete faith—was to see God himself working.[60] Even the Gospel's prologue provides the initial theological

---

57. In the same way that God's word in the OT determined the course of history and finds its fulfillment in Jesus' passion (e.g., πληρόω in John 12:38; 13:18; 15:25), so also Jesus' words determine the course of his days and find their fulfillment in his passion (πληρόω in John 18:9, 32). Also, believing Moses' words, which are ultimately God's words, is on par with believing Jesus' words (John 5:47).

58. Perceiving the uniqueness of Jesus' words, people claim that he must be a prophet (John 4:19), marvel over his teaching (John 7:15), note that "no one ever spoke like this man" (John 7:46), and charge him with blasphemy (John 10:33). Moreover, in John 18:5–6 Jesus appears to utter the name that only God bears throughout the OT, namely, ἐγώ εἰμι (e.g., Exod 3:14 LXX; cf. Isa 43:10; 46:4, 9), but uses it as a title for himself. The utterance sends Judas and the soldiers falling to the ground, much like what occurs elsewhere in Scripture when God reveals himself (e.g., Ps 27:2; Ezek 1:28; Dan 2:46). So also Ridderbos, *John*, 575–76; Köstenberger, *John*, 507–8. That is not to suggest that all the soldiers knew the full extent of what happened to them when Jesus spoke; otherwise, they would not have followed through with the arrest, so it would seem. Cf. Carson, *John*, 578. Nevertheless, by including the event—alongside previous testimony where Jesus ascribes the same title to himself (e.g., John 8:58; cf. 6:20; 8:24, 28; 13:19)—John makes a profound theological point about Jesus bearing God's name as he goes to the cross, just like Jesus said he would at the end of his prayer in John 17:26. In this way, John becomes a witness to the revelation of God's name through Jesus' words, through his answer, "I am."

59. See the examples listed on p. 82n14.

60. John reports Jesus saying, "My Father is working until now, and I myself am

Jesus as the Pierced One

framework for understanding all of Jesus' works: in the same way that the Word created the world, being ontologically equal with and still personally subordinate to God (the Father), so Jesus performs all his works as the Word-made-flesh.[61] Thus, every work is a revelation of God the Father in his equal and yet obedient Son. Such revelation becomes even more explicit[62] as, among Jesus' many other works, John focuses on a few "signs" (σημεῖον) that serve his explicit purpose to reveal Jesus as the Christ and Son of God (John 20:30–31; 21:25).[63] Six signs in particular stand out, each playing a specific role in manifesting the glory of God in his Son.[64] John witnesses such glory and writes to

---

working," and such an assertion was enough for the Jews to discern that he was making himself equal to God (John 5:17–18). Other passages that show Jesus' works directly revealing the Father's works include, e.g., John 5:19–20, 36; 9:3; 10:25, 32, 38; 12:45; 14:9. That faith, or the faith accompanying the new birth, is necessary to see Jesus' glory truly, see John 1:50–51; 3:3; 11:40. For a study on the relationship between faith/belief and Jesus' signs/works in John's Gospel, see Campbell, "Signs and Belief." Unlike some who hold that John views signs-based faith negatively, Campbell argues that John views signs-based faith positively while still criticizing any faith that refuses to confess Jesus publicly. See especially Campbell, "Signs and Belief," 84–92. Viewing John's presentation of signs-based faith more negatively is Carson, *John*, 184, 187, 347–48, 537; Carson, "Signs and Wonders," 100–101. Nevertheless, in relation to John 10:38, Carson still suggests that signs-based faith is better than no faith at all. Carson, *John*, 52, 184, 239.

61. Köstenberger and Swain, *Father, Son & Spirit*, 115. "The prologue's portrayal of the Word's creative agency thus establishes an important theme that will command the reader's attention for the rest of John's Gospel. While the Word is personally distinct *from* God, the work he performs is nonetheless nothing but the work *of* God. The two participate in one divine work (cf. 14:10–11)" (italics original).

62. Cf. Culpepper, "Cognition," 251–60. Culpepper sees the signs in John's Gospel as tokens pointing to the creative Logos of John 1:1 in the person of Jesus.

63. At times, John uses ἔργον ("work") to encapsulate all that the Father gives Jesus to perform in his earthly mission (e.g., John 5:20, 36; 17:4). Within this broader category of "work/s" are Jesus' words (John 14:10) and Jesus' σημεῖα ("signs"), the latter of which share significant semantic overlap with Jesus' ἔργα ("works") (e.g., John 2:23; 3:2; 6:26; 7:31; 11:47). Finally, however, John appears to differentiate a few select signs from the others in general, and from these select signs he then develops a deeper theological point about Jesus that contributes to the Gospel's overall purpose (e.g., John 2:11; 4:54; 6:14; 12:18; cf. also 7:21, though he uses ἓν ἔργον in reference to the healing in John 5:1–9).

64. As Köstenberger observes, Johannine scholars commonly recognize six signs: the changing of the water into wine (John 2:1–11); the healing of the official's son (John 4:46–54); the healing of the invalid (John 5:1–9); the feeding of the five thousand (John 6:1–15); the healing of the blind man (John 9); and the raising of

compel faith, a faith that sees in Jesus' works (as well as his words) what John himself has seen, namely, glory as of the one-of-a-kind Son from the Father (John 1:14; 20:31).

Jesus' Death on the Cross

A second factor is that John witnesses the glory of God in and through Jesus' death on the cross. Whereas Jesus also manifested God's glory in the works/signs he performed leading up to the cross (e.g., John 2:11; 11:4), the cross for John becomes the climactic revelation of God's glory in the Son.[65] John drives his entire narrative toward an appointed "hour" (ὥρα).[66] Jesus describes that "hour" as his own glorification and

---

Lazarus (John 11:1–44). See Köstenberger, "Seventh Sign," 88–89. While John labels only the first, second, fourth, fifth, and sixth of these miracles as "signs" (John 2:11; 4:54; 6:14; 9:16; 12:18), he ascribes the same characteristics to the healing of the invalid in his explanation in John 5:17–18 and John 7:18, 21. That is, the healing of the invalid is also a "work" whereby the Father manifests his glory through the Son for the expressed purpose of belief, as is seen in the contexts where the other signs are explicitly named. Köstenberger proposes that the temple-clearing is a seventh sign. Van Belle presents a compelling case for including the cross and resurrection within John's use of σημεῖα at least in John 20:30. See van Belle, "Meaning," 300–325.

65. That is not to minimize the glory that John also witnesses in Jesus' resurrection and ascension. John 7:39, John 12:16, and John 17:4–5 also characterize Jesus' return to the Father through resurrection and ascension as Jesus' glorification. However, the kind of glorification associated with Jesus' resurrection and ascension seems to carry a different connotation. While the glorification associated with the cross entails the glory displayed in Jesus (John 12:23–24, 28; 13:31–32; 17:1; cf. 8:54; 21:19), the glory associated with the resurrection/ascension entails the glory returned to Jesus (John 7:39; 12:16; 17:4–5). In Jesus' resurrection and ascension—both of which form Jesus' return to the Father (John 20:17)—the Father returns to Jesus the glory he had before the world existed (John 17:4–5; cf. 1:1–3, 14; 17:24). The Father does not add to Jesus an intrinsic glory he forfeited in taking on flesh. Rather, the Father returns to Jesus his right to be seen as glorious in splendor. In taking on flesh, the Son set aside his right to be seen as glorious on earth (John 1:10, 14). In returning to the Father, having accomplished all the work the Father gave him to do on earth, the Father now 're-clothes' Jesus with the observable splendor he once set aside, only then he dons it as the Word-made-flesh, the God-man.

66. John uses ὥρα with several different connotations that also include a specific time within a twenty-four hour day (John 1:39; 4:6, 52, 53; 11:9; 19:14), a short period of time (John 5:35; 16:4), a marker for the occurrence of a specific event (John 5:28; 16:21; 19:27), and an undefined period usually inaugurated by Jesus' coming (John 4:23; 5:25). See also BDAG, s.v. "ὥρα." However, none of these uses overshadow his unique use of ὥρα to mark the period encompassing Jesus' death

Jesus as the Pierced One

links the glorification with his death. For example, immediately following his assertion that "the hour [ὥρα] has come for the Son of Man to be glorified [δοξασθῇ]," Jesus likens his own death to a grain of wheat that must die to bear fruit and then prays for his Father to glorify (δόξασόν) his own name in the face of the Son's greatest distress (John 12:23-24, 27-28). Likewise, just before his arrest and trial, Jesus opens his high-priestly prayer by linking the "hour" that has arrived, and for which he was sent (John 12:27), with the mutual glorification of the Father and the Son (John 17:1; cf. 12:28).[67] Paradoxically, then, Jesus' humiliation on the cross is God's glorification of himself and of his Son.

In several OT passages, God's glory refers to the weighty manifestation of the intrinsic worth and goodness of the invisible God, if not through his theophanic presence alone, then through his acts of judgment and salvation.[68] John characterizes the Word's incarnation in terms reminiscent of God's glorious presence in the tabernacle,[69] but he also characterizes Jesus' death on the cross as both an act of God's judgment and an act of God's salvation. In the death of Jesus, God's righteousness and love become manifest as God's righteousness calls for an outpouring of wrath on sinners (i.e., judgment), and God's love makes provision in offering Jesus as a Lamb in place of those same sinners (i.e., salvation).[70] For Jesus to accomplish his Father's work in

---

(John 7:30; 8:20; 12:23, 27; 13:1; 16:32; 17:1) as well as its ongoing effects (John 2:4; 4:21; 16:2, 25).

67. While the term ὥρα does not appear in John 13:31-32, it does appear in 13:1 in relation to the arrival of Jesus' time to depart out of this world to the Father. That departure, however, would come first through the cross as indicated by Judas' betrayal in John 13:30 and Jesus' words following thereafter in John 13:31-32: "Now is the Son of Man glorified, and God is glorified in him. If God is glorified in him, God will also glorify him in himself, and glorify him at once." This stands as a third example where John links Jesus' hour with his death and the Father and Son's mutual glorification in that death.

68. E.g., Exod 16:7, 10; 33:18—34:7; 40:34-35; Num 14:22; Isa 40:1-5; Ezek 39:21. Similar conclusions from others surveying the glory of God in the OT include those of Piper, *Desiring God*, 227; Longman III, "Glory," 51-57; Hamilton, *God's Glory*, 56; Schreiner, *King in His Beauty*, 45.

69. Hoskins, *Jesus as Fulfillment*, 116-25.

70. In John's Gospel, God's wrath already abides on all sinners refusing to obey the Son (John 3:36), and those without (eternal) life will come into judgment, which is equivalent to condemnation (John 5:24). People will also die "in their sins" (John

The Pierced One's First Redeeming Advent

laying down his life for those his Father entrusted to him (John 6:39; 10:29; 17:2), Jesus reveals the glory of God's justice and love in his death. In OT fashion, therefore, the cross becomes the revelation of the invisible God. For John, to see Jesus dying is to see God himself judging, God himself loving, and, therefore, God himself revealed.[71]

Also contributing to this display of glory in the cross is the theme of the Son of Man being 'lifted up' (ὑψόω; John 3:14; 8:28; 12:32). The idea contains a double entendre: the Romans will physically "lift up" Jesus' body on a cross, but in that event God will simultaneously "lift up" his Son in a sense of exaltation.[72] John seems to be alluding to language that Isaiah normally applies to Yahweh and his temple mount being "lifted up" or exalted (e.g., Isa 2:2, 11, 17; 5:16; 12:4; 30:18), with one exception where Isaiah applies it to the Suffering Servant (Isa 52:13).[73] As others have noted, such an allusion suggests that Jesus' suffering and dying on behalf of others paradoxically becomes for John the point

---

8:21, 24), an OT expression when someone suffers death because they are guilty of rebellion against God (e.g., Num 16:26; Ezek 3:18; 18:18, 24, 26). However, despite the judgment that the world deserves, God still chooses to love the world by sending his only Son (John 3:16). God's love then manifests itself in offering up his Son as the true Passover lamb (John 1:29; 19:36; cf. 1 John 3:16; 4:9–10), which, according to the careful study by Hoskins, also serves as an atoning sacrifice. Hoskins, "Deliverance," 286–89. Moreover, Jesus characterizes his own pending death in terms of willingly drinking "the cup" (John 18:11), an OT metonymy for God's wrath (e.g., Ps 11:6; 75:8; Isa 51:17; Jer 25:15; 49:12; 51:7). It is also in his death on the cross that Jesus judges the world and the ruler of this world (John 12:32; cf. 16:11). By believing in Jesus, by appropriating the benefits of his death for oneself (John 6:51–58), one passes from death (i.e., judgment) to life (John 5:24). In this way, John characterizes the cross as both an event of God's judgment and an expression of God's love for the world.

71. Showing how John and Paul's understanding of the cross relate, similar conclusions appear in Stott, *The Cross of Christ*, 200–212.

72. The double meaning in John's use of ὑψόω is widely recognized. E.g., Cullmann, "Gebrauch doppeldeutiger Ausdrücke," 176–86; Wead, "Double Meaning," 108–10; Nicholson, *Descent-Ascent*, 75–160; Hoskins, *Jesus as Fulfillment*, 148; Köstenberger, *Theology*, 132.

73. See especially the discussion in Hoskins, *Jesus as Fulfillment*, 148–59. Hoskins carefully shows how John's (or Jesus') use of ὑψόω not only carries a double meaning, but implies a deep unity between Jesus' death on the cross, his ascension into heaven, and his exaltation. Hoskins, *Jesus as Fulfillment*, 148–49. Such a unity will also contribute to the development of the third factor below.

where God discloses his glory supremely.⁷⁴ Commenting on John 8:28, Köstenberger and Swain rightly conclude that "the event [of the cross] will constitute at once [Jesus'] 'exaltation' as God's true Servant *and* his self-revelation as the one true God and Saviour of the world."⁷⁵ Indeed, it is only in the "lifting up" of Jesus that others will discern that he is "I AM" (John 8:28).⁷⁶ Nevertheless, such discernment does not come apart from Jesus' further glorification to the Father, and this leads to another factor in John's theological convictions.

Jesus' Spirit Giving Post-resurrection Understanding

The third factor is that John witnesses the glory of God in and through Jesus' Spirit granting a post-resurrection understanding of the Scriptures. According to John, Jesus' subsequent glorification to the Father in resurrection and ascension plays an instrumental role and serves as a decisive turning point in the disciples' understanding of the Scripture. Only after Jesus' glorification do the disciples truly believe and understand what the Scriptures teach concerning the Christ and the significance of his work (John 2:17, 22; 12:16; 20:9). Such true understanding comes after Jesus' glorification, because only then do the Father and Son send the Holy Spirit, and only then do the disciples receive the promised Holy Spirit (John 7:39; 14:26; 15:26; 16:7; 20:22).⁷⁷ The Spirit then guides the disciples into all truth, teaches them all things, reminds

---

74. Carson, *John*, 444; Bauckham, *Jesus and the God of Israel*, 32–48; Köstenberger and Swain, *Father, Son & Spirit*, 41–43, 125–26.

75. Köstenberger and Swain, *Father, Son & Spirit*, 125.

76. While it is difficult to determine whether Jesus intended to equate himself with God in every occurrence of ἐγώ εἰμι ("I am") in John's Gospel, the grammar and context in some cases, especially the absolute statements, suggest Jesus is doing just that (e.g., John 6:20; 8:24, 28, 58; 13:19; 18:6). See Ball, *"I AM" in John's Gospel*; Bauckham, *Testimony*, 239–52.

77. Cf. Bynum, *Fourth Gospel*, 183. Bynum likewise concludes that "John's Gospel is the result of his and the other disciples' reflection upon the meaning of Christ under the Spirit's leadership ... The profound *post factum* interpretation of the passion events by John is the realisation of Jesus' promise that the Paraclete would transform their view of the cross, as seen in John 14:26, 15:26, 16:7, 16:13." More recently, see Bynum, "Quotations," 61–62. For a study developing the eschatological gift of the Spirit spoken of in John 7:38–39 in comparison to the experience of God's people in under the old covenant, see Hamilton, *God's Indwelling Presence*, 100–126.

The Pierced One's First Redeeming Advent

them of all that Jesus spoke to them, and enables them to bear witness about Jesus (John 14:26; 15:26–27; 16:13), witness that also manifests itself in what John has written (John 15:27; cf. 19:35; 21:24).[78] All of this—that is, all of the Spirit's illuminating work—John characterizes in terms of the glorification of Jesus: "[the Spirit] will glorify [δοξάσει] me, for he will take what is mine and declare it to you" (John 16:14).

The Spirit's post-resurrection work of glorifying Jesus by reminding them of Jesus' words and giving them insight into the OT becomes apparent as John's Passion narrative unfolds. Composing his Gospel after Jesus' glorification, John includes explicit instances of Jesus teaching how particular OT passages become fulfilled in his own betrayal (John 13:18; 15:25).[79] When John proceeds to find the same fulfillment of particular OT passages in John 19:24, John 19:28, and John 19:36–37, it is reasonable to see these instances as the Spirit reminding John of Jesus' teaching and John then following Jesus' interpretation of the OT.[80] Therefore, because of the Spirit's post-resurrection work of glorifying Jesus, Jesus' teaching from the OT about himself becomes John's hermeneutical control and presupposition when he reads and interprets the OT.[81] The possession of the Holy Spirit has bearing on whether or not John finds in the Scriptures what Jesus apparently thinks people

---

78. On the unique redemptive-historical role the apostles possess in writing Scripture, especially as it relates to John's presentation of the Spirit, see Ridderbos, *Redemptive History*, 14, 23, 28–30, 59–60, 64–68.

79. The two texts referred to by Jesus in John 13:18 and 15:25 are most likely Ps 41:9 and Ps 69:5 (ET 69:4), respectively. Though Ps 35:19 includes the same phrase found in 69:5 (οἱ μισοῦντές με δωρεάν), John makes repeated references to Ps 69 elsewhere in his Gospel (John 2:17 [Ps 69:10 LXX]; 19:29 [Ps 69:22 LXX]). This prominence leads me to conclude that Jesus' quotation stems from Ps 69. So also Schmidt, "Typology," 82–83, 114–16.

80. Moo concludes his study of the OT in the Passion narratives of all for Gospels stating, "two fundamental presuppositions dominated the approach to the OT: the new revelational basis in the life and teaching of Jesus and a view of Scripture which understood Jesus (and his passion) to have been foreseen and foreshadowed in many OT passages." Moo, *Old Testament*, 386–87. Schmidt likewise concludes, "The NT identifies Jesus as the 'source' and 'paradigm' for the proper application and understanding of the OT." Schmidt, "Typology," 51. See also the examples provided in Schmidt, "Typology," 51–55.

81. After numerous examples from John's Gospel and Acts, a fellow student recently drew the same conclusion about Jesus modeling for the disciples a hermeneutic of prophetic David typology. See Schmidt, "Typology," 304.

Jesus as the Pierced One

ought to have found there before.[82] As the Holy Spirit glorifies Jesus by bearing witness to Jesus from the OT, John himself becomes a witness and then writes a Gospel that develops connections between the Christ Scripture expects and the person Jesus is.[83]

One of the ways the Spirit glorifies Jesus from the OT, and thereby enables John to bear witness to that glory in his Gospel, is by applying to Jesus several OT concepts reserved exclusively for God/Yahweh. For example, John alludes to Gen 1:1 in developing how the Word not only existed with God and as God "in the beginning," but also belongs in the category of Creator, since he made all things that are not God (John 1:1, 3; cf. Gen 1:1).[84] John also refers to Jesus as "the light" (John 1:5, 7–8; 3:19), an OT concept applied very often to Yahweh, in whose presence light abounds and by whose presence light often came to his people, whether visibly or morally.[85] Using language reminiscent of Yahweh's glory filling the tabernacle in the OT, John casts the eternal Word's incarnation in terms of him dwelling, or "tabernacling" (σκηνόω), among us (John 1:14).[86] John's use of Isa 40 in John 1:23 also appears to link

---

82. Cf. Carson, "Understanding," 59–91. At least three examples buttress this claim. (1) Jesus expects the teacher(s) of Israel to understand what he says about the Spirit bringing new birth (John 3:1–10; cf. Ezek 36:25–27). (2) Jesus exposes that Jewish unbelief, rooted in a desire for self-praise, makes them unable to understand the words Moses wrote concerning himself (John 5:37–46). (3) Jesus argues that a person cannot rightly hear the words of God—i.e., the Scriptures and Jesus' own testimony—apart from being born of God/Spirit (John 8:41, 47 [γεγεννήμεθα . . . ἐκ τοῦ θεοῦ]; cf. 1:13 [ἐκ θεοῦ ἐγεννήθησαν]; 3:5 [γεννηθῇ ἐξ ὕδατος καὶ πνεύματος]; 1 John 4:2 [ἐκ τοῦ θεοῦ]; 5:1 [ἐκ τοῦ θεοῦ γεγέννηται]).

83. John's interpretation of the OT, then, serves a unique role in the composition of his Gospel. John's chief aim is to write a Gospel, so that others might believe that the Scripture's Christ is Jesus (John 20:31). See Carson, "Purpose," 639–51; Carson, "Observations on John 20:30–31," 693–714.

84. Both Gen 1:1 of the LXX and John 1:1 open with ἐν ἀρχῇ, as has been noted by others. Schwarz, "Ein Vergleich," 136–37; Carson, *John*, 113–14; Köstenberger, "John," 421.

85. E.g., Exod 13:21; Pss 27:1; 36:9; 89:15; 104:2; Isa 10:17; 60:20; Dan 2:22; Hab 3:4; cf. 1 Tim 6:16. Other places where John (or Jesus) use "light" in the Fourth Gospel include John 3:20, 21; 8:12; 9:5; 11:9, 10; 12:35, 36, 46. See also the discussions in Achtemeier, "Light," 439–49; Hoskins, *Jesus as Fulfillment*, 160–70; Köstenberger, *Theology*, 178–81, 344–48.

86. While the verb, σκηνόω ("to take up residence"), appears only here and in Rev 7:15, 12:12, 13:6, and 21:23, the noun, σκηνή ("tent"), appears in the LXX in

Yahweh with Jesus. Whereas Isaiah envisions Yahweh returning to establish Zion (Isa 40:9), gather his sheep (Isa 40:10–11), and display his glory before all flesh (Isa 40:5), John 1:23 indicates that John the Baptist is the prophetic forerunner announcing Yahweh's eschatological glory now appearing in the person and work of Jesus.[87] Also, just as living waters flow from Yahweh's presence in the eschatological temple of Ezek 47:1–12 and Zech 14:8, so the same waters come from Jesus to benefit the believer (John 4:10; 7:38).

Still more, and likely the most compelling example besides John 19:37 where John's post-resurrection understanding of the OT enables him to include Jesus in the identity of Yahweh, is the double quotation from Isaiah's prophecy in John 12:38–41. After quoting from Isa 53:1 regarding the rejection of the Suffering Servant, and from Isa 6:10 regarding the people's obduracy to Yahweh's word, John then concludes that Isaiah "said these things [i.e., these things about rejection and obduracy] because he saw his glory [i.e., Jesus' glory] and spoke of him."[88] Daniel J. Brendsel has demonstrated that the logic of John 12:41, the immediate context, and John's overall theology of exaltation through suffering suggests that Isaiah received a prophetic vision of Christ's future glory revealed in rejection, and the people's obduracy that leads to it.[89] Nevertheless, recognizing John's contextual use of Isa 6, Brendsel keenly adds that

---

reference to the tabernacle and God's glory dwelling there (e.g., Exod 40:34–35; Num 9:15; 2 Sam 7:6; 22:12). See the discussions in Keener, *John*, 1:408–10; Hoskins, *Jesus as Fulfillment*, 116–25. Also, see BDAG, s.v. "σκηνόω."

87. Cf. John 1:14. Among the elements in Isa 40:3 that resonate with its use in John 1:23 is "the coming revelation of God's glory through his visible coming and bringing of salvation, not merely to Israel, but to all humanity." Köstenberger, "John," 427.

88. Both the αὐτόν of John 12:37 and the αὐτοῦ of John 12:41 have Jesus as their antecedent in 12:36. Moreover, as Brendsel observes, "there is no reason to think a shift in the referent of αὐτός has occurred between vv. 41 and 42." Brendsel, "Use of Isaiah," 171.

89. Brendsel, "Use of Isaiah," 171–83. That John lacks any explicit reference to the Servant of Isa 53:2–12 does not weaken the argument. His verbal and thematic allusions to the broader context of Isaiah's "Servant Songs" show John's familiarity with the Servant's role in redemptive humiliation and glorification, something 53:2–12 exposits further (e.g. John 11:52 [Isa 49:5]; 12:23 [Isa 52:13]; 13:31 [Isa 49:3]; 18:22 [Isa 50:6]). Dodd makes these connections in Dodd, *According to the*

Jesus as the Pierced One

> ... the glory seen by Isaiah, to which John refers, also includes the glory filling the temple at the time of Isaiah's calling (LXX Isa 6:1; cf. MT Isa 6:3). This temple-filling glory is also rightly named 'his [i.e., Christ's] glory,' since John presents Jesus as the speaker of the Isa 6:10 quotation ... apparently reading Isaiah 6 as an encounter with the pre-incarnate Christ. But John interprets this Isaiah 6 glory as being identified with and further revealed in the glory of the Servant ... Isaiah said "these things" in advance (both Isa 53:1 and Isa 6:10) because he was a prophetic witness to a glory that would both incorporate rejection and death and reveal its possessor to be included in the identity of Yahweh himself.[90]

Such examples sufficiently demonstrate how Jesus' Spirit not only grants John a post-resurrection understanding of the OT, but also bears witness to Jesus' glory from the OT by ascribing to Jesus concepts once reserved for Yahweh.[91]

In sum, John witnesses God's glory revealed through Jesus' words and works, through Jesus' revelatory death on the cross, and through Jesus' Spirit granting post-resurrection understanding to the OT. These three factors serve John's conviction that Jesus is God, and, therefore, serve his hermeneutical axiom in appropriating OT texts like Zech 12:10. The warrant for John's appropriation of a text like Zech 12:10, which justifiably speaks of Yahweh's piercing, rests in his Spirit-given theological presupposition that Jesus is God, that he is the revelation of God's glory.

By reading Zech 12:10 in light of what he witnesses about Jesus' divine glory, therefore, John cannot help but conclude that Jesus' piercing must fulfill the eschatological contours of Yahweh's mission to save

---

Scriptures, 88–96.

90. Brendsel, "Use of Isaiah," 179, 182. Cf. Bauckham, *Jesus and the God of Israel*, 46–51.

91. Additional supporting examples from John's use of the OT may also include the following: like Yahweh in the OT, Jesus' word/Spirit gives life to the dead (John 5:25; 11:43–44; 20:22; cf. Gen 2:7; Ezek 37:4), he proves his kingship over creation by controlling the waters (John 6:16–21; cf. Ps 107:25–32), he gathers his sheep such that his own unwavering hand is equivalent to God the Father's hand (John 10:10–18, 28–30; cf. Isa 40:11; Ezek 34:13; Zech 10:8).

his people. That does not mean that he imports to Zech 12:10 a meaning never present before, but that he sees what was always present before now revealed in Jesus. What he now knows of God through Jesus Christ enables him to understand and articulate the meaning always present in Zech 12:10. As stated before, John answers the *sui generis* problem of Zech 12:10, God is pierced, with the *sui generis* answer, Jesus is God (the Son). If the narrower reading of Zech 12:10 suggests that the Pierced One is not only a human messianic figure but Yahweh himself (see chapter 2), then Zech 12:10 befits both the high Christology saturating John's Gospel and the unique piercing of Jesus' side. In fact, John even seems to clarify the tension of Zech 12:10 by translating the Hebrew construction as simply εἰς ὅν—that is, "on him" instead of "on me"—with ὅν referring to the now incarnate God, Jesus.[92] Because

---

92. Interpreting John 19:37 along similar Christological lines, see O'Rourke, "Fulfillment Texts," 441; Schnackenburg, *John*, 3:293. Brown argues against O'Rourke: "we reject the suggestion of O'Rourke . . . that because in the MT Yahweh himself is pierced, possibly John is referring the text to Jesus to imply the divinity of Jesus. The fact that John does not cite the text according to the MT shows that he is not thinking in this way." Brown, *John XIII–XXI*, 956. A more mediating position appears in Bynum, *Fourth Gospel*, 177. Bynum explains the change from the first person of Zech 12:10 ("to me") to the third person in John 19:37 ("to him") like so: "If John had desired in this citation to identify Jesus directly with Yahweh who is speaking in the original citation, it would have been a simple matter to do so by following that vocalisation tradition. The fact that he does not do so allows him to continue to hold Jesus' humanity and divinity in creative tension, without drifting into a form of Docetism or resolving the issue into a facile identity of Jesus with God that would minimize his humanity and his suffering." Bynum is right that John carefully maintains the humanity and divinity of Jesus. However, a change to the third person does not seem to exclude the possibility that John identifies Jesus directly with Yahweh. The exegesis in chapter 2 demonstrated that the figure that receives the people's piercing is also the one upon whom they look, namely, Yahweh. John seems just as concerned with interpreting the looking upon Yahweh as he does the piercing of Yahweh, both of which he finds fulfilled in the event of Jesus' cross (see chapter 5 regarding the looking). So, whether in the looking or the piercing, John connects Jesus with Yahweh directly, all the while maintaining Jesus' humanity through other contextual features (e.g., the blood and water flowing from Jesus' side). A similar point appears in Kubiś, *Zechariah in John*, 189n322. Moreover, other NT authors occasionally make similar changes to the vocalization tradition when linking Jesus directly with Yahweh. See, e.g., Paul's use of Isa 45:23 ("to me [Yahweh] every knee shall bow") in Phil 2:9–10 ("God has highly exalted him . . . so that at the name of Jesus every knee should bow"; cf. Rom 15:11), and the discussion in Yeago, "Nicene Dogma," 154–57. Also, see Paul's use of Ps 68:19 [ET 68:18] ("you [Yahweh] ascended on high") to refer to Jesus in Eph 4:8 ("when he [Jesus] ascended on high"),

the one-of-a-kind Son exists at the Father's side, John recognizes the Pierced One of Zechariah not as a mere human representative distinct from God (i.e., in essence), but as God (the Son) himself now come in the flesh.

STEP FOUR: THE THEOLOGICAL SIGNIFICANCE OF ZECH 12:10 FOR JESUS' IDENTITY AND MISSION

According to the Gospel of John, therefore, what is the theological significance of Zech 12:10 for Jesus' identity and mission? Limiting the question to Jesus' identity and mission is not intended to minimize the other theological implication regarding those who pierce and look upon God/Jesus. Several studies have emphasized that the participants in piercing Jesus—whether direct (i.e., Roman soldiers) or indirect (i.e., the Jews)—and the participants in looking upon Jesus (e.g., the soldiers, the women, the eyewitness of John 19:35), all prove significant for the fulfillment of Zech 12:10.[93] These same studies also emphasize that John uses Zech 12:10 to build on his Gospel's overarching motif of seeing/looking upon Jesus for deliverance.[94] The emphasis of these studies appropriately addresses some of the details surrounding John 19:37, but they have simultaneously given much less attention to Jesus' identity and mission.

Therefore, I have chosen to limit the aforementioned question to Jesus' identity and mission, and postpone developing the theological

---

and the commentary by O'Brien, *Ephesians*, 289. Granted, the change in Eph 4:8 is from the second person to the third person, but it still shows an example outside of John where changes occurred to the vocalization tradition while still identifying Jesus with Yahweh.

93. The most extensive treatment of the theological significance of the onlookers in relation to the Fourth Gospel belongs to Kubiś, *Zechariah in John*, 194–216. Kubiś argues that the two verbs of the Zechariah quotation have different subjects. Those looking upon the pierced Jesus include "the Roman soldiers, the Jews, ὁ ἑωρακώς [i.e., the eyewitness of John 19:35], Jesus' mother, the women, and present and future believers." Those who actually pierce Jesus, however, is a much smaller group including "only the Roman soldiers and the Jews." Other studies include Schuchard, *Scripture within Scripture*, 146–48; Menken, "Textual Form," 504–11; Tuckett, "Zechariah 12:10 and the NT," 115–19; Bynum, *Fourth Gospel*, 176–79.

94. Menken, "Textual Form," 507–8; Tuckett, "Zechariah 12:10 and the NT," 115–16; Kubiś, *Zechariah in John*, 198–213; Bynum, *Fourth Gospel*, 176–79.

The Pierced One's First Redeeming Advent

significance of the onlookers until after treating Rev 1:7. Whereas previous studies develop the significance of the onlookers in relation to John's Gospel only, I will develop their significance in light of John 19:37 and Rev 1:7 simultaneously, so that the contours of inaugurated and consummated eschatology stand out as well as their implications for John's readers. Thus, questions surrounding the piercers/onlookers must wait until chapter 5.[95] Nevertheless, at least three theological contributions are worth considering here in relation to the Fourth Gospel quite apart from Revelation.

The Divine Identity of Jesus

To begin, John uses Zech 12:10 to identify Jesus, not merely with God but as God. John's concern is not merely to disclose Jesus as God's human representative—even though he is that too—but to disclose Jesus' divinity and do so from a most fitting OT witness. Indeed, John passes over the rather popular and clear OT passages where Yahweh's representative is pierced in favor of the enigmatic Zech 12:10, where it seems most likely that Yahweh is pierced. The use of Zech 12:10 builds on John's understanding of God's self-disclosure in Jesus by showing that the pierced Jesus he beheld is the pierced God Zechariah promised.

The theological import of Zech 12:10 does not even necessarily require reinterpretation "in a totally new way," as Kubiś has stated for example, but simply elucidation in light of the self-revelation of God in Jesus Christ.[96] John is not reinterpreting Zech 12:10 by adding a divine

---

95. Some questions to be answered include the following. Who are the subjects that pierce Jesus, and should they be limited to the Roman soldiers or broadened to include others such as the Jews? Should the subjects who look upon Jesus be limited to the subjects who participated in the actual piercing of Jesus? How does the eyewitness of John 19:35 relate to those who look upon Yahweh in Zech 12:10, especially in light of the outpouring of God's Spirit? What is the relationship between the onlookers in John 19:37 and the onlookers in Rev 1:7, and how do the two comings of Jesus affect them?

96. Kubiś, *Zechariah in John*, 189. "According to Zech 12:10, regardless of the textual tradition in which this oracle is conveyed (MT, OG, *Tg.*, etc.), the one on whom they look is *always* identified as *God*. The contention is that the author of the [Fourth Gospel] identifies the pierced one with the one who is looked upon and the one on whom they have looked was *God*. John embraces the messianic interpretation of the oracle, but he also interprets it in a totaly [sic] new way: the pierced one is the Messiah who is the same as the one on whom they have looked, i.e., God" (italics

Jesus as the Pierced One

dimension to the merely human messianic dimension of the original prophecy. Rather, John uses Zech 12:10 because of the divine dimension that was always explicitly there in the original prophecy and now made obvious in the piercing of God's only Son, Jesus Christ. That is to say, his understanding of Jesus' identity stems from a process of mutual interpretation: God's word-revelation in Zech 12:10 and God's Word-revelation in Jesus mutually interpret one another, the former revealing how Jesus must belong to who God is, and the latter revealing how God himself actually gets pierced (i.e., in the person of God the Son).[97]

Such a theological point aligns with the Christology of John's Prologue as well as his chief aim to identify the OT's Christ and Son of God as Jesus. Others have rightly emphasized that John's use of Zech 12:10 reveals Jesus' messianic role, but the emphasis has at times overshadowed the more stunning theological point John appears to be making: Yahweh fulfills his redeeming mission first in the human flesh of Jesus. In short, Jesus is God. Of course, John's presentation is always careful to decipher between the persons of Father and Son—that is, God the Son was pierced and not God the Father—but the shared essence between Father and Son means that Jesus is no less than God in his being pierced.[98] Stated differently, Yahweh's ancient and inexplicable

---

original).

97. Bauckham makes the same point in relation to John's use of Isa 52:13 and Isa 6:1 in John 12:38–41: "The [early Christians] did not, of course, read the Jewish Scriptures in the historicizing manner of modern Old Testament scholarship, but nor did they, as some accounts of New Testament interpretation of the Old seem to suggest, simply read into the Old Testament ideas they held in any case independently of the Old Testament. They brought the Old Testament text into relationship with the history of Jesus in a process of mutual interpretation from which some of their profoundest theological insights sprang." Bauckham, *Jesus and the God of Israel*, 33.

98. As developed above, John explains that the Word not only existed with God (πρὸς τὸν θεόν) in the beginning—showing personal distinction between the Word and God the Father—but even what God the Father was, that the Word was too (θεὸς ἦν ὁ λόγος)—showing an identity of being, a unity in divine essence (John 1:1). From eternity the Word shares the one divine nature with the Father as a distinct person from the Father (and Spirit). Yet the Word also took to himself a human nature: "the word became [ἐγένετο] flesh" (John 1:14). As the Council of Chalcedon (AD 451) would later assert, Jesus Christ the Word/Son must be acknowledged "in two natures" (ἐν δύο φύσεσιν). Being fully God and fully man, he is one person with two natures. From the perspective of Christian orthodoxy, such observations distance

The Pierced One's First Redeeming Advent

self-revelation, "and they will look upon me whom they have pierced," culminates and receives clarity in the actual piercing of Jesus. To pierce Jesus is to pierce God the Son, thus including Jesus within the divine identity. By equating Jesus with the pierced God of Zech 12:10, John articulates some of the highest Christology in the NT.

The Divine Revelation in Jesus' Death

Still, John articulates that highest Christology in a surprising manner, namely, from the event of Jesus' crucifixion. As stated above, John views the cross as the climax of God's revelation in his Son. The piercing of God in Zech 12:10 serves to develop John's understanding of the cross as God's revelation. At perhaps the greatest point of humiliation—the piercing of Jesus' side after he was already dead—John sees the greatest point of God's self-revelation. Zechariah 12:10 teaches John's readers to look at the death of Jesus through a particular theological lens, namely, the lens of God's own piercing. To look at the death of Jesus through

---

my conclusions above from several ancient heresies. Arianism claims that the Son is not fully God, but John 1:1 is clear that there is a unity in divine essence. Modalism claims that Father and Son are different modes of divine revelation, but John 1:1 again clarifies that Father and Son are distinct persons eternally subsisting in the one divine nature. Patripassianism claims that God the Father suffered in the crucifixion, but John's presentation is clear that only God the Son, the one whom God the Father sent and who always does the Father's will, suffered the crucifixion. Theopaschitism claims that the divine nature suffered on the cross and stems from another heresy, monophysitism, which understands Christ to possess only one nature, the human nature being absorbed into the divine nature. However, it is clear from above that Jesus is one person with two natures, divine and human (John 1:1, 14). Christian orthodoxy maintains (1) the person-nature distinction, (2) that even as the properties of both natures become common to the one person of the Son (i.e., *communicatio idiomatum*), the two natures themselves never intermingle (e.g., Chalcedon: "inconfusedly, unchangeably"), and (3) that the person of the Son acts through his divine and human natures according to their respective capacities such that whatever is asserted of either nature can be asserted about the person of the Son, but not the other nature. See especially Turretin, *Institutes*, 2:321–32; Wellum, *God the Son*, 437–40. Thus, while the person of the Son subsists eternally in the divine nature, he experienced the sufferings of his crucifixion through his (*hypostatized*) human nature. Thus, though his human nature was pierced and not the divine nature, one can say that God was pierced because, acting through his human nature, the divine person of the Son suffered the piercing. I am indebted to my dear friend and partner in ministry, Michael Wilkinson, who took the time to help me think through these matters historically and theologically.

Jesus as the Pierced One

such a lens is to see in his person and work the very revelation of God, a redemptive theophany.

Such a view would also seem to complement the expectation that John established for his readers to believe that Jesus is I AM (ἐγώ εἰμι) when they lifted up the Son of Man (John 8:28), a lifting up that certainly included the crucifixion (John 12:32–33). John's use of Zech 12:10 helps his readers understand that to look upon Jesus lifted up is to look upon God himself. The I AM's self-revelation climaxes in the piercing of Jesus' side. Theologically speaking, the reader thus observes the extent to which God himself is willing to go in the salvation of his people. The manner in which, and even the degree to which,[99] God the Father loves the world thus manifests itself in his Son's death and subsequent piercing. Perhaps this is also why Thomas confesses that Jesus is "my Lord and my God" immediately upon witnessing Jesus' hands and his pierced side (John 20:27–28). Thomas sees the true God only in the pierced Jesus.

Moreover, like the first and only other double OT quotation toward the beginning of John's Passion narrative (i.e., John 12:38–41), the second double OT quotation in John 19:36–37 seems to function in a similar manner. As noted above, John's use of Isaiah in John 12:38–41 suggests that Isaiah is a "prophetic witness to a glory that would both incorporate rejection and death and reveal its possessor to be included in the identity of Yahweh himself."[100] Thus, two OT themes interrelate and reach their fulfillment in the onset of Jesus' Passion, namely, the humiliation of Jesus with the revelation of God's glory in Jesus. John's use of Exod 12:46 (or Num 9:12)[101] alongside Zech 12:10 in John 19:36–37

---

99. The use of οὕτως in John 3:16 most likely refers to the manner in which God loved the world. That is, "For God loved the world *in this way* that he gave his one-of-a-kind Son . . ." However, translating the verse to express the manner in which God loved the world should not leave one minimizing the degree of God's love for the world either. Rather, it is in understanding how God loved the world that we gain greater clarity about the degree to which he loved the world. God's love was of the kind that, despite the world's rebellion against him, he gave up his only Son.

100. Brendsel, "Use of Isaiah," 182.

101. After several contextual observations, Hoskins concludes that "the Scripture quote in [John] 19:36, 'a bone of him/it will not be broken' surely points to Exod 12:10, 46 and Num 9:12, even if it may also point to Ps 34:20." Hoskins, "Deliverance," 296.

seems to unite the same two OT themes: in Jesus' humiliating death as the ultimate Passover lamb,[102] the reader simultaneously beholds the pierced God.[103] Both double OT quotations in John 12:38–41 and in John 19:36–37 meld the revelation of God with the humiliation of Jesus. John uses Zech 12:10, therefore, to help his readers interpret Jesus' death on the cross within a theological framework of divine revelation in humiliation.

The Divine Mission of Jesus

John also reveals in his use of Zech 12:10 that Jesus' mission is equivalent to Yahweh's mission. Zechariah's prophecy consistently emphasizes Yahweh's return to his people (Zech 1:3, 16; 8:3, 15; 9:8). When he returns, Yahweh will establish a new temple-city,[104] gather for himself a remnant from Israel and the nations,[105] forgive/cleanse their sins and

---

102. Hoskins, "Deliverance," 295–99.

103. Other connections between the double OT quotations in John 12:38–41 and John 19:36–37 include the following. (1) These OT quotations are the first and the last place where John employs the explicit fulfillment formula. (2) These are the only two places in John's fulfillment motif that include a pair of OT quotations connected by πάλιν. (3) John's testimony in John 19:35 starkly contrasts the people's state of unbelief in John 12:37–40. John sees and believes and proclaims in John 19:35, but the people of John 12:37–40 do not see or believe or, therefore, proclaim. In this regard, John seems more like Isaiah who had seen and spoke concerning the glory of Jesus Christ.

104. Zech 1:14, 16–17; 2:5–9, 14–16 [ET 2:1–5, 10–12]; 4:7; 6:12–15; 8:3–5; 14:10, 20–21.

105. Zech 2:8, 10–15 [ET 2:4, 6–11]; 8:6–8, 11–13, 20–23; 9:7, 12, 16; 10:8–10; 13:9; 14:2, 16.

Jesus as the Pierced One

idolatry upon a new covenant,[106] conquer their enemies completely,[107] and bless them with his royal, life-giving presence in a sanctified land.[108] Some of these intended blessings associated with Yahweh's eschatological return seem contingent on his piercing. For example, Yahweh graciously pours out "a spirit of grace and pleas for mercy" for the specific purpose of causing the people to look upon him after their piercing of him. The inward change likely comes from the gracious outpouring of Yahweh's Spirit (Ezek 36:26–28; Zech 4:6–7).[109] The outpoured Spirit that causes his people to look upon the pierced God must follow the piercing of God. Or, as established in chapter 2, there exists a close connection between the piercing of God in Zech 12:10 and the fountain

---

106. Zech 2:16 [ET 2:12]; 3:1–9; 5:5–11; 8:8; 9:7, 11; 13:1–6, 9; 14:20–21. At this juncture, I am familiar with fourteen differing interpretations of Zech 3:9 listed here. E.g., see the list by Klein, *Zechariah*, 145. I will mention the two most commonly held views before offering another proposal. One common view is that the stone in Zech 3:9 refers directly to the messiah. While the broader context may point to the messiah, a Branch, and while the OT links the messiah with a stone elsewhere (e.g., Isa 26:18; Ps 118:22), this view never provides a very good explanation for the engraving. Another view is that the stone with the engraving recalls the various stones on the priestly garments—whether that is the stones with the names of Israel engraved on them, or the one gold plate on the priests turban with the engraving, "Holy to the Lord." While the preceding context deals with the priesthood and while the engraving even matches the way the stones are described in Exod 28, difficulties persist. Such a view requires one to translate "the seven eyes" as "seven *pairs of eyes*," equaling fourteen eyes and refer symbolically to the fourteen stones on the priestly garments. Yet Zech 3:9 mentions only one stone. Or better, some translate "the seven eyes" as seven *facets* of a single stone (cf. Ezek 1:4, 7, 16), thus referring to the one stone in the priest's turban. Even still, the priest's turban had a gold plate and not a stone (Exod 28:36). My own view is that the engraved stone represents the promise of the new covenant: "I will remove the iniquity of this land in a single day" (cf. Jer 31:34; Heb 8:7–13). The only other place in Scripture where God himself writes something on stone is when he writes the old covenant on two tablets of stone and gives them to Moses (e.g., Exod 24:12; 31:18; 34:1, 4; Deut 4:13). But the reason he brings the Branch in Zech 3:8 is to establish a new covenant with the forgiveness of sins in a single day (cf. Zech 9:11; Matt 26:28). In this case, the seven eyes are the "eyes of Yahweh, which range through the whole earth" (Zech 4:10); and his eyes never cease to gaze upon (cf. the idiom in 2 Sam 22:28; 2 Chr 20:12; Jer 16:17; 24:6) the stone representing the new covenant until the Branch ratifies the new covenant.

107. Zech 1:15; 2:1–4, 12–13 [ET 1:18–21; 2:8–9]; 6:1–8; 9:1–6, 13–15; 10:3–5, 11; 11:1–3; 12:1–9; 14:3–5, 12–15, 18–19.

108. Zech 1:16; 2:9, 15–16 [ET 2:5, 11–12]; 3:10; 6:13; 8:3, 12, 18–19; 9:8, 16–17; 12:10; 13:1–2; 14:6–9, 16, 20–21.

109. Regarding Yahweh's Spirit changing the human spirit, see p. 27n6.

The Pierced One's First Redeeming Advent

opened for cleansing in Zech 13:1. Thus, part and parcel to Yahweh's return-mission is his own piercing for the people's benefit.

John's use of Zech 12:10 appears to carry these prophetic threads of Yahweh's return-mission to their intended consummation in the person of God's Son, Jesus Christ. In some real sense, then, the piercing of Jesus reveals the onset of Yahweh's eschatological return. John's readers must know both who Jesus is as Yahweh in the flesh and what Jesus is doing to carry out Yahweh's return-mission. By forging a link to the Pierced One of Zech 12:10, the Spirit, through John's writing, glorifies Jesus as the one carrying out Yahweh's eschatological return. Thus, in connection to the aforementioned themes running through Zechariah, John understands that Jesus inaugurates the building of God's eschatological temple-city by coming, dying, and raising his own body from the dead (John 1:14; 2:19–22).[110] Jesus also gathers for himself the remnant from both the Jews and the nations (John 10:16; 11:52; 12:32; 17:20–21).

Furthermore, by dying on the cross, Jesus provides atonement, forgiveness, and cleansing for sin (John 1:29; 8:24; cf. 20:23).[111] Indeed, as I. de la Potterie and Adam Kubiś keenly develop, John's use of Zech 12:10 just following the outpoured water and blood from Jesus' pierced side in John 19:34 seems to evoke the wider context of Zech 13:1, wherein God opens a fountain for cleansing from sin.[112] In other words,

---

110. For the connections to Jesus as the fulfillment of the ideal temple set forward in Zechariah, see Hoskins, *Jesus as Fulfillment*, 83–89, 108–16, 165–66.

111. Contrary to the Bultmann-Käsemann paradigm, others have sufficiently demonstrated that Jesus' death is best understood as an atoning event. E.g., Morris, "Atonement," 49–64; Turner, "Atonement," 99–122; Metzner, *Sünde Im Johannesevangelium*, 131; Thielman, *Theology*, 201; Dennis, "Jesus' Death," 331–63; Hoskins, "Deliverance," 287–89. According to these studies, John 1:29 stands as a programmatic text for understanding the mission of Jesus, who takes away sins. John 20:23 also becomes programmatic for the mission of Jesus' church, the newly gathered community who benefit from the forgiveness of sins through Jesus' atoning death. Moreover, John uses the preposition ὑπέρ ("for") to portray Jesus' death as substitutionary and atoning (e.g., John 6:51; 10:11, 15; 11:50; 15:13; 17:19; 18:14), much like other NT writers do (e.g., Mark 14:24; Luke 22:19; Rom 5:6, 8; 8:32; 14:15; 1 Cor 1:13; 11:24; 15:3; 2 Cor 5:14; Gal 2:20; 3:13; Eph 5:25; 1 Thess 5:10; 1 Tim 2:6; Titus 2:14; Heb 2:9; 6:20; 1 Pet 2:21; 3:18; 1 John 3:16).

112. de la Potterie, "Il Costato Trafitto," 625–49; Kubiś, *Zechariah in John*, 191–94. Also interpreting John 19:34 and John 19:37 in connection with the fountain

the blood and water from Jesus' side is not merely further historical proof that Jesus is dead. John's use of Zech 12:10 also leads the reader to discover the theological significance of the blood and water using the broader context of Zech 13:1, namely, God opened the fountain for cleansing from sin and uncleanness in Jesus' death.[113]

Jesus' "lifting up" on the cross is also the place where God conquers the true enemies of his people, enemies such as death caused by sin (John 8:24, 36) as well as the devil himself (John 12:31b; 14:30; 16:11; cf. 1 John 3:8). Yet perhaps one can assert even more. If John understands the repeated eschatological "day" of Zech 12 receiving its fulfillment in two episodes—the first episode occurring in the death

---

opened in Zech 13:1 are Barrett, *John*, 557; Brown, *John XIII-XXI*, 954–55; Carson, *John*, 628; Ridderbos, *John*, 623–24; Malina and Rohrbaugh, *John*, 275; Vanhoozer, "Body Piercing," 299–302; Minear, *John*, 78, 80; Kubiś, *Zechariah in John*, 191–94; Carnazzo, *Seeing Blood and Water*, 69–72. Interestingly, the Vulgate translates John 19:34, *sed unus militum lancea latus eius aperuit* ("but one of the soldiers with a spear opened his side"). Does the idea of "opening" instead of "piercing" suggest an early interpretation of what was happening in that event, namely, that Jesus was in fact opening the fountain of salvation for his people? Cf. Hoskyns, *Fourth Gospel*, 536.

113. "Blood," within the context of John 6:51–56, seems to signify Jesus' sacrificial death. As Hoskins explains, one must "appropriate ('eat' and 'drink') the benefits of [Jesus'] sacrificial death ('flesh' and 'blood') in order to have eternal life." Hoskins, "Deliverance," 297. John regularly uses "water," however, to signify the gift/age of the Holy Spirit (e.g., John 3:5; 4:10, 14; 7:38–39). It is the Spirit who cleanses from sin and gives eternal life by applying the benefits of Jesus' death to his people. Likewise, Schnackenburg, *John*, 3:294; Carson, *John*, 628; Jones, *Water*, 211; Hoskins, "Deliverance," 298. See also the study on blood and water in John's Gospel by Carnazzo, *Seeing Blood and Water*, 31–61, 69–72. Carnazzo develops conceptual links between Zech 13:1b (i.e., "sin and uncleanness") and John 19:34b (i.e., "blood and water"). Carnazzo argues, "With this correlation, the 'blood' (αἷμα) provides the prophesied purification of 'sin' (חַטָּאת), and the 'water' (ὕδωρ) provides the prophesied purification of 'uncleanness' (נִדָּה)." Carnazzo, *Seeing Blood and Water*, 72. In a similar vein, Hoskyns observes, "The Beloved Disciple does not merely bear witness against the Docetists to the evident proof of the actual death of Christ, nor merely to the miraculous occurrence which followed His death, but rather to the significance of that occurrence. He perceived that purification (water) and new life (blood) flow from the completed sacrifice of the Lamb of God . . ." Hoskyns, *Fourth Gospel*, 533. So also Devillers observes that John's "insistance ne porte pas tant sur la materialite des faits que sur l'importance theologique et symbolique qu'il leur accorde ("[John's] focus is not so much on the materiality of the facts as on the theological and symbolic importance which he grants them"). Devillers, "L'interprétation," 140.

The Pierced One's First Redeeming Advent

of Jesus and the second in the return of Jesus[114]—then John may also view the cross as episode one in the revelation of God's eschatological judgment. Indeed, even though John acknowledges a judgment at the end of history (John 5:27–29), he still presents Jesus' death as an end-time event wherein God judges the rebellious world (John 12:31a; 16:33). The major difference is that while Zechariah anticipates God's judgment of the world to manifest itself in military defeat at the end of history (Zech 12:2–9),[115] John understands the cross to manifest God's

114. See chapter 4 below for further development, but several observations persuade me to understand the fulfillment of the events in Zech 12 through two advents of Jesus and not just his final advent. (1) Like Zech 12:1–9, Ps 2 describes the nations vainly gathering against God. Yet the apostles, John included (cf. Acts 4:19, 21, 23), use Ps 2 to explain Jesus' cross as well as Jesus' return. For instance, Acts 4:25–28 quotes Ps 2:1–2 to say that the nations gathered against God and his messiah at the cross of Jesus. However, Rev 19:15–19 alludes to Ps 2:1–2 to explain Jesus' final return (cf. Rev 2:26–27; 12:5). Apparently, the apostles understood God's victory against the nations to unfold with two advents of Jesus and not just one. Could John's understanding of Zech 12 be similar? (2) Zech 12 describes an eschatological "day" when the nations would gather against God (Zech 12:1–4), when God would judge the nations (Zech 12:2, 9), when God would act decisively to save his own covenant people (Zech 12:4, 7–8), when God would make even the feeblest of his people glorious and mighty because of their union with David's house (Zech 12:6–7), and when God's people would be reestablished at Jerusalem (Zech 12:6). According to the NT, Jesus inaugurates that "day" in his death on the cross. The nations did gather against God in his Son (John 18:3, 28–32; 19:1–16; cf. Acts 4:25–28). God did judge the nations (John 12:31). Through the death of Jesus, God also acted decisively to save his own covenant people (John 10:16; 17:2; 20:17; Rom 15:8–9). Through Jesus' resurrection God also made his people mighty for the spiritual battle they would face against the nations (John 12:31; 14:30; 15:18–27; 16:33; 20:21–22; cf. Eph 6:10–18; 1 John 5:4–5, 18). Still more, God established his people as an unshakable, heavenly Jerusalem, the church (John 4:23; cf. Matt 16:18; Gal 4:26; Heb 12:22). Thus, even if a final battle remains at Jesus' second advent, God's victory for his people has begun. (3) The phrase "on that day" recurs six times in Zech 12:1–9 and then again in Zech 12:11, suggesting that the events of vv. 1–9 and the events of v. 10 fall within the same eschatological time-frame of that "day." Interestingly enough, the Apostle John uses Zech 12:10 to explain Jesus' cross in John 19:37 and Jesus' return in Rev 1:7. That "day," therefore, appears to be temporally expansive enough to include within its purview Jesus' victory at the cross and at his return. For a similar view of the NT's use of Zech 12, see Petterson, *Zechariah*, 268. Further discussion on the nature of the inter-advent age in relation to John's use of Zech 12:10 will transpire in chapter 5.

115. Zechariah 12 describes an eschatological "day" when God would, among other redemptive acts, pour out his wrath on the nations (Zech 12:2, 9). One metaphor employed was the "cup of staggering" (Zech 12:2). See the remarks in on p. 28n11.

judgment of the world first within history (John 12:31). In a word, God inaugurates the rebellious world's demise in Jesus' death/glorification well before the end of history. Simultaneously, Beasley-Murray states that "the sentence of judgment passed on this world is endured by the One whom this world murders. This turns awful news of judgment on sin at the cross into the good news of deliverance from condemnation through the cross."[116] Prior to the final revelation of God's judgment, one may trust in Jesus the substitute to experience freedom from God's abiding wrath (John 3:16, 36; 5:24; 1 John 2:20; 4:10)[117] and to experience the life-giving waters of the eschatological kingdom even now through the sent Spirit (John 7:38–39; 14:15–26; 15:26–27; 16:7–15). While Zechariah's sanctified land remains future, God's presence in Jesus is already living water, or eternal life, for the soul (John 4:10, 14; 7:38–39; 17:3). Yet, and this is the key, it is the piercing of God in Jesus the Son that enables John to link Jesus' life, death, and resurrection with these other elements of Yahweh's return-mission.

Along similar lines, William Randolph Bynum has argued that Zech 9–14 provides John with the theological framework for articulating his passion narrative. Indeed, rather than seeing with others[118] a literary *inclusio* formed by the double OT quotations at John 12:38–40 and John 19:36–37, Bynum argues for an *inclusio* formed by John's explicit quotations of Zechariah in John 12:15 and John 19:37. "When taken together," Bynum writes, "the two citations demonstrate John's

---

116. Beasley-Murray, *John*, 213.

117. What John leaves implicit in his Gospel he makes explicit in his first letter, presenting Jesus as the propitiatory sacrifice (ἱλασμός) for the world in 1 John 2:2 and 1 John 4:10. On John's presentation of Jesus' death as both expiating sin and propitiating God in his Gospel and Letters, see Marshall, *Epistles of John*, 117–18; Stott, *Letters of John*, 86–92; Turner, "Atonement," 109, 114, 118; Kruse, *Letters of John*, 75–76; Yarbrough, *1–3 John*, 75–78; Rainbow, *Johannine Theology*, 110–11, 212–13. Cf. also Morris, "Atonement," 49–64. Morris sees John's Gospel presenting Jesus' death as a substitution that both saves from sin and averts God's judgment. In an earlier work, Morris sets John's use of ἱλασμός in 1 John 2:2 and 1 John 4:10 within the broader teaching of the NT on Christ's propitiatory sacrifice. See Morris, *Apostolic Preaching*, 144, 206.

118. E.g., Manns, "Zacharie 12,10," 309; Meyers, *Characterizing Jesus*, 169.

The Pierced One's First Redeeming Advent

dialogue with Zechariah as he encloses the passion narrative in the hope, joy, and the irony of Zech 9–12."[119] Bynum then continues,

> In viewing the events of Christ's passion in the light of Zechariah, John grasps the essential meaning of Zech 9–14, which promises divine hope and salvation for postexilic Judah along with a call for renewed relationship to God, and applies it to the events of Christ's entrance into Jerusalem, his death, and resurrection. Thus, in his view, God has truly returned; the promised humble king has arrived; the new era of his lordship has begun; the era of renewal envisioned by Zechariah has come.[120]

Whether or not one agrees with his literary *inclusio*, Bynum rightly concludes that, according to John's use of Zechariah, God has truly returned. The present study makes such a conclusion even more explicit: God has truly returned in the person of his Son, Jesus Christ. John connects the pierced Yahweh with the pierced Son, who is no less than μονογενὴς θεός (John 1:18). God has truly returned in that Jesus himself is not only the humble king of Zech 9:9, a king who certainly represents God, but Jesus is also the pierced God of Zech 12:10, the covenant Lord of Israel on mission to return to his people and return his people to himself through a piercing that puts into effect the mutual reconciliation. He will dwell with his people, and they with him, but not without God first opening a fountain to fit them for his holy presence.

Not all interpreters will welcome the aforementioned theological developments, especially those interpreters who deny that Jesus should be included within Yahweh's divine identity. However, apart from the aforementioned Christological interpretation given by John, whereby Jesus, as God, fulfills the redemptive piercing set forward in Zech 12:10, the prophecy remains an enigma. Apart from the incarnation of God's one-of-a-kind Son, it was not possible to pierce God. Yet since the incarnation of God's Son occurred, the pierced God of Zech 12:10 can be known more fully and rightly. God's self-revelation in the word of Zech

---

119. Bynum, "Quotations," 73.
120. Bynum, "Quotations," 73.

12:10 finds its only and full embodiment in the incarnate Word, Jesus Christ. He alone explains the piercing of God.

Yet another tension may also persist for those following the argumentation thus far. The narrative elements surrounding the prophecy of Zech 12:10, where expectation emerges for God to work in a final cataclysmic way against the nations, do not seem to transpire within John's passion narrative despite his fulfillment motif. However, knowing that the prophets often viewed the events of the eschatological drama on the same horizon helps resolve some of this tension.[121] That is, their proclamation includes an accumulation of end-time events, which they leave chronologically undefined. The eschatological "day" of God's return is temporally expansive to include a number of end-time events within its purview.[122] Moreover, John regularly employs an inaugurated eschatology in his Gospel without losing sight of consummated eschatology.[123]

---

121. Waltke, *Old Testament Theology*, 821–22.

122. E.g., Joel 2:28–32 anticipates (i.e., אַחֲרֵי־כֵן, "after this") that Yahweh will pour out the Spirit of prophesy on all flesh without distinction (Joel 2:28–29). On the same horizon, however, Yahweh will also show wonders in the heavens and on the earth, blood and fire and columns of smoke, and the sun will be turned to darkness and the moon to blood (Joel 2:30–31). Luke certainly interprets the outpouring of the Spirit at Pentecost as the realization of the former, while the latter prophecies associated with cosmic upheaval and judgment are yet to come (cf. Acts 2:16–21 with Luke 21:25; Matt 24:29; Mark 13:24–25; Rev 6:12). Some have argued that Peter sees the whole of Joel 2:28–32 fulfilled in the death and exaltation of Jesus and his sending of the Spirit. E.g., see Schnabel, *Acts*, 138–39. It is true that similar imagery of cosmic upheaval surrounds Luke's description of the crucifixion in Luke 23:44–45a (e.g., darkness and the sun's light fading), but the imagery serves as a fitting description of what the cross truly is, God's eschatological wrath endured by Jesus in the present before the "great and awesome day of the Lord comes" (cf. Joel 2:31). So Bock, *Acts*, 116–17. Also, the "wonders and signs" performed by Jesus (cf. Acts 2:22) and by the apostles (cf. Acts 2:43) seem to differ from those cosmic signs that Joel describes, though could still be viewed as precursors to them. Cf. Marshall, "Acts," 535; Peterson, *Acts*, 143. Thus, the events of Pentecost may very well inaugurate the end-time fulfillment of Joel's prophecy, but the use of the same Joel prophecy in other places suggests there is more still to come, especially when read in light of Luke 21:25–28.

123. John 5:25–29 likely stands as the clearest example: "Truly, truly, I say to you, an hour is coming, and is now here [i.e., inaugurated eschatology], when the dead will hear the voice of the Son of God, and those who hear will live . . . Do not marvel at this, for an hour is coming [i.e., consummated eschatology] when all who are in the tombs will hear his voice and come out, those who have done good to the resurrection of life, and those who have done evil to the resurrection of judgment." While

Such an awareness grants insight to how John may understand Jesus fulfilling Zech 12:10. The Pierced One, upon whom Zechariah expects the people to look "on that day," must first meet his prerequisite. That is, Yahweh must be pierced; the piercing must be historically realized.[124] According to John, this becomes possible only when the Word becomes flesh, when God the Son takes to himself a human nature (John 1:14). Jesus' historical piercing realizes the prerequisite of Zechariah's prediction that the people will look upon him whom they pierced. At the same time, Jesus' piercing shows that God is carrying out the process of his redemptive purposes yet to be consummated. John has seen the Pierced One firsthand (John 19:35), but his readers should expect to see more from him as God's return-mission continues transpiring in all Jesus' activity (e.g., John 5:27–29; 6:39–40; 14:2–3; 21:23). This ushers us nicely into John's use of Zech 12:10 in Rev 1:7. However, some concluding remarks on John 19:37 will help gather the scattered pieces.

CONCLUSION

In order to identify Jesus and interpret the closing events of his crucifixion, John says that Jesus' piercing took place in order to fulfill the Scripture from Zech 12:10. Vital to the redemption of God's people, the prophet expected Yahweh to endure the actual piercing from them. John has witnessed God's glory revealed through Jesus' words and works, through Jesus' death on the cross, and through Jesus' Spirit granting post-resurrection insight to the Scriptures. In short, John has a theological conviction that Jesus is God in the flesh. As the pre-existent Word now incarnate, Jesus is God's ultimate self-revelation, and that self-revelation enables John to see in Zech 12:10 a meaning that

---

interpreters such as C. H. Dodd introduced the notion of "realized" eschatology in relation to the Gospel of John, others have demonstrated that it is more accurate to speak in terms of "inaugurated" eschatology, since "realized" suggests that there is "no future tense to salvation." Smalley, *Evangelist and Interpreter*, 236. Similarly, see the discussions in Ladd, *Theology of NT*, 308; Cook, "Eschatology," 79–99; Köstenberger, *Theology*, 295–98.

124. Cf. Hoskyns, *Fourth Gospel*, 536. Hoskyns similarly argues that " . . . the author of the Fourth Gospel sees the anticipation of the eschatological scene in the concrete situation in which the soldiers and the crowd beheld the pierced side of the crucified Christ."

was always present before, even though mysterious. That is to say, John answers the *sui generis* problem of Zech 12:10, God is pierced, with the *sui generis* answer, Jesus is God.

Such a conclusion differs from the more popular interpretation that links John 19:37 to Zech 12:10 along merely human, messianic lines. From the representative or "functional-identity" perspective, God is pierced in his authorized, messianic representative. That perspective may very well fit a wider contextual reading of Zech 12:10 and also find a place within John's identification of Jesus as the Messiah or Christ. However, John's principal emphasis on Jesus' equality with God the Father provides the overall framework for understanding Jesus' messiahship. Moreover, as chapter 2 demonstrated, Zech 12:10 does not clearly point to the piercing of God's human representative—an inference usually drawn to figure out a difficult text—but to the piercing of God himself. Also, while John had available to him more popular and less ambiguous OT passages, where God's representative gets pierced, he deliberately chose Zech 12:10 to advance a theological element not made as explicit by these other messianic passages, namely, God himself gets pierced. Therefore, not only does John identify Jesus as God from an OT witness, he also magnifies the revelatory nature of the cross-event, and demonstrates that Jesus is carrying out Yahweh's return-mission. The prophet's words, however, also expect more from the Pierced One, a consummated eschatology which John's Gospel does not suppress and to which Rev 1:7 draws attention.

4

The Pierced One's Second Redeeming Advent
Rev 1:7

JOHN 19:37 PROVIDED THE initial insight to how God's self-disclosure in Jesus' first redeeming advent enables John to link the piercing of Jesus' side with the fulfillment of Zech 12:10. When the one-of-a-kind Son who shares God's essence while being distinct in person gets pierced, God gets pierced. Jesus' historical piercing realizes the prerequisite of Zechariah's prediction that the people will look upon God whom they pierced. At the same time, Jesus' piercing indicates that God is carrying out the process of his redemptive purposes yet to be consummated. Revelation 1:7 becomes a unique contribution in explaining Zech 12:10 along the lines of consummated eschatology.

Chapter 4 will seek to demonstrate how Rev 1:7 provides further insight into John's use of Zech 12:10, but from the viewpoint of God's self-disclosure in Jesus' second redeeming advent. God, the Pierced One, has already revealed himself in Jesus' Passion, but is there enough evidence to say that Rev 1:7 anticipates God to reveal himself in Jesus' Parousia, doing so again as the Pierced One? The research below will show that is indeed the case. Understanding the Pierced One of Zech 12:10 as God, and not simply God's human representative, aligns with the divinity of Jesus the Lamb in Revelation. Moreover, if Rev 1:7 is describing Jesus' second coming in terms of Zech 12:10, a prophecy

Jesus as the Pierced One

associated with God's eschatological return, then identifying Jesus' second coming as God's return also seems warranted.

In order to develop these aforementioned connections, the following research will unfold in four main steps. Step one, we must establish that John is alluding to Zech 12:10 in Rev 1:7. Step two, we must understand the broader literary framework of Revelation, especially Rev 1:1–20, in order to grasp the message of Rev 1:7. Step three, we must examine Rev 1:7 itself and then determine how John's use of Zech 12:10 develops what Jesus' coming is. Step four, we will need to determine how John's use of Zech 12:10–14 contributes to his biblical-theological presentation of Jesus' identity and mission in the book of Revelation. John interweaves a supporting redemptive-historical thread from the prophet Daniel that will also receive treatment, though only enough treatment to illuminate John's use of Zech 12:10.

STEP ONE: ESTABLISHING THE ALLUSION

Unlike the formal quotation in John 19:37, John only alludes to Zech 12:10 in Rev 1:7. An allusion lacks an introductory formula and only gives an indirect reference to an OT passage with less than exact wording.[1] Still, the basic elements of the prophecy are discernable: a people look upon (ὄψεται) the Pierced One (i.e., αὐτὸν) whom they themselves were complicit in piercing (οἵτινες . . . ἐξεκέντησαν).[2] Moreover, Rev 1:7 adds the mourning (κόψονται) of the onlookers, an element further

---

1. Beale, *Handbook*, 31. A commonly observed phenomenon is that John never uses formal OT quotations in Revelation even though it contains more OT references than any other NT book. See, e.g., Trudinger, "Observations," 82–88; Paulien, "Allusions," 3, 53.

2. John's vocabulary differs from the LXX here (e.g., ὄψεται instead of ἐπιβλέψονται; αὐτὸν instead of πρός με); and in the case of οἵτινες . . . ἐξεκέντησαν ("those who . . . pierced"), John's words better reflect the Hebrew. As noted about the quotation in John 19:37, such differences may reveal John's desire to represent his Hebrew *Vorlage* more accurately against the LXX. Nevertheless, Moyise's evaluation of whether John favored Greek or Semitic sources should temper such a conclusion. John surely knew and used both, but evidence is lacking to say he favored one over the other for his discourse in Revelation. Moyise, "Language," 97–113.

The Pierced One's Second Redeeming Advent

developed in Zech 12:10–14.[3] Thus, an allusion to Zech 12:10 in Rev 1:7 is apparent.[4]

Yet John notably combines the allusion to Zech 12:10 with another OT text that bears some level of affinity and becomes mutually interpretive.[5] Considering its influence, the allusion to Dan 7:13 merits some attention as well. The verbal connections to Dan 7:13 appear evident regardless of which Greek version one favors.[6] Both Rev 1:7

---

3. Note especially the mourning language in the LXX (κόψονται ... κόψονται in Zech 12:10, 12). However, in Zech 12:11–14 the mourning spreads tribe by tribe until covering all the remaining clans within the covenant community, while Rev 1:7 envisions all the tribes of the earth mourning on account of the Pierced One. This universalization will receive further attention below.

4. Though less certain, Jesus is also "the firstborn [ὁ πρωτότοκος]" in Rev 1:5, the same vocabulary used by the LXX in Zech 12:11 ("and they shall be pained with pain as for a firstborn [πρωτοτόκῳ]"). Cf. Beale and McDonough, "Revelation," 1090. They observe John's allusion to πρωτότοκος in light of Ps 89:28 (ET 89:27; LXX 88:28). In light of Zech 12:11 likening Israel's mourning over the Pierced One to Israel's mourning over King Josiah (2 Kgs 23:29; 2 Chr 35:24–25), a significant king in David's line, it is possible that Zech 12:10 is alluding to Ps 89:27 with πρωτότοκος to recall the Davidic hope.

5. Indeed, most of the OT references in Revelation appear intertwined with each other, and such a use presents its challenges methodologically and hermeneutically as noted by Paulien, "Allusions," 49–55; Beale, "Revelation," 319–21; Beale, *John's Use*, 13–128. With challenges noted, Vanhoye's work on the use of Ezekiel in Revelation concludes as follows: "Il est rare que l'Apocalypse se contente de puiser à une seule source; en général, elle fusionne plusieurs textes et fait souvent preuve d'un sens admirable des affinités qu'ils ont entre eux ... Les éléments qu'il lui emprunte sont choisis avec un discernement très sûr. Jean excelle à trouver les textes qui se complètent ou se corrigent mutuellement de façon à exprimer avec plus de fidélité l'accomplissement chrétien" ("It is rare that the Apocalypse is content to draw from a single source; in general, it merges several texts and frequently demonstrates an admirable sense of affinity that they have between them ... The elements that [the Apocalypse] borrows are chosen with a very careful discernment. John excels in finding texts that complement or correct each other so as to express the Christian fulfillment more faithfully."). Vanhoye, "L'utilisation," 467–68.

6. Daniel has two distinct textual traditions usually referred to as Septuagint-Daniel (or Old Greek-Daniel) and Theodotion-Daniel, the latter presupposing and thus post-dating the former. See Bruce, "Daniel," 22–40; Di Lella, "Textual History," 586–607. With its use of μετά ("with") versus ἐπί ("upon"), Rev 1:7 appears to reflect Theodotion-Dan 7:13, καὶ ἰδοὺ μετὰ τῶν νεφελῶν τοῦ οὐρανοῦ ὡς υἱὸς ἀνθρώπου ἐρχόμενος ἦν ("and behold, with the clouds of heaven, there was coming [one] like the son of man"). Yet even Septuagint-Daniel contains the same basic components: καὶ ἰδοὺ ἐπὶ τῶν νεφελῶν τοῦ οὐρανοῦ ὡς υἱὸς ἀνθρώπου ἤρχετο ("and behold, upon the clouds of heaven, there was coming [one] like the son of man").

and Dan 7:13 use the interjection "behold" (ἰδοὺ) to introduce a heavenly figure who is in process of coming (ἔρχεται) with/upon the clouds (τῶν νεφελῶν). Furthermore, Rev 1:5–6 describes the universal dominion of Jesus, a description analogous to the "son of man" figure in Dan 7:13–14.[7] Also, in close proximity to Rev 1:7, John describes the exalted Jesus as ὅμοιον υἱὸν ἀνθρώπου ("one like a son of man," Rev 1:13; cf. ὡς υἱὸς ἀνθρώπου in Dan 7:13). On verbal and thematic grounds, therefore, Rev 1:7 also connects with Dan 7:13. Having established the allusions to Zech 12:10 and Dan 7:13 in step one, the study of how John uses them to build on an understanding of God's self-disclosure in Jesus' second advent will prove valuable to the present project, but not without addressing the question of context.

STEP TWO: REV 1:7 IN THE PROLOGUE OF JOHN'S REVELATION

We must understand the broader literary framework of Revelation, especially Rev 1:1–20, in order to grasp the message and significance of Rev 1:7. Revelation is unique when compared with the other NT literature, especially in the way John intertwines genres of apocalyptic, prophecy, and letter.[8] As Richard Bauckham summarizes, " . . . Revelation seems to be an apocalyptic prophecy in the form of a circular letter to seven churches in the Roman province of Asia."[9] All three genres

---

7. In Rev 1:5 Jesus is "ruler of kings on earth," and Rev 1:6 concludes, "to him belongs glory and dominion forever and ever." While an allusion to Ps 88:28 in the LXX could also be present in Rev 1:5 (cf. ὑψηλὸν παρὰ τοῖς βασιλεῦσιν τῆς γῆς), it is still important to observe that, the Ancient of Days in Dan 7:14 gives the "son of man" figure "dominion and glory and a kingdom" and his "dominion is an everlasting dominion."

8. The prophetic nature of John's message is both explicit (e.g., τοὺς λόγους τῆς προφητείας, "the words of this prophecy" in Rev 1:3; cf. 10:11; 22:7, 10, 18, 19) and implicit (e.g., τῶν ἀδελφῶν σου τῶν προφητῶν, "your brothers the prophets" in Rev 22:9). Revelation 1:4 (cf. Rev 1:11; 2:1, 8, 12, 18; 3:1, 7, 14) and Rev 22:21 contain features representative of other letters in the first century (e.g., Rom 1:7; 16:20; 1 Cor 1:3; 16:23). While the opening term of Rev 1:1, ἀποκάλυψις, is not a label identifying the book's genre, some of its literary features are comparable to Jewish apocalyptic and its biblical prototypes in Isa 24–27, Ezek 37–48, Zechariah, and Daniel. For further development, see the discussions in Bauckham, *Theology of Revelation*, 2–17; Collins, *Apocalyptic*, 1–42, 256–79; Gradl, *Buch Und Offenbarung*, 104–22.

9. Bauckham, *Theology of Revelation*, 2. Cf. Ladd, "Prophetic-Apocalyptic,"

become evident within the opening chapter, and their literary devices contribute toward an initial breakdown of the book's structure. While a number of differing proposals exists for the structure of Revelation,[10] widespread agreement persists that Rev 1:1–20 forms the introductory material, with a few suggesting a three-part prologue: vv. 1–3 introduce the book as a whole; the dense salutation in vv. 4–8 then frames the book within a letter; and vv. 9–20 describe John's visionary, prophetic commission.[11] In order to grasp how Rev 1:7 functions in relation to the whole three-part prologue, we will summarize vv. 1–3 and vv. 9–20 before treating more thoroughly vv. 4–8.[12]

General Introduction (Rev 1:1–3)

Revelation 1:1–3 opens the three-part prologue, providing the general introduction to the nature of the book. The burden of the book is ἀποκάλυψις Ἰησοῦ Χριστοῦ ("the revelation *given by* Jesus Christ") with the ultimate source of that revelation being God the Father— ἔδωκεν αὐτῷ ὁ θεὸς ("God gave [the revelation] to him [i.e., Jesus]").[13] Fol-

---

192–200; Aune, *Revelation*, lxxiii. However, Ladd's study uses prophetic-apocalyptic to describe an eschatological outlook more than a body of literature. Combined with Bauckham's observations, one might say that apocalyptic is the vehicle for John's prophecy in Revelation, and that prophecy contains what Ladd calls a "prophetic-apocalyptic" eschatology.

10. Bauckham, *Climax*, 1–37; Beale, *Revelation*, 108–51.

11. Many would limit the prologue to Rev 1:1–8, including Rev 1:9–20 with the letters of chs. 2–3. E.g., Ladd, *Revelation*, 19; Schüssler Fiorenza, "Composition," 344–66; Bauckham, *Climax*, 21; Smith, "Structure," 373–93; Aune, *Revelation*, 5; Osborne, *Revelation*, 50; Hamilton, *Revelation*, 19. However, others have shown that Rev 1:9–20 belong with Rev 1:1–8 in that it furthers the book's provenance (cf. Rev 1:1–2, 9–10), identifies the seven churches (cf. Rev 1:4, 11), explains John's prophetic commission (cf. Rev 1:3, 12–19; Ezek 1:26–28), details the general structure of John's visions (cf. Rev 1:2, 19; 4:1), and parallels Rev 22:6–21. E.g., Muñoz León, "La Estructura," 125–72; Morris, *Revelation*, 45; Snyder, "Combat Myth," 84–85; Giesen, *Offenbarung*, 53; Mounce, *Revelation*, 31–32, 39; Beale, *Revelation*, 181; Günther, *Enderwartungshorizont*, 65. Hübenthal also observes that the typographical division in NA27 suggests a three-part prologue. Hübenthal, *Transformation*, 171.

12. Reviewing Rev 1:9–20 prior to Rev 1:4–8 also presupposes that John's audience would have read or listened to the book (cf. Rev 1:3) multiple times. Thus, they would re-read/hear Rev 1:7 in the light of what came after it as well, seeing more clearly how it serves John's prologue.

13. That God the Father is in view as the ultimate source seems clear from the

lowing a pattern similar to what we observed in the Fourth Gospel—though using different vocabulary—God the Father chooses to reveal himself and his saving purpose through his Son, Jesus Christ. The contents of the revelation includes disclosing ἃ δεῖ γενέσθαι ἐν τάχει ("the things that must soon take place"), a referent which the remainder of Revelation appears to fill with end-time events that, temporally speaking, are both near and distant to John and his readers.[14] Granting a well-recognized allusion to Dan 2:28–29,[15] such events include those Daniel himself anticipated in God's everlasting kingdom supplanting the beastly world empires that oppose God and oppress God's people (Dan 2; 7; 9; 10–12; cf. Rev 11; 13; 19–20).

Similar to prophets before him, especially Daniel and Zechariah (Dan 7:12; Zech 1–6), John receives the divine revelation through heavenly visions (ὅσα εἶδεν, "even to all that he saw") interpreted by an angelic intermediary (καὶ ἐσήμανεν ἀποστείλας διὰ τοῦ ἀγγέλου αὐτοῦ τῷ δούλῳ αὐτοῦ Ἰωάννῃ, "and [Jesus] had it made known by his angel to his servant John"). The stated goal is not mere foresight into God's unfolding plan, but to awaken obedience in God's people and to assure divine favor upon those who act accordingly until God's plans are complete (Rev 1:3).

---

larger context of v. 6: καὶ ἐποίησεν ἡμᾶς βασιλείαν, ἱερεῖς τῷ θεῷ καὶ πατρὶ αὐτοῦ ("and he [i.e., Jesus Christ, cf. 1:5] made us a kingdom, priests to his God and Father").

14. Beale treats the clause, ἃ δεῖ γενέσθαι ἐν τάχει ("things which must soon take place"), in light of Dan 2:28–29. Essentially, Dan 2:28–29 follows other OT prophets who speak of God's end-time salvation in terms of the "last days." For Beale, John interprets the "last days" as occurring ἐν τάχει ("quickly"), in the sense that God has already begun the "defeat of cosmic evil" and is "ushering in the divine kingdom" (cf. Mark 1:15). Beale, *Revelation*, 152–54, 181–82. I agree with Beale insofar as I view the "last days" as a temporally expansive referent. It is also true that the progression of historical events within Revelation includes the recent past (e.g., Jesus' death and resurrection), the current situation (e.g., John's vision, the tribulation, the state of the seven churches), the near future (e.g., persecution and martyrdom, gospel proclamation), and the more distant future (e.g., Jesus' return and the new heavens and earth). At the same time, Beale's emphases do seem to empty the phrase ἐν τάχει of its primarily future connotation. See the fair criticisms of Beale in Jauhiainen, "Climax?," 101–3; Poythress, "Review," 143–46.

15. E.g., Beale, *Revelation*, 152–70; Hamilton, *With the Clouds*, 202. See also the previous footnote.

The Pierced One's Second Redeeming Advent

Prophetic Commissioning (Rev 1:9–20)

Revelation 1:9–20 finishes the three-part prologue with a theophanic vision of Jesus' kingship followed by John's prophetic commissioning to write the revelation he witnesses.[16] As the Lord did for prophets like Ezekiel, Isaiah, and Daniel (Ezek 1; Isa 6; Dan 7), so also the Lord unveils for John a glimpse of his royal majesty during turbulent times. The tribulation on earth (Rev 1:9) is not reason for the church to question Jesus' past victory or present reign. Rather, the vision John receives confirms Jesus' victory and reign, which he describes with a mosaic of OT images. I will demonstrate below that several of these images recall the majesty of Yahweh, the Ancient of Days, but John applies them directly to the "one like a son of man." The "son of man" figure unveiling his glory to John also died and now lives forevermore with authority over the grave (Rev 1:18), a clear reference to the crucified but risen Jesus Christ (cf. Rev 1:5). The glorified state Jesus possesses never overshadows the humble state he once took; it was in and through death that he conquered and established his people (cf. Rev 1:5–6; 5:6–10). Now the risen Jesus not only bears authority likened to that of Yahweh, but he upholds the churches with his right hand (Rev 1:20; 2:1), walks among them (Rev 1:13; 2:1), and commissions John to write for their benefit (Rev 1:4, 11, 19).

Dense Salutation (Rev 1:4–8)

The dense salutation of Rev 1:4–8 links[17] John's general introduction (Rev 1:1–3) to his prophetic commissioning (Rev 1:9–20).[18] Verses

---

16. Revelation 1:9–20 shares many similarities with Ezekiel's experience in Ezek 1:1—2:10 and Daniel's experience in Dan 10:1—12:4 (e.g., receiving a heavenly vision, falling faint before majesty, and being strengthened by a heavenly being to speak/write the message). In that sense, God appears to be commissioning John in a way that aligns with earlier prophetic commissionings. Likewise, see the remarks in DeSilva, *Seeing*, 119.

17. Cf. Haukaas, "Revelation 1:7–8," 49–57. Further developing the literary connections between Rev 1:7–8 and 1:9–20, Haukaas shows how the vision from Dan 7:13 holds both units together: "he is coming with the clouds" (Rev 1:7) forms a 'chain-link interlock' with the "one like a son of man" (Rev 1:13).

18. As others have shown, vv. 4 and 8 form an *inclusio* recalling ὁ ὢν καὶ ὁ ἦν καὶ ὁ ἐρχόμενος ("he who is and he who was and he who is to come"). E.g., Giesen, *Offenbarung*, 80–81; Beale, *Revelation*, 196.

4–8 set John's revelation within the framework of a circular letter, the closing of which must wait until Rev 22:21. Thus, the seven churches to whom John writes should appropriate the whole of Rev 1:4—22:21 for their present situation and not limit their appropriation to the one letter addressed to their church specifically. The more accurate perspective is for each church to see itself as one with the other churches, all of whom face the onslaught of temptation within and persecution without, and desperately depend on Jesus' victory for their own. Hence, John's salutation also points the churches collectively to the only sovereign Lord, Yahweh, "him who is and who was and who is coming [ὁ ἐρχόμενος],"[19] and to what Yahweh will soon accomplish for the church through Jesus' first and second comings. Indeed, it seems that John can hardly ponder "the coming one [ὁ ἐρχόμενος]" of Rev 1:4 without also announcing Jesus' coming in Rev 1:7: "behold, he is coming [ἔρχεται]."[20]

Still, John does not pass over the redeeming significance of Jesus' first coming. As in Rev 1:9–20, so also here: Jesus' present glory never forgets his former humility. Jesus is ὁ μάρτυς, ὁ πιστός ("the faithful witness"). Like John's Gospel (e.g., John 3:11; 8:14, 18; 18:37), Revelation also presents Jesus as the one who faithfully and truthfully bore witness to God throughout his earthly ministry, even when such pure witness would require willingly sacrificing his life.[21] Jesus is also ὁ πρωτότοκος

19. After a vision of God's throne, Rev 4:8 combines the three-fold title that appears in Rev 1:4 with the same words, "Holy, holy, holy," repeated for Yahweh in Isa 6:3. The general consensus is that the divine name, Yahweh, stands behind the three-fold formula (or *Dreizeitenformel*), ὁ ὢν καὶ ὁ ἦν καὶ ὁ ἐρχόμενος. E.g., see McDonough, *YHWH at Patmos*, 1–5.

20. Others have made the same literary connection. E.g., McDonough, *YHWH at Patmos*, 233; Gradl, *Buch Und Offenbarung*, 152–55. Whether John sees Jesus' coming as Yahweh's coming merits further attention below, but the literary context is ripe for an association.

21. The "faithfulness" characterizing Jesus' witness, then, reached its perfect display in the cross. To associate the title "faithful witness" with Jesus' cross appears obvious in that John then advances to a second title implying Jesus' resurrection. Bauckham further observes, "The word 'witness' (*martys*) does not yet, in Revelation, carry the technical Christian meaning of 'martyr' (one who bears witness by dying for the faith). It does not refer to death itself as witness, but to verbal witness to the truth of God (cf. the association of witness with 'the word of God': 1:2, 9; 6:9; 20:4; cf. also 12:11) along with living obedience to the commands of God (cf. the association witness with keeping the commandments: 12:17). But it is strongly implied that faithful witness will incur opposition and lead to death (2:13; 11:7; 12:17). That

τῶν νεκρῶν ("the firstborn from the dead") in that he not only conquers death itself but also inaugurates the end-time resurrection by being the first among many others whom God will raise to glory with Jesus (cf. Rev 20:4–6).[22] Such victory over death also qualifies Jesus to stand as ὁ ἄρχων τῶν βασιλέων τῆς γῆς ("the ruler of the kings of the earth"). While death always terminates the reign of earthly rulers (e.g., Rev 6:15–17; 17:12–14; 19:16–18), here John celebrates Jesus as the sole ruler who conquered death itself.[23]

Shifting to the dative of recipient (Τῷ ἀγαπῶντι ἡμᾶς … αὐτῷ ἡ δόξα, "to him who loves us … to him [give] the glory"), Christology progresses to doxology (Rev 1:6).[24] Jesus' faithful witness, victorious resurrection, and present reign have secured a redemption for the church that is too glorious to ignore and compels worship until Jesus comes again. The church's redemption includes Jesus' enduring love for them,[25] Jesus' sacrificial death liberating them from their sins (Rev

---

Jesus' witness led to his death is suggested by the sequence of titles in 1:5." Bauckham, *Theology of Revelation*, 72.

22. The OT expected a final resurrection at the end of time (Dan 12:2; cf. Isa 26:19; Ezek 37:1–10). However, Jesus' resurrection separates one end-time event into two episodes: episode one, Jesus rises; episode two, the people Jesus represents rise. For God to raise Jesus "from the dead" means for him to raise Jesus from all the dead ones who will one day also be raised. Jesus not only beat death itself, but also beat everybody else out of the grave (cf. 1 Cor 15:20; Col 1:18). For further treatment of the subject, see Beale, *NT Biblical Theology*, 227–355; Wright, *Resurrection*, 333, 372–73, 448, 477, 681. If an allusion to Ps 89:27 is present, both in πρωτότοκος and in ὁ ἄρχων τῶν βασιλέων τῆς γῆς, then the resurrection fulfills the prayer of Ps 89 and makes Jesus the Davidic ruler *par excellence*.

23. Revelation 1:18 develops Jesus' victory over death further by asserting that he has the keys of death and hades (i.e., the grave), with keys signaling authority over a particular realm (cf. Isa 22:22 with Matt 16:19 and Rev 3:7). Jesus rules from a glorified state that will never end and with an absolute supremacy that leaves no earthly king beyond the bounds of his control. Indeed, John presents Jesus' sacrificial death as "God's decisive victory over evil" (e.g., Rev 5:5–6; 12:10–11). Bauckham, *Theology of Revelation*, 73. To be sure, the victory is only assured in that the once slain Lamb is now standing (Rev 5:6), the one who died is now alive forevermore (Rev 1:18). There is no victory in the death of Christ without the resurrection of Christ.

24. The use of the dative in a sentence like this would normally be the indirect object (e.g., δὸς δόξαν τῷ θεῷ, "Give glory to God," John 9:24). But the dative appears here in a verbless construction and "it is used to indicate the person(s) who receives the object stated or implied." Wallace, *Grammar*, 148.

25. For the present tense stressing continual action, see Wallace, *Grammar*,

1:5),[26] and Jesus' conversion of them into a kingdom and priesthood (Rev 1:6).[27] Such descriptions of Jesus' redeeming work in Rev 1:6, when joined to the revelation of his person from Rev 1:5, become fitting preludes to themes John will intertwine and develop throughout the book. The descriptions in Rev 1:5–6 also provide the framework in which the churches must heed the Lord's repeated calls to repentance and endurance.[28]

Even more pertinent to the present study is how Rev 1:5–6 also serves John's allusion to Zech 12:10. As stated before, Jesus' piercing in his first advent becomes the prerequisite for God's further eschatological work in Jesus' second advent. John's three-fold description of Jesus in Rev 1:5, especially the phrase ἐν τῷ αἵματι αὐτοῦ ("by his blood"), reminds the reader of Jesus' sacrificial death. That sacrificial death included Jesus' historical piercing as indicated by οἵτινες αὐτὸν ἐξεκέντησαν ("those who pierced him") in Rev 1:7. Yet Rev 1:5 also

---

519–20.

26. Often in the NT, "blood" is a euphemism for death, especially Jesus' sacrificial death that benefits others (e.g., Acts 20:28; Rom 3:25; 5:9; 1 Cor 10:16; Eph 1:7; Rev 5:9; 12:11). See Morris, *Apostolic Preaching*, 112–28. In the first Exodus, Yahweh manifested his love for his people by delivering them from slavery to Egypt through the blood of the Passover lamb and by establishing them as a kingdom of priests (Exod 12–14; 19:6; cf. Exod 15:13; Deut 4:37). Likewise, Jesus manifests his love for the church by delivering them from slavery to sin through his own blood—he is the true Passover lamb—and by establishing the church as God's kingdom and priests (Rev 1:6; cf. Rev 5:10; 20:6; 1 Pet 2:5, 9). That Passover is the most likely OT background for Rev 1:5 and for the lamb symbolism applied to Jesus throughout Revelation (e.g., Rev 5:9–10), see the extensive discussion in Isbell, "Exodus Typology," 135–76. Isbell also answers common objections to a Passover background, including how the Passover lamb was viewed as an atoning sacrifice. Isbell's study advances earlier observations by Bauckham, *Theology of Revelation*, 70–72; Beale, *Revelation*, 350–52.

27. See also Sanchez, "People of God," 36–38, 58–59, 85–89, 133–36. Sanchez traces the theme of priesthood from the creation narrative, through its place in Israel, to the new covenant, Jesus Christ, and finally the church. While Sanchez stops with 1 Pet 2:5–9 and its implications for the church's present mission, his biblical-theological conclusions befit the kingdom and priests mentioned in Rev 1:5.

28. The saints must live in accordance with who they are in union with Jesus (cf. ἐν Ἰησοῦ in Rev 1:9), namely, the loved and liberated kingdom of priests (Rev 1:5–6). Simultaneously, if the King who stands triumphant over sin and death loves them, then the saints can rest assured that Jesus will provide them with the grace and peace needed to persevere in all that he commands of them (cf. Rev 1:4).

The Pierced One's Second Redeeming Advent

prepares the reader for Jesus' further work of redemption articulated by Rev 1:7, since Jesus' resurrected status explains how people can look upon him once more in his far more glorious state. The historical piercing that, according to John 19:37, linked the pierced Jesus with the pierced God of Zech 12:10 was only episode one in God's end-time salvation. The past resurrection and the present rule of Jesus prepare the way for episode two when Jesus, the Pierced One, comes again. Until his arrival, the church acknowledges his glory and dominion forever (Rev 1:6), a doxology that only makes sense if Jesus' present heavenly reign eventually manifests itself fully on earth.

Within this setting, John reassures the churches of Jesus' coming by alluding to Zech 12:10–14 and Dan 7:13 in Rev 1:7:

	GNT	Translation
1:7a	Ἰδοὺ ἔρχεται μετὰ τῶν νεφελῶν	Behold, he is coming with the clouds,
1:7b	καὶ ὄψεται αὐτὸν πᾶς ὀφθαλμὸς καὶ οἵτινες αὐτὸν ἐξεκέντησαν	and every eye will see him, even those who pierced him,
1:7c	καὶ κόψονται ἐπ' αὐτὸν πᾶσαι αἱ φυλαὶ τῆς γῆς	and all the tribes of the earth will mourn on account of him.
1:7d	ναί, ἀμήν	Even so, amen.

The literary context of Rev 1:7, summarized in step two above, intertwines several key themes that the reader expects John to develop:

1. God inaugurated his end-time salvation in the cross and resurrection of his Son, Jesus Christ (Rev 1:5–6, 18).

2. God reveals his end-time salvation through and will soon consummate his end-time salvation in Jesus Christ (Rev 1:1–3, 19).

3. That end-time salvation includes God's everlasting kingdom supplanting all rebel kingdoms (Rev 1:2, 5; cf. Dan 2:28–45).

4. God's final coming to consummate the end-time salvation seems closely connected with Jesus' coming (Rev 1:4, 7, 8).

5. The aim of revealing the end-time salvation in the present age is to keep the church persevering in humble obedience to Christ until his arrival to close the age (Rev 1:3, 4, 6b, 9–11).

These key themes prepare the reader to understand Rev 1:7, but we must take yet another step in our study to determine how John's use of Zech 12:10 aligns with and develops these key themes.

STEP THREE: THE PIERCED ONE'S SECOND ADVENT IN REV 1:7

We must now examine Rev 1:7 itself, in order to determine how John's use of Zech 12:10 develops what Jesus' coming is. Essentially, four main elements stand out in Rev 1:7, namely, Jesus coming (Rev 1:7a), every eye beholding (Rev 1:7b), all tribes mourning (Rev 1:7c), and the Amen resounding (Rev 1:7d). Each of the four main elements will receive treatment below.

Jesus Coming (Rev 1:7a)

The first element to address is Jesus coming: ἰδοὺ ἔρχεται μετὰ τῶν νεφελῶν ("behold, he is coming with the clouds"). That John names Jesus in Rev 1:5a, directs doxology to Jesus in Rev 1:5b-6, and recalls the piercing of Jesus in Rev 1:7b (cf. Rev 1:5b, 18), all clarify that Jesus is the one coming with the clouds. However, answering when Jesus comes has become a matter of debate. Since the present tense of ἔρχομαι leaves the matter ambiguous,[29] context must decide.

Some limit Jesus' coming to a heavenly event, as Dan 7:13 envisions "one like a son of man" only being presented before the Ancient of Days. Such interpreters also tend to associate Jesus' coming with Jerusalem's destruction in 70 CE.[30] However, the interpretation of Dan

---

29. Grammatically, one may translate ἔρχεται as a progressive present ("he is coming right now") or a futuristic present ("he is soon going to come" or "he is coming"). Cf. Wallace, *Grammar*, 518-19, 535-37.

30. See, e.g., Chilton, *Days of Vengeance*, 64-66; Gentry, *Before Jerusalem Fell*, 121-32. According to this view, Rev 1:7 supports a coming in 70 CE, since Zech 12:10-14 envisages a setting where only Jews mourn over the judgment befalling them. Jesus' coming may certainly entail judgment for the Jews who reject their Messiah (see more below), but Zech 12 is a prophecy about God saving Jerusalem from the nations (Zech 12:1-9), strengthening the house of David (Zech 12:8), and causing the Jews' repentance (Zech 12:10-14), which hardly represents the situation in 70 CE. So also Beale, *Revelation*, 26. Moreover, to limit the mourning to Jews alive in 70 CE does not recognize the textual indicators that John is appropriating Zech 12:10 in a universalizing manner (see further discussion below). Also, Dan 7:19-27

7:19–27 and John's further clarification of the same end-time events in Rev 19–20,[31] indicate that the heavenly presentation in Dan 7:13 is only part of the story. Indeed, the heavenly enthronement that Dan 7:13–14 depicts will eventually manifest itself in an earthly defeat of and reign over the four beastly kingdoms (Dan 7:11–12, 22, 27).[32] That Jesus comes with the clouds in heaven does not mean that he will never come with the clouds to earth (cf. Mark 13:26; Acts 1:9–11). Moreover, the fact that every human eye will witness his coming (cf. Rev 1:7b) seems to preclude a strictly heavenly coming. More likely is that John combines Dan 7:13 with Zech 12:10, because the coming of the "son of man" figure explains how every eye will eventually see the one who was also pierced. That is, the one wretchedly pierced now comes with royal power to culminate God's heavenly kingdom on earth.

Others have understood Jesus' coming in Rev 1:7 as progressive. Based on Jesus' conditional comings within history (e.g., Rev 2:16; 3:11) and Jesus' final coming at the end of history (e.g., Rev 22:7, 12, 20), Beale views Jesus' coming as a "process occurring throughout history; the so-called 'second coming' is actually a final coming concluding the whole process of comings."[33] However, even without minimizing the implications of Jesus' present reign, Jauhiainen argues that "the six other instances [of the 'I am coming' formula] clearly refer to [Jesus'] final coming," and "Beale's view also militates against John's overall emphasis

---

envisages an end-time situation where the saints of God enjoy victory in the exalted Son of Man's consummated and earthly kingdom. That earthly kingdom transpires with the return of Jesus (cf. Rev 19–20), not with the fall of Jerusalem. Additionally, rather than an invisible coming in 70 CE, as proponents of the 70 CE view suggest, Jesus' coming in Rev 1:7 is clearly visible to all: ὄψεται αὐτὸν πᾶς ὀφθαλμός ("every eye will see him"). One further argument is that the past view of Jesus' coming dates Revelation prior to 70 CE, but others have sufficiently demonstrated that "no compelling reason exists to reject Irenaeus's testimony [in *Adversus Haereses* 5.30.3] to the date [being at the end of the reign of Domitian]." Collins, "Dating," 33–45; Giesen, *Offenbarung*, 41–42; Beale, *Revelation*, 4–27.

31. See especially Hamilton, *With the Clouds*, 212–20.

32. See Hamilton, "Appreciation," 68–69; Hamilton, *With the Clouds*, 90–93, 135–54.

33. Beale, *Revelation*, 198, following Brütsch, *La Clarté de l'Apocalypse*, 31.

on the imminent consummation of God's kingdom, which would leave little time for repeated local comings."[34]

Moreover, several observations demonstrate that John's emphasis in Rev 1:7 itself is on the future, consummating arrival of Jesus Christ.[35] One, Dan 7 envisages an eschatological horizon wherein the "son of man" figure's heavenly rule eventually manifests itself in his earthly rule together with the saints (Dan 7:19–27; cf. Rev 19–20).[36] Two, the only other occasion where John describes the "one like a son of man" (ὅμοιον υἱὸν ἀνθρώπου) appearing with a cloud (νεφέλη) comes in Rev 14:14, a context that describes Jesus' return at the end of the age to initiate the final harvest for judgment.[37] To clarify, John alludes to the "one like a son of man" in Rev 1:13 as well. However, the emphasis in Rev 1:13 seems to be Jesus' present heavenly rule ensuring the manifestation of his future earthly rule, which John later describes in Rev 14:14 using the similar cloud imagery already used in Rev 1:7. Three, when read in light of the universal effect of Jesus' coming and the similar vocabulary used elsewhere in passages where Jesus' final arrival is more apparent (i.e., Rev 22:7, 12, 20; cf. 16:15), the future tense verbs (i.e., ὄψεται and κόψονται) seem indicative of Jesus' final, second coming.

---

34. Jauhiainen, *Use of Zechariah*, 148n40. Cf. Merkle, "Imminence," 279–92.

35. So also Ladd, *Revelation*, 28; Morris, *Revelation*, 49; Aune, *Revelation*, 59; Giesen, *Offenbarung*, 79; Mounce, *Revelation*, 50; Keener, *Revelation*, 72; Kistemaker, *Revelation*, 86–87; Johnson, *Triumph*, 52–53; Prigent, *Apocalypse*, 122; Osborne, *Revelation*, 69; Hamilton, *Revelation*, 38; Koester, *Revelation*, 219; Thomas and Macchia, *Revelation*, 78; Hoskins, *Revelation*, 54. Cf. Bauckham, *Theology of Revelation*, 63–64. Also significant is that Justin Martyr used Zech 12:10 (sometimes alongside Dan 7:13) as one of his primary texts to explain the second advent of Christ. E.g., see Justin, *Dial.* 14.8; 32.2; 1 *Apol.* 52.10–12 and the careful treatment by Skarsaune, *Proof from Prophecy*, 78, 154–56, 311. Justin's hope for the repentance and conversion of a few Jews at Jesus' Parousia, which he bases on Zech 12:10–12, will differ from the way I treat "all the tribes of the earth" mourning (see the discussion below). Still, I find it significant that Justin, who was connected with the community of John the apostle in Ephesus and who was familiar with the revelation John received (see Justin, *Dial.* 81.4), uses the same biblical tradition present in Rev 1:7 to speak of the second and public advent of Jesus.

36. Again, see Hamilton, *With the Clouds*, 90–93, 135–54.

37. So also Beale, *Revelation*, 770–72; Hultberg, "Messianic Exegesis," 101–4. That the ὅμοιον υἱὸν ἀνθρώπου in Rev 14:14 is not another angel but Jesus, see Reynolds, *Apocalyptic Son of Man*, 83–85.

The Pierced One's Second Redeeming Advent

Four, ὁ ἐρχόμενος ("he who is coming") appears in Rev 1:4 and 1:8 as part of the three-fold formula describing God/Yahweh (cf. Rev 4:8). The title seems reminiscent of the way God revealed himself in the OT as the one coming to save and to judge in a final, eschatological day.[38] Inserted between the two appearances of ὁ ἐρχόμενος in Rev 1:4 and 1:8 is the "coming" (ἔρχεται) of Jesus in Rev 1:7.[39] Indeed, the fact that Rev 11:15–18 equates the arrival of the Lord's kingdom with the arrival of his Christ's kingdom, suggests that John envisages God's future coming as being one and the same with Christ's future coming.[40]

Five, the announcement of Jesus' coming in Rev 1:7 receives further confirmation by τὸ ἄλφα καὶ τὸ ὦ ("the Alpha and the Omega") in Rev 1:8. The unique title receives further clarification as ἡ ἀρχὴ καὶ τὸ τέλος ("the beginning and the end") and ὁ πρῶτος καὶ ὁ ἔσχατος ("the first and the last") in Rev 21:6 and Rev 22:13. Such clarifications link the divine title in Rev 1:8 to passages in Isaiah that distinguish Yahweh from the nations and their idols. Unlike the nations and their idols, Yahweh, as "the first and the last" (Isa 41:4; 44:6; 48:12),[41] knows the future before it takes place and creates the future by his sovereign word (Isa 44:7–9, 18–19; 48:3, 6–8, 11–16; cf. 41:22–24; 42:9; 43:9b; 45:21;

---

38. E.g., see Isa 40:10; 66:15; Zech 14:5. Cf. also the treatment of Hab 2:3–4 LXX by Heb 10:37: "For, 'Yet a little while, and the coming one [ὁ ἐρχόμενος] will come and will not delay.'"

39. Arguing that ἔρχεται is better understood as a futuristic present is Thompson, *Apocalypse*, 34–35.

40. McDonough, *YHWH at Patmos*, 216–17, 233; Gradl, "Buch Und Brief," 421. As further support for understanding Jesus' coming in Rev 1:7 as primarily future, Bauckham argues that the end of the prologue (i.e., Rev 1:8) and the beginning of the epilogue (i.e., Rev 22:13) are "both preceded by an announcement of the Parousia (1:7: 'Behold, he is coming . . . '; 22:12: 'Behold, I am coming . . . ')." Bauckham, *Theology of Revelation*, 57.

41. For Isa 41:4 the title in Hebrew is אֲנִי יְהוָה רִאשׁוֹן וְאֶת־אַחֲרֹנִים אֲנִי־הוּא ("I am Yahweh, the first and the last, I am he"), with the LXX rendering the following translation: ἐγὼ θεὸς πρῶτος καὶ εἰς τὰ ἐπερχόμενα ἐγώ εἰμι ("I God, the first and for all things to come, I am"). For Isa 44:6 the title in Hebrew is אֲנִי רִאשׁוֹן וַאֲנִי אַחֲרוֹן ("I am the first and I am the last"), with the LXX rendering the following translation: ἐγὼ πρῶτος καὶ ἐγὼ μετὰ ταῦτα ("I am first and I am after these things"). For Isa 48:12 the title in Hebrew is אֲנִי רִאשׁוֹן אַף אֲנִי אַחֲרוֹן ("I am the first even [more] I am the last"), with the LXX rendering the following translation: ἐγώ εἰμι πρῶτος καὶ ἐγώ εἰμι εἰς τὸν αἰῶνα ("I am first and I am forever").

46:10).⁴² Such an emphasis on God's ability to know and create the future would also point to a future coming of Jesus in Rev 1:7. The Alpha and the Omega is once again telling the end from the beginning and confirming Jesus' future coming with his sovereign word.

Six, Jesus alludes to Dan 7:13 as well as Zech 12:10–14 in Matt 24:30–31.⁴³ The passage certainly stands as one of the most difficult to interpret, especially since Jesus mingles prophecy regarding Jerusalem's destruction in 70 CE with prophecy regarding the close of the entire inter-advent age. Some have attempted to explain Matt 24:30–31 as solely a reference to Jerusalem's destruction in 70 CE,⁴⁴ but others have demonstrated serious weaknesses with that interpretation.⁴⁵ On

---

42. I am indebted to Paul Hoskins for providing the insight into how Isaiah's use of the title "the first and the last" contrasts Yahweh with the false gods of the nations in the manner specified here. Cf. also Stuhlmueller, "'First and Last,'" 495–511; Williamson, "First and Last," 95–108. While his point is to address questions of literary coherency/dependency with Isa 1–39 in general, and Isa 8:23 in particular, Williamson notes the polemical thrust behind "the first and the last." Williamson, "First and Last," 100–101. Likewise, see Oswalt, *Isaiah 40–66*, 171; Motyer, *Isaiah*, 252–53, 277, 303. Stuhlmueller's article tries to determine whether a relationship exists between Yahweh as "Creator" and Yahweh as "First and Last." He concludes that they seem separated, with one of his reasons stated as follows: "The reason for this unexpected separation is probably to be found in the fact that 'first and last' qualify predictions of the future." Stuhlmueller, "'First and Last,'" 204. Hoskins's remarks in a personal conversation helped me combine the polemical thrust with God's ability to predict the future and not simply with God's eternal existence (though the latter may also be implied).

43. After alluding to the personal arrival of the Son of Man along with the signs preceding his coming, Jesus explains, "Then will appear in heaven the sign of the Son of Man, and then all the tribes of the earth will mourn, and they will see the Son of Man coming [ἐρχόμενον] on the clouds of heaven with power and great glory. And he will send out his angels with a loud trumpet call, and they will gather his elect from the four winds, from one end of heaven to the other" (Matt 24:30–31). For the allusion to Dan 7:13 see Blomberg, "Matthew," 87–88. For the allusion to Zech 12:10–14, see Ham, *The Coming King*, 135–40.

44. E.g., following others, see Wright, *Victory*, 339–68.

45. See the extensive criticisms by Carson, *Matthew*, 552–55. France also holds to a fulfillment of Matt 24:30–31 in 70 CE, but acknowledges that the Gospel writers use Dan 7:13–14 to refer to three different stages in Jesus' work: "It was applied (a) to his exaltation to authority immediately after the resurrection, (b) to a manifestation of that authority in the lifetime of his contemporaries, and (c) to the culmination of the same authority in the final judgment." France, *Jesus and the OT*, 235. France then concludes, "Which of these three stages of application is here in view the context must decide." In my estimation, the context of Matt 24:30–31

The Pierced One's Second Redeeming Advent

the contrary, if one accepts that Jesus combines Dan 7:13 with Zech 12:10–14 in order to describe events surrounding his second coming,[46] then it seems reasonable to conclude that John is imitating Jesus when he does the same in Rev 1:7. Like the coming referenced in Rev 1:7, Matt 24:30–31 envisions Jesus' coming as public, visible, and having universal effects. Yet Matt 24:30–31 adds further details (e.g., angels, the trumpet blast) that the NT elsewhere associates with Jesus' final arrival to end the present, inter-advent age with judgment (e.g., Matt

---

suggests that the culmination of Jesus' authority in judgment is in view. (1) Matthew 24:27–28 explains Jesus' return, not as secret and hidden (per Matt 24:23–26), but as visible as lightning flashing and vultures circling (cf. with the visible judgment in Luke 17:22–37). So also Carson, *Matthew*, 565–66. See even France, *Matthew*, 911. France acknowledges the Parousia is in view in vv. 27–28 though not in vv. 30–31. (2) Matthew 24:29 describes the cosmic upheaval often characteristic of the Lord's final day of judgment (cf. Isa 13:9–11; Joel 2:31; Rev 6:12–17). See especially Adams, "Son of Man," 39–61; Adams, *Cosmic Catastrophe*, 133–82. Adams's 2005 article deals with the Olivet Discourse in Mark 13, but his 2007 work clarifies the parallels with Matt 24. (3) Matthew 24:30 describes the universal impact of the Son of Man's coming: "all the tribes of the earth will mourn" (cf. with πᾶσαι αἱ φυλαὶ τῆς γῆς in Gen 12:3; 28:14; Ps 72:17). (4) Some will argue that the temporal indicator in Matt 24:29, Εὐθέως δὲ μετὰ τὴν θλῖψιν τῶν ἡμερῶν ἐκείνων ("and immediately after the tribulation of those days"), limits the events of Matt 24:29–31 to Jerusalem's destruction in 70 CE, and that the coming of Jesus is invisible. However, Blomberg has shown how "the 'great tribulation' of which Jesus speaks begins with the events of 70 CE and continues until Christ's public return at the end of the age." See Blomberg, "Matthew," 88. (5) The question of ἡ γενεὰ αὕτη ("this generation") in Matt 24:34 will also lead others to restrict the events of Matt 24 to 70 CE, since πάντα ταῦτα ("all these things") must take place within the generation to whom Jesus is speaking. However, Blomberg also points out that πάντα ταῦτα in Matt 24:33 excludes Jesus' coming (cf. Matt 24:30–31), and, therefore, πάντα ταῦτα in Matt 24:34 must include all the events spanning the inter-advent age until Jesus' Parousia. Blomberg, "Matthew," 87. Moreover, see the studies by Lövestamm, *This Generation*; Nelson, "This Generation," 369–85. Building on Lövestamm, Nelson argues from a literary-critical perspective that "'this generation' (24:34) represents an evil class of people who will oppose Jesus' disciples until the day he returns." Nelson, "This Generation," 385.

46. See, e.g., Ridderbos, *Coming*, 477–510; Blomberg, *Matthew*, 363–65; Beasley-Murray, *Last Days*, 350–476; Carson, *Matthew*, 556–57. Also, based on linguistic similarities between Matthew's and Daniel's description of "the end" (cf. Dan 11:27, 29, 35, 40; Matt 24:6, 13, 14) and "what must soon take place" (cf. Dan 2:28–29, 45; Matt 24:6), Hamilton calls Matt 24 (along with Mark 13) "a commentary on what Daniel indicates about the consummation of the ages." See Hamilton, *With the Clouds*, 184.

13:41, 49; 16:27; 1 Thess 4:14-17; 2 Thess 1:7-10; Rev 19:11-16).⁴⁷ Such details would seem to prepare readers of the Christian canon to associate Jesus' coming with the clouds in Rev 1:7 with his final, second coming.⁴⁸ For all these reasons, therefore, the emphasis of Rev 1:7a appears to fall on Jesus' second advent.

Every Eye Beholding (Rev 1:7b)

The second element needing interpretation in Rev 1:7 is every eye beholding Jesus: καὶ ὄψεται αὐτὸν πᾶς ὀφθαλμὸς καὶ οἵτινες αὐτὸν ἐξεκέντησαν ("and every eye will see him, even those who pierced him"). The phrase πᾶς ὀφθαλμὸς ("every eye") appears nowhere else in Scripture, but similar imagery appears in Isaiah, wherein both Israel and the nations witness the universal glory of the Lord's eschatological judgment and/or salvation.⁴⁹ Zechariah 9:1b seems to sharpen the universal connotation of πᾶς ὀφθαλμὸς even further. Zechariah 9:1-8 envisions Yahweh judging the proud, self-reliant nations and yet still showing mercy to a remnant. Yahweh acts in judgment and mercy for the following reason: כִּי לַיהוָה עֵין אָדָם וְכֹל שִׁבְטֵי יִשְׂרָאֵל ("for to Yahweh [belongs] the eye of humanity, especially all the tribes of Israel").⁵⁰ That

---

47. Cf. Glasson, "Theophany," 259-62.

48. On the hermeneutical role of the canon for readers of Scripture, see the study by Spellman, *Canon*, 46-220.

49. Examples include the following: "then the glory of Yahweh shall be revealed, and all [כָל / πᾶσα] flesh shall see [וְרָאוּ / ὄψεται] it together ... " (Isa 40:5); " ... for eye to eye [עַיִן בְּעַיִן / ὀφθαλμοὶ πρὸς ὀφθαλμούς] they shall see [יִרְאוּ / ὄψονται] the return of Yahweh to Zion" (Isa 52:8); "all [כָל / πάντα] the ends of the earth shall see [וְרָאוּ / ὄψονται] the salvation of our God" (Isa 52:10); " ... the time is coming to gather all [כָל / πάντα] nations and tongues, and they shall see [וְרָאוּ / ὄψονται] my glory" (Isa 66:18).

50. The NASB translation renders Zech 9:1b, " ... for the eyes of men, especially of all the tribes of Israel, are toward the Lord." Likewise, see the translations by NIV and NET. Similar uses of ל prefixed to יהוה following כִּי in a verbless clause appear elsewhere and carry the sense we have adopted here (e.g., 1 Sam 2:8; 17:47; Pss 22:29 [ET 22:28]; 89:19 [ET 89:18]). The ESV opts for a different and much rarer (see *IBHS* 11.2.10) understanding of the prefixed ל: " ... for the Lord has an eye on mankind and on all the tribes of Israel." If taken in the latter sense, Zech 9:1 would be saying that the reason judgment is coming against the nations is that the Lord is watching the world. However, Petterson shows the strength of the translation provided above. See Petterson, *Zechariah*, 217-18.

is, both Israel and the nations owe God their total attention. Since Zech 9:1 initiates a parallel oracle to Zech 12,[51] John may be attempting to reflect the same universal imagery but now setting it within the context of Jesus' second coming.[52] Every eye belongs to Yahweh, and now every eye will turn to Yahweh in the second coming of Jesus, the Pierced One. As he did in John 19:37, John substitutes the pierced Jesus (i.e., αὐτὸν) for the pierced God of Zechariah's prophecy once again. Where Zech 12:10 expected them to look on God, the people look upon Jesus now in his second coming. Linking the pierced God with the pierced Jesus also furthers the aforementioned observation that John seems to equate God's coming with Jesus' coming.

John's universal referent also includes a subgroup. Taking the second καὶ in Rev 1:7b ascensively,[53] John includes οἵτινες αὐτὸν ἐξεκέντησαν ("even those who pierced him [i.e., Jesus]"). As noted by others before, it is difficult to limit the referent to Israel/Jews, as Zech 12:10 itself may suggest (i.e., "the house of David and the inhabitants of Jerusalem"), since Roman soldiers actually pierced Jesus (John 19:31, 34).[54] At the same time, it is also difficult to limit the referent to the Roman soldiers, since the Jews instigated Jesus' arrest, trial, crucifixion, and what happened to his body thereafter (John 18:3, 14, 31; 19:6–7, 31). Moreover, if the piercers are those present at the second coming of Jesus, a coming that involves the universal manifestation of his glory

---

51. Zechariah 9:1 and Zech 12:1 begin with מַשָּׂא דְבַר־יְהוָה ("the oracle of the word of the Lord"), dividing the structure of Zech 9–14 into two parts (i.e., Zech 9:1—11:17 and 12:1—14:21).

52. Cf. Devillers, "L'interprétation," 137. Devillers observes that the eschatological context of Revelation compels one to widen the population concerned as far as possible. He concludes, "C'est toute l'humanité aui *verra le Fils de l'Homme* venant avec les nuées du ciel" ("It is all humanity that *will see the Son of Man* coming with the clouds of heaven"). Italics are original to the author. Devillers, "L'interprétation," 137.

53. For the ascensive use of καί, see Wallace, *Grammar*, 670–71. Treating the piercers as a subgroup is also Hoskins, *Revelation*, 55.

54. See, e.g., Schuchard, *Scripture within Scripture*, 146–48; Kubiś, *Zechariah in John*, 194–216; Bynum, *Fourth Gospel*, 176–79. Also pertinent for the discussion is that John reports that only "one [εἷς] of the soldiers pierced [Jesus'] side with a spear" (John 19:34), but he preserves the plural ἐξεκέντησαν in John 19:37 and in Rev 1:7. One must say that John at least broadens the referent to include more than the one soldier who actually pierced Jesus.

Jesus as the Pierced One

to πᾶς ὀφθαλμὸς, then οἵτινες αὐτὸν ἐξεκέντησαν would seem to include a group extending beyond those who actually pierced Jesus' side. Far more likely, the referent is to those who are hostile to the Lord and his Christ in every age, whether belonging to Israel or to the nations.[55] Indeed, if it is characteristic for those belonging to the Beast's kingdom to shed the blood of God's people (e.g., Rev 11:7–10; 12:7; 16:6), then it would seem that the piercers who shed Jesus' blood refers to all who participate in the works that characterize the Beast's kingdom.[56] Understood in this manner, that is, as a collective referent for all who oppose Christ, John would be emphasizing that even the Lord's enemies will witness Jesus' second coming.[57]

By doing so, would John thereby prove unfaithful to Zech 12:10, which specifies the piercers as the house of David and the inhabitants of Jerusalem? To the contrary, John could maintain the original sense of Zech 12:10 while broadening the piercers to include the rest of the sinful world. Zechariah 12:10 belongs to an oracle concerning Israel (cf. Zech 12:1), but John is developing what the oracle implies for an audience extending beyond Israel to πᾶς ὀφθαλμὸς.[58] Vanhoye and Beale

---

55. So also Swete, *Apocalypse*, 9; Ladd, *Revelation*, 28; Morris, *Revelation*, 50; Mounce, *Revelation*, 51; Kistemaker, *Revelation*, 86; Osborne, *Revelation*, 70. Beale draws a different conclusion about the nature of the mourning than the present study will draw, but he still agrees that "those who mourn are not those who literally crucified Jesus but those who are guilty of rejecting him." Beale, *Revelation*, 197. Cf. the point here with the early church's understanding of Ps 2:1–4 in Acts 4:23–30.

56. For this point, I am indebted to some personal correspondence with Paul Hoskins. Later, I found his commentary on the piercers/mourners in Rev 1:7 helpful as well: "In Revelation, John sets forth two kingdoms, the kingdom of God and the kingdom of the Beast. 'Every tribe' can refer to the numerous followers of God (5:9; 7:9) or to the followers of the Beast (13:7, also 11:9). In Rev 11–20, the Dragon, the Beast, the Harlot, and their kingdom are presented as persecutors and murderers of the people of God. In 11:8, Jesus was crucified in the Beast's city, the Harlot of Rev 17. His piercing would thus be associated with the Beast and his people. Therefore, in Rev 1:7, it would appear likely that John is viewing the piercers of Christ as the people of the Beast." Hoskins, *Revelation*, 56.

57. Thus, while John could be referring to both the redeemed and the rebellious community together witnessing Jesus' return (i.e., "every eye"), those who still stand as enemies of Jesus seem to be the focus in the latter phrase. Such a view seems to align with 2 Thess 1:7–10, wherein believers are expected to marvel at Jesus' return while the enemies of Jesus suffer judgment at his return.

58. The context surrounding God's covenant people looking upon the Pierced

The Pierced One's Second Redeeming Advent

demonstrate that such a move belongs to a pattern of interpretation in Revelation called universalization, wherein John applies "to the world what the OT applied only to Israel or to other entities."[59] In this particular case, piercing God is the sinful act in Zech 12:10 over which sinful Israel was expected to mourn and from which sinful Israel was expected to repent. In the book of Revelation, however, John sometimes applies sinful actions once committed by sinful Israel in the OT to a group that includes sinners in general (e.g., Rev 2:14, 20; 6:8).[60] If such a pattern also holds true in Rev 1:7, then the sinners from Israel

One in Zech 12:10 includes God's eschatological judgment on the rebel nations (Zech 12:1–9), even a day when Yahweh himself would personally return to war against the nations and establish his universal kingdom on the earth (Zech 14:2–5, 9). Thus, a universal beholding of Yahweh in the second coming of Jesus could even fit within a contextual reading of Zech 12–14.

59. Vanhoye, "L'utilisation," 446–67; Beale, *Revelation*, 91–92.

60. In Rev 2:14, John compares the teaching of the Nicolaitans to the teaching of Balaam, "who taught Balak to put a stumbling block before the sons of Israel, so that they might eat food sacrificed to idols and practice sexual immorality," an allusion to Num 25:1–9 and Num 31:16. Cf. Beale and McDonough, "Revelation," 1094. In Rev 2:20, John says that some in the church "tolerate that woman Jezebel, who calls herself a prophetess and is teaching sexual immorality and to eat food sacrificed to idols," an allusion to 1 Kgs 16:31–32, 1 Kgs 21:25–26, and 2 Kgs 9:22. Cf. Beale and McDonough, "Revelation," 1095. In both cases, what once referred to sinful Israel, John applies to those within the church whose sinful practices align with the rebellious world (see Rev 9:20–21) and from which they must repent (Rev 2:16, 21). John envisions time for the sinful people within the church to repent, but refusing repentance would prove they do not actually belong to God's kingdom and priesthood but still belong to the world who eventually sides with and worships the beast (cf. Rev 9:20–21 with Rev 16:2, 9–11). As a further example, Rev 6:8 seems to allude to Ezek 14:12–23 (though see Jer 14:12 as well). Cf. Beale and McDonough, "Revelation," 1103. Wherein the fourfold judgment of sword, famine, pestilence, and beasts seems to fall against sinful Israel in Ezek 14:12–23 (cf. Ezek 5:5–17), John broadens the judgment to fall on a fourth of humanity. This example from Rev 6:8 becomes especially relevant for the present discussion since it occurs in connection with the universal judgment Christ exercises at his Parousia. These examples seem to suggest a pattern in Revelation, wherein the actions of or judgments against sinful Israel become associated with the actions of or judgments against sinners in general. Again, I am indebted to Paul Hoskins for helping me see this connection in Revelation. Also, commenting on Armageddon in Rev 16:16 in light of OT passages such as Zech 12:10–11, Osborne concludes, "The force would be that those who stand against God (broadening apostate Israel to depict all the nations, a method used often in the Apocalypse) will mourn as they face God's judgment." Osborne, *Revelation*, 596.

who pierced God in Zech 12:10 could represent sinners from the entire world who oppose God in general.[61] As I will attempt to demonstrate below with respect to the tribes mourning, these universal implications of Jesus' second coming will also force John to a reversed appropriation of Zech 12:10. To that we now turn.

All the Tribes Mourning (Rev 1:7c)

The third element in Rev 1:7 is all the tribes mourning: καὶ κόψονται ἐπ' αὐτὸν πᾶσαι αἱ φυλαὶ τῆς γῆς ("and all the tribes of the earth shall mourn on account of him"). John's universalization appears to continue in that Zech 12:12–14 refers to a mourning spreading to all clans within Israel while John mentions "all the tribes of the earth [τῆς γῆς]" mourning. The phrase πᾶσαι αἱ φυλαὶ τῆς γῆς ("all the tribes of the earth") occurs three times in the LXX, each one anticipating God blessing all nations through the Abrahamic covenant/seed (Gen 12:3; 28:14; Ps 71:17).[62] Using the same vocabulary with only slight changes, Zech 14:17 threatens God's judgment upon πασῶν τῶν φυλῶν τῆς γῆς if they fail to worship Yahweh the King.[63] Like the previous three references related to the Abrahamic covenant, πασῶν τῶν φυλῶν in Zech 14:17 is equivalent to πάντων τῶν ἐθνῶν ("all the nations") in Zech 14:16 and 14:19. However, what distinguishes Zech 14:17 from the first three references is that it expects severe judgment to fall on πασῶν τῶν φυλῶν τῆς γῆς for refusing Yahweh's kingship when he arrives to establish his earthly kingdom.

What do these observations mean for John's allusion to the mourning of Zech 12:12–14 in Rev 1:7c? They demonstrate that John is clearly universalizing the mourning by following a standard universal referent from the OT, and that one need not limit πασῶν τῶν φυλῶν to ethnic Israel. Nor is it necessary to limit τῆς γῆς to the land of Israel.[64] Using the

---

61. Likewise, Koester observes that "Taken literally, those who pierced Jesus would be those who carried out his crucifixion (cf. John 19:37). But Revelation broadens this to encompass all of Jesus' adversaries, including those of John's own time (cf. 1 Cor 2:8; Col 2:14–15; Giesen)." Koester, *Revelation*, 229.

62. Cf. Bauckham, *Climax*, 323–26.

63. Koester, *Revelation*, 219, adds Ezek 20:23 as another example.

64. Such an interpretation does not minimize the Lord's purposes to deliver ethnic Israel in the eschaton (i.e., "on that day"). See, e.g., the concerns for ethnic

The Pierced One's Second Redeeming Advent

plural of φυλή ("tribe") as a universal referent also appears elsewhere in Revelation to identify either the redeemed community (e.g., Rev 5:9; 7:9) or the rebellious community (e.g., Rev 11:9; 13:7; 14:6).

The previous observations also demonstrate that one should exercise caution before equating πᾶσαι αἱ φυλαὶ τῆς γῆς so strictly with the redeemed and explaining their mourning as repentance. Again, as it does in Zech 14:17, φυλή in Revelation can also refer to the rebellious community (Rev 11:9; 13:7; 14:6). The question is which community does πᾶσαι αἱ φυλαὶ τῆς γῆς represent in Rev 1:7c, especially if Jesus' coming issues the occasion of their mourning? G. B. Caird, Richard Bauckham, and others identify πᾶσαι αἱ φυλαὶ τῆς γῆς with the repentant nations who join themselves to the Lord in fulfillment of God's promise to Abraham.[65] Strengthening this interpretation is the fact that Zech 12:10–14 anticipates God's Spirit moving the entire covenant people to heartfelt contrition over the Pierced One and to desperate pleas for mercy.[66] By universalizing the prophecy, John would then be including all the peoples of the earth within "the role of repentant Israel."[67]

However, while agreeing that John universalizes Zech 12:12–14, several factors lead me to favor the interpretation that πᾶσαι αἱ φυλαὶ

Israel in Luter, "Preaching Texts," 23–47. As chapter 5 will demonstrate, John's use of Zech 12:10 shows that the eschatological salvation of ethnic Israel occurs in tandem with the salvation of Gentiles throughout the entire inter-advent period until Jesus returns. For complementary observations from Rom 11, see Merkle, "Romans 11," 709–21; Gentry and Wellum, *Kingdom*, 499–501.

65. Caird, *Revelation*, 18–19; Bauckham, *Climax*, 319–22; Beale, *Revelation*, 196–97; Osborne, *Revelation*, 69–70; Blount, *Revelation*, 37–38. Osborne also lists Sweet, Kraft, Harrington, Boring, and Wall. For more substantial critiques of Bauckham's proposal that the conversion of the nations is the center of Revelation's message, see Jauhiainen, "Climax?," 105–9; Schnabel, "Future of the Nations," 243–71.

66. The two images of an "only child" and a "firstborn" in Zech 12:10 recall the account of Abraham and Isaac (Gen 22:2, 12, 16), or possibly God killing the firstborn in Egypt (Exod 4:22, 23; 11:5; 12:12, 29–30). In either case, Zechariah would be depicting the corporate mourning as one of great sorrow. In Zech 12:11–14, the mourning progressively spreads throughout the covenant people, moving from the city of Jerusalem (Zech 12:11) to the royal line (Zech 12:12; cf. 2 Sam 5:14; 1 Chr 3:4; Luke 3:31), the priestly line (Zech 12:13; cf. Exod 6:17; Num 3:21), and then to everyone else (Zech 12:14).

67. Beale, *Revelation*, 197.

τῆς γῆς represent the rebellious community who will mourn in dread at Jesus' return in judgment.[68] First, as demonstrated above, Rev 1:7a pictures Jesus' Parousia. When expounded elsewhere in Revelation, Jesus' Parousia enacts an immediate gathering of the redeemed who already belong to the Lamb (Rev 14:4, 14–16; 19:14)[69] and an immediate judgment upon the rebellious community with no further chance for repentance (e.g., Rev 6:16–17; 14:17–20; 19:15–21). Indeed, secondly, the rebellious community would not repent even if they were given the opportunity (Rev 9:20–21; 16:9; cf. 22:11). Yet the redeemed community responds to Jesus' coming by practicing repentance before Jesus arrives (Rev 2:5, 16, 22; 3:3, 19), which then prepares them to celebrate the final arrival of Jesus' kingdom rather than mourn (e.g., Rev 15:2–4; 19:1–3, 6–8).[70] Third, the prologue indicates that God's everlasting kingdom would supplant all rebel kingdoms (Rev 1:2; cf. Dan 2:28–29; 7; 10–12) with the coming of God/Jesus (Rev 1:4, 7, 8). Viewing the mourning negatively in the sense of deep regret and dread would seem consistent with Jesus' kingdom finally usurping their evil empires and leaving them exposed to his scrutiny and wrath (cf. Rev 6:16–17).

68. Interpreters who view the mourning in a negative sense include, e.g., Lenski, *Revelation*, 50–51; Ladd, *Revelation*, 29; Morris, *Revelation*, 50; Aune, *Revelation*, 59–60; Mounce, *Revelation*, 51; Kistemaker, *Revelation*, 87; Smalley, *Revelation*, 37–38; Hamilton, *Revelation*, 38. Osborne sees deliberate ambiguity and a double meaning in Rev 1:7, where some respond in repentance and others in dread. Osborne, *Revelation*, 69–71. Taking a more nuanced position is Hultberg, "Messianic Exegesis," 101–4. With Bauckham, Hultberg sees the inclusivism of the nations, and, in that sense, treats the mourning in a positive sense. However, he tempers the inclusivism with an allusion to Zech 9:1, which speaks of God's judgment against the nations. He writes, " . . . the parousia is a moment of terror for all the hostile nations of the earth, including unrepentant Jews, whom John views as enemies of the new people of God. In this case the lamentation is not in repentance over Christ's fateful death but in dread of his magisterial coming." Hultberg, "Messianic Exegesis," 104. Cf. Keener, *Revelation*, 73; Boxall, *Revelation*, 34–35. Keener and Boxall also acknowledge the ambiguity.

69. Cf. also Matt 24:30–31; 1 Thess 4:14–17; 2 Thess 1:7–10. When taken together, these passages seem to indicate that only the elect are saved at Jesus' coming while the rest of the nations are immediately judged.

70. All this is not to deny that some from among all peoples will repent as the church preaches the gospel prior to Jesus' coming (e.g., Matt 24:14; Rom 1:5; 16:27), but only that Jesus' coming removes any further opportunity for repentance. See also the critique of Bauckham's treatment of "all the nations" from Rev 15 in Rogers, "Zechariah in Revelation," 168.

One key objection to viewing πᾶσαι αἱ φυλαὶ τῆς γῆς as the rebellious community and their mourning as negative is that Zechariah's prophecy clearly envisions the mourning as something positive. To say that John views the mourning as something negative would seem to suggest that John dismisses the original sense of Zech 12:10–14. However, viewing the mourning as negative can still be consistent with the original sense of Zech 12:10–14, if one allows for a reversed appropriation[71] in light of Jesus' second coming. Further clarification ensues.

As chapter 5 will seek to demonstrate further, John sees a period in redemptive history when God does pour out his Spirit upon sinful Israel and the nations and causes their repentance (e.g., John 7:39; 14:26; 15:26; 16:7–14).[72] Jesus inaugurated that period when he was historically pierced (or "glorified" in John's Gospel), and the blood and water flowing from his side signified the outpouring of God's cleansing work by the Spirit (John 19:34; cf. 20:22–23).[73] When Jew and Gentile alike who receive God's Spirit look upon the Pierced One rightly by faith, God establishes them as his covenant people.[74] In that sense, John concurs

---

71. The type of interpretation I have in mind is also called an "inverted use" of the OT. See Beale, *Handbook*, 92–93. Beale also lists examples of John's inverted use of the OT within the book of Revelation in Beale, *Revelation*, 94–96. In addition to Beale's examples, another example of reversed appropriation appears in 1 Cor 15:55. For Paul, Jesus' final victory over death transforms the invitation for death to conquer Israel in Hos 13:14 into a taunt against death as it loses all power against the redeemed. By reversing the meaning, Paul does not undermine God's word of judgment in Hos 13:14 when he turns it into the taunt. Rather, he sees the judgment of death defeated in Jesus' cross and the final resurrection.

72. Notice especially in these references how the sending of the Spirit comes in conjunction with the glorification of Jesus, a glorification that encompasses the "hour" of his death, resurrection, and exaltation/return to the Father.

73. On the water from Jesus' side, see pp. 113–14 above under the section titled "The Divine Mission of Jesus." Building on studies by I. de la Potterie and Adam Kubiś, we concluded that John's use of Zech 12:10 just following the outpoured water and blood from Jesus' pierced side in John 19:34 seems to evoke the wider context of Zech 13:1, wherein God opens a fountain for cleansing from sin. See, e.g., de la Potterie, "Il Costato Trafitto," 625–49; Kubiś, *Zechariah in John*, 191–94. As also noted from John's Gospel, it is the Spirit who cleanses from sin and gives eternal life by applying the benefits of Jesus' death to his people. Likewise, Hoskins, "Deliverance," 298.

74. Further support for such an assertion will come in chapter 5, but it is sufficient at this point to note several places where John teaches his readers how to look on Jesus, the Pierced One, rightly. In each case, "seeing" is equivalent to believing.

Jesus as the Pierced One

with the positive sense of the mourning in Zech 12:10–14.[75] However, the redemptive-historical period in which Israel and the nations have opportunity to repent ends at Jesus' second coming.[76] Already we have observed that John seems to understand the repeated eschatological "day" of Zech 12 receiving its fulfillment in two episodes,[77] the first episode occurring in the death of Jesus (John 19:37) and the second in the return of Jesus (Rev 1:7). At the return of Jesus, the period for the rebellious community to repent has ended. All who remain from Israel and the nations who did not find repentance will face judgment (e.g., John 5:24, 27, 29; Rev 6:16–17; 14:7, 10; 19:15; cf. 1 John 4:17). These new circumstances force John to reverse the type of mourning that Jesus' second coming will effect among the rebellious.[78] Such an

---

E.g., one must believe in Jesus to escape death, just as the Israelites looked upon the bronze serpent (John 3:14–15; cf. Num 21:9). Only by looking on the Son and believing in him does one gain eternal life (John 6:40). The blind man already sees Jesus rightly, prior to his second encounter with Jesus (John 9:37–38). Whoever believes and sees Jesus also believes and sees that the Father sent him (John 12:44–45). The correct look, then, is the look in faith upon Jesus, the Pierced One. Some physically see Jesus, but by looking in unbelief, the persons prove they are in fact blind (John 6:36; 9:39–41; 15:24). Thus, the Fourth Gospel prepares the readers to look upon Jesus' crucifixion in faith, not unbelief. For this reason, John's testimony in John 19:35 deliberately connects what he has seen with what his readers should believe.

75. John, a Jew, was himself an onlooker (John 19:35), who also mourned Jesus' death (John 16:20, 22), and who would also receive the outpoured Spirit (John 20:22). However, John does not look upon the pierced Jesus like those who seem to look with terror in Rev 1:7. Instead, John gained the joy of eternal life by looking rightly upon the Pierced One. Only those with faith see the pierced Jesus rightly, and say with Thomas, "my Lord and my God!" (John 20:28). Moreover, the episode with Thomas in John 20:24–29 shows that all generations who look upon Jesus rightly in this present age may belong to the covenant community. On the last sentence, cf. also Menken, "Textual Form," 508.

76. That John envisions a limited time for repentance seems evident not only in his letters to the seven churches (e.g., Rev 2:5, 16, 21; 3:3, 19), but also in how those who side with the Beast fail to repent before the day of wrath finally arrives (Rev 9:20–21; 16:9, 11).

77. See the section titled "The Divine Mission of Jesus" on pp. 111–19 above.

78. The emphasis in the Fourth Gospel, however, is different. There is no need for a reversed appropriation; for there John reflects on the OT passage with respect to the Pierced One's first coming. The divine presence in Jesus was revealed through his humble state: God became a man to suffer a cross for enemies. At the second coming, the divine presence in Jesus will be revealed through his glorious state: God, as a man, will conquer and judge all his remaining enemies.

interpretive move by John, if indeed present, may even grow out of his reflection on the broader context of Zech 12–14, wherein God destroys the nations when he comes to establish his earthly rule (Zech 12:1–9; 14:2–5). If John equates God's coming with Jesus' coming, characterizing the mourning as negative for πᾶσαι αἱ φυλαὶ τῆς γῆς seems to align with the awful judgment that God/Jesus exercises when his kingdom arrives fully.

The Amen Resounding (Rev 1:7d)

The fourth and last element in Rev 1:7 is the Amen resounding: ναί, ἀμήν ("Even so, Amen!"). The vision of Rev 1:7a–c merits a response from both the reader and the hearers of the prophecy (cf. Rev 1:3).[79] Often appearing at the end of a doxology in the NT, ἀμήν signals a strong affirmation (e.g., Rom 11:36; 16:27; Gal 1:5; 1 Tim 1:17; 6:16; Jude 25). Adding the particle ναί strengthens the affirmation further. In Rev 1:5b–6 (simply ἀμήν), John led the church to affirm what Jesus' past redeeming work inaugurated for God's people and what Jesus' present reign sustains. Now, at the end of Rev 1:7, the church must further affirm (ναί plus ἀμήν) what Jesus' future coming will consummate. In light of the way John uses Zech 12:10–14 and Dan 7:13 to illuminate the nature of Jesus' coming, the church must affirm that the anticipated return of Yahweh in judgment will soon reach full expression in the universal manifestation of Jesus' kingship on earth. In this manner, Rev 1:7 anticipates a main thrust of the entire book, wherein God's heavenly kingdom will soon reach full disclosure in the personal arrival of Jesus in judgment.[80] This too the church must solemnly affirm and obediently await.

---

79. Regarding the liturgical dialogue between reader and hearer, see Vanni, "Un Esempio," 453–67; Aune, *Revelation*, 56.

80. Ladd refers to Rev 1:7 as "the theme of the book." Ladd, *Revelation*, 28. Also Luter, based on what he discerns are a series of literary chiasms, argues that Dan 7:13 and Zech 12:10 "are signaling in the introductory segment of the book that the remainder of the Apocalypse is, at least to some significant extent, an exposition of how Dan 7:13 and Zech 12:10 will be fulfilled at the end of the age." Luter, "Preaching Texts," 23. Cf. also Herghelegiu, *Siehe, Er Kommt*, 87; Jauhiainen, *Use of Zechariah*, 142–43; Haukaas, "Revelation 1:7–8," 40–153.

JESUS AS THE PIERCED ONE

We might summarize the four elements of Rev 1:7 in the following manner. Using Zech 12:10–14 (alongside Dan 7:13), John reassures the church (Rev 1:7d) that Jesus' Parousia will soon consummate Yahweh's eschatological mission, thus closing the inter-advent age (Rev 1:7a). The return will be universal in scope, as every eye beholds the one once pierced (Rev 1:7b). The return will also be awful in affect as the divine authority Jesus bears and the final judgment Jesus exercises cause the remaining rebellious community to wail in terror (Rev 1:7c). How John's use of Zech 12:10–14 in Rev 1:7 contributes to his broader theological agenda in the book of Revelation still needs further development. Onward, then, to step four.

STEP FOUR: THEOLOGICAL CONTRIBUTION OF ZECH 12:10–14 TO JESUS' IDENTITY AND MISSION

We need to determine how John's use of Zech 12:10–14 contributes to his biblical-theological presentation of Jesus' identity and mission in the book of Revelation.[81] Two key contributions will receive attention in the section below, namely, the divine identity and the divine mission of Jesus in Revelation. Theological contributions stemming from what unfolded above in relation to the onlookers must wait until chapter 5, where I will seek to determine how the entire drama from Zech 12:10 to John 19:37 to Rev 1:7 impacts John's present readers and their own mission to the nations. Until then, we move first to Jesus' divine identity.

The Divine Identity of Jesus in Revelation

Once again John's use of Zech 12:10 appears to align with his conviction that Jesus is God.[82] Whereas in Zech 12:10 the people look upon

---

81. Regarding the significant influence of Zechariah's prophecy on John's message in Revelation, see especially the observations and tables by Jauhiainen, *Use of Zechariah*, 2, 100, 130. In addition to the OT allusions marked by UBS4 and NA27, Jauhiainen also observes that the scholarly literature has shown that "Revelation alludes to more than three-quarters of Zechariah" (2).

82. Assuming that John is the common author behind the Fourth Gospel and Revelation, it would seem odd that his theological convictions about Jesus being God would have changed between works. Nevertheless, by assessing whether John's theological convictions about Jesus being God persist in Revelation, we will stand in a better place to determine whether his use of Zech 12:10 in Rev 1:7 is similar

the pierced God, in Rev 1:7 the people look upon the returning Christ whom they once pierced. Gleaning such high Christology from Rev 1:7 seems warranted by the way John presents God's self-disclosure in Jesus the Lamb throughout Revelation. Stated differently, for John to equate the pierced Jesus with the pierced God would align with the way John seems to equate Jesus with God in other ways throughout Revelation.

Jesus' Words and God's Words

First, John presents Jesus' words as equivalent to God's very words. God the Father stands as the source of Jesus' revelation, which Jesus then has his angel deliver to John (Rev 1:1). Yet in Rev 1:2, τὸν λόγον τοῦ θεοῦ ("the word given by God") parallels τὴν μαρτυρίαν Ἰησοῦ Χριστοῦ ("the testimony given by Christ") such that Jesus' testimony further describes God's self-revelation (Rev 1:2, 9; 20:4).[83] Angels, John, and God's servants also bear testimony (Rev 1:1–2; 6:9; 11:7; 12:11, 17; 20:4; 22:16), but John distinguishes Jesus' testimony from these other witnesses. Jesus delivers God's word in a manner far superior to God's angels and prophetic servants. The superiority appears evident in the prophetic oracles spanning Rev 2–3. Each oracle to the seven churches contains the phrase, τάδε λέγει ("thus says"; Rev 2:1, 8, 12, 18; 3:1, 7, 14), which is the same introductory formula used throughout the LXX to introduce prophetic utterance (i.e., "thus says the Lord").[84] When

---

to his use in the Gospel. Such a pursuit can also serve those who disagree with my conclusions about common authorship by demonstrating that the same theological assumptions about Jesus among the NT writers (or "communities") are driving a particular reading and use of the OT. Nevertheless, for the issues of common authorship between the Johannine corpus, see "Presuppositions" in chapter 1 above and also the discussion in Rainbow, *Johannine Theology*, 42–51.

83. The καί seems to function in an explanatory manner: "the word of God, that is, the testimony of Jesus." Cf. Wallace, *Grammar*, 673. See also De Smidt, "Meta-Theology," 183–208. While de Smidt adds that John's point in Rev 1:2 is not primarily Christology, he still admits that Rev 1:2 could still serve Christology indirectly.

84. E.g., Exod 4:22; 2 Sam 7:5; Isa 1:24; Jer 2:2; Ezek 2:4; Amos 1:6, 9, 11, 13; Mic 2:3; 3:5; Obad 1; Zech 1:3, 4, 14, 16, 17. Cf. BDAG, s.v. "τάδε." In the LXX τάδε λέγει stands most often as the translation for the Hebrew expression כֹּה אָמַר ("thus says"), and on occasion נְאֻם ("says"). For readers acquainted with the Greek version(s) of the OT, the connection of Jesus' words with those of Yahweh would be unmistakable.

Jesus as the Pierced One

the prophets used "thus says the Lord," their audience knew to receive their message as the very words of God, but not because the words originated with the prophets. What distinguishes the oracles in Rev 2–3, however, is that they come directly from the glorified Jesus Christ, who revealed his theophanic glory in Rev 1:9–20. It is not merely a matter of "thus says the Lord," but a matter of "thus says the first and the last, who died and came to life" (Rev 2:8), and "thus says the Son of God" (Rev 2:18). In short, it is a matter of "thus says Jesus Christ."

Further, the prophets explained how Yahweh, not the prophet, would judge those who refused to heed their words and how Yahweh would reward those who obeyed their words. Yet in Rev 2–3 Jesus explains how he himself would judge those who failed to repent and how he himself would reward those who endured.[85] In that sense, John elevates the authority of Jesus and his words to a category reserved only for Yahweh throughout the OT. Similarly, Larry W. Hurtado observes the following:

> It is utterly remarkable ... that these oracles all represent the words of the glorified Jesus, for in the biblical tradition that the author obviously reveres the only legitimate source of prophetic inspiration is the one God (e.g., Deut 13:1–5). Indeed the prophet John is strongly antagonistic against those whom he regards as false prophets, both in the churches (e.g., 2:20–23) and in the larger religious environment of the time (19:20–21). Therefore, for him [i.e., John] to unhesitatingly present his prophetic oracles as the words of Jesus indicates a profound inclusion of Jesus within the sphere of action otherwise restricted to God.[86]

Nevertheless, even with such a high view of Jesus' words, where John views them on par with God's words, John still maintains Jesus' distinction from God the Father (cf. Rev 1:6; 2:28; 3:5, 21). As in the Fourth Gospel, Jesus' testimony in Revelation manifests God's self-revelation directly and immediately. Angels simply deliver it, John writes it, and the church must keep it.

---

85. For Jesus threatening his own judgment, see Rev 2:5, 16, 22–23; 3:3, 16. For Jesus promising his own reward, see Rev 2:7, 10–11, 17, 26–27; 3:5, 12, 18, 21.

86. Hurtado, *Lord Jesus Christ*, 591. See also Hurtado, *God*, 61.

The Pierced One's Second Redeeming Advent
Jesus and OT Metaphors Ascribed to God

Second, as alluded to in the summary of Rev 1:9–20 above, John interweaves several OT metaphors that were unique to Yahweh and applies them to the glorified Christ he witnesses. As noted before, the title "the first and the last" clarifies the title "the Alpha and the Omega" (esp. Rev 21:6; 22:13) and also alludes to a divine title in Isaiah that distinguishes Yahweh, who creates the future, from the nations and their idols, who lack any power to determine the future (Isa 41:4; 44:6–28; 46:10; 48:11–16). Quite strikingly, however, in John's Revelation both God and Jesus the Lamb self-identify as "the Alpha and the Omega" or "the first and the last" (God: Rev 1:8; 21:6; Jesus: Rev 1:17; 22:13).[87]

Daniel 7:9 also describes the Ancient of Days as one whose hair was like pure wool (LXX: ὡσεὶ ἔριον λευκὸν καθαρόν). The description of his fiery throne/chariot matches the vision of Yahweh's glory in Ezek 1:15–29, confirming that the Ancient of Days refers to Yahweh.[88] John, however, applies the same description to Christ: "the hairs of his head were white, like white wool [ὡς ἔριον λευκόν]" (Rev 1:14).[89]

Also, Ezek 1:24 describes the sound of the wings of the four living creatures before Yahweh's throne as "the sound of many waters, like the voice of the Almighty [כְּקוֹל־שַׁדַּי]."[90] Thus, to hear God Almighty speak was comparable to a tumult of waters.[91] John similarly says of Christ

---

87. Bauckham, *Theology of Revelation*, 25–28, 54–58. Oswalt also makes the following assertion in his commentary on Isaiah: "That this language (*first and last*) is applied to Christ not once but four times in Revelation (1:17; 2:8; 21:6; 22:13) is some indication of the force of the early church's conviction that Jesus Christ was Yahweh incarnate." Oswalt, *Isaiah 40–66*, 171.

88. Baldwin, *Daniel*, 141; Longman III, *Daniel*, 186–87.

89. Beale, *Revelation*, 209–10.

90. See also Ezek 10:5, "And the sound of the wings of the cherubim was heard as far as the outer court, like the voice of God Almighty [כְּקוֹל אֵל־שַׁדַּי בְּדַבְּרוֹ] when he speaks" (cf. Ezek 43:2). The LXX drops the entire clause, "like the voice of the Almighty," in Ezek 1:24 and instead simply says, ὡς φωνὴν ὕδατος πολλοῦ καὶ ἐν τῷ ἑστάναι αὐτὰ κατέπαυον αἱ πτέρυγες αὐτῶν (" . . . as the sound of much water; and when they stood, their wings were let down"). Nevertheless, the LXX preserves the phrase in Ezek 10:5 stating, καὶ φωνὴ τῶν πτερύγων τῶν χερουβιν ἠκούετο ἕως τῆς αὐλῆς τῆς ἐξωτέρας ὡς φωνὴ θεοῦ Σαδδαι λαλοῦντος ("and the sound of the cherubs' wings was heard as far as the outer court, as the voice/sound of God the Almighty speaking").

91. Wright, *Ezekiel*, 50.

that "his voice [was] like the sound of many waters [ὡς φωνὴ ὑδάτων πολλῶν]" (Rev 1:15). In other words, Jesus' voice is being likened to the voice of God Almighty.

Further still, Exod 19:16 and Exod 20:18 associate a great trumpet blast with Yahweh speaking his word to the prophet Moses on Mount Sinai (cf. also Heb 12:19). In Rev 1:10, John also hears behind him "a great voice like a trumpet [φωνὴν μεγάλην ὡς σάλπιγγος]" (cf. also Rev 4:1). It is possible that the great voice could represent that of an angelic figure (e.g., Rev 5:2; 6:1; 7:2). However, the commission to write in Rev 1:11 and the parallel commission to write in Rev 1:19, where the voice clearly belongs to Christ (cf. Rev 1:17–18), suggests that the voice in Rev 1:10 is that of Christ. As Beale and Osborne both note, the imagery evokes the Sinai theophany but applies it to Christ in ways that make his presence and speech theophanic.[92]

It is true that John also applies to Jesus imagery from heavenly beings who are less than God. Allusions to the heavenly figure in Dan 10:6, 9–17 appear evident: "eyes like a flame of fire" (Rev 1:14; cf. Dan 10:6); "feet like burnished bronze" (Rev 1:15; cf. Dan 10:6); and "fell at his feet as though dead" (Rev 1:17; cf. Dan 10:9, 10, 15). Some will argue that in Dan 10:5–6, Daniel witnessed the glory of the pre-incarnate Christ, that is, the same messianic "son of man" figure of Daniel 7.[93] Yet even if one does not accept the figure of Dan 10:5–6 as the pre-incarnate Christ, Hamilton has demonstrated how other heavenly beings often reflect aspects of Christ's glorious appearance.[94] Hamilton's point seems further buttressed in that Dan 7:13 has כְּבַר אֱנָשׁ ("one like a son of man") versus כִּדְמוּת בְּנֵי אָדָם ("one as the likeness of the sons of man"). That is, there is enough to associate their likeness but not enough to equate them. The angel only reflects the "son of man" figure's likeness. Hultberg suggests this is why John is able to use aspects of the angel's description for Jesus.[95] In other words, by applying to Jesus imagery of beings who are less than God, one need not conclude that Jesus is therefore less than God. Rather, these beings reflect aspects of his own

---

92. Beale, *Revelation*, 203; Osborne, *Revelation*, 84.
93. E.g., Steinmann, *Daniel*, 497–501.
94. Hamilton, *With the Clouds*, 144–46.
95. Hultberg, "Messianic Exegesis," 127.

divine glory as God. Even if the angelic imagery placed Jesus only in a category closer to God, when taken with the additional metaphors ascribed solely to Yahweh, one can see that John intends to state more.

Jesus and OT Motifs Ascribed to God

Third, equating Jesus with the pierced God of Zech 12:10 would also align with the way John applies to Jesus entire OT motifs that were once reserved for Yahweh. For example, John depicts the great day of Jesus the Lamb's wrath with OT images of terror and cosmic upheaval often describing Yahweh's end-time arrival in judgment (Rev 6:12–17; cf. Isa 13:10–13; Joel 2:30–31; 3:15–16; Hab 3:6–11).[96]

Also, the title donned by Jesus in Rev 19:16, βασιλεὺς βασιλέων καὶ κύριος κυρίων ("King of kings and Lord of lords"), alludes to an OT motif from Dan 4:37 LXX (cf. also Rev 17:14).[97] The Most High receives praise as θεὸς τῶν θεῶν καὶ κύριος τῶν κυρίων καὶ βασιλεὺς τῶν βασιλέων ("God of gods and Lord of lords and King of kings") in Dan 4:37 LXX for his power to remove the reign of kings and set others in their place. However, John envisions Jesus removing all rebel kings at his second coming and establishing his own people to reign in his earthly kingdom (Rev 19:19–21; 20:4). In this way, Jesus fulfills the role of the Most High who refuses to share his glory with another (cf. Deut 10:17).

Further, both Ezekiel and Zechariah anticipated a river of life flowing from the midst of Yahweh's glory in the temple (Ezek 43:1–12; 47:1–12; Zech 2:10–12; 14:8–9). However, John's vision in Rev 22:1 depicts the river of the water of life flowing from the one throne of God and of the Lamb (Rev 22:1). That both God and the Lamb share the one throne of glory seems evident as the throne scene develops across Revelation. Jesus' own throne (τῷ θρόνῳ μου) is simultaneously his Father's throne (Rev 3:21). Jesus, the Lamb, approaches the throne and all heaven includes him in the worship of God (Rev 5:11, 13). The Lamb is then seen in the midst of the throne, carrying out God's care for his

---

96. See, e.g., Beale and McDonough, "Revelation," 1104–6.

97. Beale, *Revelation*, 881, 963–64. See also Osborne, *Revelation*, 686. Osborne writes, " . . . this is another place where the divinity of Christ is stressed—the Warrior Messiah is God himself!"

people (Rev 7:17). Finally, John calls the throne, ὁ θρόνος τοῦ θεοῦ καὶ τοῦ ἀρνίου ("the throne of God and of the Lamb"; Rev 22:3; cf. 22:1). That is, God and the Lamb share the one, single throne,[98] making them both the one source of the river of life.[99]

Jesus and the Worship of God

Fourth, Jesus also receives worship in the book of Revelation. The doxology in Rev 1:5b-6 encourages the church to ascribe to Jesus δόξα ("glory"). To render Jesus δόξα is not to give him something he lacks, but to recognize the worth he has.[100] What may surprise John's readers, however, is that δόξα is something regularly attributed to God in Revelation. Indeed, God not only possesses glory that manifests his inherent worth (Rev 15:8; 21:11, 23), but his creatures must recognize his glory (Rev 4:9, 11; 7:12; 11:13; 15:4; 19:1, 7; 21:24, 26), and terrible

---

98. On the shared throne, see the study by Choi, "The Lamb," 223-31.

99. John's vision of the Lamb sharing the throne of Yahweh may even have precedent in Zechariah. The Hebrew is difficult, but Zech 6:13 may also suggest that, in his dual role as priest-king, the Branch will sit on Yahweh's throne once he comes. Zechariah's use of צֶמַח ("branch") recalls the general imagery of a king's son taking his father's place on the throne (e.g., 2 Sam 10:1; 2 Chr 1:8) and the specific imagery applied to the hope for a Davidic king (e.g., Isa 4:2; 10:33-34; Jer 23:5; 33:15; Ps 132:17; cf. Isa 11:1). That he bears royal honor and sits on a throne also reveals his kingly role (Zech 6:13). But the Branch also serves in a priestly role, made evident both in Zech 3:8-9, where Joshua and his priestly cohort serve as types of the coming Branch, and in Zech 6:13, where it says וְהָיָה כֹהֵן עַל־כִּסְאוֹ ("and he shall be a priest on his throne"). Thus, the coming Branch will have a dual role as priest-king. Therefore, I do not take the end of v. 13—וַעֲצַת שָׁלוֹם תִּהְיֶה בֵּין שְׁנֵיהֶם ("and the counsel of peace shall be between them both")—as referring to two persons, a priest, and a king separate from each other but who serve peacefully side by side. Rather, I understand it to be saying that the counsel of peace shall be between the Branch as priest-king and Yahweh. It is Yahweh's temple that the Branch will build (Zech 6:13a), and it is Yahweh's throne "on/by" (עַל) which the Branch will sit and rule (Zech 6:13b). Further precedent for this interpretation comes with Ps 110, one of the few places in the OT that also mentions a Davidic priest-king ruling "on/by" (עַל) Yahweh's "right hand," the conceptual equivalent of Yahweh's throne (Ps 110:1, 5). Petterson, *Zechariah*, 187. Cf. Jauhiainen, "Turban and Crown," 509.

100. The hymn-like devotion in Rev 5:12 also suggests that Jesus' worth/worthiness is in view: "Worthy [ἄξιόν] is the Lamb who was slain to receive power and wealth and wisdom and might and honor and glory [ἄξιόν] and blessing." That the heavenly court bows in homage to the Lamb further annunciates Jesus' worth (Rev 5:13-14).

judgments fall on those who refuse to give him glory (Rev 14:7; 16:9; 18:7).¹⁰¹ Still, John does not hesitate to call the church to render to Jesus δόξα on earth (Rev 1:6) just as the creatures already do in heaven (Rev 5:12, 13).¹⁰² Even within John's strict monotheism, where to worship anything else alongside God would merit judgment, Jesus can somehow receive glory simultaneously without compromising true worship.¹⁰³ Echoes of Jesus' words in John 5:23 seem apparent: "[The Father] has given all judgment to the Son, in order that all may honor the Son, just as they honor the Father."

Furthermore, by encouraging the church to recognize Jesus' κράτος ("might") alongside his δόξα (Rev 1:6)—and even stating the duration of his might as εἰς τοὺς αἰῶνας τῶν αἰώνων ("forever and ever"; cf. also Rev 5:13)—John is at one with Paul, Peter, and Jude who also include Jesus as the object of their doxology and worshipful devotion

---

101. Other heavenly beings display δόξα as well (e.g., Rev 18:1), even enough δόξα to make John bow to worship (Rev 19:10; 22:8). However, in each case the angel rebukes John and commands him to worship God alone (Rev 19:10; 22:9), and never does the book of Revelation call earth or heaven to ascribe δόξα to anyone except God and Jesus/the Lamb. Regarding the τὴν δόξαν αὐτῶν ("the glory of them" [i.e., kings] in Rev 21:24) and τὴν δόξαν ... τῶν ἐθνῶν εἰς αὐτήν ("the glory of the nations" in Rev 21:26), the genitives appear to be genitives of source (i.e., "the glory arising from the kings and from the nations"). Beale, *Revelation*, 1095. The kings and nations are coming as worshipers of God (cf. Isa 66:18–24; Zech 14:16).

102. Crucial to notice, at least in the cases of Rev 1:5b–6 and Rev 5:9–14, is that what Jesus accomplished through his redemptive sacrifice produces the doxology and devotion. His victorious (ἐνίκησεν in Rev 5:5), redeeming (ἠγόρασας in Rev 5:9) death proves that he is worthy to receive adoration. He is not only worthy to receive adoration from people on earth, since the death he died redeemed people for God (Rev 5:9b–10), but he is also worthy to receive adoration from all heavenly creatures, since the death he died qualifies him alone to bring God's redemptive-historical purposes to fruition (Rev 5:9a). Likewise, Bauckham observes, "It was because Christians owed salvation to Jesus Christ that he was worshipped. An overwhelming religious debt to one who was regarded as living in heaven and indeed an experienced presence in the Christian community was naturally expressed in worship. The salvation was too closely connected with Jesus himself for Jesus to be bypassed in worship offered to God for it, but at the same time it was salvation from God that Jesus gave and so Jesus was not treated as an alternative object of worship alongside God. He was included in the worship of God." Bauckham, *Theology of Revelation*, 62.

103. Cf. Rev 19:10; 22:9. See also Hurtado, *Origins*, 7–38. Hurtado demonstrates how radical the call to worship Jesus truly is in the face of the religio-political claims of Rome.

Jesus as the Pierced One

(1 Tim 6:16; 1 Pet 4:11; 5:11; Jude 25).[104] In fact, not to recognize Jesus in such elevated fashion would be to trivialize the glory that John truly witnessed in his visions. Doxology and worshipful devotion is appropriate for the Lamb who uniquely shares God's heavenly throne and uniquely receives worship by angels and all creation (e.g., Rev 5:12–13; 7:10–12; 14:1–3; 22:3).[105]

In sum, concluding that John equates Jesus with the pierced God of Zech 12:10 aligns with John's larger testimony in Revelation that includes Jesus the Lamb within the divine identity. The way John presents Jesus' words, applies OT metaphors and OT motifs to Jesus, and encourages the worship of Jesus, all seem to warrant that John could be reading Zech 12:10 along divine messianic lines and not simply human messianic lines.[106] In fact, John's use of Zech 12:10 may function as one text in the prologue that anticipates more OT associations, wherein Jesus reveals some attribute of God or fulfills some aspect of the mission of God. To the latter we now turn.

The Divine Mission of Jesus in Revelation

John's Christology also informs his eschatology. Since John witnesses God's self-disclosure in Jesus Christ—even to the degree that he

---

104. For further discussion on the worship of Jesus by the early church, see Bauckham, *Climax*, 118–48; Choi, "The Lamb," 200–205; Hurtado, *Lord Jesus Christ*, 134–54; Bauckham, *Jesus and the God of Israel*, 127–81; Dunn, *Worship Jesus*, 91–150; Hurtado, *One God, One Lord*, 105–8, 119–30.

105. For the significance of the "throne of God" in monotheistic Judaism during the Second Temple period, see Bauckham, *Jesus and the God of Israel*, 152–72. Bauckham then goes on to develop the implications of the NT writers viewing Jesus as the one who shares God's throne of glory. Bauckham, *Jesus and the God of Israel*, 172–81. Moreover, as others have demonstrated, Rev 4–5 forms a single literary unit wherein the worship of God in Rev 4 is further explained by the inclusion of the worship of Christ in Rev 5. Hurtado, "Revelation 4–5," 109; Morton, "Glory to God," 102–3; Stuckenbruck, "Revelation 4–5," 241, 246, 247. A point of disagreement with Stuckenbruck, however, is his assertion that "Jews and Christians worship the same God." Stuckenbruck, "Revelation 4–5," 247. However, see texts like John 5:23 and 1 John 2:23.

106. That is not to say that John imports on Zechariah a theology that was never present before. Rather, God's self-disclosure in Jesus Christ, which the Spirit conveys through prophetic vision, enables John to see a theology that was always present in Zechariah but impossible to discern fully apart from the incarnate, crucified, and risen-to-return Jesus Christ.

The Pierced One's Second Redeeming Advent

identifies the pierced God of Zech 12:10 as the pierced Christ in Rev 1:7—then John also interprets Zechariah's prophecies about God's end-time coming in terms of Jesus' coming.[107]

Jesus and God's Coming in the Salutation

The salutation's literary structure and vocabulary strongly suggests that Yahweh's coming and Jesus' coming are one and the same event. Giesen, Beale, and McDonough have observed an *inclusio* in Rev 1:4 and 1:8 where the three-fold formula for God's name appears twice: ὁ ὢν καὶ ὁ ἦν καὶ ὁ ἐρχόμενος ("he who is and who was and who is to come").[108] The well-recognized, tripartite reflection on God's covenant name from Exod 3:14 (LXX: ἐγώ εἰμι ὁ ὤν, "I AM the one who is"), thus frames the salutation. Many commentators explain the tripartite reflection in terms that emphasize God's eternality. Important to note here is that the third element in the tripartite reflection (i.e., ὁ ἐρχόμενος) reflects numerous OT passages expecting God's eschatological coming to earth both to save and to judge.[109]

---

107. Hultberg, "Significance," 29.

108. Giesen, *Offenbarung*, 80; Beale, *Revelation*, 196; McDonough, *YHWH at Patmos*, 217. Cf. Schüssler Fiorenza, "Redemption," 222; Gradl, *Buch Und Offenbarung*, 152–55. Schüssler Fiorenza and Gradl observe the literary significance of the repeated divine name in vv. 4 and 8 but do not call it an *inclusio*. See also Vanni, "Un Esempio," 456–57. Vanni suggests a chiasm in Rev 1:4–8 that sets in motion the liturgical dialogue between the reader and hearers of Revelation (cf. Rev 1:3). Vanni arranges the chiasm as follows: A: ὁ ὢν καὶ ὁ ἦν καὶ ὁ ἐρχόμενος (Rev 1:4–5a); B: ἀμήν (Rev 1:5b–6); B': ἀμήν (Rev 1:7); A': ὁ ὢν καὶ ὁ ἦν καὶ ὁ ἐρχόμενος (Rev 1:8).

109. See, e.g., the following OT passages: " . . . before the presence of the Lord, for he is coming [ἔρχεται], for he is coming [ἔρχεται] to judge the earth" (Ps 95:13 LXX [ET 96:13]); "Comfort the discouraged in mind, be strong [and] do not fear; behold, our God renders judgment, and he will render [judgment]; he will come [ἥξει] and save us" (Isa 35:4 LXX); "Behold the Lord! The Lord is coming [ἔρχεται] with strength, and [his] arm is with power: behold, his reward is with him, and his work before him" (Isa 40:10 LXX); "For, behold, the Lord will come [ἥξει] as fire, and his chariots as a storm, to render his vengeance with wrath, and his rebuke with a flame of fire" (Isa 66:15 LXX); "let us pursue knowing the Lord: we shall find him ready as the morning, and he will come [ἥξει] to us as the early and latter rain to the earth" (Hos 6:3 LXX); "For still the vision [is] for a time, and it shall spring forth for the end and not for vain; if he should delay, wait for him; for the coming one will come [ἐρχόμενος ἥξει], and will not delay" (Hab 2:3 LXX; cf. also Heb 10:37 which adds the definite article: ὁ ἐρχόμενος ἥξει); " . . . and the Lord my God shall come [ἥξει], and all the holy ones with him" (Zech 14:5 LXX); " . . . 'and the Lord,

Jesus as the Pierced One

Nevertheless, within the framework of God's eschatological coming, John inserts a litany of clauses celebrating Jesus' past redemption (i.e., "faithful witness"; "by his blood"; "pierced"; "firstborn from the dead"), present reign (i.e., "ruler of kings on earth"), and future return (i.e., "is coming"; "will see"; "will wail"). While the early church certainly viewed Jesus' first coming as inaugurating God's eschatological rule (e.g., Mark 1:15), the main element to observe here in relation to ὁ ἐρχόμενος from Rev 1:4 and 1:8 is that John says of Jesus, "Behold, he [i.e., Jesus] is coming [ἔρχεται] with the clouds." By framing Jesus' coming (ἔρχεται) within the framework of God's coming (ἐρχόμενος), John urges the reader to understand God's coming in light of Jesus' coming.[110] Even more pointed, he seems to be saying that Jesus' coming is God's eschatological coming.

A similar emphasis may (and I want to stress "may" due to the well-known ambiguities) be present in John's combined allusion to Dan 7:13. As noted above, Dan 7:13 bears some level of affinity with Zech 12:10 in that Dan 7:13 provides the occasion for every eye to see the Pierced One. However, other affinities may exist. Both passages appear within larger prophecies about God's eschatological coming to save his people (Dan 7:14, 22–27; Zech 12:10—13:1) and judge the nations (Dan 7:11–12, 15–21, 26; Zech 12:1–9; 14:2–5). Moreover, both passages seem to present a divine (instead of merely a human) figure[111]

---

whom you seek, shall suddenly come [ἥξει] into his temple ... behold, he is coming [ἔρχεται]; says the Lord Almighty" (Mal 3:1 LXX).

110. Likewise, Swete observes that John employs ὁ ἐρχόμενος "because it adumbrates at the outset the general purpose of the book, which is to exhibit the comings of God in human history; if ἔρχεσθαι is used elsewhere chiefly of the Son, the Father may also be said to come when He reveals Himself in His workings." Swete, *Apocalypse*, 5. After commenting on the three-fold title in Rev 1:4, Beasley-Murray also concludes, "How God will so come in Christ is the theme of the prophecy." Beasley-Murray, *Revelation*, 54. For more on the literary connection, see Bauckham, *Theology of Revelation*, 29; Bauckham, *Climax*, 202, 209. Zehnder points out that the same correspondence occurs in Dan 7 between Yahweh's coming and the "son of man" figure's coming. In Dan 7:13 the one like a son of man is "coming [אָתָה] with the clouds of heaven," and in Dan 7:22 "the Ancient of Days came [אֲתָה], and judgment was given for the saints of the Most High." Zehnder, "Divine Being," 342. See also Haukaas, "Revelation 1:7–8," 177–78.

111. Similarly, Caragounis, *Son of Man*, 163–64. As an additional note, I stated in chapters 2 and 3 that others have demonstrated from wider contextual grounds that

The Pierced One's Second Redeeming Advent

who achieves God's eschatological salvation and judgment.[112] We have already identified the Pierced One of Zech 12:10 as God himself, that is, at least from a narrower contextual reading (see chapter 2). We have also shown why it is fitting for John to identify Jesus as that Pierced One: Jesus is God (see chapter 3). Yet who is Daniel's "son of man" figure?[113] The description "one like a son of man" suggests a figure

---

Zechariah's Pierced One could also be a representative of Yahweh. But the narrower contextual reading suggests that the Pierced One is in fact Yahweh. Thus, just like the "son of man" figure of Dan 7:13, even the Pierced One of Zech 12:10 could be understood as both a human, Davidic representative and divine. The thrust of the present study has been to demonstrate the latter.

112. One further affinity may also include the notion of representative and substitute. Caragounis observes that much like Daniel, Ezekiel also witnessed a heavenly throne scene, and above that throne, "a likeness as the appearance of a man [כְּמַרְאֵה אָדָם]" (Ezek 1:26). Throughout the prophecy, however, the Lord refers to Ezekiel as "son of man [בֶּן־אָדָם]." For Caragounis, the connection is informative. As Ezekiel's ministry to Israel and Judah unfolds, "the role which the prophet has assumed among his people is one of representative, intercessor, and substitute ... The appellation ['son of man'] is no longer a descriptive designation, but a term denoting role or function." Caragounis, *Son of Man*, 60. If Daniel's subsequent vision builds on Ezekiel's prophecy—and there is good reason to believe that it does (Hamilton, *With the Clouds*, 148, 150)—then the pattern of representative, intercessor, and substitute that Ezekiel sets forward as "son of man" may very well "interface with Davidic hope and informs the reference in Dan 9:26 to the Messiah being cut off and having nothing." Hamilton, *With the Clouds*, 151. That is, he too will also serve as a representative substitute (cf. Dan 9:24, 26), thus explaining how a sinful people would reign with him instead of being destroyed with the rest of the nations (Dan 7:15–27). Shepherd, "Daniel 7:13," 110. Shepherd comes close to making the same association with Dan 9:26. If so, the "son of man" figure's role looks similar to the Pierced One, whose piercing opens a fountain for cleansing God's people.

113. The question has spawned a plethora of studies too numerous to interact with critically at the present. Surveys of the debate include Geza, "Debate," 19–32; Lindars, *Jesus Son of Man*; Burkett, *Son of Man Debate*, 1–124; Casey, *Solution*, 1–55; Hurtado and Owen, *Son of Man*, 159–77. Hurtado and Owen's collection of essays strongly criticize Casey's 'solution' that "son of man" is just an Aramaic idiom referring to someone in general or another way of referring to one's self. By contrast Hurtado proposes that the expression "reflected Jesus' sense that he had a particular, even unique, vocation in God's redemptive purposes ... that Jesus saw himself as having a special role and mission ... but that ['son of man'] did not indicate what that mission was, and did not lay claim to any office or previously defined status." Hurtado, "Summary," 175. Cf. Hurtado, *Lord Jesus Christ*, 290–306. A few observations lead me to assert more. (1) At least some of Jesus' "son of man" sayings occur in sentences that allude to particular OT passages or motifs (e.g., Dan 7:13 in Matt 24:30–31; Ps 110:1 and Dan 7:13 in Matt 26:64). See also the examples from John's

who at least bears the likeness of humanity.¹¹⁴ Also, that he comes with the clouds,¹¹⁵ approaches Yahweh's throne,¹¹⁶ and receives universal

---

Gospel in Reynolds, "Son of Man Idiom in John," 101–29. These appear to be Jesus' way of telling his disciples precisely what his mission was and what office he viewed himself taking, even if the disciples did not fully grasp that mission/office until after Jesus' resurrection. (2) Usage outside the Gospels is sparse, but the early church follows Jesus in drawing similar connections as he did. E.g., as the self-proclaimed "son of man" (e.g., Matt 20:18, 28), Jesus uses Ps 8:2 in Matt 21:16 to refer to his own ministry and seems to apply the same new-Adam-dominion motif to his resurrection in Matt 28:18. Hebrews 2:6 quotes Ps 8:4 to reveal Jesus as the truly exalted "son of man" who rules with Adam-like dominion (cf. Gen 1:28; Ps 8:4–5). Stephen also witnesses the already-enthroned Son of Man in Acts 7:56, and John seems intent to develop how his reign will come to fruition in Rev 1:7 (cf. Rev 1:13) and Rev 14:14. See also Bock, "Did Jesus Connect," 399–402. (3) Jesus regularly aligned his vocation with God's redemptive purposes as revealed according to the Scriptures (e.g., Luke 24:44–47). That revelation in Scripture includes the development of a "son of man" motif stretching from Gen 1 through 2 Sam 7, Ps 8, and Dan 7, the last of which uses vocabulary and images reminiscent of the previous three passages. E.g., see Hamilton, *With the Clouds*, 56–57, 90–91, 147. Surely, Jesus understood his mission as fulfilling the prior "son of man" motif spanning the biblical narrative. Shepherd, "Daniel 7:13," 106–10.

114. Baldwin observes, "... he is only *like* a human being, just as the beasts were 'like' a lion or a bear ... The beasts turn out to be representative of certain human beings; the one who comes with the clouds is like a human being in the sense that He is what every human being should be if he is true to type, that is, one who is made in the image of God (Gn. 1:26, 27)." Baldwin, *Daniel*, 143. Some have even observed that the language in Dan 7:13–14 seems to advance the OT hope that one from David's lineage would receive an everlasting kingdom (Dan 7:14; cf. 2 Sam 7:13) and restore the dominion Adam forfeited (cf. Gen 1:28; Ps 8:5; Heb 2:6–9). See, e.g., Hamilton, *With the Clouds*, 56–57, 90–94, 147–54.

115. Daniel 7:13 describes the son of man figure "coming with the clouds of heaven," the same imagery regularly applied to Yahweh appearing (e.g., Exod 13:21–22; 40:34–38; Lev 16:2; 2 Sam 22:12; 1 Kgs 8:10–11; Ps 97:2 [LXX 96:2]; LXX Zech 2:17; Isa 19:1; Ezek 1:4; cf. Deut 33:26; Ps 18:9 [LXX 17:10; MT 18:10]). See also Gentry, "Son of Man," 73. Granted, Rev 10:1 describes a mighty angel "clothed with a cloud." Beale identifies the angel as the Angel of the Lord, who is also Jesus Christ. Beale, *Revelation*, 522–26. Others opt for an angel who reflects some of Christ's traits but is not to be identified with Christ. E.g., Morris, *Revelation*, 137; Bauckham, *Climax*, 253; Hamilton, *With the Clouds*, 146.

116. Daniel 7:9 mentions that "thrones [pl. כָּרְסָוָן] were placed." Thrones could represent the heavenly court scene over which Yahweh presides (cf. "the court" in Dan 7:10, 26), or signify an additional throne for the "son of man" figure alongside Yahweh (Dan 7:13–14). Both interpretations have merit. Perhaps the latter interpretation becomes a stronger possibility in that Matt 26:64 records Jesus combining Ps 110:1 ("Yahweh says to my Lord, 'Sit at my right hand ...'") with Dan 7:13 ("coming

The Pierced One's Second Redeeming Advent

dominion, all suggest a figure who is highly exalted, perhaps even divine.[117] These two characteristics of Daniel's "son of man" figure remain in tension until the first coming of God's Son: in Jesus Christ the exalted Son took to himself a human nature. It is possible that by identifying the human and divinely exalted figure of Dan 7:13 as Jesus (cf. Rev 1:13 with Rev 1:5–7, 18), John helps the reader understand that Jesus'

---

with the clouds of heaven"). See the discussion in Caragounis, *Son of Man*, 140–43, 203–4; Bock, "Did Jesus Connect," 78–88; Hamilton, *With the Clouds*, 148–49. That is, the thrones of Dan 7:9 anticipate the "son of man" figure's enthronement alongside Yahweh in Dan 7:13, something Ps 110:1 had anticipated before. For further discussion on the inclusion of Jesus on Yahweh's throne and the use of Ps 110, see Bauckham, *Jesus and the God of Israel*, 169–81; Zehnder, "Divine Being," 343–44.

117. Caragounis and Gentry observe that Dan 7:15–27 interprets Dan 7:1–14 and identifies both the Ancient of Days and the "son of man" figure as Most High, though with a peculiar shift in Aramaic. Normally, Daniel uses the Aramaic adjective, עֶלְיָא ("most high"), as the standard title for Yahweh (e.g., Dan 3:26, 32; 4:14; 5:18; 7:25). However, whenever referencing "the saints of the Most High," Daniel shifts to the Hebrew adjective with an Aramaic plural ending, עֶלְיוֹנִין ("most high"; Dan 7:18, 22, 25, 27). The variations appear together in Dan 7:25: "He shall speak words against the Most High [עֶלְיָא], and shall wear out the saints of the Most High [עֶלְיוֹנִין]." Gentry suggests that the shift is a "deliberate attempt to draw some distinction between a divine figure associated with the saints and yet perhaps distinguished from Yahweh in some way." Gentry, "Son of Man," 73; cf. Caragounis, *Son of Man*, 75. As Dan 7:14 and Dan 7:27 clarify, that "divine figure associated with the saints" is the son of man. In Dan 7:14 the son of man figure enjoys "dominion and glory and a kingdom, that all peoples, nations, and languages should serve him [לֵהּ יִפְלְחוּן]; his dominion is an everlasting dominion . . ." Daniel 7:27 then states, "the kingdom and the dominion and the greatness of the kingdoms under the whole heaven shall be given to the people of the saints of the Most High [עֶלְיוֹנִין]; his [i.e., the Most High's] kingdom shall be an everlasting kingdom [just like the son of man's kingdom in Dan 7:14], and all dominions shall serve [יִפְלְחוּן] and obey him [i.e., serve and obey the Most High]." While debated, Hamilton demonstrates why the singular suffix in מַלְכוּתֵהּ ("his kingdom") and the singular suffix in לֵהּ יִפְלְחוּן וְיִשְׁתַּמְּעוּן ("serve and obey him") most likely refer to עֶלְיוֹנִין ("Most High") instead of עַם ("the people"). Hamilton, *With the Clouds*, 152. Certainly, the son of man figure rules in a representative fashion, where the saints enjoy his kingdom and dominion by virtue of their union with him (Dan 7:14; cf. 7:18, 22, 27). Yet Daniel distinguishes the "son of man" figure in that as the Most High (עֶלְיוֹנִין)—alongside the Most High (עֶלְיָא)—he alone deserves the humble obedience or worship (יִפְלְחוּן) restricted to Yahweh alone (cf. יִפְלְחוּן in Dan 3:28; 6:17, 21). See also Zehnder, "Divine Being," 340. Cf. Luke 1:31–33 where Gabriel calls Jesus, Son of the Most High, in describing his relationship with God. Gabriel was also Daniel's interpreting angel (Dan 8:16; 9:21). Cf. also Leim, "Glory," 213–32. Leim draws the same conclusion from the way Jesus uses Dan 7 but from Mark's Gospel.

coming is the very occasion when the Ancient of Days would come and supplant all rebel kingdoms with his own kingdom (cf. Dan 7:22). In this manner, Zech 12:10 and Dan 7:13 become mutually interpretive in that Yahweh's eternal kingdom comes on earth through the human and divine "son of man" figure, Jesus Christ.[118] However, that human and divine "son of man" figure establishes Yahweh's kingdom by first being pierced for the nations before coming as vindicated judge over the nations. John 19:37 pertains to the former (see chapter 3), while Rev 1:7 pertains to the latter. Again, God's eschatological judgment and kingdom finally manifests itself in Jesus' second coming.

Jesus and God's Coming Elsewhere in Revelation

Combining God's coming with Jesus' coming seems further justified by re-reading Rev 1:7–8 in light of its counterpart in Rev 22:20. In Rev 1:8, Yahweh speaks as "the Lord [κύριος] God" and identifies himself as "he who is to come [ὁ ἐρχόμενος]," while in Rev 22:20 it is Jesus who is coming and who bears the title κύριος: "'Surely I am coming [ἔρχομαι] soon.' Amen. Come, Lord [κύριε] Jesus!"[119]

That Rev 11:15 equates the arrival of the Lord's kingdom with that of Christ's kingdom also suggests that John envisages God's coming as Christ's coming: "Then the seventh angel blew his trumpet, and there were loud voices in heaven, saying, 'The kingdom of the world has become the kingdom of our Lord and of his Christ [τοῦ κυρίου ἡμῶν καὶ τοῦ χριστοῦ αὐτου], and he shall reign [βασιλεύσει] forever and

---

118. That does not mean the OT authors themselves fully understood God's incarnation. One must allow for the progress of revelation. Still, God's self-revelation in Scripture contained all the elements to discern his Son's incarnation once the post-resurrection understanding transpired for the apostles.

119. Cf. Hübenthal, *Transformation*, 173. Hübenthal draws a similar connection to Rev 22:20, but she sees a change of character between Rev 1:4 and Rev 1:8 such that Jesus (cf. Rev 1:7) is the one speaking instead of Yahweh. Also note that John uses κύριος for both God the Father and Jesus Christ (God the Father: Rev 1:8; 4:8, 11; 11:4 [cf. Zech 4:14], 15, 17; 15:3, 4; 16:7; 18:8; 19:6; 21:22; 22:5, 6; Jesus Christ: Rev 11:8; 14:13; 17:14; 19:16; 22:20, 21). In doing so, John aligns himself with the confessions of the early church (e.g., Acts 2:36; Rom 10:9; 1 Cor 8:5–6; 16:22; Phil 2:9–11; 1 Pet 3:15). Moreover, for John to use the title κύριος is consistent with Thomas' confession in John 20:28, ὁ κύριός μου καὶ ὁ θεός μου. For further discussion on substituting κύριος for the divine name, Yahweh, as well as the early church applying κύριος to Jesus, see Hurtado, *Lord Jesus Christ*, 108–17.

ever.'" In light of the address to "Lord God" in Rev 11:17, the subject of βασιλεύσει ("he shall reign") likely refers to the Lord in v. 15, but it is still significant to note that his kingdom belongs equally to Christ.

Moreover, as shown above, Rev 19:16 depicts Jesus donning a title (i.e., "King of kings and Lord of lords") once ascribed to the Most High in Dan 4:37 LXX, but the scene in which John witnesses the title is that of Jesus' Parousia. In other words, John views Jesus' final return to topple the rebellious nations and replace their kingdoms with his own as the return of the Most High himself.

The same is true in the allusion to Isa 40:10 in Rev 22:12.[120] Isaiah 40:10 anticipates Yahweh's final coming to judge the world: "Behold [ἰδοὺ] the Lord! The Lord is coming [ἔρχεται] with strength, and [his] arm is with power. Behold [ἰδοὺ], his reward [μισθός] is with him, and the work [τὸ ἔργον] before him." However, Jesus (cf. ἐγὼ Ἰησοῦς in Rev 22:16) uses the vocabulary from Isaiah's prophecy to depict his own coming in terms of Yahweh's coming: "Behold [ἰδοὺ], I am coming [ἔρχομαι] soon, bringing my recompense [μισθός] with me, to repay each one for the work [τὸ ἔργον] he has done." Again, God's coming is essentially equated with Jesus' coming.[121]

God's Coming in Zechariah and Jesus' Coming in Revelation

Such an observation becomes significant for the book of Revelation, wherein John clarifies the coming of God in Zechariah as the coming of Christ in Revelation. One of Zechariah's main themes is the end-time return of Yahweh to save his people and judge his enemies. That return is even expressed as Yahweh's coming: "Sing and rejoice, O daughter of Zion, for behold, I am coming [MT: בָא; LXX: ἔρχομαι] and I will dwell in your midst" (Zech 2:14 [ET 2:10]). Yahweh's coming not only includes the humble acceptance of piercing (Zech 12:10–14), but also the final arrival in glory to deliver his people in battle (Zech 12:2–9; 14:3–5), subject the rebellious nations to judgment (Zech 14:3, 12–15,

---

120. Beale and McDonough, "Revelation," 1156–57.

121. As an additional note, equating the coming of God with the coming of Jesus seems evident elsewhere in the NT. E.g., 2 Pet 1:16 refers to "the power and coming [παρουσίαν] of our Lord Jesus Christ," and 2 Pet 3:12 refers to "the coming [παρουσίαν] of the day of God."

17–19), and transform the earth into a cosmic sanctuary with his ruling presence (Zech 14:6–11, 16, 20–22). Of no little significance is that Jesus echoes Yahweh's words from Zechariah seven times throughout Revelation: "I am coming [ἔρχομαι]" (2:5, 16; 3:11; 16:15; 22:7, 12, 20).[122] In a book where the number seven indicates completeness,[123] Jesus' seven-fold repetition of ἔρχομαι establishes that his own coming is the completion of God's coming. In fact, it is now Jesus who comes to deliver God's people in battle (Rev 19:11–16), Jesus who subjects the rebellious nations to judgment (Rev 19:17—20:3), and Jesus who transforms the earth into a cosmic sanctuary much like the one described in Zech 14 (Rev 21:1—22:5).[124] Yet it is John's initial use of Zech 12:10 in Rev 1:7 that helps the reader anticipate the association between Jesus' coming and God's coming. The interplay between who Jesus is (i.e., God's Son and self-revelation), and what Zech 12:10 anticipated (i.e., people looking on the God once pierced), helps John to see that Jesus' coming further explains God's coming. The Almighty's coming manifests itself in Jesus' coming, since Jesus the Son is God's self-revelation.[125] Stated differently, since Jesus is God's self-revelation, it is appropriate for John to view God's coming in Zechariah as Jesus' coming.

In this manner, the eschatological contours of Zech 12 have not been lost for John by saying that Jesus fulfilled Zech 12:10 in his first advent (John 19:37). Rather, by alluding to Zech 12:10 once more, but now in relation to Jesus' second advent, John shows what Jesus' first advent guaranteed for his second advent, namely, Jesus' death and resurrection inaugurated the last days he will also consummate.

---

122. Hultberg only lists six occurrences, but he demonstrates clearly that Zech 2:10 forms the textual backdrop for "I am coming" alongside an allusion to the Lord's recompense from Isa 62:11. Hultberg, "Messianic Exegesis," 377–78.

123. On the significance on the number seven in the book of Revelation, see Bauckham, *Climax*, 28–37; Beale, *Revelation*, 58–59; Bandy, "Symbolism," 50. Moyise, however, remains unconvinced that John intends to "communicate specific theological content through word frequencies." Moyise, "Word Frequencies," 294. While Moyise's observations should encourage further caution in what one deduces from the enumeration of specific words in Revelation, even Moyise concedes that Revelation contains convincing examples for the number seven.

124. E.g., Rev 21:23–25 // Zech 14:6–7; Rev 22:1 // Zech 14:8; Rev 22:3, 11 // Zech 14:11.

125. Jauhiainen, *Use of Zechariah*, 4.

The Pierced One's Second Redeeming Advent

Jesus' historical piercing ensured his future triumph. Jesus' death set in motion eschatological events previously prophesied in Zechariah that cannot be reversed. If the Pierced One of Zech 12:10 has been pierced, then it is certain that the rest of the events in Zech 12–14 are coming to fruition. Revelation provides further detail in how they will come to fruition. By alluding to the piercing once more, John shows the so-called "already and not yet" aspect of God's eschatological coming in Jesus Christ. Already, the Pierced One suffered and rose. Already, the piercing Jesus received has opened a fountain of cleansing that transformed the church into God's kingdom and priesthood. But the Pierced One has not yet manifested God's earthly rule in full. That will take place when he comes again with the clouds. How that final coming will affect the nations then, and how that final coming should affect John's readers now, is a point that chapter 5 will address. Before doing so, however, let us summarize what we have encountered with Rev 1:7.

CONCLUSION

In Rev 1:7 we encounter a combined allusion to Zech 12:10–14 and Dan 7:13, and John uses the interplay of both to help his readers understand the nature of Jesus' second redeeming advent. As he did in the Fourth Gospel, John again substitutes Jesus for Yahweh as the object of the people's looking. John interprets the prophet's words in this way because he is convinced that Jesus is God. The way John presents Jesus' words, applies OT metaphors and OT motifs to Jesus, and encourages the worship of Jesus, all seem to warrant that John could be reading Zech 12:10 along divine messianic lines and not simply along human messianic lines. If so, then John's use of Zech 12:10 may function as one text in the prologue that anticipates more OT associations, wherein Jesus reveals some attribute of God or fulfills some aspect of the mission of God. Concerning the mission of God, John uses Zech 12:10 (alongside Dan 7:13) to reassure the church that Jesus' Parousia will soon consummate God's eschatological mission, thus closing the inter-advent age. God's heavenly kingdom will soon supplant all rebellious kingdoms with the personal arrival of Jesus. Jesus' return will be universal in scope, as every eye beholds the one once pierced. Jesus' return will also be awful in effect as the divine authority Jesus bears and the final judgment Jesus exercises cause the remaining rebellious community to wail in terror.

How, then, should readers of John's Gospel and Revelation put the pieces together and respond? How, then, should the nations respond after Jesus' first coming and before Jesus' second coming? What are the implications for the church's mission to the nations today? These questions and more will be the subject of chapter 5.

5

Looking on the Pierced One Now

The Implications for John's Readers

CHAPTER 2 SOUGHT TO demonstrate that Zech 12:10 identifies the Pierced One not merely with Yahweh but especially as Yahweh. Chapters 3 and 4 then developed how John uses Zech 12:10 to build on an understanding of God's self-disclosure in Jesus' two-fold eschatological mission. Because he believes that Jesus is God, John equates Jesus with the pierced God of Zech 12:10. Jesus' Passion and Jesus' Parousia then provide John with the two vantage points from which to interpret God's eschatological coming as prophesied by Zechariah. God's self-disclosure in Jesus' first coming fulfilled the historical prerequisite of Zech 12:10 when Jesus, God the Son, suffered the soldier's spear on the cross (John 19:37). In this way, Jesus' piercing also inaugurated the eschatological "day" of God's coming salvation and judgment. God's self-disclosure in Jesus' second coming provides the opportunity for their consummation, when Jesus the Pierced One returns to close the inter-advent age, judge the nations, and replace their kingdoms with his own (Rev 1:7).

How, then, should readers of the Fourth Gospel and Revelation put the pieces of the biblical narrative together and respond? How should the nations respond after Jesus' first coming and before Jesus' second coming? How does God's eschatological mission in Jesus' two comings affect the church's mission to the nations today? Answering these questions characterizes the substance of the present chapter. Together the answers will support a single goal, namely, to demonstrate how the redemptive-historical drama extending from Zech 12:10 to John 19:37 to Rev 1:7 ought to affect John's readers, both inside and outside the church.[1]

To achieve the stated goal, I will first outline the redemptive-historical development between Zech 12:10, John 19:37, and Rev 1:7 based on the conclusions of chapters 2 through 4 above, also determining how well the outline complements the contours of inaugurated and consummated eschatology found elsewhere in John's Gospel and Revelation.[2] Next, I will return to questions surrounding the identity of the onlookers in John 19:37;[3] and by using the identity of the pierc-

---

1. I say "ought to affect John's readers," knowing that some have attempted to make the study of the NT only a descriptive discipline to the neglect of the prescriptive. E.g., see Räisänen, *Beyond*, 151–202. However, the very nature of the NT documents themselves suggest that they be received quite differently. Not only do their authors ask to be trusted in their eyewitness testimony to Jesus' resurrection, but they also call for their readers to believe and give over their allegiances to Jesus as part of their missionary claim (e.g., John 20:30–31; Rev 1:3). In the words of my NT professor B. Paul Wolfe, "If even only the broad contours of the NT, or the inescapable central points, if you prefer, are correct, then the personal accountability to respond appropriately is a profound reality with which we must all deal. It truly is a matter of life and death, a matter of eternal consequence. Let the reader be warned, the subject at hand has a transforming claim upon your life and destiny from which you may never escape." Cf. also Stuhlmacher, *Biblical Theology*, 1; Rosner, "Biblical Theology," 5; Marshall, *New Testament Theology*, 17–20, 34–37.

2. To clarify, the term "inaugurated" eschatology attempts to capture the recognized biblical-theological tension, wherein the future age of God's kingdom breaks into the present order with the first coming of Christ (e.g., "the kingdom of God is at hand," Mark 1:15). Christ's life, death, resurrection, and exaltation create an overlap of the ages, where various realities tied to God's final kingdom are already present and continue until the second coming of Christ. The term "consummated" eschatology refers to the realities of God's kingdom that are not yet present and await their full realization with the second coming of Christ. For fuller treatments, see Ladd, *Theology of NT*, 368, 622–23; Beale, *NT Biblical Theology*, 129–356. Again, for using the term "inaugurated" over "realized" see the discussion in Smalley, *Evangelist and Interpreter*, 236. Similarly, see Ladd, *Theology of NT*, 308; Cook, "Eschatology," 79–99; Köstenberger, *Theology*, 295–98.

3. In chapter 3, I dealt specifically with the theological significance of Zech 12:10 for Jesus' identity and mission according to John's Gospel, especially as that identity and mission were further illuminated by John 19:37. My intention was never to minimize the theological significance of the onlookers. Rather, since previous

ers/mourners in Rev 1:7 as clarifying support, I will demonstrate how John's readers should "look" upon the Pierced One during the inter-advent period. Finally, I will assess how John's use of Zech 12:10 in his Gospel and Revelation coheres with and gives impetus to the church's mission to the nations.

AN OUTLINE OF GOD'S COMING IN JESUS' TWOFOLD ESCHATOLOGICAL MISSION

"What time is it?" That is a crucial question for readers of Scripture to answer, especially as they respond to the progress of God's self-revelation across the biblical narrative.[4] In order to determine how John's use of Zech 12:10 should lead his readers to respond, we must first outline the redemptive-historical drama unfolding from Zech 12:10 to John 19:37 to Rev 1:7. Doing so will underscore the inner-biblical unity between Zechariah, John, and Revelation. The outline will also enable John's readers to understand where Jesus' two advents place them within the progress of redemptive history and what that inter-advent placement implies for their lives. Only the key eschatological events surrounding the Pierced One in Zech 12–13 will receive attention in the following outline, as well as the fulfillment of these events through Jesus' two comings according to John 19:37 and Rev 1:7.

---

studies already developed the significance of the onlookers in relation to John's Gospel only, I wanted to develop their significance in light of John 19:37 and Rev 1:7 simultaneously, so that the contours of inaugurated and consummated eschatology stand out as well as their implications for John's readers. I am now returning to this subject.

4. In terms of God's progressive self-revelation in Scripture, Carson provides a helpful definition: "By 'progressive revelation' I refer to the fact that God progressively revealed himself in event and in Scripture, climaxing the events with the death-resurrection-exaltation of Christ and climaxing the Scriptures with the closing of the canon. The result is that God's ways and purposes were progressively fulfilled not only in redemption events but also in inscripturated explanation. The earlier revelation prepares for the later; the later carries further and in some ways explicates the earlier." Carson, *Collected Writings*, 133–34. See further treatments of progressive revelation in Packer, "Progressive Revelation," 143–58; Poythress, "Divine Meaning," 241–79.

Jesus as the Pierced One

Outlining Key Events from Zech 12–13

In Zech 12:1—13:1, God promised to act on behalf of his people by judging enemy nations gathered against Jerusalem (Zech 12:1–9), by pouring out the Spirit[5] and thereby causing his covenant people to look upon him, the Pierced One, with a new spirit of repentance (Zech 12:10–14), and by opening a fountain for cleansing his people from sin and uncleanness (Zech 13:1). Most striking was the fact that the prophecy included the future piercing of God (Zech 12:10),[6] a theological enigma in itself but a happening that still fit within Zechariah's broader theme of God's eschatological coming (e.g., Zech 2:10; 14:5). All these events were to transpire "on that day" (Zech 12:3, 4, 6, 8, 9, 11), a day marking the end of redemptive history with the arrival of God's kingdom on earth.

Outlining Key Events from John 19:37

After studying John's use of Zech 12:10 in his Gospel and Revelation, it seems that the eschatological "day" wherein these prophecies find their fulfillment is also temporally expansive enough to include within its purview both Jesus' death on the cross and Jesus' judgment at his return. According to John, the enigmatic piercing of God becomes possible only when God the Son takes to himself a human nature (John 1:14). As God's supreme self-disclosure in the Word, Jesus is fully man and fully God (John 1:1–3, 14, 18). For the soldier in John 19:34 to pierce Jesus, then, was for him to pierce God, that is, the person of God the Son incarnate.[7] Using Zech 12:10 to interpret the events transpiring at the cross, John shows that Jesus' historical piercing realizes the prerequisite of Zechariah's prediction that the people will look upon God whom they pierced (John 19:37).[8] Moreover, Jesus' piercing indicates

---

5. For further discussion on Yahweh's Spirit being poured out to change the human spirit in God's people, see p. 27

6. Chapter 2 sought to identify the Pierced One as Yahweh (i.e., "me" in Zech 12:10).

7. See the section titled "The Divine Identity of Jesus" on pp. 107–9. For an extensive treatment of the deity of Christ, see the study by Wellum, *God the Son*, 189–208.

8. See the section titled "The Divine Revelation in Jesus' Death" on pp. 109–11 above.

the inauguration of that eschatological "day" when God pours out his Spirit to transform his people's spirit (John 3:3, 5; 7:39; 19:34; Zech 12:10), causes his people to look upon him (John 19:37; Zech 12:10–14), and cleanses their sins (John 1:29; 20:23; 1 John 1:9; Zech 13:1).[9] In that sense, Jesus' piercing secures salvation for the nations who trust in his death for eternal life (John 3:16; 20:31). Jesus' piercing further indicates the inauguration of that eschatological "day" when God judges the rebellious world (John 12:31; Zech 12:2–9). The consummation of the world's judgment becomes John's focus in Rev 1:7.

Outlining Events from Rev 1:7

Complementing the message of John 19:37, Rev 1:7 becomes a further contribution in explaining the events of Zech 12:10–14 along the lines of consummated eschatology.[10] Based on the observations in chapter 4, the "coming" in Rev 1:7 refers to Jesus' second coming, wherein he consummates God's eschatological mission by closing the inter-advent age with final judgment (cf. Rev 1:7 with Rev 6:12–17; 19:11–21). Even more pointed, Jesus' future coming is still God's coming since Jesus the Lamb shares in the divine identity.[11] For Jesus to arrive is for God's final kingdom to usurp and replace all rebel kingdoms with his earthly rule. The period for Israel and the nations to look upon the pierced God and mourn in repentance will end upon Jesus' personal arrival, or his Parousia. Since Jesus' Parousia means no further time for repentance, John reverses, or inverts, the type of mourning that Zech 12:12–14 originally envisioned.[12] Jesus' Parousia will mean the rebellious community can

---

9. See the section titled "The Divine Mission of Jesus" on pp. 111–19 above. Cf. also the observations on cleansing according to Johannine theology in Rainbow, *Johannine Theology*, 211.

10. Again, "consummated" eschatology refers to the realities of God's kingdom that are not yet present but reach their full realization with the second coming of Christ.

11. Chapter 4 developed Jesus' divine identity along the following subheadings: "Jesus' Words and God's Words," "Jesus and OT Metaphors Ascribed to God," "Jesus and OT Motifs Ascribed to God," "Jesus and the Worship of God."

12. For more examples of John's inverted use of the OT in Revelation, or, what I am calling a reversed appropriation, see Beale, *Revelation*, 94–96.

no longer mourn in repentance; they must mourn in terror as God's judgment falls on the nations by the Pierced One.

In this manner, John's use of Zech 12:10 from the vantage points of inaugurated (John 19:37) and consummated (Rev 1:7) eschatology provides a significant contribution to understanding God's ultimate self-disclosure at the end of redemptive history. The eschatological "day" of God's coming as the Pierced One occurs in two episodes, the first episode occurring in the death of Jesus and the second in the return of Jesus. Or, God's ultimate self-disclosure transpires in the twofold eschatological mission of Jesus Christ. The figure below seeks to illustrate the aforementioned outline and how the present study understands John to be interpreting Zech 12:10 from the standpoint of Christ's (i.e., the Pierced One's) two comings.[13]

The Pierced One's Redeeming Advents

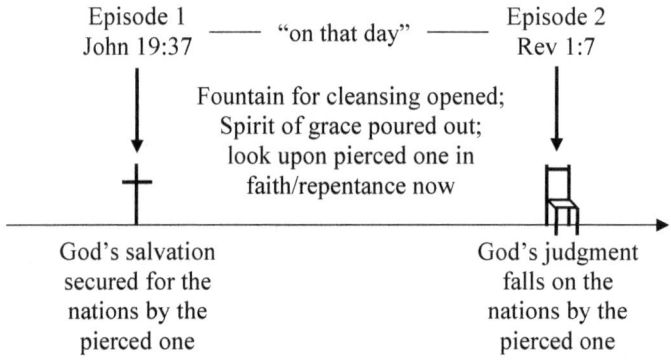

In the figure above, the eschatological "day" of God's coming in Christ extends from Jesus' first coming in which he was pierced on the cross (i.e., Episode 1) to Jesus' second coming in which people witness the one once pierced establishing his earthly rule (i.e., Episode 2). On the cross God secured salvation for the nations by Jesus the Son being pierced, whereas at Jesus' return God's judgment will fall on the nations by the Pierced One. Both episodes of God's coming in Christ then

---

13. For a similar view of the NT's use of Zech 12:10, see Petterson, *Zechariah*, 268. Such an interpretation also has historical precedent dating back to Justin Martyr. Skarsaune has demonstrated that Justin (esp. in *Dial*. 32.2) used Zech 12:10 to speak of Jesus' two comings in a manner similar to the presentation above. Skarsaune, *Proof from Prophecy*, 156, 311.

frame the inter-advent period in which John envisions some from the nations benefitting from God's gracious Spirit and responding to the Pierced One in faith/repentance.

So much for outlining the key events unfolding from Zech 12:10 to John 19:37 to Rev 1:7. Determining whether it coheres with John's eschatology elsewhere still needs further development below.

Inaugurated and Consummated Eschatology in John's Gospel and Revelation

Outlining (and illustrating) the Pierced One's redeeming advents in the manner above coheres with the way John's eschatology develops elsewhere in his Gospel and Revelation. Both John's Gospel and Revelation develop Jesus' two comings as well as what those two comings imply for the people living between them. Stated differently, John's inaugurated eschatology due to Jesus' first coming and John's consummated eschatology due to Jesus' second coming, together announce that God's end-time salvation is already available, and that it is imperative that all peoples trust in Christ in order to benefit from that end-time salvation.

In John's Gospel

John's Gospel contains several passages that advance the inaugurated and consummated eschatology associated with Jesus' two comings.[14] In John 5:25–29, for example, Jesus explains his mission as the Son of Man in terms of an hour that "is coming" and an hour that "now is."[15] John often uses "hour" (ὥρα) in a unique manner to mark the period

---

14. In the following observations, I am distancing myself from the traditions that follow C. H. Dodd and Rudolf Bultmann, who both argued for a fully "realized" eschatology in the ministry of Jesus. E.g., see Dodd, "Kingdom," 138–42; Bultmann, *Theology*, 2:75–92. By contrast, others have demonstrated the contours of both inaugurated and consummated eschatology in John's Gospel. E.g., see Ladd, *Theology of NT*, 334–44; Cook, "Eschatology," 79–99; Köstenberger, *Theology*, 295–98.

15. Jesus says in John 5:25, "Truly, truly, I say to you, an hour is coming and now is [ἔρχεται ὥρα καὶ νῦν ἐστιν], when the dead will hear the voice of the Son of God, and those who hear will live." In John 5:28, however, Jesus says that the hour is "coming" (without νῦν ἐστιν): "Do not marvel at this, for an hour is coming [ἔρχεται ὥρα] when all who are in the tombs will hear [the Son of Man's] voice . . . "

Jesus as the Pierced One

encompassing Jesus' death[16] as well as its ongoing effects.[17] John may also use "hour" to mark a specific event (e.g., John 16:21; 19:27). The hour that "is coming" in John 5:28 seems to mark the specific event of resurrection at the close of the inter-advent age.[18] Jesus explains that all who are in the tombs will hear the Son of Man's voice and will come out, "those who have done good to the resurrection of life, and those who have done evil to the resurrection of judgment" (John 5:28-29).[19] At the same time, since Jesus the Son has life in himself as the Father has life in himself, Jesus has the ability to make people sharers in eternal life even prior to the final resurrection: "Truly, truly, I say to you, an hour is coming and now is when the dead will hear the voice of the Son of God, and those who hear will live" (John 5:25).[20] The same authority and power in the Son of Man's voice to raise dead bodies at the final resurrection is the same authority and power to give spiritually dead people eternal life even before the final resurrection. Indeed, the Son of Man may give life to others, because he will soon die to secure life for others. Thus, while Jesus' death and its ongoing effects will bring people life,[21] the hour that "is coming and now is" suggests that the life stemming from his own pending death and resurrection is not merely a future gift but one that is "proleptically present" in Jesus' person and

---

16. John 7:30; 8:20; 12:23, 27; 13:1; 16:32; 17:1.

17. John 2:4; 4:21; 16:2, 25. More detailed discussion on John's use ὥρα in his Gospel appears under the section titled "Jesus' Death on the Cross" on pp. 97-100.

18. So also Carson, *John*, 258; Ridderbos, *John*, 199; Keener, *John*, 1:653; Köstenberger, *John*, 189.

19. Cf. Dan 12:2; Matt 25:31-32; Acts 24:15; 1 Cor 15:52; Rev 20:4-5, 11-15. These references also envision a future resurrection of the just and the unjust at the eschaton. That the final resurrection at the end of history is in view also appears evident by the way Jesus and Martha later refer to a resurrection on "the last day" (τῇ ἐσχάτῃ ἡμέρᾳ) in John 6:39 and John 11:24, respectively.

20. See also Carson, *John*, 256-57. Carson also notes the presence of John's "already" and "not yet" eschatology in John 5:25.

21. That Jesus' death brings life to those who are perishing seems especially evident in John 6:51c: "and the bread that I will give for the life [ζωῆς] of the world is my flesh." Jesus' death brings life in that it delivers people from the curse of death (e.g., Jesus was "lifted up" like the serpent in the wilderness to give eternal life; John 3:14-16), and in that it serves to glorify Jesus, thereby inaugurating the age of the Spirit who gives life to those who believe (cf. John 4:14; 7:38-39).

ministry.[22] Those who listen to Jesus' voice can already experience the benefits of his pending death through following him and finding in him eternal life, which is to know God and Jesus Christ whom he has sent (John 17:3). Thus, the hour that "now is" in John 5:25 refers to the redemptive-historical turning point marked by God's first coming in Jesus.[23] The benefits of God's eschatological salvation are already available in the person and ministry of Jesus.[24] In that sense, the hour that "now is" in John 5:25 highlights inaugurated eschatology. The hour that "is coming" in John 5:28 refers to the consummation of these days at the final resurrection.

What is the implied significance for those living in this overlap of the hour that is "already" and the hour that is "not yet"? Prior to the consummation, John 5:24 specifies the implications for Jesus' hearers: "Truly, truly, I say to you, whoever hears my word and believes him who sent me has eternal life. He does not come into judgment [i.e., condemnation at Jesus' return], but has passed from death to life."[25] According to John 3:36 people abide under God's wrath already (cf. also John 3:18). John 5:24 calls the desperate predicament death, and John 5:29 shows that abiding in death (or under wrath) will eventually result in the experience of final judgment at the resurrection. In short, one's current state determines their future state. John 5:24 offers hope to people abiding in death beneath God's wrath. God can change their current state "from death to life" before the last day of judgment arrives. People must listen to the Son of Man's voice and believe the Father sent him to grant eternal life and to rescue from the coming judgment through his specific mission. By listening and believing, people pass from death to life, thus changing their current state from abiding under

22. Carson, *John*, 224, 256.

23. Carson, *John*, 224.

24. See also Beasley-Murray, *John*, 76–77.

25. John appears to relate judgment with death, so that not to come into judgment means to pass from death to life. John 3:36 likewise states that "whoever believes in the Son has eternal life; whoever does not obey the Son shall not see life, but the wrath of God remains on him." Thus, death (i.e., not seeing [eternal] life) in John 3:36 is equivalent to the wrath of God remaining on the individual. As in John 5:24, then, death is not merely physical death but experiencing judgment under God's wrath. In both contexts, believing in the Son (or in the Father who sent him) delivers one from such death/judgment.

Jesus as the Pierced One

God's wrath to having eternal life with God's Son. What readers of John discern, therefore, is that Jesus' first coming (inaugurated eschatology) has both serious and beneficial implications for life prior to the last day (consummated eschatology).[26]

Likewise, in John 6:38–39 one finds Jesus explaining his mission from the Father along the lines of inaugurated and consummated eschatology. Jesus has already come down from heaven, not to do his own will but the will of the Father who sent him (John 6:38). The will of the Father includes not only all his people coming to Jesus and Jesus never losing the people entrusted to him, but also "raising" (ἀναστήσω) the same people from the dead[27] on the last day (John 6:38, 40, 44, 54). Jesus' coming down from heaven and Jesus' raising the Father's people on the last day relate to inaugurated and consummated eschatology, respectively. The implications for people living after Jesus' coming down from heaven also become clear within the same context: " . . . whoever comes to me I will never cast out" (John 6:37); " . . . everyone who looks on the Son and believes in him should have eternal life" (John 6:40); "whoever feeds on my flesh and drinks my blood has eternal life . . . " (John 6:54). People living between Jesus coming down and Jesus raising the dead on the last day must come, look, believe, feed, and drink.

The narrative of Jesus raising Lazarus presents a similar dynamic for readers of the Fourth Gospel. Still mourning the death of her brother Lazarus, Martha is aware of the resurrection on the last day, that is, at the consummation of the age (John 11:24). Jesus then responds in the following manner: "I am the resurrection and the life. Whoever believes in me, though he die, yet shall he live, and everyone who lives and believes in me shall never die. Do you believe this?" (John 11:25–26). The response not only reassures Martha of the final resurrection (i.e., "though he die, yet shall he live"), but also points Martha to the life of the resurrection age available to Martha now through believing in Jesus

---

26. Introducing comments on John 5:24–30, Keener likewise states, "Jesus returns to the claim that the Father has authorized him to give life (5:21) with the image of realized eschatology implied by 'passed from death to life' (5:24); one already abides in death until believing in the one who sent Jesus, hence in Jesus' delegated mission (cf. also 3:18)." Keener, *John*, 1:652.

27. When the use of ἀνίστημι in John 11:23, 24, 31 and John 20:9 is taken into account, it seems clear that Jesus has raising people from the grave in view.

(i.e., "everyone who lives and believes in me shall never die"). The former represents consummated eschatology and the latter inaugurated eschatology. Until the final resurrection occurs, though, the question that Jesus poses to Martha presses upon all readers of John's Gospel: "Do you believe this?" (cf. John 20:31).[28] In other words, the time to believe these things about Jesus is now, prior to the final resurrection. Other examples contribute to the same eschatological perspective in John's Gospel and show how that perspective should produce faith in Jesus' followers, including those who become followers after reading the Gospel of John (e.g., John 4:21, 23; 14:1–3).

In Revelation

Revelation shares the same two-fold eschatological perspective.[29] As noted in chapter 4, Revelation presents Christ's cross and resurrection as God's decisive victory over evil and the inauguration of God's end-time salvation. The book's focus, however, is that Christ's second coming will soon consummate God's end-time salvation.[30] Because of Christ's present reign (inaugurated eschatology) and because of Christ's coming judgment (consummated eschatology), serious implications follow for John's readers. For example, only those who "hear" and "keep" (i.e., in the sense of obey) what is written in the prophecy will receive God's blessing (Rev 1:3a–b). The reason (γὰρ) given for readers to hear and keep is that "the time is near" (Rev 1:3c). That is, the time is near for God's kingdom to supplant all rebel kingdoms through Christ (cf. Rev 1:1; Dan 2:28–29). As stated above, the purpose of revealing the end-time salvation in the present age is to keep the church persevering in humble obedience to Christ until his arrival to close the age.

---

28. See also Köstenberger, *Theology*, 321. Köstenberger writes, "Martha . . . becomes an identification figure for those readers who come to the conclusion desired by the evangelist: 'I believe the you are the Messiah, the Son of God, who was to come into the world' (John 11:27)." Cf. Köstenberger's further observations on John 20:31 in Köstenberger, *Theology*, 260.

29. For a recent theological treatment of the 'already' and 'not yet' aspects of Revelation, see Hoskins, *Revelation*, 17, 29–36.

30. Again, notice the emphasis in Rev 1:1–3, with phrases such as ἃ δεῖ γενέσθαι ἐν τάχει ("things that must soon take place"; Rev 1:1) and ὁ γὰρ καιρὸς ἐγγύς ("for the time is near"; Rev 1:3).

Jesus as the Pierced One

Also, in the letters to the seven churches, Christ issues several exhortations to repent from sinful practices (Rev 2:5, 16, 21; 3:3, 19). At least part of the motivation to repent is that Christ will soon come as judge: "I will come to you and remove your lampstand from its place" (Rev 2:5); "I will come to you soon and war against them with the sword of my mouth" (Rev 2:16; cf. 19:15, 21); "I will give to each of you according to your works" (Rev 2:23; cf. 22:12); "I will come like a thief, and you will not know at what hour I will come against you" (Rev 3:3). In other words, Christ's inaugurated victory over evil makes repentance possible for God's people, and Christ's consummating return makes repentance necessary for God's people.

Readers also find the following four imperatives at the end of John's prophecy: "The Spirit and the Bride say, 'Come [ἔρχου].' And let the one who hears say, 'Come [ἔρχου].' And let the one who is thirsty come [ἐρχέσθω]; let the one who desires take [λαβέτω] the water of life without price" (Rev 22:17). Whether the third and fourth imperatives to "come" and to "take" further serve the church's own perseverance, or openly invite the unbelieving community to partake of Christ's salvation,[31] the relevant point for our analysis is this: the inaugurated victory of Christ means that people must "come" and "take" now before the Spirit and the Bride's prayers for Christ to "come" are fully answered and realized (cf. Rev 22:12, 17, 20). Again, the inaugurated eschatology and consummated eschatology creates the inter-advent age wherein people not only can but must respond to Christ and his rule.

Thus, to outline the Pierced One's redeeming advents as I did above appears to cohere with the way John's eschatology develops elsewhere in the Fourth Gospel and Revelation. The coherent pattern is that the events associated with Jesus' first coming inaugurate the final, inter-advent age that will eventually consummate with the events associated with Jesus' second coming. Moreover, it has become even clearer that both John's Gospel and Revelation present Christ's two comings—and in the case of our study, the Pierced One's two comings—as having serious implications for the people living between them (e.g., come, drink, believe, obey), including people like John's readers. These more general observations prepare us for understanding how the overarching

---

31. See the discussion in Beale, *Revelation*, 1148–50.

Looking on the Pierced One Now

narrative between John's Gospel and Revelation urges readers to look upon the Pierced One in the present, inter-advent age.

IDENTIFYING THE ONLOOKERS OF JOHN 19:37 IN LIGHT OF THE PIERCERS/MOURNERS OF REV 1:7

That brings us to addressing the onlookers in John 19:37 and how John wants his readers to look upon the Pierced One during the inter-advent age. The quotation in John 19:37 states that "they will look [ὄψονται] on him whom they have pierced [ἐξεκέντησαν]." The subjects behind ὄψονται (i.e., the onlookers) are the primary interest of what follows, but determining the subjects behind ἐξεκέντησαν (i.e., the piercers) will also prove helpful to identifying the onlookers. Thus, the following section will address both the onlookers and the piercers with the latter helping to identify the former. As noted in chapter 3, I intentionally waited to address the onlookers in the Fourth Gospel until now. Not only had others already devoted significant and detailed research to the subject from John 19:37 specifically,[32] but I wanted to develop the onlookers' significance in light of the aforementioned contours of inaugurated and consummated eschatology in John's writings. That is, what message[33] presses upon John's readers as they consider both the onlookers of John 19:37 and the piercers/mourners of Rev 1:7 simultaneously? If John 19:37 and Rev 1:7 stand as complementary elements within John's unified, eschatological narrative, and both draw from Zech 12:10, then what conclusions might one draw about those who look upon the one they pierced?

Identifying the subjects behind ὄψονται ("they will look") in John 19:37 has proven elusive for interpreters of the Fourth Gospel,[34] even

---

32. E.g., Brown, *John XIII–XXI*, 954–55; Lindars, *John*, 591; Schnackenburg, *John*, 3:293–94; Moo, *Old Testament*, 213–14; Carson, *John*, 628; Schuchard, *Scripture within Scripture*, 146; Menken, "Textual Form," 504–10; Tuckett, "Zechariah 12:10 and the NT," 115–19; Kubiś, *Zechariah in John*, 194–98; Bynum, *Fourth Gospel*, 176–79; Bynum, "Quotations," 70–71.

33. I am using the word "message" to mean "an idea that demands a response." Waltke, *Old Testament Theology*, 49n1. I was first directed to this definition by Williams, "Message," 2–3.

34. On the uncertainty of the onlookers' identity, see the remarks by Schuchard, *Scripture within Scripture*, 146; Menken, "Textual Form," 505; Devillers, "L'interprétation," 140; Hübenthal, *Transformation*, 70. Cf. also Carson, *John*, 628.

leading some to conclude that John's interest in using Zech 12:10 lies only in the "piercing" and not the "looking."[35] At the same time, interpreters such as Lindars have stressed the importance of the onlookers' identity: "What he [the Evangelist] intends this to be [i.e., his use of Zech 12:10] can only be decided when the subject of *they shall look* has been identified."[36] Several proposals for the onlookers' identity in John 19:37 have circulated.

Proposal 1: The Onlookers as the Eyewitness of John 19:35 Alone

J. Ramsey Michaels finds no (explicit) reason to extend the identity of the onlookers beyond the eyewitness of John 19:35, whom he views as the literal fulfillment of Zech 12:10.[37] The strength of Michaels's proposal is the immediate context: the only person John records as "seeing" (cf. ὁράω in John 19:35, 37) just following Jesus' piercing is the eyewitness of John 19:35. A weakness of this proposal is that John 19–20 also present others who—whether by being bystanders at the cross (John 19:20, 25, 33) or post-resurrection witnesses to Jesus' pierced side (John 20:27–28)—become equally likely candidates for ὄψονται and better suit its plural subject ("they").[38] Another weakness is that Michaels's proposal forces one to understand the onlookers (i.e., the eyewitness in John 19:35) to differ from the piercers (i.e., the soldier in John 19:34), whereas in Zech 12:10 the onlookers are also the piercers.

Carson prefaces his own comments regarding the onlookers as follows: "If John has a referent for *They*, he does not tell us . . ."

35. Barrett, *John*, 559. So also Lenski, *John*, 1322.

36. Lindars, *John*, 591. Italics were originally bold.

37. Michaels, *John*, 977. In terms of the piercers, Michaels also sees no reason to extend the identity of the piercers beyond the soldier in John 19:34 who literally pierces Jesus.

38. See especially Kubiś, *Zechariah in John*, 194–98. Cf. Menken, "Textual Form," 508; Thompson, *John*, 405. More will be said on the plural ("they") below, especially when understood in light of Rev 1:7.

Proposal 2: The Onlookers as a Group Much Broader than the Piercers

Adam Kubiś proposes that the onlookers, while likely including the piercers, are a much broader group than the piercers.[39] Kubiś argues that the two verbs of the Zechariah quotation in John 19:37 (i.e., ὄψονται and ἐξεκέντησαν) have different subjects.[40] Those who pierced Jesus consist of "only the Roman soldiers and the Jews."[41] Nevertheless, the broader context of John's Gospel suggests that those "looking" upon the pierced Jesus encompass a larger group: "the Roman soldiers, the Jews, ὁ ἑωρακὼς [i.e., the eyewitness of John 19:35], Jesus' mother, the women, and present and future believers."[42] As support for including "present and future believers" in ὄψονται, Kubiś points to "the Johannine concept of *seeing* as an expression of *faith*," as well as to the aim of John's testimony to bring his hearers/readers to faith in Jesus (John 19:35; 20:31).[43] Indeed, Kubiś views the beloved disciple as the believer

---

39. The most extensive treatment of the onlookers in John 19:37 belongs to Kubiś, *Zechariah in John*, 194–216. Kubiś represents and builds on the work of Boismard and Lamouille, *Jean*, 451; Lindars, *John*, 591; Schnackenburg, *John*, 3:343–44; Menken, "Textual Form," 504–10; Maloney, *John*, 510; Klauck, "Schriftzitate in Der Johannespassion," 156. Kubiś's proposal is similar to that of Menken in that Kubiś broadens the onlookers in contrast to the piercers. However, Menken sees the onlookers to encompass primarily believers who see Jesus for who he really is, the first and ideal believer being John the eyewitness himself. Menken, "Textual Form," 509–10.

40. Kubiś, *Zechariah in John*, 197. See also Schnackenburg, *John*, 3:293; Menken, "Textual Form," 504–5; Devillers, "L'interprétation," 140; Hübenthal, *Transformation*, 215.

41. Kubiś, *Zechariah in John*, 197. While only one soldier literally pierced Jesus (John 19:34), John 19:37 preserves the plural verb, ἐξεκέντησαν ("they pierced"). The Roman soldiers also pierced Jesus as the result of the initial instigation by the Jews (John 18:12; 19:7, 12–14), making "the Jews" culpable in the piercing.

42. Kubiś, *Zechariah in John*, 197. The Roman soldiers "saw" that Jesus was dead (cf. εἶδον in John 19:33) and proceeded to pierce him in John 19:34. It is also clear that John is one who "has seen" the soldiers pierce Jesus (cf. ὁ ἑωρακὼς in John 19:35). Kubiś then extends the subjects behind ὄψονται to include the Jews (cf. John 19:20), several women present at the crucifixion (cf. John 19:25), and present/future believers (cf. John 19:35 with 20:31).

43. Kubiś, *Zechariah in John*, 196.

Jesus as the Pierced One

par excellence, and thus representing all believers who choose to look upon Jesus with faith.[44]

Kubiś's proposal has its strengths. In terms of identifying the piercers, the proposal resonates with the fact that only one (εἷς) of the soldiers pierced Jesus' side with a spear in John 19:34, and yet John still preserves the plural ἐξεκέντησαν ("they pierced") in John 19:37. Kubiś's proposal also accounts for the likely bystanders at the cross and frames the "look" of the Zechariah citation within the Johannine theme of "seeing,"[45] a theme that enables Kubiś to connect ὄψονται with all future readers who may "see" the Pierced One by faith as John himself has.[46]

However, a potential weakness is that Kubiś interprets the two verbs in the Zechariah citation as having different subjects whereas the onlookers are the same group as the piercers in Zech 12:10, a point that Kubiś himself admits but does not find insurmountable.[47] On the differentiation of the subjects, Kubiś finds Menken's analysis of the use of Zech 12:10 in Rev 1:7 helpful:

---

44. Kubiś, *Zechariah in John*, 196.

45. Beginning with the most obvious, the Roman soldiers "saw" that Jesus was dead (cf. εἶδον in John 19:33) and proceeded to pierce him in John 19:34. It is also clear that the eyewitness is one who "has seen" the soldiers pierce Jesus (cf. ὁ ἑωρακὼς in John 19:35). Moving to the less obvious, Kubiś extends the subjects behind ὄψονται in John 19:37 further to include the Jews (cf. John 19:20), several women (cf. John 19:25), and present/future believers (cf. John 19:35 with 20:31). Kubiś, *Zechariah in John*, 196–97. Compared with the broader NT witness, for Kubiś to include the Jews and several women alongside the Roman soldiers and John seems warranted (e.g., Matt 27:55–56; Mark 15:40–41; Luke 23:27, 47–49). Broadening the subjects behind ὄψονται to encompass present (i.e., present to John) and future believers, of course, necessitates further development of the looking in terms of a spiritual "look" with the eyes of faith. See, e.g., Obermann, *Erfüllung*, 322; Maloney, *John*, 510; Klauck, "Schriftzitate in Der Johannespassion," 156; Kubiś, *Zechariah in John*, 196; Bynum, *Fourth Gospel*, 177–79.

46. See especially Kubiś, *Zechariah in John*, 198–213. Further discussion on the theme of "seeing/looking" and how John's testimony affects future believers will ensue below.

47. Kubiś states, "The subjects of both verbs seems to be the same in the MT and OG of Zec 12:10." Kubiś, *Zechariah in John*, 197n355. For further discussion, see the analysis in chapter 2 above, where "the house of David and the inhabitants of Israel" stand as the primary subjects who look, pierce, and mourn in Zech 12:10–14.

Still more important is the fact that in Jewish and early Christian exegesis of Zech 12:10 outside John 19:37 it is often presupposed that the subjects of the two verb forms in Zech 12:10aβ are not identical. In Rev 1:7 and Matt 24:30, "every eye" and "all the tribes of the earth" are those who mourn; that implies that the subject of "looking" encompasses many more people than the subject of "piercing."[48]

Both Menken and Kubiś equate "every eye" in Rev 1:7b with the subject "they" in "they will look" of Zech 12:10.[49] They do so by understanding "every eye" seeing in Rev 1:7b to represent the same group as "all the tribes" mourning in Rev 1:7c and Matt 24:30. Accordingly, if "every eye" represents the same group as "all the tribes," then it makes sense why Menken and Kubiś would conclude that the onlookers must be a larger group than the piercers.

It is true that "every eye" is a larger group than the piercers themselves,[50] but that need not imply that "every eye" is then equivalent to "all the tribes" who mourn in Rev 1:7c. Revelation 1:7 does not necessarily equate the "they" in "they will look" of Zech 12:10 with "every eye"; nor does Rev 1:7 necessarily equate "every eye" with "all the tribes."[51] Revelation 1:7b could focus on the piercers as a subgroup within "every eye" (i.e., "every eye will see him, even/including [καὶ] those who pierced him"); and this subgroup of piercers consists of "all the tribes of the earth" who will also mourn with terror at Jesus' Parousia (Rev 1:7c). John would then understand the "they" in "they will look" of Zech 12:10 as still being the subgroup of piercers/mourners within "every eye." In this way there still remains a common subject between the verbs even in the use of Zech 12:10 in Rev 1:7.[52] For further clarity, the difference in interpretation may be illustrated as follows:

---

48. Menken, "Textual Form," 505.
49. Menken, "Textual Form," 505; Kubiś, *Zechariah in John*, 198n357.
50. Cf. also Hanson, *Prophetic Gospel*, 224.
51. In terms of Matt 24:30, the universal witness of Jesus' return seems evident from Matt 24:26–28. Nevertheless, like Rev 1:7, Matt 24:30–31 seems to differentiate between "all the tribes" who mourn with dread at the Son of Man's arrival in judgment and all the elect (i.e., the redeemed) whom are gathered from the four points of the compass (cf. 1 Thess 4:16–17; Rev 14:14–20).
52. I am indebted to Paul Hoskins for helping me untangle my thoughts over

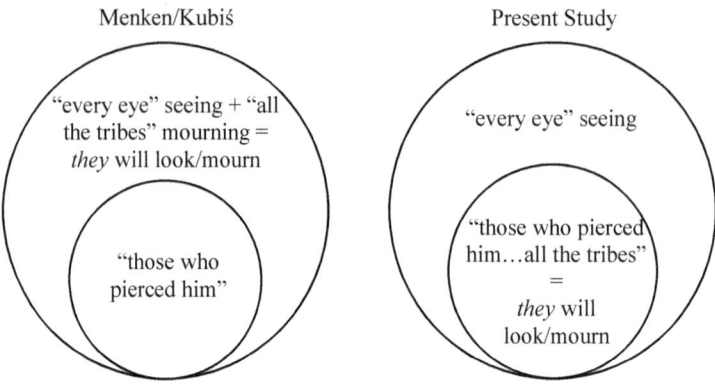

Thus, "every eye" will in fact see Jesus coming with the clouds of heaven, but within "every eye" will be the subgroup of piercers who look and mourn. Therefore, in the use of Zech 12:10 in Rev 1:7, it seems that John maintains that the onlookers are the same group as the piercers. Perhaps John is doing something similar in John 19:37.[53]

Proposal 3: The Onlookers as the Group Present at Jesus' Parousia

Another proposal for identifying the onlookers is to understand the onlookers in a strictly future sense. The onlookers consist of only those who look on the pierced Jesus at the Parousia. Taking Matt 24:30 and Rev 1:7 as their cue, Sanders and Mastin argue that the onlookers of John 19:37 must be "the opponents of the Pierced One, and it is the future occasion of Christ's return that his enemies will gaze on him."[54] For Sanders and Mastin, Jesus' piercing at the cross fulfills only the piercing aspect of Zech 12:10, while the looking awaits Jesus' final

---

this point raised by Menken and Kubiś from Rev 1:7. See also Hoskins, *Revelation*, 55–56.

53. Yes, John universalizes the piercers and mourners from "the house of David and the inhabitants of Jerusalem" in Zech 12:10 to "all the tribes of the earth" in Rev 1:7, but the onlookers still remain the same group as the piercers and mourners, only now the group is from all the tribes. Further discussion on how this broad group of piercers/mourners fits within the John's theology in the Fourth Gospel and Revelation develops below.

54. Sanders and Mastin, *John*, 414. Cf. also Lagrange, *Jean*, 502; Haenchen, *John*, 196.

Looking on the Pierced One Now

vindication.[55] In that sense, John 19:37 emphasizes the coming judgment. The primary strength of Sanders and Mastin's proposal is that it recognizes the unity between the NT's uses of Zech 12:10, and then tries to account for the future aspect of the "looking." They even interpret the onlookers as "opponents of the Pierced One," which I sought to demonstrate from Rev 1:7c in chapter 4. Nevertheless, a few weaknesses persist. John seems to indicate that the fulfillment[56] applies to both the piercing and the looking, especially since εἰς ὃν ("on him whom") links ὄψονται with ἐξεκέντησαν so closely. Indeed, one wonders how their proposal would also account for the onlookers and piercers being the same group, as they are in Zech 12:10, if they are divided by time (i.e., a partial fulfillment in Jesus' piercing awaiting a total fulfillment in the people's looking at the Parousia). Also, by identifying the onlookers with a strictly future community, Sanders and Mastin's proposal neglects how the looking may also function within John's inaugurated eschatology, a point I started to develop above and will finish doing so below.[57] Finally, Zech 12:10 expected a day when the onlookers would also mourn in repentance as the result of God's gracious initiative, but Sanders and Mastin's proposal seems to emphasize only the onlookers mourning in dread at the judgment alone.[58]

---

55. Sanders and Mastin, *John*, 414. Lenski, Brown, and Moo each recognize others who constrain the onlookers' identity to those present at Jesus' Parousia based on either the future tense of ὄψονται or the NT's use of Zech 12:10–11 elsewhere (i.e., Matt 24:30; Rev 1:7). Lenski, *John*, 1322–23; Brown, *John XIII–XXI*, 954; Moo, *Old Testament*, 213.

56. Cf. πληρωθῇ ... καὶ πάλιν in John 19:36–37. As a linking adverb, πάλιν extends the fulfillment motif in John 19:36–37 to the latter quotation (cf. also John 12:38–39). For further discussion, see the exegesis under "The Quotation of Zech 12:10 in the Narrative of John's Gospel" in chapter 3.

57. In terms of how John's inaugurated eschatology influences his use of Zech 12:10, see, in addition to below, Moo, *Old Testament*, 213–14; Menken, "Textual Form," 509–10; Köstenberger, "John," 505.

58. The proposal I offer in this chapter demonstrates how John's use of Zech 12:10 allows for a mourning in repentance during the inter-advent age and a mourning in dread at Christ's Parousia.

Jesus as the Pierced One

Proposal 4: The Onlookers as the Same Group as the Piercers

Three proposals stand evaluated so far, and one can see how the identity of the onlookers in John 19:37 is not so straightforward, especially when looking at the Fourth Gospel alone. However, one further proposal seems most promising. That proposal maintains that the onlookers are the same group as the piercers and they are a very broad group, and their identity becomes especially clear when understood in light of the piercers and mourners in Rev 1:7.[59] In other words, the following proposal attempts to account for what the other proposals are hesitant to accept, namely, that the onlookers and piercers in John 19:37 are the same group, just as they are in Zech 12:10. Some interpreters have recognized the potential for this proposal, but then dismiss it based on rabbinic interpretation of Zech 12:10,[60] or based on a differentiation of subjects in the looking and the piercing,[61] or based on the absence of the Romans and Jews explicitly "looking" after Jesus' piercing in John

---

59. Neither Schuchard, de Boer, nor Bynum would likely articulate the fourth proposal as I have just done, especially since I am including the influence of Rev 1:7 in understanding John 19:37. Still, how they explain the collective responsibility of the world in Jesus' death, Jew and Gentile alike, fits well with the proposal I am suggesting. Cf. Schuchard, *Scripture within Scripture*, 146; de Boer, *Death of Jesus*, 300–301; Bynum, *Fourth Gospel*, 178. Schuchard indicates on p. 146n21 how Rev 1:7 could influence one's interpretation of John 19:37, but stops short of allowing it to do so. I do not affirm the way de Boer treats John 19:35 as a later insertion that leaves the eyewitness out of the onlookers/piercers.

60. E.g., Lindars writes, "It is not a foregone conclusion that [the subject of *they will look*] is the same as the subject of *they have pierced*. It is true that both Mt. 24.30 and Rev. 1.7 take it this way, so that in the eschatological judgment it is those who have crucified Jesus who look on him in his glory and mourn for their wicked deed, according to the continuation of the passage, which describes a mourning ceremony (Zech. 12.10–14). But in the rabbinic tradition, in which the prophecy is applied to the slaying of the Messiah ben Joseph (*B. Sukkah*, 52a), it is not taken this way, and there seems no reason to do so here." Lindars, *John*, 591. See also Menken, "Textual Form," 504–5.

61. E.g., Menken writes, "In the original text of Zechariah, they [i.e., those who look and those who pierce] seem to be identical. It was quite possible in Jewish and early Christian exegesis, however, that the obvious but not explicitly indicated subject of a verb form was replaced by another subject in the explanation of the biblical text." For a treatment of Menken's argumentation on Rev 1:7 in particular, see the critique of the third proposal above.

19,[62] or based on the difficulty of demonstrating it from John's Gospel alone.[63]

Nevertheless, proposing that ὄψονται and ἐξεκέντησαν share a common subject finds support in the following observations. One, the onlookers, piercers, and mourners are the same group in the original prophecy of Zech 12:10–14, namely, "the house of David and the inhabitants of Jerusalem" (cf. also "Israel" in 12:1; "Judah" in 12:3). Upon a gracious act of God, sinful Israel collectively looks upon Yahweh whom they themselves have collectively pierced. The same Israelites then collectively mourn. It is true that NT authors will sometimes change or broaden the subjects of OT Scriptures when appropriating them for their new, eschatological context. However, the question in John 19:37 is whether John's use of Zech 12:10 evidences a differentiation between the onlookers and piercers, or a broadening to both the onlookers and piercers. If the latter is in view (see further below), then the subjects in ὄψονται and ἐξεκέντησαν would remain the same even if John broadens their referent.

Two, Rev 1:7 presents the piercers and the mourners as the same group, and these are also among those who will "see" Jesus at his return. As argued above, Rev 1:7b focuses on the piercers as a subgroup

---

62. E.g., Tuckett writes, "In one way the most 'obvious' way to read the text is to interpret the subject of the ὄψονται as the same as that of the ἐξεκέντησαν. The 'they' will then be the Roman soldiers. Alternatively one could extend this slightly to include the Jews present at the cross as well. However, nothing is said in the immediate context of either the Roman soldiers or the Jews specifically 'looking at' or 'seeing' Jesus at this point." Tuckett, "Zechariah 12:10 and the NT," 116.

63. E.g., Schuchard writes, "If this is what John has in mind in John 19:37 [i.e., the whole world], then all the possible referents identified above [i.e., the Roman soldiers, the Jews, the eyewitness, etc.] are intended in John's 'they.' Such a solution is attractive, but its likelihood is, again, admittedly difficult to demonstrate." Schuchard, *Scripture within Scripture*, 146. Also, Devillers writes, "Mais Jean identifie-t-il ceux qui vont regarder avec ceux qui ont transpercé? Ce n'est pas certain, et a mon avis c'est improbable. À moins d'imaginer une responsabilité collective de toute l'humanité dans la mise a mort de Jésus, ce qui n'apparaît pas comme une préoccupation johannique" ("But does John identify those who will look with those who have pierced? It is not certain, and in my opinion it is unlikely. Unless we imagine a collective responsibility of all mankind in the putting to death of Jesus, which does not seem like a Johannine preoccupation"). Devillers, "L'interprétation," 140. In light of Rev 1:7 and a Johannine theology of the world, this is precisely what I will attempt to develop below.

Jesus as the Pierced One

within "every eye" who will see. This subgroup of piercers consists of "all the tribes of the earth" who will also mourn at Jesus' return (Rev 1:7c).[64] By including the subgroup of piercers/mourners within "every eye" who will also "see" (ὄψεται) the Pierced One at his return, Rev 1:7 becomes another Johannine text that maintains a common subject between those who pierce/mourn and those who look. Stated differently, within "every eye" there is also the subgroup who, as Zech 12:10 anticipated, look upon the one they pierced and then mourn.[65] If John maintains the common subject in his use of Zech 12:10 in Rev 1:7, then it seems likely that he is doing the same in John 19:37 as well. Based on Zech 12:10 itself and John's use of the prophecy in Rev 1:7, then, it seems best to view the onlookers and piercers as the same group. Yet who are they?

The Piercers Consist of "All the Tribes"

The piercers are likely a very broad group, a group that includes but extends well beyond the immediate referents in John 19. John 19:34 recounts that a Roman soldier pierced Jesus' side, but the soldier does so at the instigation of "the Jews,"[66] who want the bodies removed before the Sabbath (John 19:31). Indeed, throughout John 18–19, "the Jews" are the primary instigators behind Jesus' crucifixion,[67] a role already anticipated by the earlier parts of John's Gospel.[68] In that sense, the un-

---

64. See the exegesis under "Every Eye Beholding" in chapter 4.

65. Again, see the discussion in Hoskins, *Revelation*, 55–56. Also, see the figure on p. 184, which compares the view of Menken and Kubiś with that of the present study.

66. By enclosing the Jews within quotation marks (i.e., "the Jews"), I am attempting to highlight a particular group of Jews that John has in mind, namely, the unbelieving Jews who reject their Messiah. Unless otherwise qualified, I will continue using "the Jews" to refer to unbelieving Israel. Further discussion on "the Jews" in relation to the unbelieving world appears below.

67. John 18:12, 14, 31, 36; 19:7, 12, 16 (i.e., αὐτοῖς), 31. On the ominous αὐτοῖς ("to them") in John 19:16, thereby reinforcing that "it was the machinations of the Judean aristocracy, not the specific hostility of Rome, that would bring about Jesus' execution (18:31–32; 19:6)," see Keener, *John*, 2:1127, 1132–33.

68. E.g., "This was why the Jews were persecuting Jesus, because he was doing these things on the Sabbath" (John 5:16); "This was why the Jews were seeking all the more to kill him, because he was even calling God his own father, making himself equal with God" (John 5:18); " . . . [Jesus] would not go about in Judea, because the

believing Jews also belong to the initial piercers of John 19:37 alongside the Roman soldiers.⁶⁹ One could even argue that by presenting "the Jews" who rejected Jesus as responsible for his crucifixion, John maintains the prophetic expectation that sinful Israel would pierce Yahweh and then look upon him (Zech 12:10).⁷⁰

Of no less importance, however, is that within Rev 1:7 John presents the piercers as a very diverse people. Like the mourners, they consist of "all the tribes of the earth."⁷¹ The piercers are also a people who have opposed Jesus, the piercing itself standing as their act of hostility against Jesus.⁷² Treating Rev 1:7 as a clue to understanding the piercers in John 19:37, "the Jews" are certainly not alone in their rejection and piercing of Jesus. "All the tribes of the earth" pierce Jesus, according to John's appropriation of Zech 12:10 in Rev 1:7.

Such a universal reading of John 19:37 would certainly complement the way John's Gospel presents the sinful world's hostility to Jesus and his inclusion of the unbelieving Jews as key participants within that sinful world. "The Jews" who refuse to believe in Jesus and eventually crucify Jesus (cf. John 19:16) may even be said to represent the entire unbelieving world in its hostility to Jesus.⁷³ For instance, Jesus

---

Jews were seeking to kill him" (John 7:1); ". . . but now you [i.e., the Jews] seek to kill me [Jesus], a man who has told you the truth that I heard from God" (John 8:40; cf. 8:31); "The Jews picked up stones again to stone him" (John 10:31).

69. The plural verb, ἐξεκέντησαν ("they have pierced"), would also imply a collective referent beyond the one soldier who pierced Jesus. Westcott, *John*, 280; Schuchard, *Scripture within Scripture*, 146; de Boer, *Death of Jesus*, 300; Kubiś, *Zechariah in John*, 195; Bynum, *Fourth Gospel*, 178. Such an observation also aligns with the broader NT witness that, while Gentiles were certainly involved and just as guilty, the Jews were responsible for crucifying Jesus (cf. "you" killed/crucified in Acts 2:23, 36; 3:15; 4:10; 5:30).

70. That sinful Israel is in view in Zechariah's original prophecy seems evident in that Israel pierces Yahweh (Zech 12:10), Israel mourns over their wretched deed (Zech 12:11), and Israel needs their sin/uncleanness removed (Zech 13:1).

71. Hoskins, *Revelation*, 55.

72. Ladd, *Theology of NT*, 28–29; Mounce, *Revelation*, 51; Hoskins, *Revelation*, 55–56.

73. Keener, *John*, 1:216–28; Rainbow, *Johannine Theology*, 130–36. Keener observes that "John's characters . . . are sometimes flatter, theological representatives of the realm 'above' (especially Jesus) or of 'the world.' 'The Jews' in the Fourth Gospel are often a flat composite character, representing the evil attitudes of the world." Keener, *John*, 1:217. That is not to say that John always refers to "the Jews" in this

came to his own people, the Jews, but many did not receive him (John 1:11). In doing so, these unbelieving Jews (cf. John 1:12) exemplify the rest of the morally dark world, who did not know Jesus when he entered their habitation as the true light (John 1:9–10; 3:19; 8:12).[74] Also, sharing Abraham's physical lineage (John 8:38) made "the Jews" (John 8:31) no morally better than the rest of the sinful world, who were still slaves of sin (John 8:21, 24, 34) and who needed their sin taken away (John 1:29; cf. 16:8). Furthermore, by desiring to kill Jesus, the unbelieving Jews evidence that they belong to their murderous father, the devil himself (John 8:44; cf. 1 John 3:12). Their will is to do the devil's desires just as the rest of "the world" stands under the devil's deceptive sway and powerful influence (John 12:31; 14:30; 16:11; cf. 1 John 5:19). Jesus also reveals and testifies that the unbelieving world's works are evil (John 3:19; 7:7; 15:18). For this reason the unbelieving world hates Jesus (John 3:20; 7:7; 15:18), and hates him so much that those within it rejoice over Jesus' death instead of mourning (John 16:20). By wanting to kill Jesus, and eventually succeeding, despite his revelatory words and works (cf. John 12:37), the unbelieving Jews thereby exemplify the same profound hatred for Jesus that characterizes the unbelieving world (cf. John 7:1, 7).[75]

---

negative light, such as when he more neutrally describes Jewish feasts (e.g., John 2:13; 5:1; 7:2) and customs (e.g., John 2:6; 18:20), or when he more positively describes God's favor toward them (e.g., John 4:22) and, on occasion, their favorable response toward God's Son (e.g., John 11:45; 12:11). It is only to say that more often than not in the Fourth Gospel, "the Jews," especially when they consist of the unbelieving religious elite and their followers, represent the same sinful attitudes of "the world" in its hostility to Christ. In other words, John's Gospel is not anti-Semitic, but written, in part, to expose the profound irony of "the Jews" rejecting their own Messiah with the rest of the unbelieving world and then to appeal for faith in the one to whom their own Scriptures pointed for centuries.

74. Speaking to the unbelieving Jews in John 8:23, Jesus says directly, "You are from below; I am from above. You are of this world; I am not of this world." Pryor's study on John 1:11 concludes as follows: "So here at the very beginning of the gospel is a theme which is developed in the ensuing chapters: Israel, though acknowledged as the πατρίς of Jesus, his own people by race, have shown by their rejection of him to belong totally to the world." Pryor, "Jesus and Israel," 218.

75. The world's hatred in John 7:7 seems to be that of the Jews in John 7:1. Moreover, that Jesus refers to "their Law" (i.e., the Jews' Law in John 15:25) in the context of the world's hatred of Jesus indicates that "the Jews" are implicated with the unbelieving world in hating Jesus (John 15:23–25). In this way, John's Gospel reflects

Looking on the Pierced One Now

According to his Gospel's presentation of the world's hostility to Jesus—the Satanic and murderous pursuits of the unbelieving Jews being included—it appears that John would view the entire sinful world as those who pierce Jesus. John makes such a view of the world more explicit in Rev 1:7, namely, that Jesus' opponents from "all the tribes of the earth" stand responsible for his piercing. Just as Zech 12:10 anticipated, John indicates that sinful Israel, otherwise known as the unbelieving Jews, did in fact pierce Jesus. Nevertheless, these unbelieving Jews did so as allies within and representatives of the broader sinful world that opposes Jesus.[76] In that sense, the entire sinful world is responsible for Jesus' death and piercing, especially as that world's unbelieving disposition toward Jesus aligns with that of the actual Jewish and Roman perpetrators.[77]

---

a similar outlook found in Revelation. Indeed, Jews who refuse to follow Jesus and instead kill him and persecute his people are not really Jews at all. Instead, the unbelieving Jews are no less than a "synagogue of Satan" (Rev 2:9; 3:9). The unbelieving Jews are like the citizens of that great city of the Beast, where their Lord was crucified (Rev 11:8). They rejoice over the death of God's witnesses just as they rejoiced over the death of Jesus (Rev 11:10; John 16:20), proving that they belong to that world whom the Dragon deceives (Rev 12:9). Hoskins, *Revelation*, 56, 201.

76. Such an observation also aligns with Acts 4:27, where the early church interprets the rebellious "peoples" (LXX: λαοὶ) of Ps 2:1 as "the peoples [λαοῖς] of Israel" who gathered with the nations against the Lord and his Christ at the cross. As Marshall puts it, "The inclusion of Israel among the foes of the Messiah marks the beginning of the Christian understanding that insofar as the people of Israel reject their Messiah they cease to be the Lord's people and can be ranked with unbelieving Gentiles." Marshall, *Acts*, 106. The observation is important because the Apostle John is among the group who interpret Ps 2 in this manner (cf. Acts 4:19–21, 23).

77. To repeat the words of Schuchard, "In the broadest possible sense ... John understands the entire world to be responsible for the piercing (cf. 1.29)." Schuchard, *Scripture within Scripture*, 146. Similarly, after highlighting the responsibility of both the Jews and the Romans in Jesus' death, Bynum argues from the context of Zech 12 as follows: "Further, since John is sensitive to the scriptural context from which his citations come, which in this case is Zech 12, then the entire public can be seen as participating to some extent in the rejection and piercing of Jesus. This would include both the Jewish community and nascent Christian community, particularly those 'secret' disciples who were unwilling to confess their faith publicly." Bynum, *Fourth Gospel*, 178.

Jesus as the Pierced One

The Onlookers Consist of "All the Tribes"

Simultaneously, if John views the piercers and the onlookers as the same group, it follows that the onlookers in John 19:37 would stretch beyond the initial onlookers to include people from all the tribes of the earth. John's use of Zech 12:10 in Rev 1:7 certainly suggests the possibility of broadening the onlookers to people from all the tribes of the earth. Granting that the piercers and the mourners are the same subgroup within "every eye,"[78] the "they" in "they who look" of Zech 12:10 are explicitly identified in Rev 1:7 as "all the tribes of the earth." All the tribes who pierced Jesus will mourn when they literally see Jesus in his eschatological glory. If John broadens the onlookers to all the tribes of the earth in Rev 1:7, perhaps he understands the onlookers in John 19:37 in a similar fashion. Interpreters of John 19:37 often seek to broaden the onlookers to some extent anyway, and they usually do so based on what they perceive is implicit to the Fourth Gospel.[79] Nonetheless, the most explicit reason to broaden the onlookers in John 19:37 may be John's own broadening in Rev 1:7. Beyond the initial onlookers such as the Roman soldiers, the Jews, and the eyewitness, John

---

78. See the critique of Menken and Kubiś on pp. 181–84.

79. E.g., Schnackenburg broadens the onlookers grammatically by leaving the "they" of "they will look" indefinite. Schnackenburg, *John*, 3:293. Brown broadens the onlookers by suggesting that "they" who look upon Jesus include two groups. "First, 'the Jews,' who are [Jesus'] enemies, are defeated by the very act they instigated; for as they look upon Jesus who died on the cross, there flows forth, along with his life blood, a stream of life-giving water . . . However, a second group also looks upon the pierced Jesus, since in the person of the Beloved Disciple those who have faith in Jesus (xix 35) behold the scene." Brown, *John XIII–XXI*, 954–55. A similar approach to Brown's appears in Manns, "Zacharie 12,10," 308. Kubiś broadens the onlookers by pointing to the Roman soldiers (John 19:33) and various Jews (John 19:20, 25, 31, 35) in the surrounding context, and by viewing John as the believer *par excellence* who represents all future believers looking upon Jesus with faith. Kubiś, *Zechariah in John*, 196. Along with Menken, Kubiś follows Boismard and Lamouille, *Jean*, 451; Lindars, *John*, 591; Schnackenburg, *John*, 3:343–44; Maloney, *John*, 510; Klauck, "Schriftzitate in Der Johannespassion," 156. Bynum broadens the onlookers to both the Jewish and nascent Christian communities based on his reading of the entire public mourning in Zech 12. Bynum, *Fourth Gospel*, 178. Devillers broadens the onlookers to "all" because in John's Gospel Jesus died for "all." Devillers, "L'interprétation," 140, 143. Devillers cites John 3:16–17, John 4:42, and John 10:10. Further remarks on Jesus' death for the world appear below.

Looking on the Pierced One Now

envisions people from all the tribes of the earth among those who will look on the one they pierced. Yet how does he do so?

Since the eschatological situation between John 19:37 and Rev 1:7 differs, further clarification is necessary. Zechariah 12:10 anticipated God's formerly rebellious people looking upon him and mourning with great sorrow over their piercing of him (Zech 12:12—13:1).[80] As argued in the exegesis of Rev 1:7, Jesus' Parousia leads John to grant a reversed appropriation of Zech 12:10, so that a repentant mourning is no longer in view. Instead, the rebellious nations will mourn with great dread as Jesus comes to judge and replace their kingdoms with his own (Rev 1:7; cf. 6:12–17; 19:11–21).[81] However, the eschatological situation differs in John 19:37 where Jesus' first and humble redeeming advent is in view. Therefore, it seems that the reversed appropriation is unnecessary to John 19:37 and that John does leave room for the sorrowful mourning over the Pierced One by all disciples who look on Jesus and believe prior to the Parousia. The following observations support this conclusion.

The Initial Disciples Mourn, Look, and Believe

First, John certainly presents the initial disciples mourning over Jesus' death. In John 16:20, Jesus indicates that the sinful world would rejoice over Jesus' death, while the disciples would weep and lament over Jesus' death until Jesus' resurrection turned their sorrow into joy (John 16:20, 22).[82] Jesus' disciples would rightly mourn over Jesus' death, while Jesus' enemies would wrongly rejoice. If the eyewitness of John 19:35 is

---

80. Baldwin, *Zechariah*, 205; McComiskey, "Zechariah," 1214; Klein, *Zechariah*, 364; Petterson, *Zechariah*, 263.

81. The broader theology of Revelation reveals that those who pierced Jesus belong to the people of the Beast rather than the people of God, and these in particular will mourn upon Jesus' arrival to judge them. See, e.g., Hoskins, *Revelation*, 55–56. Thus, instead of the look engendering repentance for the covenant community as in Zech 12:10, the look in Rev 1:7 engenders great dread for the rebellious community.

82. That the mourning refers to what the disciples experience between Jesus' death and resurrection, versus a mourning that would characterize Jesus' disciples until Jesus' Parousia, see Beasley-Murray, *John*, 285; Carson, *John*, 543–44. Cf. also with Luke 23:27, which uses the same vocabulary as Zechariah's prophecy: "And there followed him a great multitude of the people and of women who were mourning [ἐκόπτοντο] and wailing for him."

John the Beloved Disciple and numbered among the remaining eleven disciples in John 14–16,[83] one may infer from John 16:20 that the eyewitness both looked on the pierced Jesus and mourned his death. One may also infer that the eyewitness looked on the pierced Jesus and believed (John 19:35).[84] Thus, John seems to indicate that the disciples of Jesus, and John the eyewitness in particular, did respond to the pierced Jesus with heartfelt sorrow and faith as Zech 12:10 anticipated.[85]

The Initial Disciples Represent the New Believing Community

Second, the disciples were not just Jews but now believing Jews, whom Jesus chose to represent the new believing community.[86] The disciples are unlike the unbelieving Jews that proved to be part of the evil world system. Throughout John's Gospel, the disciples[87] differ from the un-

---

83. Many infer that the eyewitness in John 19:35 is none other than the beloved disciple (John 13:23; 19:26, 27; 20:8; 21:20) and author of the Fourth Gospel (John 21:24–25; cf. 20:30–31). E.g., see Morris, *John*, 725; Carson, *John*, 625–26; Ridderbos, *John*, 620; Lincoln, "Beloved Disciple," 12–14; Köstenberger, *John*, 553; Köstenberger and Stout, "Witness," 11, 13. Against this view, some may argue from John 19:27 that the beloved disciple could not have been present at Jesus' piercing since "from that hour the disciple took her to his own home." E.g., Michaels, "Centurion's Confession," 103; Thyen, "Johannes Und Die Synoptiker," 103–4. Nevertheless, the language in John 19:27 need not be pressed to suggest that the beloved disciple took Jesus' mother to his home at that very moment. See especially the reasons set forward in Lincoln, "Beloved Disciple," 13–14.

84. John's use of καί in the final clause of John 19:35 seems best understood as adjunctive: "in order that you also [καί] may believe." Cf. Wallace, *Grammar*, 651. The adjunctive καί implies that John numbers himself among those who have believed in Jesus (cf. John 20:8).

85. That is not to ignore the fact that earlier in the Passion narrative, nearly all of the disciples seem to scatter (Matt 26:56; Mark 14:27 [cf. Zech 13:7; Mark 14:50]; John 16:32). At the same time, it remains unclear how long, or in what sense, they all remained scattered as one eventually finds Peter near the court of the high priest with "another disciple" (John 18:15–16) and also John the Beloved Disciple near the cross with Jesus' mother (John 19:26–27) and then at the piercing (John 19:35).

86. See especially Pryor, "Covenant and Community," 47–50; Köstenberger, *Theology*, 500–502.

87. John often uses the term μαθητής ("disciple") to refer to Jesus' inner circle of followers, especially the Twelve (e.g., John 2:2, 11; 4:8, 27; 6:22, 24; 9:2; 11:7, 8, 12; 12:4, 16; 13:5, 22; 16:17; 18:1; 20:18, 19, 25, 26), but at other times it refers to a broader group of followers (e.g., John 4:1; 6:60, 61; 7:3; 9:27, 28; 18:17, 19, 25; 19:38). Some within this broader group of disciples (μαθητῶν) take offense at Jesus' words

believing world in that Jesus chose them out of the world (John 15:19), manifested God's name to them instead of the world (John 17:6), and set them apart by God's word from the world (John 17:14). The disciples are those who formerly belonged to the unbelieving world, but who now receive Jesus, believe in Jesus' name, and gain the right to become God's children (John 1:10–13; 6:68–69; 17:8).

Also, while many from the unbelieving world witnessed Jesus' signs/works, their obstinate unbelief kept them from seeing God's glory revealed in Jesus' signs/works (John 6:36; 9:39–41; 12:40).[88] By contrast, the disciples' faith in Jesus as God's sent one enabled them to see the glory of God in Jesus (John 1:14; 2:11; 6:68–69; 17:8, 22; cf. 11:40). Moreover, the unbelieving world cannot receive the Spirit, because it neither sees him nor knows him (John 14:17). However, as believers in Jesus, the disciples receive the Spirit once Jesus is glorified (John 7:38–39; cf. 20:22). The Spirit causes the new birth so they can see/enter the kingdom of God (John 3:3–6).[89] The Spirit also bears witness to Jesus' glory (John 16:14) by granting the disciples a post-resurrection understanding of all that Jesus taught them, including what Jesus taught them from the OT about himself (John 14:26; 16:13; cf.

(John 6:60) and eventually turn away from following Jesus (John 6:66). I am using "disciples" to refer to those within Jesus' inner circle who truly believe in Jesus (John 6:69) and abide in Jesus' word (John 8:31). For further discussion on "disciples" in John's Gospel, see Köstenberger, *Theology*, 482–96.

88. In John 12:40, John describes the people's unbelief from Isaiah 6:10: "He has blinded their eyes and hardened their heart, lest they see with their eyes, and understand with their heart, and turn, and I would heal them." Accordingly, true blindness is not perceiving God's redemptive activity with the heart. As in Deut 29:2–4, it is not being able to spiritually perceive the revelation of God's redemptive activity even while one may be physically perceiving the events. Similarly, in John 9:39–41 Jesus condemns the Jewish authorities for thinking they "see" (i.e., spiritually perceive) who Jesus is, when they truly do not know him or the nature of his mission. For those who claim to see Jesus but in truth do not see God's glory in him, their guilt remains (John 9:41). Likewise, all who were present at Lazarus' tomb saw (i.e., with their physical eyes) Jesus raise Lazarus from the dead, but some in the crowd did not actually "see the glory of God," which Jesus said the miracle would display (cf. John 11:40 with the differing responses in John 11:45–46). Morris rightly observes that "the real meaning of what He would do is accessible only to faith. All there, believing or not, would see the miracle. But Jesus is promising Martha sight of the glory." Morris, *John*, 560.

89. Belleville, "Water and Spirit," 125–41.

JESUS AS THE PIERCED ONE

2:22; 12:16).⁹⁰ Because the disciples benefit from Jesus and the Spirit's mission in so many ways that the unbelieving world does not, the disciples get to see the glory of God's self-revelation in Jesus (John 1:14 ["we"]; 2:11; 11:40; 17:22).

Such observations are crucial since Zech 12:10 also expected formerly rebellious Israel to look upon the Pierced One in conjunction with the outpouring of God's Spirit to change their spirit.⁹¹ With such insight granted by the Spirit, even the ignominy of Jesus' death became for the disciples the revelation of God's glory in judging the world and cleansing his people in fulfillment of the Scriptures (John 1:29; 12:28, 31–32; 13:31–32; 19:36–37).⁹² Eternal life belongs solely to those dis-

---

90. John is one of the disciples to whom Jesus promised to give the Holy Spirit after returning to the Father (John 15:26–27; cf. 1 John 3:24; 4:1–6, 13–14; 5:6, 20). That John the son of Zebedee authored the Fourth Gospel, see Köstenberger and Stout, "Witness," 209–31. Yet even where questions of authorship persist, the Fourth Gospel seems to connect the trustworthy witness of the author (John 19:35; 21:24) with the trustworthy witness of "the Spirit of truth" (John 14:17; 15:26; 16:13). The trustworthy testimony of the Fourth Gospel is a product of the post-resurrection ministry of "the Spirit of truth," whom Jesus sent.

91. In conjunction with the people looking upon the Pierced One, God promised to pour out "a spirit of grace and pleas for mercy" (Zech 12:10). For further discussion regarding the s/Spirit in Zech 12:10, see the "Literary Context" in chapter 2 above, especially p. 27n6. Formerly sinful Israel would experience inward change leading to repentant mourning and cleansing from sin (Zech 12:12—13:1). According to the narrative of John's Gospel, God pours out the Spirit on believers following Jesus' death/glorification: "Now this he said concerning the Spirit, whom those who believed in him were to receive, for the Spirit was not yet [given/sent (cf. John 14:16, 26; 15:26)], because Jesus was not yet glorified" (John 7:39). As observed in chapter 3, the occasion for Jesus' glorification refers either to Jesus displaying the Father's glory through his death on the cross, or to the Father clothing Jesus with glory upon his ascension. John 7:39 indicates the latter, especially when the giving or the sending of the Spirit is contingent on Jesus' return to the Father in John 14–16. Once Jesus completed his earthly mission and returned to his glorified state alongside the Father, both the Father and Son would send the Spirit (John 14:16; 15:26; 16:7). Thus, the eschatological "day" when God pours out the Spirit begins when Jesus returns to his Father in glory after his piercing (cf. Luke 24:49 with Acts 1:4, 8; 2:33). For further discussion on the Fourth Gospel's presentation of the Spirit's work once Jesus was glorified, see Ladd, *Theology of NT*, 344; Hamilton, *God's Indwelling Presence*, 100–126. According to the redemptive-historical outline above, that places the outpouring of God's Spirit between the Pierced One's two redeeming advents where both John and his readers find themselves living.

92. For further discussion of God's self-revelation in Jesus' death, see the section titled "Jesus' Death on the Cross" on pp. 97–100.

ciples who see the glory of God's self-revelation in Jesus and believe (John 3:16; 20:31).

The Initial Disciples Multiply as Others Look and Believe

Third, Jesus' initial disciples would also multiply (John 10:16; 12:24; 15:16; 17:20; 20:21, 23). Jesus' initial disciples represent many others who would also leave the unbelieving world to follow Jesus, as they too believed John's testimony about Jesus for salvation (John 4:35; 17:20; 20:21, 31).[93] John himself even appeals to all his readers directly in relation to Jesus' piercing: "He who saw it has borne witness—his testimony is true, and he knows that he is telling the truth—that you also [i.e., you the reader] may believe" (John 19:35).[94] If any reader of John's Gospel learns to look and believe that Jesus' piercing is the piercing of God according to Zech 12:10, then they too will find eternal life in Jesus' name (John 20:30–31).[95]

It is true that later disciples cannot look on the pierced Jesus literally, as the initial disciples were privileged to do (John 19:35; 1 John 1:1–3). It is also true that Jesus himself blessed those who would not see him physically but would still believe in him (John 20:29). Nevertheless, seeing/looking in John's writings is not always limited to physical perception. There exists in John a type of seeing that involves spiritually perceiving the significance of Jesus' person and redeeming work.[96]

---

93. See Köstenberger, *Theology*, 486–90. Köstenberger clarifies that what is "*primarily* true for Jesus' original followers extends *derivatively* also to later believers" (italics are original). Köstenberger, *Theology*, 489.

94. Köstenberger, *John*, 553.

95. Kubiś also concludes: "In fact, the aim of the testimony, i.e., of the Gospel (a written record of this witness) is defined as bringing its readers and/or its hearers (ὑμεῖς) to faith in Jesus (19:35; 20:31). Hence, the subject of ὄψονται, expressed in the future tense, may encompass all potential readers and hearers of the [Fourth Gospel] who will believe in Jesus." Kubiś, *Zechariah in John*, 196.

96. Some have argued that ὄψονται ("they will look") in John 19:37 also includes future disciples looking in the sense of spiritual sight, but they have done so poorly by ascribing a spiritual connotation to the verb ὁράω in John's Gospel. E.g., see Abbott, *Johannine Vocabulary*, 104–5; Hübenthal, *Transformation*, 170; Bynum, *Fourth Gospel*, 177. The fact is that John, as with his use of other vocabulary (e.g., terms related to "love"), employs different verbs of "seeing" (ὁράω, θεωρέω, βλέπω) interchangeably. Sufficient examples appear in Kubiś, *Zechariah in John*, 204–5.

Jesus as the Pierced One

In John's Letters, for example, those who believe in Jesus are also those who "have seen" Jesus: "No one who abides in [Jesus] keeps on sinning; no one who keeps on sinning has seen [ἑώρακεν] him or known him" (1 John 3:6). Likewise, 3 John 11 states that "anyone who does what is evil has not seen [ἑώρακεν] God." While it is true that the initial disciples literally saw Jesus (1 John 1:1–3), it seems safe to conclude with Marshall that "few, if any, of John's readers could have seen the earthly Jesus . . . Clearly, 'seeing' with the eyes is not meant [in 1 John 3:6]. John is thinking rather of 'seeing' the significance of Jesus as the one who reveals the unseen God."[97] In other words, while it may be true that John had the unique privilege of literally seeing Jesus (John 19:35; 1 John 1:1–3), and his eyewitness testimony plays an important role in the ongoing life of the church (1 John 1:1–4), disciples who followed John could still see Jesus in the sense described in 1 John 3:6 and 3 John 11 (i.e., spiritually).

In his Gospel, John understands Jesus to be God's self-revelation (John 1:14, 18), the Light of the world (John 1:9; 8:12), whose glory becomes known to those who believe John's testimony even without literally seeing (John 20:29–31, esp. 20:29). Disciples of the inter-advent age see Jesus as the Pierced One (i.e., spiritually, with the eyes of their heart)[98] to the degree that they believe John's eyewitness testimony to God's self-revelation in Jesus. That is, John's future disciples see the glory of God's salvation through Jesus' piercing when they believe the fact of Jesus' piercing (John 19:35) as well as its meaning (John 19:36–37). Indeed, seeing God the Father rightly belongs not just to the initial disciples (e.g., John 1:14), but also to whomever else might see God's self-revelation in Jesus.[99] Indeed, John 6:40 says, "For this is the will of my Father, that everyone [πᾶς] who looks on [ὁ θεωρῶν] the Son and

---

97. Marshall, *Epistles of John*, 183–84. Also, see Stott, *Letters of John*, 126; Yarbrough, *1–3 John*, 186.

98. John 9:39, 41; 12:40; cf. Isa 6:10; 42:7, 18–20. See also the discussion on p. 145n74 on how these passages apply to spiritual sight.

99. Note especially the generic ὁ θεωρῶν ("whoever sees") in John 12:45: "And whoever sees me sees him who sent me." See also the generic ὁ ἑωρακὼς ("whoever has seen") in John 14:9: "Jesus said to him, 'Have I been with you so long, and you still do not know me, Philip? Whoever has seen me has seen the Father. How can you say, "Show us the Father"?'"

believes in him should have eternal life, and I will raise him up on the last day." The Father's will is that "everyone" who looks on the Son and believes in him will have eternal life, and Jesus will raise him up on the last day (John 6:40).[100]

The notion of spiritual seeing also appears in Rev 3:18, where those who are spiritually blind "must appeal to Christ to heal their spiritual blindness."[101] Based on these observations, ὄψονται ("they will look") in John 19:37 likely includes future disciples of the inter-advent age looking on the Pierced One in the same sense of spiritual seeing/looking in John 6:40, 1 John 3:6, 3 John 11, and Rev 3:18. If so, any believer will find themselves numbered among those who, although formerly belonging to the rebellious world, have now looked upon the Pierced One in faith and found cleansing for their sins and eternal life.[102]

---

100. The context surrounding John 6:40 involves two types of seeing, physical sight and spiritual sight. Some look on Jesus' signs only with physical sight, seeing only the bare miracle while missing its true significance (John 6:36). Jesus wishes that the people move beyond physical sight to spiritual sight, to seeing what his works truly signify about his person and work (John 6:26). The "look" in John 6:40 best represents the latter type of seeing. That is, those who look on the Son, truly discerning the significance of God's saving work, and believe in him will have eternal life. See Brown, *John I–XII*, 264, 270, 502; Morris, *John*, 358, 368–69; Bruce, *John*, 150, 154; Ridderbos, *John*, 224, 231. Cf. also Keener, *John*, 1:247–51. With two groups of people who look on Jesus, one group looking with faith (John 6:40) and another looking with unbelief (John 6:36; 12:37), one may wonder if John could envision both groups standing behind ὄψονται in John 19:37. However, to suggest that ὄψονται in John 19:37 includes both would mean that some unbelievers who pierced Jesus do not actually look upon him with faith and repentance as the fulfillment of Zech 12:10 demands. To be clear, only those disciples who once belonged to the rebellious world that pierced Jesus, but who now look on and believe in Jesus, only these disciples fulfill Zech 12:10 as it is appropriated in John 19:37. That is, all disciples of the inter-advent age who look on the pierced Jesus and believe fulfill the anticipated looking and repentant mourning of Zech 12:10. The rest of the rebellious world who pierced Jesus and who maintain their state of unbelief, will find themselves among those who look and mourn with great dread as John's appropriation of Zech 12:10 in Rev 1:7 suggests.

101. Hoskins, *Revelation*, 115. Likewise, see Beale, *Revelation*, 306; Osborne, *Revelation*, 210.

102. Thus, John's writings place people in one of two categories in relation to Jesus: either someone belongs to the unbelieving world that does not see God's glory in Jesus, or someone belongs to Jesus' believing disciples who, because of the Spirit, do see God's glory in Jesus. The same division appears in John's letters. There are those who love the sinful world, which itself lies under the power of the evil one (1 John

Jesus as the Pierced One

Disciples Look and Believe because of Jesus' Universal Mission

Fourth, John's Gospel presents Jesus' death and exaltation bringing salvation to the world.[103] In John's Gospel, the Father entrusts the Son with a universal mission. As God's true Passover Lamb, Jesus does not merely take away Israel's sin but the whole world's sin (John 1:29; cf. John 19:36). In love, the Father sends his Son not to condemn the world, but so that the world might be saved through him (John 3:16-17). As the true manna from heaven, Jesus gives the world eternal life through offering his own flesh as a sacrifice (John 6:51). Jesus lays down his life for sheep within Israel and even beyond the fold of Israel (John 10:15-16).[104] Jesus also dies as a substitute for all God's children scattered abroad and not for the nation of Israel only (John 11:51-52; cf. 1 John 2:2).[105] Truly, Jesus is the Savior of the world (John 4:42).

Thus, while it is true that the unbelieving world stands responsible for piercing Jesus (see above), it is also true that Jesus came to save that same rebellious world through his death, the piercing included. Indeed, Jesus came down from heaven to do the will of the Father who sent him by losing none of all the Father gave him (John 6:39) and instead bringing (John 10:16), gathering (John 11:52), and drawing "all" (πάντας) of

---

5:19), produces sinful desires (1 John 2:15-16), and embraces the spirit of antichrist (1 John 4:1, 3; cf. 2:18-19). However, because of the Spirit's work (1 John 3:24; 4:2; cf. 2:27), some overcome the world by "seeing" Jesus (1 John 3:6; 3 John 11) and believing John's testimony about Jesus (1 John 5:4-5, 19). These who "see" and believe in Jesus no longer belong to the world but the world hates them (1 John 3:1, 13).

103. John uses ὁ κόσμος to refer to (1) the physical universe (e.g., John 1:10a-b; 6:14; 9:5a; 16:21; 17:5; 21:25), (2) the inhabitants of earth in general (e.g., John 1:10c; 7:4; 8:26; 12:19), and, more often, (3) the sinful and unbelieving community in particular (e.g,. John 1:29; 3:16-17, 19; 4:42; 6:51; 7:7; 12:47; 14:17, 19, 22, 27; 15:18, 19; 16:8, 20). The ensuing observations primarily have referent (3) in mind, while also acknowledging that those in referent (2) make up those in referent (3).

104. That Jesus' "other sheep" likely refers to Gentiles and not simply Jews of the Diaspora, see the discussion in Beasley-Murray, *John*, 171; Carson, *John*, 388, 390; Keener, *John*, 1:818-19; Köstenberger, *John*, 306.

105. On the substitutionary nature of Jesus' death in John's Gospel, see Morris, "Atonement," 58, 63; Metzner, *Sünde Im Johannesevangelium*, 131. Regarding how the scattered children likely includes Gentiles as well the Jews of the Diaspora, see the discussion in Carson, *John*, 422-23. Cf. also Isa 56:3-8.

Looking on the Pierced One Now

them to himself once he was "lifted up" (John 12:32).[106] "All" in John 12:32 likely means all peoples without distinction.[107]

If the point of Jesus' death/exaltation is to save "the world" (John 3:16–17) and draw "all" peoples to himself (John 12:32), then John likely envisions a people from the whole world, even from all the tribes,[108] looking on Jesus who was pierced for their salvation and believing for eternal life. Zechariah 12:10 had anticipated a day when a formerly rebellious Israel would collectively look on the Pierced One and also find cleansing from their sin (Zech 12:10; 13:1). By understanding that Jesus' death brings cleansing for the world and not just for Israel, John broadens the application of Zech 12:10 from Israel to the whole world

---

106. The "lifting up" in John 12:32 has in view Jesus' exaltation through death (John 12:33; cf. 12:23, 28), by which Jesus judges the sinful world and ousts the ruler of this world (John 12:31). Jesus will draw "all" peoples to himself, because he claims victory over the sinful world and its evil ruler through his death and exaltation. Other Johannine passages on Jesus' mission to judge the rebellious world and conquer the devil, so that his own people might overcome the world themselves, are numerous (e.g., John 14:30–31; 16:11, 33; 1 John 3:8; 5:4–5, 18; Rev 12:1–17).

107. As Keener remarks, " . . . the context is the Pharisaic complaint that 'the world' was now following him (12:19), and Gentiles were now ready to approach Jesus (12:20)." Keener, *John*, 2:881. Thus, "all" need not imply all individuals without exception, especially since the wrath of God remains on those who continue in unbelief (John 3:36; 5:29), but all peoples without distinction (John 4:42; 10:16; 11:52; cf. Rev 5:9). So also Carson, *John*, 444. Regarding the text-critical decision between πάντας (P75^{vid} ℵ² B L W Θ Ψ) or πάντα (P66 ℵ* D it Vg syrs, p, pal), Metzger's comments seem reasonable: "A majority of the Committee . . . favored the reading πάντας because of the weight of its external attestation and because it appears to be more congruent with Johannine theology. The reading πάντα, which suggests ideas of a cosmic redemption, may have arisen under the influence of Col 1.16–17 and/or Gnostic speculation." Metzger, *Textual Commentary*, 202.

108. According to our study of Rev 1:7, some from "all the tribes" belong to the Beast's followers (Rev 11:9; 13:7), and they will mourn with great dread when Jesus returns to replace their kingdom with his own (Rev 1:7; 6:12–16). However, there are also some from "all tribes" who belong to the Lamb's worshipers (Rev 5:9; 7:9), and they will rejoice when Jesus returns to bring them into his kingdom (Rev 15:2–4; 19:1–3, 6–8). According to Rev 5:9 and Rev 7:9, therefore, John envisions some from "all the tribes" as those who turned from their hostility toward the Lamb and joined the worshipers of the Lamb. The present proposal alongside John 19:37 is suggesting that those who repent and join the worshipers of the Lamb are those who, prior to Jesus' Parousia, behold God's glory in Jesus and believe like the initial disciples did in John's Gospel.

Jesus as the Pierced One

looking on the pierced Jesus to find cleansing from their sin as well (cf. John 1:29; 1 John 1:9; 2:2).[109]

Disciples Must Look Before Jesus Consummates His Mission

Still, the reader must also learn that the time to look and believe in Jesus for eternal life will end. By juxtaposing John 19:37 with Rev 1:7, we see that readers must look on the Pierced One now, during the interadvent age, instead of waiting to look on him at the consummation.[110] The Pierced One is still to come for his final advent (Rev 1:7). When Jesus returns to establish God's kingdom on earth, the "day" for looking upon the Pierced One in sorrowful mourning and faith will draw to a close. Thus, it is needless to wait and pertinent for John's readers to believe.[111]

---

109. Interesting to note is that John the Baptist calls two of his disciples to "Behold [ἴδε], the Lamb of God who takes away the sin of the world" (John 1:29; cf. 1:36). Because of the heavenly revelation given to John the Baptist by the Spirit (John 1:32–34), he exhorts his followers to "behold" (or "look on") Jesus as the Lamb who takes away the world's sin. Now, at the end of John's Passion Narrative, another disciple, the Apostle John (possibly even one of the two disciples who heard John the Baptist in John 1:37; see Ridderbos, *John*, 621) "sees" Jesus' death (ὁ ἑωρακὼς in John 19:35). John also comprehends Jesus' death in terms of the Passover lamb (John 19:36) and the piercing of God (John 19:37), which we know that he too eventually discerns by the Spirit (John 14:26; 16:12–14). At least from a literary perspective, John the apostle beholds (i.e., he sees) at the cross precisely what John the Baptist had invited others to behold from the beginning. Having seen it, John now invites his readers to believe (John 19:35).

110. Cf. Keener, *John*, 2:1156–57. Keener writes, "Even if John interprets this text eschatologically, however, it is more likely, given his emphasis on realized eschatology . . . [John] suggests that Jesus' side was pierced so that the soldiers and Jewish leaders who handed Jesus over to them would look at him on the day of his death rather than at his second coming." Also, see Moo, *Old Testament*, 214. Moo does not consider John 19:37 to depict the fulfillment of Zech 12:10 as I have done above in chapter 3, but he still observes that "The use of a text from an eschatological passage [i.e., Zech 12:10; cf. Matt 24:30; Rev 1:7] is in keeping with John's emphasis on 'realized eschatology.'" Similarly, Köstenberger observes that " . . . the Fourth Evangelist does not place the 'looking on' the Messiah in faith exclusively in the distant future . . . but rather, in keeping with his inaugurated-eschatological outlook, he projects a believing vision of the Messiah into the present and immediate future from a precrucifixion vantage point . . . If so, the evangelist himself is the first who has seen Jesus pierced and has believed." Köstenberger, "John," 505.

111. In reference to Justin Martyr's use of Zech 12:10–12 to explain Jesus' two advents, Skarsaune concludes as follows: "In the *Apology*, the idea is the following:

Looking on the Pierced One Now

Jesus, the perfect revelation of the Father's character and will, has already come (John 1:18; 14:9). Since God has decisively revealed himself in Jesus, people from all tribes must look upon the Pierced One now (John 6:40; cf. 3:14–16). By looking upon him rightly with faith, they will be joined to God's new, believing community whose salvation the Pierced One procured in his death (John 10:16; 11:52). The wrath of God already abides on any that do not look and believe (John 3:16–17, 36).

Taking John 19:37 and Rev 1:7 both into account, therefore, the message for John's readers is to look upon the Pierced One now by faith, so that they will gain eternal life and not have to look upon the Pierced One later with dread. The message is to turn from the sinful world that rejoices over Jesus' death now but will mourn with dread at his return. Instead, join the believing disciples who mourn over Jesus' death now but rejoice in his resurrection life and eventual return. In fact, accounting for the two opposing kingdoms in Revelation, the combined message of John 19:37 and Rev 1:7 becomes a plea for all mankind to flee the kingdom of the Beast and join themselves to the kingdom of God by looking upon the Pierced One rightly while there is still time.

Such a message infuses John's overarching message with great urgency: the opportunity to look upon Jesus for eternal life is now, during the inter-advent age. Because Jesus' piercing set in motion the events connected with that eschatological "day" in Zechariah, it is certain that Yahweh's return to destroy his enemies and replace their kingdoms with his own will soon also come to fruition (Zech 12:1–9; 14:1–9; Rev 19–20). Yet, as a result of Jesus' death and exaltation, God has also poured out his Spirit to apply the benefits of Jesus' death to any who will look upon him and believe in him (John 3:15–16, 36; 6:40; 7:38; 12:46; 20:31). The implication for readers of John's Gospel and Revelation is to look upon the Pierced One now by faith before Yahweh's coming in

---

Since the prophecies covering the first coming of Christ can be shown to have been fulfilled in great detail, we may safely conclude that those prophecies which predict His glorious second coming will also be fulfilled. The thrust of the argument is directed toward Gentile readers; the purpose of the argument is to convince them that Christ's return is imminent, and that all men must repent in order to be justified when Christ comes to judge the living and the dead." Skarsaune, *Proof from Prophecy*, 156.

Jesus' return closes the inter-advent age and consigns the kingdom of the Beast to eternal punishment (Rev 14:10–11; 20:10).

THE PIERCED ONE'S REDEEMING ADVENTS AND THE CHURCH'S MISSION TO THE NATIONS

With Rev 1:7 striking such a note of urgency for John's readers, the church's mission to all nations now enters the purview of our study. Having established the way John uses Zech 12:10 to build on God's self-disclosure in Jesus' two-fold eschatological mission, and having established the implications for John's readers living between Jesus' two advents, the question we now address is how these implications shape the church's witness and mission to the nations.[112]

The question of mission to the nations has been lingering in the background, especially since Bauckham and others have interpreted Rev 1:7 to portray the future conversion of the nations.[113] If, to the contrary, the present study has interpreted Rev 1:7 to portray the final judgment of the nations, how does God's mission to convert the nations fit within the aforementioned presentation? The purpose of the present section is to show how the conversion of the nations takes place during the inter-advent age through the witness of the church.

Setting John's Use of Zech 12:10 within God's Mission to the Nations

Zechariah himself anticipated a day when Yahweh's new city would become like a village without walls, not only because Yahweh's glorious

---

112. Because of the ambivalence in studies on mission, Köstenberger sees the need to define "mission" more carefully. Based on the Gospel of John, he defines mission as "the specific task which a person or group (as sender or sent ones) seeks to accomplish, involving various modes of movement." Köstenberger, "Mission," 447. Since I am drawing conclusions based on the mission of God across Zechariah, John, and Revelation, and how God includes his people in that mission, the definition by Wright is more encompassing: "[the church's] mission means . . . our committed participation as God's people, at God's invitation and command, in God's own mission within the history of God's world for the redemption of God's creation." Wright, *Mission of God*, 23.

113. E.g., see Bauckham, *Climax*, 318–22; Caird, *Revelation*, 18–19. Although, see the substantial criticisms by Schnabel, "Future of the Nations," 243–71.

presence would return to protect the citizens within,[114] but also because a new multitude of inhabitants from many nations would swell the city beyond its regular boundaries (Zech 2:8–9, 14–16 [ET 2:4–5, 10–12]).[115] True, Yahweh's return also meant judgment against the nations who grew arrogant over Israel's exilic downfall.[116] Nevertheless, Yahweh's covenant to bless all nations through Abraham (cf. Zech 8:13) still meant that mercy would extend to some from the "far off" nations[117] such that they too would become a remnant[118] joining the true, restored

---

114. The pairing of "fire" and "glory" in Zech 2:5 recalls the Exodus. In the Exodus, the Lord manifests his glory to Israel in the pillar of fire leading them out of slavery (Exod 13:21), protecting them at the Red Sea (Exod 14:24), and then dwelling among them in the tent of meeting (Exod 40:38). In the new city of Zech 2, the Lord's glory isn't limited to a tent but fills the city from the center (i.e., "glory in your midst") to the edges (i.e., "wall of fire all around"). Like the glory-fire burned to protect Israel in the Exodus, so here it constantly works for his people's good. There may be a sense in which the "wall of fire all around" also portrays a reversal of the curse (cf. Gen 3:24).

115. So also Petterson, *Zechariah*, 128. The pairing of "man and beasts" likely recalls the blessings of Gen 1:24–27 and how the curses of exile have removed such blessings (Jer 7:20; 21:6; 32:43; 36:39; Ezek 14:13; 25:13; 29:8; Zeph 1:3). The promise of Zech 2:8 (ET 2:4) reveals a divine reversal wherein God not only removes the curse but lavishes blessings beyond what the previous city would have held. The blessings of the new age are superabundant (cf. also Jer 31:27; 33:6–16; Ezek 36:11).

116. Zech 1:15; 2:4 [ET 1:21]; 6:1–8; 9:1–6; cf. Isa 47:5–11. The idea behind these passages is that the nations took Israel into exile, but then they grew arrogant and went too far in punishing Israel. Rather than acknowledging God's sovereignty in using them to judge Israel, and rather than humbling themselves before a God who judges covenant breakers like Israel, the nations boasted in Israel's fall.

117. Zechariah 6:15 states, "And those who are far off [וּרְחוֹקִים] shall come and help to build the temple of the Lord." The "far off" could be the Jewish remnant still scattered among the nations (cf. Zech 2:10 [ET 2:6]; 10:9) or, more likely, the Gentile nations who will become a remnant (cf. Zech 2:8, 15 [ET 2:4, 11]; 8:22). Because God chose Israel and gave them the covenants and the privileges of God's revelation, Israel is the one nation that was viewed as being "near" (e.g., Ps 148:14; Isa 57:19). The Gentile nations were viewed as being "far off" (e.g., Deut 28:49; 1 Kgs 8:41; Isa 5:26; 57:19; Jer 5:15). Paul advances the same idea by viewing the Gentiles as "far off" (Eph 2:11–13), and yet whom God eventually uses to build his household, temple, and dwelling place (Eph 2:19–22).

118. In Zech 9:7–8, the prophet anticipates God mercifully redeeming a people from Philistia by cleansing them from idolatry (i.e., "I will take away [Philistia's] blood from its mouth, and its abominations from between its teeth"), making them part of his people (i.e., "[Philistia] too shall be a remnant for our God ... "), and bringing them into his protecting presence (i.e., "I [Yahweh] will encamp at my

Israel in the rebuilding of his eschatological temple and the worship of Yahweh as king (Zech 6:15; 8:20–23; 9:7–8; 14:16). Thus, God's mission to redeem a people beyond Israel to then include them within a true, restored Israel in the future age seems evident from Zechariah's broader prophetic concerns. The *missio Dei* involves rescuing a multiethnic people in conjunction with Yahweh's coming in the eschaton.

The Fourth Gospel and Revelation develop within this larger framework of the *missio Dei*,[119] with both books revealing God's purpose to redeem and gather a people from all nations during the interadvent age. The Fourth Gospel develops Jesus' first coming in terms reminiscent of Zechariah's prophecy wherein God's presence comes to indwell a superior temple (John 2:18–22; cf. Zech 2:10)[120] in conjunction with God's humble king bringing salvation for Zion (John 12:15; cf. Zech 9:9).[121] The Fourth Gospel also anticipates an ingathering of Jew and Gentile alike into one people under Jesus' rule and in Jesus' presence (cf. John 6:37; 10:16–18; 11:52; 17:20–24). Moreover, once Jesus was "lifted up" on the cross (John 12:33; cf. John 3:15)—his resurrection life and exaltation also presupposed in the glorification (cf. John 10:16–18)—he then promises to draw all peoples to himself (John 12:32), so that they might know him as the exalted I AM (John 8:28).[122]

Jesus' disciples would also become instrumental in drawing the nations to Jesus through their Spirit-filled witness (John 15:27; 17:20). By belonging to Jesus, the disciples enter Jesus' own labors of gathering

---

house as a guard . . . no oppressor shall again march over them [including Philistia]"). For a similar treatment, see Petterson, *Zechariah*, 220, 226.

119. For a more comprehensive treatment of the *missio Dei* across Scripture, see Wright, *Mission of God*, 71–188, 454–530. For the *missio Dei* in John's Gospel, see Köstenberger, *Missions*, 45–50, 141–98. For the *mission Dei* in Revelation, see Bauckham, *Theology of Revelation*, 83–104; Flemming, "Missio Dei," 161–78.

120. For further treatment of John 2:18–22, see Beale, *Temple and Church's Mission*, 192–200; Hoskins, *Jesus as Fulfillment*, 108–16.

121. Bynum, "Quotations," 52–65.

122. The Greek in John 12:32 only specifies πάντας ἑλκύσω πρὸς ἐμαυτόν ("I will draw all to myself"). Πάντας ("all") refers not to every single individual without exception, since people must believe in order to be saved (John 1:12; 3:16), be born again in order to come (John 1:13; 3:1–8; 6:44), be part of God's sheep to hear Jesus' voice (John 8:47; 10:16, 26–27), and part of God's elect people (John 11:52; 17:24). Rather, πάντας best refers to all people without distinction (hence "peoples" above), whom the Father has given the Son to save (John 6:39; 10:16, 29; 11:52; 17:2).

fruit for eternal life (John 4:38), an evangelistic activity for which Jesus specifically chose them and sent them into the world (John 15:16, 27; 17:18, 20; 20:21–23).[123] What then becomes explicit in their testimony is that since Jesus is God, the piercing of Jesus fulfills the expected piercing of Yahweh in Zech 12:10, and it is through his piercing that the fountain for cleansing from sin comes for Jew and Gentile alike who believe.

Likewise, the book of Revelation describes the Lamb's sacrificial death—a death that includes Jesus' historic piercing (Rev 1:7b)—as ransoming a multiethnic people for God and securing their future reign upon the earth (Rev 1:5–6a; 5:9–10). Nevertheless, the assumption throughout is that those ransomed by Jesus the Lamb have, at some point during the inter-advent age, also embraced Jesus' testimony and responded to the Spirit's invitation through the church (cf. Rev 1:3; 2:13, 19; 22:17).[124] Indeed, Jesus' testimony becomes the motivation for their exclusive worship and the content of their own prophetic witness, even among the nations who will persecute and martyr them throughout the inter-advent age.[125] Their end is not without vindication, however,

---

123. The concept of "bearing fruit" (καρπός) in John's Gospel also includes activity that glorifies the Father (John 15:8), depends upon the Son (John 15:2, 4–5), and shows love toward the brethren (cf. John 15:8–12). At the same time, these activities also serve the purpose of winning new converts (John 4:38; 12:24–26; 15:16; cf. 20:21–23). Spending our life for others unto death, as Jesus himself did to glorify the Father, multiplies fruit and brings the nations to Jesus. For a similar presentation, see Köstenberger, *Missions*, 133. Paul uses similar terminology in Col 1:6: "[the gospel] has come to you, as indeed in the whole world it is bearing fruit [καρποφορούμενον] and growing."

124. Revelation 22:17 is significant in its allusion to Isa 55:1. Revelation 22:17 says, "The Spirit and the Bride say, 'Come [ἔρχου].' And let the one who hears say, 'Come [ἔρχου].' And let the one who is thirsty come [ὁ διψῶν ἐρχέσθω]; let the one who desires take the water of life without price [ὁ θέλων λαβέτω ὕδωρ ζωῆς δωρεάν]." Isaiah 55:1 says, "Come, everyone who thirsts [οἱ διψῶντες], come to the waters [ὕδωρ]; and he who has no money, come, buy and eat! Come, buy wine and milk without money and without price." The offer of the witness in Isa 55:1, however, eventually extends in Isa 55:4–5 beyond Israel to all peoples (i.e., ἔθνεσιν).

125. E.g., Rev 1:9; 2:13; 6:9–11; 11:3–7; 12:11, 17; 20:4. Revelation 11:3–7 is especially important since it portrays the prophetic witness of the church throughout the inter-advent age, the period portrayed as "1,260 days" (Rev 11:3; 12:6), "forty-two months" (Rev 11:2; 13:5), or "time, and times, and half a time" (Rev 12:14). While some interpret the mysterious time period more literally, others have demonstrated more consistently on typological grounds from Daniel and on exegetical grounds

Jesus as the Pierced One

as John envisions the Pierced One returning to judge the unrepentant nations (Rev 1:7; cf. 6:9–11; 11:11–13).[126] Consistent with Zechariah, Revelation develops the *missio Dei* in terms of God's redemption of a multiethnic people through the Lamb (also the one pierced) and God's judgment of the rebellious nations who reject the Lamb.

According to John, then, Jesus fulfills the *missio Dei* that Zechariah anticipated by bringing us the presence of God, being pierced for Israel and the nations, and drawing the nations through the prophetic testimony of his disciples, disciples who bear witness to his piercing and then promise the Pierced One's return to judge all who reject their testimony. Since the inter-advent age continues at the present, and since Jesus continues the *missio Dei* through the church today, how might we say that John's use of Zech 12:10 in John 19:37 and Rev 1:7 shapes the church's witness to the nations?

Jesus' Divine Identity Is Necessary for the Church's Witness and Worship

First, with great urgency the church must proclaim to the nations that Jesus is the divine Messiah. Many have interpreted John's use of Zech 12:10 along the lines of Jesus fulfilling the role of Yahweh's human,

---

from the events transpiring in Rev 12 that the 1,260 day period "begins with Christ's exaltation and ends with his second coming in judgment." Hoskins, *Revelation*, 190–93, 216. See also Mounce, *Revelation*, 236; Beale, *Revelation*, 565–68, 646–47; Keener, *Revelation*, 318–20; Hamilton, *With the Clouds*, 105–33, 212–19. Studies supporting that Rev 11:3–7 portrays the church's prophetic witness are numerous, even if disagreement persists on whether Rev 11:13 envisions a future conversion of the nations. E.g., see Bauckham, *Climax*, 273–83; Beale, *Revelation*, 572–90; Keener, *Revelation*, 291–93; Schnabel, "Future of the Nations," 247–57; Hoskins, *Revelation*, 193–203. Hoskins helpfully observes how John envisions his own witness in writing Revelation as belonging to the church's prophetic witness. Hoskins, *Revelation*, 195–96, 199.

126. Hoskins is especially helpful in connecting the revivification/rapture of the two prophets in Rev 11:11–12 to the rapture of the church at Jesus' return (cf. 1 Thess 4:16–17), and in connecting the response of the nations in Rev 11:13 to God forcing them to give/recognize his glory at the judgment (cf. Rev 6:17; Phil 2:10–11). Hoskins, *Revelation*, 202–3. See also Beale, *Revelation*, 607; Schnabel, "Future of the Nations," 254–55. For presentations showing that "they gave glory to the God of heaven" signals true repentance and not forced confession, see Caird, *Revelation*, 140; Bauckham, *Climax*, 278–79; Blount, *Revelation*, 218; DeSilva, *Seeing*, 77; Flemming, "Missio Dei," 173.

messianic representative. Such an interpretation may receive support on broader contextual grounds, but it overlooks the fact that John selects the more ambiguous OT passage, Zech 12:10, which does not clearly point to the piercing of God's representative. Rather, Zech 12:10 points to the piercing of God himself. As established from the perspectives of the Fourth Gospel and Revelation, John not only includes Jesus within the divine identity but such a conviction shapes John's hermeneutical axiom: the Christ is himself Yahweh. Indeed, John interprets the OT convinced that Yahweh's eschatological self-revelation culminated in the person of Jesus, the Christ. Because the one-of-a-kind Son exists at the Father's side (John 1:14, 18), John recognizes the Pierced One of Zechariah not as a mere human representative distinct from God (i.e., in essence), but as God (the Son) himself now come in the flesh. The use of Zech 12:10 builds on John's understanding of God's self-disclosure in Jesus by showing that the pierced Jesus he beheld is the pierced God Zechariah promised. As stated before, by equating Jesus with the pierced God of Zech 12:10, John articulates some of the highest Christology in the NT.[127]

Objections to Jesus' divinity will surely persist, but John's use of Zech 12:10 should embolden the church to continue persuading the nations that Jesus is more than a human representative; he is God. Like other NT authors who take OT passages concerning Yahweh and apply them to Jesus,[128] John also does not hesitate to substitute Jesus for Yahweh when using Zech 12:10. Part of the church's witness, therefore, is to demonstrate for the nations the divine glory that John witnesses in the person of Jesus. Through Jesus' words and works, Jesus' revelatory death on the cross, Jesus' Spirit giving post-resurrection insight to the OT (see chapter 3), and through the way Jesus receives worship and takes to himself OT metaphors and motifs once applied only to Yahweh (see chapter 4), John has given the church plenty to build a positive

---

127. Although, the high Christology John articulates coheres with other places where the NT treats Jesus as God (e.g., Rom 9:5; Phil 2:5–11; Titus 2:13; Heb 1:8–9; 2 Pet 1:1; 1 John 5:20). For further treatment, see Brown, "Call Jesus God," 545–73; Harris, *Jesus as God*, 21–299; Yeago, "Nicene Dogma," 152–64; Hurtado, *Lord Jesus Christ*, 79–153, 349–426; Bauckham, *Jesus and the God of Israel*, 1–59, 127–268.

128. For an overview with numerous NT examples, see Hurtado, *Lord Jesus Christ*, 108–17.

Jesus as the Pierced One

case for Jesus' divinity and how Jesus alone could fulfill a text like Zech 12:10. Jesus alone is God in the flesh, and unless he is God in the flesh, he can be no true Messiah for Israel or Savior for the world. Only the piercing of God the Son incarnate saves.

Moreover, as God in the flesh, Jesus deserves the nations' exclusive worship. Not only had the disciple Thomas begun to recognize Jesus' divine worth (see "My Lord and my God" in John 20:28) when he looked upon Jesus' pierced hands and side following Jesus' resurrection, but the multitudes in heaven still honor the slain but risen Lamb just as they honor God the Father (Rev 5:9–14; cf. Rev 4:11; John 5:23). Part of the church's witness, therefore, is also urging the nations to surrender all their loyalties to Jesus Christ, an act of faith they will hardly be able to privatize in a world hostile to Jesus (cf. John 15:18–19; 17:14; Rev 2:13).[129] Still the change in inward allegiance must give way to proactive resistance of all that compromises the worship of Jesus and public witness to all that supports the worship of Jesus. Taking John's vision in Revelation as our cue, the church's worship of Jesus on earth corporately resists the rebellious world's idolatry opposed to Jesus' worth (e.g., Rev 9:20–21; 13:4, 8), faithfully represents what the heavenly multitudes already see of Jesus' worth (e.g., Rev 5:9–14; 7:9–12), and expectantly prefigures what God's final kingdom on earth will reveal about Jesus' worth (e.g., Rev 21:22–26). The time is now for the church to expose the folly of the people who worship the Beast, a people the Pierced One will return to condemn (Rev 1:7; 14:11; 19:19–20), and to explain the hope of the people who worship God and the Lamb, a people the Pierced One bled to save (John 19:37).

Jesus' Death to Fulfill the Scriptures Shapes the Church's Proclamation and Hope

Furthermore, with great urgency the church must proclaim to the nations that Jesus died to fulfill the Scriptures. The Apostle Paul explained to the Corinthian believers that, as a matter of first importance, Christ died in accordance with the Scriptures (1 Cor 15:3). John aligns himself with this apostolic tradition by testifying that Jesus died in such a way

---

129. Cf. Flemming, "Missio Dei," 174–75.

that fulfills the prophecy of Zech 12:10. By doing so, John encourages his readers both to interpret the OT in light of God's self-revelation in Jesus Christ and to understand Jesus Christ's person and work in light of the OT.

When witnessing to the nations, the church must announce both the historical facts of Jesus' death as well as the theological meaning gleaned from the Scriptures.[130] The church must announce Jesus' unbroken legs and piercing alongside the meaning John introduces for these events with γὰρ ("for") in John 19:36–37. It is insufficient merely to present the facts of Jesus' death. Alongside the historical apologetic, remaining faithful to John's testimony means preserving and announcing the complete—and oftentimes more offensive—message of what texts like Zech 12:10 help explain about Jesus' death: as God in his own right, Jesus fulfills the eschatological mission of Yahweh by first being pierced. The enigmatic prophecy that Yahweh would be pierced receives clarification in that Jesus is God the Son incarnate. The piercing of God only makes sense in light of the piercing of God the Son, Jesus Christ.

By persuading people from all nations that the piercing of Jesus is the piercing of God, the nations not only learn of Jesus' inclusion within the divine identity, but they gain an accurate understanding of what the death of Christ is, namely, the revelation of God in the saving of sinners. In Jesus' death people can look upon the revelation of Yahweh's salvation (i.e., Jesus was pierced for the nations), and then discern from Zech 12:10—13:1 that the outpoured blood and water from Jesus' side is God's fountain for cleansing from sin through the Spirit. By looking upon the pierced Jesus in this sense and believing what God achieved in him, the nations will gain eternal life.

Moreover, if Jesus died to fulfill the Scriptures, then his death was not an end to an otherwise noble life. The crucifixion of God's Son was not an accident of history. Rather, Jesus' death was central to

---

130. Cf. Köstenberger, who also explains in the context of mission in John, "What John therefore gives us is not merely a historical narrative of Jesus' passion, but a theological interpretation of it. It is true that Jesus' contemporaries saw in his cross a shameful curse. In hindsight, however, the cross was a place of glory and exaltation where the Son of Man was 'lifted up,' not humiliated (cf. 3:14; 8:28; 12:32; see also 17:1, 4–5)." Köstenberger, "Mission," 450.

Jesus as the Pierced One

God's sovereign design, crucial to God's redemptive-historical drama outlined in prior revelation like Zech 12:10.[131] The cross is first and foremost God's plan (John 13:18–19), God's charge (John 10:18), God's purpose (John 12:27), and God's demonstration of love (John 3:16–17; cf. 1 John 4:10). Not only does such unity between God's promise in the OT and its fulfillment in the NT serve to buttress the veracity of the church's biblical witness; the unity also reveals that history is not an endless cycle. Rather, history is linear. God is truly directing all things towards the final consummation in Christ. If God was truly pierced in Jesus (John 19:37) to fulfill the expectations of Zech 12:10, then the church can rest assured—and the world should be warned—that the Pierced One shall also come again in glory (Rev 1:7). The same sovereign God who promised his piercing in history, entered history in his Son and orchestrated history to fulfill his word.

Peoples Will Look on the Pierced One to Obtain Life before the Judgment

A corollary to Jesus' piercing, which proves God's faithfulness to achieve his sovereign plan, is that God's promise in Zech 12:10 then extends to the people's looking. According to Zech 12:10, the Lord's gracious Spirit would work pleas of mercy into the hearts of his people, the result being that they would in fact look upon him with repentance and receive his salvific cleansing (cf. Zech 12:12–14; 13:1). If it is true that God has been pierced in Jesus Christ, then it is just as true that the Spirit will cause God's elect people to look rightly upon Jesus during the inter-advent age.

While not all will look upon Jesus and believe (John 1:10–11; Rev 9:20; 16:9), many from the nations have and will look and believe for eternal life (John 1:12–13; 6:37, 40; 1 John 3:6). Indeed, the Father has given these people to the Son, and the Father will not fail to draw them

---

131. Affirming that God designed/ordained the crucifixion of Jesus, including the sinful acts of the Jews and Gentiles gathered against Jesus (John 13:18–19; cf. Acts 2:23; 4:27–28), need not imply that God himself is culpable of sin (cf. Jas 1:13) or that the people involved are not responsible for their actions. God is able to ordain evils such as the cross *through* human acts and not be blamed for the evil. For a helpful treatment of these tensions in the Gospel of John, see the study by Carson, *Divine Sovereignty*, 125–222.

(John 6:37, 40), nor will the Son fail to redeem and raise them (John 6:39; 10:16–18; 17:1–5, 24).[132] As established above, John seems to number himself among those who have already looked and believed, in order to receive eternal life (John 19:35; cf. 2:11, 22; 16:27; 20:8).

The broader theology of the Fourth Gospel shares the same ambiance: "I [Jesus] have other sheep that are not of this fold. I must [δεῖ][133] bring them also, and they will listen to my voice" (John 10:16); "[Caiaphas] prophesied that Jesus would die . . . not for the nation only, but also for the purpose of [ἵνα][134] gathering into one the children of God who are scattered abroad" (John 11:52); "I [Jesus], when I am lifted up from the earth, will draw [ἑλκύσω][135] all to myself" (John 12:32). The Revelation then offers further assurance, by giving John a vision of the final redeemed community of peoples gathered into God's glorious presence (cf. λαοὶ in Rev 21:3). All for whom Jesus the Lamb bled to save (Rev 1:5b–7; 5:9–10) will respond to Jesus' voice (John 10:16) through the church's prophetic witness (John 20:21–23; Rev 11:3–7), and God will grant them eternal life and healing (Rev 22:1, 2, 14).

The church must take courage in the assurance of God's prophetic word and God's sovereignty[136] to fulfill his prophetic word. Even in the face of great obstinacy and rebellion among the nations (John 12:37),

---

132. On God's gracious initiative and election of his people in John's Gospel, see Yarbrough, "Divine Election," 47–62; Carson, *Divine Sovereignty*, 125–200; Köstenberger, *Theology*, 458–63.

133. Drawing from the definition provided in BDAG, s.v. "δεῖ," Jesus' act of bringing all his elect 'sheep' into God's fold is "under necessity of happening" (cf. Isa 56:3–8; Jer 23:3; Ezek 34:13; 36:24; Zech 10:8, 10). The determined will of the Father is in view, and the Son must bring these other sheep into the fold, so that through his death and resurrection life the sheep become unified. Morris, *John*, 512; Ladd, *Theology of NT*, 106, 318; Thielman, *Theology*, 713.

134. The context of Caiaphas's prophecy (though unbeknown to him), and the emphasis throughout John's Gospel on the Father's intent to save all he gave to the Son by giving up the Son, lead me to understand the ἵνα in John 11:52 as purpose. Cf. Wallace, *Grammar*, 472. Jesus would die with the divine intent to gather the children of God.

135. The verb ἑλκύσω is best understood as a predictive future. Cf. Wallace, *Grammar*, 568. That is, there is no question of whether Jesus will draw the "all" to himself. The drawing will happen, and is part and parcel to the intent of his "lifting up" or glorification through crucifixion, resurrection, and exaltation.

136. Cf. Köstenberger and O'Brien, *Ends of the Earth*, 223.

Jesus as the Pierced One

Jesus' piercing at the hands of godless men (John 19:34; cf. Acts 2:23) serves as an ongoing reminder that God's sovereign plan to save his people will never fail. The nations may persecute and even martyr Jesus' disciples as they did to Jesus (e.g., John 15:20; Rev 1:9; 11:7–10), but people will in fact look upon the Pierced One rightly during the inter-advent age, in order to enjoy eternal life with God (John 6:40; cf. 1 John 3:6). John had done so, as well as many others whom God made to be a kingdom and priesthood (Rev 1:5–6).

Such assurance gives impetus to continue preaching John's testimony about the piercing of Jesus and about the redemption and cleansing his spilled blood implies for all who believe (cf. John 20:30–31). The church must further trust that God's Spirit will give all God's elect people a contrite spirit that pleas for mercy from God (Zech 12:10) and that receives what God's grace provided in piercing his Son for them. Just as the Spirit enabled John to discern God's self-revelation and salvation in Jesus Christ, so also we see throughout the mission of the early church that the Spirit—also using the OT through the apostles to explain Jesus' identity and mission—enabled others to discern the same.[137] Far from hindering the church's mission, the divine assurance that others will look on the Pierced One with faith and repentance keeps disciples witnessing to those outside the church.

The Church Must Keep Looking on the Pierced One for Eternal Life

At the same time, the hope that others outside the church will in fact look upon the Pierced One must never imply that those inside the church cease to look. For John, faith involves continuous trust in Jesus,[138]

---

137. E.g., Acts 2:16–37, 41; 6:7; 8:32–39; 13:48; 16:14. For an overview of the work of Jesus' Spirit through the witness of the church, see Thompson, *Acts*, 88–102.

138. E.g., see Thompson, "Signs," 95. After defining faith in the Fourth Gospel as "faithfulness in trusting the God who is made known in Jesus Christ," Thompson observes the following: "There is in the Fourth Gospel an emphasis on the importance of persevering, continuing, being steadfast in faith. That is the burden of John's use of the word *menein*, for example. It is those disciples who 'continue' in Jesus' word who will know the truth and be set free (8:31); those who 'abide' in the vine who will bear fruit (15:4–7). Jesus' farewell discourses are intended to keep the disciples from falling away (16:1), from becoming like the disciples of chapter 6 who 'withdrew and no longer went about with him' (6:66)."

and therefore involves an ongoing and transformative[139] look upon the Pierced One to behold all that God is in him and all that God achieved through him. The Gospel according to John was not written simply to win people to faith but also to keep people in the faith, a faith that grows by coming to Jesus (John 6:37; 7:37), eating and drinking from Jesus (John 4:13–14; 6:54, 56), abiding in Jesus (John 8:31; 15:4, 6), and, as demonstrated above, looking upon Jesus (John 6:40; 19:37; cf. 3:14; 1 John 3:6).[140] If eternal life is to know the one true God and Jesus Christ whom he has sent (John 17:3), and thus also has a qualitative dimension to it that believers can experience in the present (John 4:14; cf. 7:38) by means of looking (John 6:40; 1 John 3:6), then the church must keep looking upon the pierced Jesus in order to know God truly and experience eternal life with him. Part and parcel to God's self-revelation of his glory and grace (John 1:14) is God sending Jesus to suffer the expected piercing (John 19:37), but in order to know that glory truly, the church must look.

Revelation shares a similar approach by consistently presenting Jesus as the slain but risen Lamb. Though risen, the Lamb's wounds go unforgotten by the worshipers in heaven and the saints on the earth (Rev 1:5b–6; 5:9–10). Indeed, the blood of the Lamb is central to the saints' victory over the Dragon/Satan (Rev 12:7–12). John receives and writes such a revelation to keep these truths about the Lamb and his

139. Describing the look as "transformative" comes from Bynum, "Quotations," 71. Bynum writes, "Well beyond the physical looking of those present at the crucifixion, this 'seeing' and 'looking' is best understood as a directive on John's part to gaze upon the crucified Christ in transformative contemplation. Nor need it be seen as unidirectional in a vision that simply leads to faith, but as interactive, as both vision and faith lead toward one another in mutually enriching dynamics."

140. While some have debated whether John's Gospel was written to evangelize unbelieving Jews or to strengthen those who already believe, Carson is correct to assert that such decisions cannot be based on verb tense alone (e.g., πιστεύ[σ]ητε in John 20:31). Carson, *John*, 662. Contra Fee, "Meaning of John 20,30–31," 2193–2205. With that consideration in mind, others have demonstrated that John's purpose to engender/strengthen faith among his readers remains true whether those readers are believers or unbelievers. E.g., see Bauckham, *Gospels for All Christians*, 10; Keener, *John*, 2:1215–16; Köstenberger, *John*, 582. Cf. also Bynum, who adds that "it [i.e., the events of Jesus entering Jerusalem and Jesus' piercing] requires a theological interpretation to see the enduring spiritual significance for believers of the figure of Christ entering Jerusalem and then 'lifted up' on the cross." Bynum, "Quotations," 73.

saving wounds—including the piercing (Rev 1:7)—circulating among the churches for their edification and endurance in the mission (Rev 1:4, 11; 22:16).

In this way, John is not too far from Paul's teaching in 2 Corinthians. God not only opens people's eyes to see his glory in the face of Christ (cf. 2 Cor 4:4, 6), but God also transforms believers "from glory to glory [ἀπὸ δόξης εἰς δόξαν]" insofar as they continue beholding the glory of God in the person of Jesus (2 Cor 3:18).[141] As it was for John, the beholding occurs when the Spirit enables the "heart" (2 Cor 4:6) or the "mind" (2 Cor 4:4) to perceive the glory of Christ in the apostolic gospel.[142] Therefore, as God's people offer the benefits of Jesus' death to the nations, they too must keep looking upon Jesus, whose piercing serves to manifest the very glory of Yahweh coming to redeem his own before judging the world.

CONCLUSION

In conclusion, the present chapter has outlined the redemptive-historical drama unfolding from Zech 12:10 to John 19:37 to Rev 1:7. When taking these passages together, one sees that the eschatological "day" of God's coming as the Pierced One occurs in two episodes, the first episode occurring in the death of Jesus and the second in the return of Jesus. On the cross Jesus was pierced to secure God's salvation for the nations, whereas at Jesus' return God's judgment will fall on the nations by the Pierced One. John's inaugurated eschatology due to Jesus' first coming and John's consummated eschatology due to Jesus' second coming, together announce that God's end-time salvation is already available to all peoples and their faithful trust in Christ is imperative. By juxtaposing John 19:37 with Rev 1:7, John's message is that his readers must look on the Pierced One now, during the inter-advent age, instead of waiting to look on him at the consummation when Jesus condemns the nations.

---

141. Cf. Barnett, *2 Corinthians*, 204–9, 218–20, 223–26; Piper, *God Is the Gospel*, 59–74. Cf. also 1 John 3:2, where the believer's future perception of Jesus' unveiled glory will produce final glorification.

142. Notice the "gospel" in 2 Cor 4:4 and the preaching of Christ in 2 Cor 4:5. See also Barnett, *2 Corinthians*, 206.

Looking on the Pierced One Now

  Looking rightly upon Jesus and his death includes believing what the prophetic Scriptures expected his piercing to be and what God's self-revelation in Jesus make possible to understand through the Spirit. The Spirit enables people to understand that Jesus' piercing is the very revelation of God's glory in the salvation of sinners, the very piercing of God that opens a fountain of cleansing for his people. The Spirit further empowers the church to involve themselves in the *missio Dei* by gathering the nations through their prophetic witness to Jesus' divine identity and to Jesus' death fulfilling the Scriptures, all the while trusting God's sovereign power to fulfill his word and "looking" upon the Pierced One for edification and endurance in the task. In writing the Fourth Gospel and the Revelation, therefore, John joins the rest of the apostolic witness in commending to all Jesus, who died for our sins in accordance with the Scriptures, was buried, and was raised on the third day in accordance with the Scriptures (1 Cor 15:3–4). Shall we, those readers to whom John offers eternal life (John 20:30–31), not all the more hearken to the Pierced One's testimony, "Behold, I am coming quickly" (Rev 22:7, 12, 20; cf. 1:7)? There is no one else who can save except Jesus, God the Son once pierced and coming again. Look on him and believe!

6

Conclusion

THE AFOREMENTIONED STUDY INVESTIGATED John's use of Zech 12:10 in John 19:37 and Rev 1:7. The purpose for bringing John 19:37 and Rev 1:7 into a single study was to understand how God's self-revelation in Jesus provides John the interpretive key that unlocks the mysterious promise of Zech 12:10, and to understand how both passages complement one another within John's unified, eschatological narrative. The present chapter will summarize the findings of chapters 1 to 5 and then comment briefly on the implications of those findings.

SUMMARY OF THE PROJECT

Chapter 1 established the thesis of the project, namely, to examine how John's use of Zech 12:10 builds on an understanding of God's self-disclosure in Jesus' two-fold eschatological mission. In order to pursue such a thesis, it was necessary to investigate the identity of the Pierced One in Zech 12:10, demonstrating the validity of understanding the Pierced One's identity as Yahweh. The study would then need to investigate how John uses Zech 12:10 in John 19:37 and Rev 1:7, giving special attention to the fact that John applies the same OT prophecy to two separate events in Jesus' eschatological mission, his death, and his return. The history of research exposed that no in-depth study yet exists that develops the mission of the Pierced One in Zechariah, John's Gospel, and Revelation as a coherent whole, not to mention the effects

Conclusion

such a mission must have on people living between the Pierced One's two advents.

Chapter 2 then sought to investigate the identity of the Pierced One in Zech 12:10. Numerous observations led to the conclusion that identifying the Pierced One as Yahweh and not merely with Yahweh is a valid interpretation. First, the most historically viable and contextually supported reading is that of the MT, אֵלַי, with Yahweh standing as the object of the preposition and focus of the verbal action in וְהִבִּיטוּ. Second, the clause אֵת אֲשֶׁר־דָּקָרוּ modifies the first-person suffix in אֵלַי, also making Yahweh the object of דְּקָרוּ. Third, taking the alternation of suffixes as a stylistic feature, Yahweh remains the central object throughout the entire text, whether the people look, pierce, or mourn. Fourth, the wider context and the seeming aversion by the LXX to Yahweh's piercing, both suggest that the use of the verb דָּקַר conveys a literal piercing of Yahweh. Fifth, the wider context of Zech 12:10 suggests that Zechariah's audience should have understood the piercing, looking, and mourning to accompany the eschatological "day" of God's redeeming mission. Still, interpreting Zech 12:10 to suggest that God experiences the piercing certainly presents a *sui generis* problem. How can anyone pierce God?

With this question in mind, chapter 3 shows that John 19:37 provides the first clue to understanding the mysterious prophecy. According to John, Jesus' piercing took place in order to fulfill the Scripture from Zech 12:10. More popular is the interpretation that links John 19:37 to Zech 12:10 along merely human, messianic lines. One must also recognize, however, that John's principal emphasis on Jesus' equality with God the Father provides the overall framework for understanding Jesus' messiahship. John has witnessed God's glory revealed through Jesus' words and works, through Jesus' death on the cross, and through Jesus' Spirit granting post-resurrection insight to the Scriptures. In short, John has a theological conviction that Jesus is God (the Son) in the flesh. As the pre-existent Word/Son now incarnate, Jesus is God's ultimate self-revelation, and that self-revelation enables John to see in Zech 12:10 a meaning that was always present before though mysterious. That is to say, John answers the *sui generis* problem of Zech 12:10, God is pierced, with the *sui generis* answer, Jesus is God

Jesus as the Pierced One

(the Son). Therefore, not only does John identify Jesus as God from an OT witness, he also magnifies the revelatory nature of Jesus' death and demonstrates that Jesus has inaugurated Yahweh's eschatological mission.

Chapter 4 then develops John's use of Zech 12:10 in Rev 1:7 and finds that Jesus, as the Pierced One, will also consummate Yahweh's eschatological mission. The way John presents Jesus' words, applies OT metaphors and OT motifs to Jesus, and encourages the worship of Jesus, all seem to warrant that John could be reading Zech 12:10 along divine messianic lines and not simply along human messianic lines. If so, then John uses Zech 12:10 to reassure the church that Jesus' Parousia will soon consummate God's eschatological mission, thus closing the inter-advent age. God's heavenly kingdom will soon supplant all rebellious kingdoms with the personal arrival of Jesus. The consummating eschatological moment signifies that the time for repentance has drawn to a close and leads John to a reversed appropriation of the mourning in Zech 12:10. Jesus' return will be awful in effect as the final judgment he exercises causes the rebellious community not to repent but to wail in terror.

Chapter 5 then closed the study by outlining the redemptive-historical drama extending from Zech 12:10 to John 19:37 to Rev 1:7. Chapter 5 also sought to demonstrate how John's interpretation of Zech 12:10 from the vantage points of inaugurated and consummated eschatology ought to affect John's readers, both inside and outside the church. The eschatological "day" of God's coming as the Pierced One occurs in two episodes, the first episode occurring in the death of Jesus and the second in the return of Jesus. On the cross Jesus was pierced to secure God's salvation for the nations, whereas at Jesus' return God's judgment will fall on the nations by the Pierced One. John's inaugurated eschatology due to Jesus' first coming and John's consummated eschatology due to Jesus' second coming, together announce that God's end-time salvation is already available to all peoples and their faithful trust in Christ is imperative. By juxtaposing John 19:37 with Rev 1:7, John's message is that his readers must look on the Pierced One and believe now, during the inter-advent age, instead of waiting to look on him at the consummation when Jesus condemns the nations. Until

Conclusion

Jesus comes again, the church announces from the Scriptures that Jesus is God, and that God has been pierced in his Son to open a fountain of cleansing and eternal life for all who look on him and believe.

IMPLICATIONS OF THE PROJECT

Treating Zech 12:10, John 19:37, and Rev 1:7 in a single study reveals several implications serving hermeneutics, biblical theology, Christology, eschatology, missiology, and doxology. First, the present study serves hermeneutics by exemplifying how John's theological convictions—what Moo would call John's "hermeneutical axioms"[1]—drove his appropriation of Zech 12:10. John witnessed the glory of God's self-revelation in the person of God the Son, Jesus Christ. That self-revelation in Jesus' first advent led John to see the fulfillment of Zech 12:10. In the historical piercing of Jesus, God (the Son) was pierced, and that piercing inaugurated God's eschatological mission to secure the salvation of all who look on Jesus and believe. God's self-revelation in Jesus' second advent then led John to a reversed appropriation of Zech 12:10, since the pierced Jesus was returning to consummate God's eschatological mission, drawing the opportunity for repentance to a close (Rev 1:7). In both cases that John uses Zech 12:10, it becomes clear that God's final self-revelation in Jesus Christ was the key to interpreting the OT and its promises.[2]

John's conviction that Jesus was God and that the age of fulfillment had dawned in Jesus' two-fold eschatological mission, helped him to explain earlier parts of God's revelation in Scripture. John does not impose on Zech 12:10 a meaning that was never present. Rather, God's fuller revelation in Jesus Christ clarifies the earlier revelation and even draws out the implications for a new and broader audience on whom the end of the ages has come.[3] Interpreters of Scripture would do well to pay attention to the theological convictions driving the apostles' use of the OT. These convictions help one to discern the redemptive-historical rationale behind the NT's use of the OT, and keep one from too hastily accusing the apostles of misusing the OT to serve their own

---

1. Moo, *Old Testament*, 56; Moo, "Problem of Sensus Plenior," 194.
2. Beale, *Handbook*, 97.
3. Moo, *Old Testament*, 386–87.

ends. Moreover, they help one to discern that no passage of Scripture has been fully understood until it has been read in light of God's fuller and climactic self-revelation in Jesus Christ, to whom the apostles bear witness in their writings.

Second, John's use of Zech 12:10 contributes to biblical theology by validating the unity of the Testaments. The present study has attempted to show that Zech 12:10, John 19:37, and Rev 1:7, all form a coherent narrative. John's explanation of Zech 12:10 does not contradict the meaning of the original prophecy. Even where John broadens the audience to include "all the tribes of the earth," the meaning of the original prophecy persists in that sinful Israel can represent the sinful world, just as believing Israel (i.e., Jesus' disciples) can represent the new, believing community.[4] A proper method will be open to this inner-biblical unity and allow the salvation-historical framework of the canon to shape its exegetical conclusions instead of discarding such unity as an ahistorical imposition on the biblical text.

Unity also exists between the Fourth Gospel and Revelation. The present study has argued that this is partially due to the Apostle John being their common author. Others have doubted that John and Revelation share a common authorship, and one line of support is the theological differences between the two works. However, the present study demonstrates a coherent narrative that develops between John 19:37 and Rev 1:7. Indeed, the use of Zech 12:10 in both John 19:37 and Rev 1:7 should at least be considered an additional piece of evidence on the list of the theological affinities between John and Revelation.[5] Alongside the interest in Zechariah's Pierced One, the formulation of a high Christology and the strikingly similar contours of inaugurated and consummated eschatology also show deep unity between these two NT

---

4. Respectively, see the discussion on pp. 188–91 (The Piercers Consist of "All the Tribes") and pp. 194–97 (The Initial Disciples Represent the New Believing Community).

5. Listing the theological affinities between the Fourth Gospel and Revelation, Hoskins includes that "in John 19:37 and Rev 1:7, Jesus is the fulfillment of Zech 12:10, which says, 'They will look on him whom they pierced.'" Hoskins, *Revelation*, 18. Similarly, Mounce observes that "The prophecy of Zech 12:10 regarding Jerusalem looking on the one they have pierced is quoted in both Rev 1:7 and John 19:37 using the same Greek verb (*ekkenteō*), which in turn is not used by the LXX and is found nowhere else in the NT." Mounce, *Revelation*, 14.

books. In terms of developing a Johannine theology, those who include Revelation within the Johannine corpus stand on solid ground,[6] as do those who allow the Fourth Gospel to help with the interpretation of Revelation and vice versa.[7] Perhaps the present study will also lead those opposed to the Apostle John authoring both works to reconsider their position.

Third, the implications of the present study also serve Christology. While others have rightly emphasized that John's use of Zech 12:10 reveals Jesus' messianic role, the emphasis has at times overshadowed the more stunning theological point John appears to be making: God fulfills his eschatological mission first in the human flesh of Jesus. In short, Jesus is God. To pierce Jesus is to pierce God the Son, thus including Jesus within the divine identity. By equating Jesus with the pierced God of Zech 12:10, John articulates some of the highest Christology in the NT, and he does so while drawing from an OT witness. Thus, John's use of Zech 12:10 shows that the Fourth Gospel and Revelation should be read not merely along the lines of God working through his human, messianic representative, true as that may be, but along lines of God himself fulfilling his eschatological mission in the person of Jesus the divine Son.

Studies on the high Christology of the NT, like those of Bauckham[8] and Hurtado,[9] could add John's use of Zech 12:10 to their list of passages wherein a NT writer takes what once applied to Yahweh and applies it to Jesus Christ. Moreover, John's use of Zech 12:10 would fall into a category comparable to Paul's use of Isa 45 in Phil 2:10–11, which led Yeago to demonstrate that the Trinitarian and Christological doctrines of the early church were not something "imposed *on* the New Testament texts, nor distantly deduced *from* the texts, but rather [describe] a pattern of judgments present *in* the texts, in the texture of scriptural discourse concerning Jesus and the God of Israel."[10] Indeed, how else can the immortal God say, "they will look on me whom

---

6. E.g., see Rainbow, *Johannine Theology*, 42–52.
7. E.g., see Hoskins, *Revelation*, 17–20, 41–42.
8. Bauckham, *Jesus and the God of Israel*.
9. Hurtado, *Lord Jesus Christ*.
10. Yeago, "Nicene Dogma," 153.

they have pierced," unless inherent to that self-revelation was its future fulfillment in the gift of his Son, the eternal Word who would take to himself a human nature.

Fourth, the present study joins many others in affirming the inaugurated and consummated eschatology of the NT, especially that of John's writings. However, the present study may challenge some to reconsider how the fulfillment of Zech 12:10 squares with God's eschatological plan for Israel. Dispensationalists will sometimes argue that Zech 12:10 points to ethnic Israel's conversion during, or near the end of, the great tribulation, often being paired with Paul's interpretation of Isa 59:20–21 in Rom 11:26–27.[11] Dispensationalists rightly explain that the prophecy of Zech 12:10 anticipates God's eschatological salvation for Israel. However, they stop short of understanding the way John develops the prophecy's fulfillment for Israel, as well as the whole world, based on Jesus' two-fold eschatological mission. The present study has argued that John interprets Jesus' piercing to fulfill Zech 12:10, thereby inaugurating the "day" when God pours out the Spirit and cleanses his people as they look on Jesus and believe. Moreover, the present study has argued that John's reversed appropriation of Zech 12:10 in Rev 1:7 signals not a repentant mourning by ethnic Israel in conjunction with Jesus' Parousia, but a dreadful mourning by people from all the tribes of the earth who remain hostile to Jesus. If the present study is correct, then the "day" for the conversion of ethnic Jews, as well as people from every tribe, spans the entire inter-advent age, as God's Spirit transforms their spirit to look on Jesus and believe in response to the church's preaching of the gospel.[12]

Such an observation leads to a fifth implication, namely, the present study has implications for the church's mission. Through Jesus' death and piercing, God inaugurated his end-time salvation, securing for his people the gift of his Spirit and opening a fountain for cleansing their sins as they look on the Pierced One and believe. Until the

---

11. E.g., see Archer, "Rapture," 132; MacArthur, *Revelation 1–11*, 33; MacArthur, *Second Coming*, 42; Baron, *Zechariah*, 454; Pentecost, *Things to Come*, 298–99.

12. Such an interpretation aligns rather well with the way others have demonstrated that "all Israel" in Rom 11:26 best represents the elect ethnic Jews throughout history. See especially Robertson, "Distinctive Future," 209–27; Merkle, "Romans 11," 709–21; Gentry and Wellum, *Kingdom*, 499–501.

Conclusion

Pierced One returns to close the inter-advent age with judgment, the church must declare this good news of God's salvation in Jesus Christ to the nations. People from all the tribes of the earth must look on Jesus and believe to receive eternal life (John 6:40), but "how are they to believe in him of whom they have never heard? And how are they to hear without someone preaching?" (Rom 10:14). John and the initial disciples testified to Jesus' death and its saving significance according to the Scriptures (John 19:37; 1 Cor 15:3). Their witness continues now through the church (John 20:21; 3 John 7; Rev 11:3).

Lastly, the present study has implications for doxology, that is, the worship of God in the Lord Jesus Christ. What Jesus accomplished through his redemptive sacrifice, his piercing included, produces doxology in Rev 1:6 and Rev 5:9–10. He is not only worthy to receive adoration from people on earth, since the death he died redeemed people for God (Rev 1:6; 5:9b–10), but he is also worthy to receive adoration from all heavenly creatures, since the death he died qualifies him alone to bring God's redemptive-historical purposes to fruition (Rev 5:9a). Accordingly, John's use of Zech 12:10 shows not only the immense significance of Jesus' death for the salvation of God's people, but also the way Jesus was bringing God's purposes to fruition in his two-fold eschatological mission. Therefore, to Jesus belong power and wealth and wisdom and might and honor and glory and blessing (Rev 5:12)!

Appendix 1

Comparative Analysis of Zech 12:10, 12a in John 19:37 and Rev 1:7

John 19:37	Rev 1:7	Zech 12:10, 12a	
NA²⁷	NA²⁷	LXX (Göttingen)	BHS
καὶ πάλιν ἑτέρα γραφὴ λέγει			
	Ἰδοὺ ἔρχεται μετὰ τῶν νεφελῶν		
		καὶ ἐκχεῶ	וְשָׁפַכְתִּי
		ἐπὶ τὸν οἶκον Δαυιδ	עַל־בֵּית דָּוִיד
		καὶ ἐπὶ τοὺς κατοικοῦντας Ιερουσαλημ	וְעַל יוֹשֵׁב יְרוּשָׁלַם
		πνεῦμα χάριτος καὶ οἰκτιρμοῦ	רוּחַ חֵן וְתַחֲנוּנִים
ὄψονται	καὶ ὄψεται αὐτὸν πᾶς ὀφθαλμὸς	καὶ ἐπιβλέψονται	וְהִבִּיטוּ
εἰς ὃν ἐξεκέντησαν	καὶ οἵτινες αὐτὸν ἐξεκέντησαν	πρός με	אֵלַי אֵת אֲשֶׁר־דָּקָרוּ
		ἀνθ' ὧν κατωρχήσαντο	
	καὶ κόψονται ἐπ' αὐτὸν	καὶ κόψονται ἐπ' αὐτὸν κοπετόν	וְסָפְדוּ עָלָיו

Appendix 1

John 19:37	Rev 1:7	Zech 12:10, 12a	
NA²⁷	NA²⁷	LXX (Göttingen)	*BHS*
		ὡς ἐπ' ἀγαπητὸν	כְּמִסְפֵּד עַל־הַיָּחִיד
		καὶ ὀδυνηθήσονται ὀδύνην	וְהָמֵר עָלָיו
		ὡς ἐπὶ πρωτοτόκῳ	כְּהָמֵר עַל־הַבְּכוֹר
		[...]	[...]
		καὶ κόψεται ἡ γῆ	וְסָפְדָה הָאָרֶץ
	πᾶσαι αἱ φυλαὶ τῆς γῆς	κατὰ φυλὰς φυλάς	מִשְׁפָּחוֹת מִשְׁפָּחוֹת
	ναί, ἀμήν		

Appendix 2

Comparative Analysis of Early Greek Translations of Zech 12:10

LXX	καὶ	ἐπιβλέψονται	πρός με ἀνθ' ὧν	κατωρχήσαντο
Aquila	-	-	σὺν ᾧ	ἐξεκέντησαν
Symmachus	-	-	ἔμπροσθέν	ἐπεξεκέντησαν
Theodotion	καὶ	ἐπιβλέψονται	πρός με [εἰς] ὃν	ἐξεκέντησαν
Lucian	-	-	εἰς ὃν	ἐξεκέντησαν
John 19:37	-	ὄψονται	εἰς ὃν	ἐξεκέντησαν

Appendix 3

Proposed Identifications of the Pierced One

	1. Past	2. Present	3. Future
Collective	Benjaminites	Jewish Martyrs Prophetic Figures Visionary Disciples of Second Isaiah Oppressed Judahites	-
Singular	King Josiah Jeremiah Uriah, son of Shemiah Gedaliah Zechariah, son of Jehoiada	Zerubbabel, the Davidide Someone killed in the war of Zech 12:1–8 YHWH's prophet Simon Maccabeus Onias III Joshua, the High Priest	Messiah ben Ephraim/Joseph The Shepherd of Zechariah Isaiah's Suffering Servant Person of Messiah

Bibliography

Abbott, Edwin A. *Johannine Vocabulary: A Comparison of the Words of the Fourth Gospel with Those of the Three*. London: Adam and Charles Black, 1905.
Achtemeier, Elizabeth R. "Jesus Christ, the Light of the World: The Biblical Understanding of Light and Darkness." *Interpretation* 17 (1963) 439–49.
———. *Nahum–Malachi*. IBC. Atlanta: John Knox, 1986.
Adams, Edward. "The Coming of the Son of Man in Mark's Gospel." *TynBul* 56 (2005) 39–61.
———. *The Stars Will Fall from Heaven: Cosmic Catastrophe in the New Testament and Its World*. LNTS 347. London: T. & T. Clark, 2007.
Aland, Barbara, et al. *Novum Testamentum Graece*. 27th ed. Stuttgart: Deutsche Bibelgesellschaft, 1993.
Archer, Jr., Gleason L. "The Case for the Mid-Seventieth-Week Rapture Position." In *Three Views on the Rapture: Pre-, Mid-, or Post-Tribulational?*, edited by Gleason L. Archer, Jr., 113–45. Counterpoints. Grand Rapids: Zondervan, 1984.
Aune, David Edward. *Revelation 1–5*. WBC 52a. Dallas: Word, 1997.
Baker, David L. *Two Testaments, One Bible: A Study of Some Modern Solutions to the Theological Problem of the Relationship between the Old and New Testaments*. Downers Grove, IL: IVP, 1976.
Baldwin, Joyce G. *Daniel: An Introduction and Commentary*. TOTC 21. Downers Grove, IL: IVP, 1978.
———. *Haggai, Zechariah, Malachi: An Introduction and Commentary*. TOTC 28. Downers Grove, IL: InterVarsity, 1972.
Ball, David Mark. *"I AM" in John's Gospel: Literary Function, Background and Theological Implications*. JSNTSup 124. Sheffield: Sheffield Academic, 1996.
Balla, Peter. *Challenges to New Testament Theology: An Attempt to Justify the Enterprise*. Peabody, MA: Hendrickson, 1997.

Bibliography

Bandy, Alan. "The Hermeneutics of Symbolism: How to Interpret the Symbols of John's Apocalypse." *SBJT* 14 (2010) 46–58.

Barnett, Paul. *The Second Epistle to the Corinthians*. NICNT. Grand Rapids: Eerdmans, 1997.

Baron, David. *Zechariah: A Commentary on His Visions and Prophecies*. Grand Rapids: Kregel, 2001.

Barrett, C. K. *The Gospel according to St. John: An Introduction with Commentary and Notes on the Greek Text*. 2nd ed. Philadelphia: Westminster, 1955.

———. "The Old Testament in the Fourth Gospel." *JTS* 48 (1947) 155–69.

Barthélemy, Domonique. *Critique Textuelle de l'Ancien Testament*. Vol. 3. OBO 50. Fribourg: Editions universitaires, 1992.

Bauckham, Richard. *The Climax of Prophecy: Studies on the Book of Revelation*. Edinburgh: T. & T. Clark, 1993.

———. *Jesus and the Eyewitnesses: The Gospels as Eyewitness Testimony*. Grand Rapids: Eerdmans, 2006.

———. *Jesus and the God of Israel: God Crucified and Other Studies on the New Testament's Christology of Divine Identity*. Grand Rapids: Eerdmans, 2008.

———. *The Testimony of the Beloved Disciple: Narrative, History, and Theology in the Gospel of John*. Grand Rapids: Baker, 2007.

———. *The Theology of the Book of Revelation*. New Testament Theology. Cambridge: Cambridge University Press, 1993.

Bauckham, Richard, ed. *The Gospels for All Christians: Rethinking the Gospel Audiences*. Grand Rapids: Eerdmans, 1998.

Beale, G. K. *The Book of Revelation: A Commentary on the Greek Text*. NIGTC. Grand Rapids: Eerdmans, 1999.

———. "Did Jesus and His Followers Preach the Right Doctrine from the Wrong Texts? An Examination of the Presuppositions of Jesus' and the Apostles' Exegetical Method." In *The Right Doctrine from the Wrong Texts? Essays on the Use of the Old Testament in the New*, edited by G. K. Beale, 387–404. Grand Rapids: Baker, 1994.

———. *Handbook on the New Testament Use of the Old Testament: Exegesis and Interpretation*. Grand Rapids: Baker, 2012.

———. *John's Use of the Old Testament in Revelation*. JSNTSup 166. Sheffield: Sheffield Academic, 1998.

———. "Questions of Authorial Intent, Epistemology, and Presuppositions and Their Bearing on the Study of the Old Testament in the New: A Rejoinder to Steve Moyise." *IBS* 21 (1999) 152–80.

———. *A New Testament Biblical Theology: The Unfolding of the Old Testament in the New*. Grand Rapids: Baker, 2011.

Bibliography

———. "A Response to Jon Paulien on the Use of the Old Testament in Revelation." *AUSS* 39 (2001) 23–34.

———. "Revelation." In *It Is Written: Scripture Citing Scripture, Essays in Honor of Barnabas Lindars*, edited by D. A. Carson and H. G. M. Williamson, 318–36. New York: Cambridge, 1988.

———. *The Temple and the Church's Mission: A Biblical Theology of the Dwelling Place of God.* NSBT 17. Downers Grove, IL: InterVarsity, 2004.

———. *The Use of Daniel in Jewish Apocalyptic Literature and in the Revelation of St. John.* Lanham, MD: University Press of America, 1984.

Beale, G. K., ed. *The Right Doctrine from the Wrong Texts? Essays on the Use of the Old Testament in the New.* Grand Rapids: Baker, 1994.

Beale, G. K., and D. A. Carson, eds. *Commentary on the New Testament Use of the Old Testament.* Grand Rapids: Baker, 2007.

Beale, G. K., and Sean M. McDonough. "Revelation." In *Commentary on the New Testament Use of the Old Testament*, edited by G. K. Beale and D. A. Carson, 1081–1161. Grand Rapids: Baker, 2007.

Beasley-Murray, G. R. *The Book of Revelation.* Eugene, OR: Wipf & Stock, 1981.

———. *Jesus and the Last Days: The Interpretation of the Olivet Discourse.* Peabody, MA: Hendrickson, 1993.

———. *John.* WBC 36. Waco, TX: Word, 1987.

Beauchamp, P. "Lecture Christique de l'Ancient Testament." *Bib* 81 (2000) 105–15.

Beckwith, Isbon T. *The Apocalypse of John.* New York: Macmillan, 1919.

Beckwith, Roger T. *The Old Testament Canon of the New Testament Church, and Its Background in Early Judaism.* Grand Rapids: Eerdmans, 1985.

Bekins, Peter Joseph. "Information Structure and Object Marking: A Study of the Object Preposition *'et* in Biblical Hebrew." PhD diss., Hebrew Union College—Jewish Institution of Religion, 2012.

Belle, Gilbert van. "The Meaning of Sēmeia in Jn 20,30–31." *ETL* 74 (1998) 300–25.

Belleville, Linda. "'Born of Water and Spirit': John 3:5." *TrinJ* 1 (1980) 125–41.

Bilić, Niko. *Jerusalem an Jenem Tag: Text Und Botschaft von Sach 12–14.* FB 117. Würzburg: Echter, 2008.

Black, Mark. "Messianic Use of Zechariah 9–14." In *Scripture and Traditions: Essays on Early Judaism and Christianity in Honor of Carl R. Holladay*, edited by Patrick Gray and Gail R. O'Day, 97–114. NovTSup 129. Leiden: Brill, 2008.

Black, Mark C. "The Rejected and Slain Messiah Who Is Coming with His Angels: The Messianic Exegesis of Zechariah 9–14 in the Passion Narratives." PhD diss., Emory University, 1990.

Bibliography

Blomberg, Craig L. *Matthew*. NAC 22. Nashville: Broadman & Holman, 1992.

———. "Matthew." In *Commentary on the New Testament Use of the Old Testament*, edited by G. K. Beale and D. A. Carson, 1–110. Grand Rapids: Baker, 2007.

Blount, Brian K. *Revelation: A Commentary*. NTL. Louisville: Westminster John Knox, 2009.

Bock, Darrell L. *Acts*. BECNT. Grand Rapids: Baker, 2007.

———. "Did Jesus Connect Son of Man to Daniel 7? A Short Reflection on the Position of Larry Hurtado." *BBR* 22 (2012) 399–402.

Bockmuehl, Markus. *Seeing the Word: Refocusing New Testament Study*. Studies in Theological Interpretation. Grand Rapids: Baker, 2008.

Boda, Mark J. *Haggai, Zechariah*. NIVAC. Grand Rapids: Zondervan, 2004.

———. "Quotations and Allusions." In *Dictionary of Biblical Criticism and Interpretation*, edited by Stanley E. Porter, 296–98. New York: Routledge, 2005.

———. *"Return to Me": A Biblical Theology of Repentance*. NSBT 35. Downers Grove, IL: InterVarsity, 2015.

Boer, M. C. de. *Johannine Perspectives on the Death of Jesus*. CBET 17. Kampen: Kok Pharos, 1996.

Boismard, M. É., and A. Lamouille. *Synopse Des Quatre Évangiles En Français, Tome III: L'Evangile de Jean*. Paris: Le Éditions du Cerf, 1977.

Borchert, Gerald L. *John 12–21*. NAC 25b. Nashville: B&H, 2002.

Boxall, Ian. *The Revelation of Saint John*. BNTC. Peabody, MA: Hendrickson, 2006.

Brandenburg, Hans. *Die Kleinen Propheten*. Lebendige Wort. Giessen u. Basel: Brunnen, 1963.

Brendsel, Daniel J. "'Isaiah Saw His Glory': The Use of Isaiah 52–53 in John 12." PhD diss., Wheaton College, 2013.

Brodie, Thomas L. *The Gospel according to John: A Literary and Theological Commentary*. New York: Oxford University Press, 1993.

Brooke, George J. "The Biblical Texts in the Qumran Commentaries: Scribal Errors or Exegetical Variants?" In *Early Jewish and Christian Exegesis: Studies in Memory of William Hugh Brownlee*, edited by Craig A. Evans and William F. Stinespring, 85–100. Atlanta: Scholars, 1987.

Brown, Raymond E. *The Community of the Beloved Disciple*. New York: Paulist, 1979.

———. "Does the New Testament Call Jesus God?" *TS* 26 (1965) 545–73.

———. *The Gospel According to John I-XII*. AB 29. New York: Doubleday, 1966.

———. *The Gospel according to John XIII-XXI*. AB 29a. New York: Doubleday, 1970.

Bibliography

Bruce, F. F. "The Book of Zechariah and the Passion Narrative." *BJRL* 45 (1961) 336–53.

———. *The Gospel of John*. Grand Rapids: Eerdmans, 1983.

———. "The Oldest Greek Version of Daniel." In *Instruction and Interpretation: Studies in Hebrew Language, Palestinian Archaeology and Biblical Exegesis*, 22–40. OTS 20. Leiden: Brill, 1977.

Brunner, Fredrick Dale. *The Gospel of John*. Grand Rapids: Eerdmans, 2012.

Brütsch, Charles. *La Clarté de l'Apocalypse*. 5th ed. Genève: Éditions Labor et fides, 1966.

Bultmann, Rudolf. *The Gospel of John: A Commentary*. Translated by George R. Beasley-Murray et al. Philadelphia: Westminster, 1971.

———. *Theology of the New Testament*. Translated by Kendrick Grobel. 2 vols. Waco, TX: Baylor University Press, 2007.

Burge, Gary M. *John*. NIVAC. Grand Rapids: Zondervan, 2000.

Burkett, Delbert. *The Son of Man Debate: A History and Evaluation*. SNTSMS 107. Cambridge: Cambridge University Press, 1999.

Burridge, Richard A. *Four Gospels, One Jesus? A Symbolic Reading*. 2nd ed. Grand Rapids: Eerdmans, 2005.

Butterworth, Mike. *Structure and the Book of Zechariah*. JSOTSup 130. Sheffield: JSOT, 1992.

Bynum, William Randolph. *The Fourth Gospel and the Scriptures: Illuminating the Form and Meaning of Scriptural Citation in John 19:37*. NovTSup 144. Leiden: Brill, 2012.

———. "Quotations of Zechariah in the Fourth Gospel." In *Abiding Words: The Use of Scripture in the Gospel of John*, edited by Alicia D. Myers and Bruce G. Schuchard, 47–74. SBLRBS 81. Atlanta: SBL, 2015.

Caird, G. B. *A Commentary on the Revelation of St. John the Divine*. New York: Harper and Row, 1966.

Calvin, John. *Commentary on the Gospel according to John*. Translated by William Pringle. Vol. 18. Calvin's Commentaries. Edinburgh: Calvin Translation Society, 1843.

———. *Commentaries on the Twelve Minor Prophets*. Translated by John Owen. Vol. 15. Calvin's Commentaries. Grand Rapids: Baker, 2003.

Campbell, W. Thomas. "The Relationship of the Thomas Pericope to Signs and Belief in the Fourth Gospel." PhD diss., Southwestern Baptist Theological Seminary, 2000.

Caragounis, Chrys C. *The Son of Man: Vision and Interpretation*. WUNT 8. Tübingen: Mohr, 1986.

Carnazzo, Sebastian A. *Seeing Blood and Water: A Narrative-Critical Study of John 19:34*. Eugene, OR: Wipf & Stock, 2012.

Carson, D. A. *Collected Writings on Scripture*. Edited by Andrew David Naselli. Wheaton: Crossway, 2010.

———. "Current Issues in Biblical Theology: A New Testament Perspective." *BBR* 5 (1995) 17–41.

———. *Divine Sovereignty & Human Responsibility: Biblical Perspectives in Tension*. Eugene, OR: Wipf & Stock, 2002.

———. *The Gospel according to John*. PNTC. Grand Rapids: Eerdmans, 1991.

———. *Jesus the Son of God: A Christological Title Often Overlooked, Sometimes Misunderstood, and Currently Disputed*. Grand Rapids: Crossway, 2012.

———. "John and the Johannine Epistles." In *It Is Written: Scripture Citing Scripture, Essays in Honor of Barnabas Lindars, SSF*, edited by D. A. Carson and H. G. M. Williamson, 245–64. Cambridge: Cambridge University Press, 1988.

———. *Matthew*. EBC 9. Grand Rapids: Zondervan, 2010.

———. "The Purpose of Signs and Wonders in the New Testament." In *Power Religion: The Selling Out of the Evangelical Church?*, edited by Michael S. Horton, 89–118. Chicago: Moody, 1992.

———. "The Purpose of the Fourth Gospel: John 20:31 Reconsidered." *JBL* 106 (1987) 639–51.

———. "Syntactical and Text-Critical Observations on John 20:30–31: One More Round on the Purpose of the Fourth Gospel." *JBL* 124 (2005) 693–714.

———. "Systematic Theology and Biblical Theology." In *NDBT* 89–104.

———. "Understanding Misunderstandings in the Fourth Gospel." *TynBul* 33 (1982) 59–91.

———. "Unity and Diversity in the New Testament: The Possibility of Systematic Theology." In *Scripture and Truth*, edited by D. A. Carson and John D. Woodbridge, 65–95. Grand Rapids: Baker, 1992.

Carson, D. A., and H. G. M. Williamson, eds. *It Is Written: Scripture Citing Scripture. Essays in Honour of Barnabas Lindars*. Cambridge: Cambridge University Press, 1988.

Carson, D. A., et al. *An Introduction to the New Testament*. Grand Rapids: Zondervan, 1992.

Casey, Maurice. *The Solution to the "Son of Man" Problem*. LNTS 343. London: T. & T. Clark, 2007.

Cathcart, Kevin, and R. P. Gordon, eds. *The Targum of the Minor Prophets*. Vol. 14. ArBib. Wilmington: Michael Glazier, 1989.

Chary, Théophane. *Aggée–Zecharie, Malachie*. SB. Paris: J. Gabalda et Cie, 1969.

Childs, Brevard S. *Introduction to the Old Testament as Scripture*. Philadelphia: Fortress, 1979.

Chilton, David. *The Days of Vengeance: An Exposition of the Book of Revelation*. Fort Worth: Dominion, 1987.

Choi, Byong Kie. "The 'ἀρνίον', Lamb, as a Christological Figure in the Visions of the Apocalypse (4:1—22:5): A Christological Study of the Book of Revelation." PhD diss., Drew University, 2001.

Cirafesi, Wally V. "The Johannine Community Hypothesis (1968–Present): Past and Present Approaches and a New Way Forward." *CBR* 12 (2014) 173–93.

Clark, David J., and Howard A. Hatton. *A Handbook on Haggai, Zechariah, and Malachi*. UBS Handbook Series. New York: United Bible Societies, 2002.

Cohen, A. *The Twelve Prophets: Hebrew Text, English Translation and Commentary*. Soncino Books of the Bible. Bournemouth: Soncino, 1948.

Collins, Adela Yarbro. "Dating the Apocalypse of John." *BR* 26 (1981) 33–45.

Collins, John J. *The Apocalyptic Imagination: An Introduction to Jewish Apocalyptic Literature*. 2nd ed. Biblical Resource Series. Grand Rapids: Eerdmans, 1998.

Condamin, A. "Le Sens Messianique de Zecharie, XII, 10." *RSR* 1 (1910) 52–56.

Conrad, Edgar W. *Zechariah*. Readings: A New Biblical Commentary. Sheffield Academic, 1999.

Cook, Stephen. "The Metamorphosis of a Shepherd: The Tradition History of Zechariah 11:17 + 13:7–9." *CBQ* 55 (1993) 453–66.

Cook, W. Robert. "Eschatology in John's Gospel." *CTR* 3 (1988) 79–99.

———. "The 'Glory' Motif in the Johannine Corpus." *JETS* 27 (1984) 291–97.

Cooke, George A. "The Unknown Martyr: A Study of Zechariah 11 and 12." *ATR* 6 (1923) 97–105.

Cullmann, Oscar. "Der Johanneische Gebrauch Doppeldeutiger Ausdrücke Als Schlüssel Zum Verständnis Des Vierten Evangeliums." In *Vorträge Und Aufsätze, 1925–1962*, edited by Karlfried Fröhlich, 176–86. Tübingen: Mohr Siebeck, 1966.

Culpepper, R. Alan. "Cognition in John: The Johannine Signs as Recognition Scenes." *PRSt* 35 (2008) 251–60.

Dahms, John V. "The Johannine Use of Monogenēs Reconsidered." *NTS* 29 (1983) 222–32.

Dahood, Mitchell. "A Note on Third Person Suffix -Y in Hebrew." *UF* 4 (1972) 63–64.

Davies, G. I. "The Use and Non-Use of the Particle ʾet in Hebrew Inscriptions." In *Studies in Hebrew & Aramaic Syntax: Presented to Professor J. Hoftijzer on the Occasion of His Sixty-Fifth Birthday*, edited by K. Jongeling et al., 14–26. Leiden: E. J. Brill, 1991.

Deissler, Alfons. "Sach 12,10—Die Große Crux Interpretum." In *Ich bewirke das Heil und erschaffe das Unheil (Jesaja 45,7): Studien zur Botschaft der*

Propheten: Festschrift für Lothar Ruppert zum 65. Geburtstag, edited by Friedrich Diedrich and Bernd Willms, 49–60. FB 88. Würzburg: Echter, 1998.

Delcor, M. "Un Problèm de Critique Textuelle et D'exégèse, Zach 12:10: Et Aspicient Ad Me Quem Confixerunt." *RB* 58 (1951) 189–99.

Delling, Gerhard, "πληρόω." In TDNT 6:295–97.

Dempster, Stephen G. *Dominion and Dynasty: A Theology of the Hebrew Bible.* NSBT 15. Downers Grove, IL: InterVarsity, 2003.

Dennis, John. "Jesus' Death in John's Gospel: A Survey of Research from Bultmann to the Present with Special Reference to the Johannine Hyper-Texts." *CBR* 4 (2006) 331–63.

DeSilva, David Arthur. *Seeing Things John's Way: The Rhetoric of the Book of Revelation.* Louisville: Westminster John Knox, 2009.

Devillers, Luc. "I. 'Le Transpercé': L'oracle de Zacharie 12,10 Dans Son Contexte Biblique et Dans La Tradition Juive." In *Centenaire Du Monastère Des Bénédictines de Notre-Dame Du Calvaire Au Mont Des Oliviers 1896–1996*, edited by J. B. Livio, 87–104. Carouge-Genève: Éd. Choisir, 1997.

———. "II. L'interprétation de Za 12,10 Dans Le Nouveau Testament, in Particulier Dans Le Quatrième Évangile." In *Centenaire Du Monastère Des Bénédictines de Notre-Dame Du Calvaire Au Mont Des Oliviers 1896–1996*, edited by J. B. Livio, 135–44. Carouge-Genève: Éd. Choisir, 1997.

Di Lella, Alexander A. "The Textual History of Septuagint-Daniel and Theodotion-Daniel." In *The Book of Daniel: Composition and Reception*, edited by John J. Collins and Peter W. Flint, 2:586–607. VTSup 83. Leiden: Brill, 2002.

Dodd, C. H. *According to the Scriptures: The Substructure of New Testament Theology.* London: Nisbet, 1952.

———. "The Kingdom of God Has Come." *ExpTim* 48 (1936) 138–42.

———. *The Parables of the Kingdom.* New York: Scribner, 1961.

Dogniez, Cécile. "Some Similarities between the Septuagint and the Targum of Zechariah." In *Translating a Translation: The LXX and Its Modern Translations in the Context of Early Judaism*, edited by H. Ausloos and J. Cook, 89–102. BETL 213. Paris: Uitgeverij Peeters, 2008.

Dolezal, James E. *All That Is in God: Evangelical Theology and the Challenge of Classical Christian Theism.* Grand Rapids: Reformation Heritage, 2017.

Driver, S. R. *The Minor Prophets: Nahum, Habakkuk, Zephaniah, Haggai, Zechariah, Malachi.* Century Bible. New York: Oxford University Press, 1904.

Duguid, Iain. "Messianic Themes in Zechariah 9–14." In *The Lord's Anointed: Interpretation of Old Testament Messianic Texts*, edited by Philip E.

Bibliography

Satterthwaite et al., 265–80. Tyndale House Studies. Grand Rapids: Baker, 1995.

Duhm, D. Bernh. *Anmerkungen zu den zwölf Propheten*. ZAW. Giessen: Alfred Töpelmann, 1911.

Dunn, James D. G. *Did the First Christians Worship Jesus? The New Testament Evidence*. London: T. & T. Clark, 2010.

Ellis, E. Earle. *The Old Testament in Early Christianity: Canon and Interpretation in the Light of Modern Research*. Grand Rapids: Baker, 1991.

Erdmann, Martin. "Mission in John's Gospel and Letters." In *Mission in the New Testament: An Evangelical Approach*, edited by William J. Larkin and Joel F. Williams, 207–26. Maryknoll: Orbis, 1998.

Evans, Craig A. "Old Testament in the Gospels." In *Dictionary of Jesus and the Gospels*, edited by Joel B. Green et al., 579–90. Downers Grove, IL: IVP, 1992.

———. "On the Quotation Formulas in the Fourth Gospel." *BZ* 26 (1982) 79–83.

———. "Scripture within Scripture: The Interrelationship of Form and Function in the Explicit Old Testament Citations in the Gospel of John." *CBQ* 55 (1993) 822–24.

———. *Word and Glory: On the Exegetical and Theological Background of John's Prologue*. JSNTSS 89. Sheffield: JSOT, 1993.

Fee, Gordon D. "On the Text and Meaning of John 20,30–31." In *The Four Gospels 1992: Festschrift Frans Neirynck*, edited by F. van Segbroeck et al., 2193–2205. BETL 100. Leuven: University Press, 1992.

Feuillet, A. *The Apocalypse*. New York: Alba House, 1965.

Fishbane, Michael. *Biblical Interpretation in Ancient Israel*. Oxford: Clarendon, 1985.

Flemming, Dean. "Revelation and the Missio Dei: Toward a Missional Reading of the Apocalypse." *JTI* 6 (2012) 161–78.

Floyd, Michael H. *Minor Prophets, Part 2*. FOTL 22. Grand Rapids: Eerdmans, 2000.

Ford, J. Massyngberde. *Revelation: Introduction, Translation and Commentary*. AB 38. Garden City: Doubleday, 1975.

France, R. T. *The Gospel of Matthew*. NICNT. Grand Rapids: Eerdmans, 2007.

———. *Jesus and the Old Testament: His Application of Old Testament Passages to Himself and His Mission*. Vancouver: Regent College Publishing, 1998.

Freed, E. D. *Old Testament Quotations in the Gospel of John*. NovTSup 11. Leiden: Brill, 1965.

Fritsch, Charles T. *The Anti-Anthropomorphisms of the Greek Pentateuch*. Princeton: Princeton University Press, 1943.

Bibliography

Fuller, Russell E. "4QXIIe." In *Qumrân Cave 4. X. the Prophets*, edited by Eugene C. Ulrich et al., 258–65. DJD 15. Oxford: Clarendon, 1997.

Gentry, Kenneth L. *Before Jerusalem Fell: Dating the Book of Revelation: An Exegetical and Historical Argument for a Pre-AD 70 Composition*. Tyler, TX: Institute for Christian Economics, 1989.

Gentry, Peter J. "The Son of Man in Daniel 7: Individual or Corporate?" In *Acorns to Oaks: The Primacy of Biblical Theology*, 59–75. Toronto: Joshua, 2003.

Gentry, Peter J., and Stephen J. Wellum. *Kingdom through Covenant: A Biblical-Theological Understanding of the Covenants*. Wheaton: Crossway, 2012.

Geza, Vermes. "The 'Son of Man' Debate." *JSNT* 1 (1978) 19–32.

Giesen, Heinz. *Die Offenbarung Des Johannes*. RNT. Regensburg: F. Pustet, 1997.

Glasson, T. Francis. "Theophany and Parousia." *NTS* 34 (1988) 259–70.

Goldsworthy, Graeme. "Relationship of Old Testament and New Testament." In *NDBT* 81–89.

Gordon, Robert P. "The Ephraimite Messiah and the Targum(s) to Zechariah 12.10." In *Reading from Right to Left: Essays on the Hebrew Bible in Honor of David J. A. Clines*, edited by J. Cheryl Exum and H. G. M. Williamson, 184–95. JSOTSup 373. Sheffield: Sheffield Academic, 2003.

Goshen-Gottstein, Moshe H. "Hebrew Biblical Manuscripts: Their History and Their Place in the HUBP Edition." In *Qumran and the History of the Biblical Text*, edited by Frank M. Cross and Shemaryahu Talmon. Cambridge: Harvard University Press, 1975.

Gradl, Hans-Georg. "Buch und Brief: Zur motivischen, literarischen und kommunikativen Interdependenz zweier medialer typen in der Johannes-Offenbarung." In *Die Johannesapokalypse: Kontext-Konzepte-Rezeption*, edited by Jörg Frey et al., 414–33. WUNT 287. Tübingen: Mohr Siebeck, 2012.

———. *Buch und Offenbarung: Medien und Medialität der Johannesapokalypse*. HBS 75. Freiburg: Herder, 2014.

Gren, Conrad R. "Piercing the Ambiguities of Psalm 22:16 and the Messiah's Mission." *JETS* 48 (2005) 283–99.

Günther, Hans Werner. *Der Nah- und Enderwartungshorizont in der Apokalypse des heiligen Johannes*. FB 41. Würzburg: Echter, 1980.

Haenchen, Ernst. *John: A Commentary on the Gospel of John*. Translated by Robert W. Funk. Hermeneia. Philadelphia: Fortress, 1984.

Haily, Homer. *A Commentary on the Minor Prophets*. Grand Rapids: Baker, 1972.

Ham, Clay Alan. *The Coming King and the Rejected Shepherd: Matthew's Reading of Zechariah's Messianic Hope*. New Testament Monographs. Sheffield: Phoenix, 2005.

———. "Reading Zechariah and Matthew's Olivet Discourse." In *Biblical Interpretation in Early Christian Gospels: Volume 2: The Gospel of Matthew*, edited by Thomas R. Hatina, 85–97. LNTS 310. New York: T. & T. Clark, 2008.

Hamilton, James M. "Appreciation, Agreement, and a Few Minor Quibbles: A Response to G. K. Beale." *MwJT* 10 (2011) 58–70.

———. *God's Glory in Salvation through Judgment: A Biblical Theology*. Wheaton: Crossway, 2010.

———. *God's Indwelling Presence: The Holy Spirit in the Old and New Testaments*. NAC Studies in Bible & Theology. Nashville: Broadman & Holman, 2006.

———. *Revelation: The Spirit Speaks to the Churches*. Preaching the Word. Wheaton: Crossway, 2010.

———. *With the Clouds of Heaven: The Book of Daniel in Biblical Theology*. NSBT 32. Downers Grove, IL: InterVarsity, 2014.

Hanson, Anthony Tyrrell. *The Prophetic Gospel: A Study of John and the Old Testament*. SEBS. London: T. & T. Clark, 1991.

Hanson, Paul D. *The Dawn of Apocalyptic*. Philadelphia: Fortress, 1975.

Harris, Murray J. *Jesus as God: The New Testament Use of Theos in Reference to Jesus*. Eugene, OR: Wipf & Stock, 1992.

Haukaas, Mark A. "'Indeed, He Is Coming with the Clouds': A Study of Revelation 1:7–8 as the Multivalent Thematic Statement of the Apocalypse." MA Thesis, Trinity Western University, 2013.

Hays, Richard B. "Can the Gospels Teach Us How to Read the Old Testament?" *ProEccl* 11 (2002) 402–18.

———. *The Conversion of the Imagination: Paul as Interpreter of Israel's Scripture*. Grand Rapids: Eerdmans, 2005.

———. *Echoes of Scripture in the Letters of Paul*. New Haven: Yale University Press, 1989.

Hendriksen, William. *Exposition of the Gospel according to John*. New Testament Commentary. Grand Rapids: Baker, 1954.

Hengel, Martin. "Die Schriftauslegung des 4. Evangeliums auf dem Hintergrund der urchristlichen Exegese." In *"Gesetz" als Thema biblischer Theologie*, edited by Ingo Baldermann and Dwight R. Daniels, 249–88. JBT 4. Neukirchen-Vluyn: Neukirchener, 1989.

———. "The Effective History of Isaiah 53 in the Pre-Christian Period." In *The Suffering Servant: Isaiah 53 in Jewish and Christian Sources*, edited by Bernd Janowski and Peter Stuhlmacher, 75–146. Translated by Daniel P. Bailey. Grand Rapids: Eerdmans, 2004.

———. "The Prologue of the Gospel of John as the Gateway to Christological Truth." In *The Gospel of John and Christian Theology*, edited by Richard Bauckham and Carl Mosser, 265–94. Grand Rapids: Eerdmans, 2008.

Bibliography

Herghelegiu, Monica-Elena. *Haggai, Zechariah and Malachi*. TOTC 28. Downers Grove, IL: InterVarsity, 2012.

———. *Siehe, Er Kommt Mit Den Wolken!: Studien Zur Christologie Der Johannesoffenbarung*. Europäische Hochschulschriften. New York: Lang, 2004.

Hill, Andrew E. "Dating 'Second Zechariah': A Linguistic Reexamination." *HAR* 6 (1982) 105–34.

Hirsch, E. D. *Validity in Interpretation*. New Haven: Yale University Press, 1967.

Hofius, Otfried. "'Der in des Vaters Schoß Ist' Joh 1,18." *ZNW* 80 (1989) 163–71.

Hoftijzer, J. "Remarks Concerning the Use of the Particle *et* in Classical Hebrew." *OtSt* 14 (1965) 1–99.

Hoskins, Paul M. "Deliverance from Death by the True Passover Lamb: A Significant Aspect of the Fulfillment of the Passover in the Gospel of John." *JETS* 52 (2009) 285–99.

———. *Jesus as the Fulfillment of the Temple in the Gospel of John*. Paternoster Biblical Monographs. Waynesboro: Paternoster, 2006.

———. *That the Scripture Might Be Fulfilled: Typology and the Death of Christ*. LaVergne: Xulon, 2009.

———. *The Book of Revelation: A Theological and Exegetical Commentary*. North Charleston, SC: ChristoDoulos, 2017.

Hoskyns, Edwyn Clement. *The Fourth Gospel*, edited by Francis Davey Davey. London: Faber and Faber, 1947.

Hübenthal, Sandra. *Transformation Und Aktualisierung: Zur Rezeption von Sach 9–14 Im Neuen Testament*. SBB 57. Stuttgart: Katholisches Bibelwerk, 2006.

Hultberg, Alan D. "Messianic Exegesis in the Apocalypse: The Significance of the Old Testament for the Christology of Revelation." PhD diss., Trinity Evangelical Divinity School, 2001.

———. "The Significance of Zechariah 12:10 for the Theology of the Apocalypse." In *Evangelical Theological Society Papers 1996*, 1–39. Philadelphia, PA: TREN, 1995.

Hurtado, Larry W. *At the Origins of Christian Worship: The Context and Character of Earliest Christian Devotion*. Grand Rapids: Eerdmans, 1999.

———. *God in New Testament Theology*. LBT. Nashville: Abingdon, 2010.

———. *Lord Jesus Christ: Devotion to Jesus in Earliest Christianity*. Grand Rapids: Eerdmans, 2003.

———. *One God, One Lord: Early Christian Devotion and Ancient Jewish Monotheism*. 3rd ed. London: T. & T. Clark, 2015.

———. "Revelation 4–5 in the Light of Jewish Apocalyptic Analogies." *JSNT* 25 (1985) 105–24.

Bibliography

———. "Summary and Concluding Observations." In *"Who Is This Son of Man?" The Latest Scholarship on a Puzzling Expression of the Historical Jesus*, edited by Larry W. Hurtado and Paul L. Owen, 160–77. LNTS 390. New York: T. & T. Clark, 2011.

Hurtado, Larry W., and Paul L. Owen, eds. *"Who Is This Son of Man?" The Latest Scholarship on a Puzzling Expression of the Historical Jesus*. LNTS 390. New York: T. & T. Clark, 2011.

Isbell, Barbara Ann. "The Past Is Yet to Come: Exodus Typology in the Apocalypse." PhD diss., Southwestern Baptist Theological Seminary, 2013.

Jacobs, Alan. *A Theology of Reading: The Hermeneutics of Love*. Boulder, CO: Westview, 2001.

Jansma, T. "Inquiry into the Hebrew Text and the Ancient Versions of Zechariah 9–14." In *OtSt*, edited by P. A. H. de Boer, 7:1–142. Leiden: E. J. Brill, 1950.

Jauhiainen, Marko. "ΑΠΟΚΑΛΥΨΙΣ ΙΗΣΟΥ ΧΡΙΣΤΟΥ (Rev. 1:1): The Climax of John's Prophecy?" *TynBul* 54 (2003) 99–117.

———. "Turban and Crown Lost and Regained: Ezekiel 21:29–32 and Zechariah's Zemah." *JBL* 127 (2008) 501–11.

———. *The Use of Zechariah in Revelation*. WUNT 199. Tübingen: Mohr Siebeck, 2005.

Jobes, Karen H., and Moisés Silva. *Invitation to the Septuagint*. Grand Rapids: Baker, 2000.

Johnson, Dennis E. *Triumph of the Lamb: A Commentary on Revelation*. Phillipsburg: P&R, 2001.

Jones, Larry Paul. *The Symbol of Water in the Gospel of John*. JSNTSup 145. Sheffield: Sheffield Academic, 1999.

Jonge, Marinus de. "The Gospel and the Epistles of John Read Against the Background of the History of the Johannine Communities." In *What We Have Heard from the Beginning: The Past, Present, and Future of Johannine Studies*, edited by Tom Thatcher, 127–44. Waco, TX: Baylor University Press, 2007.

Joosten, Jan. "To See God: Conflicting Exegetical Tendencies in the Septuagint." In *Die Septuaginta—Texte, Kontexte, Lebenswelten: Internationale Fachtagung Veranstaltet von Septuaginta Deutch (LXX.D), Wuppertal 20.–23. Juli 2006*, edited by Karrer Martin and Wolfgang Kraus, 287–99. WUNT 219. Tübingen: Mohr Siebeck, 2008.

Josephus. *The Works of Flavius Josephus*. Translated by William Whiston. 1828. In *BibleWorks 7* [CD-ROM]. Norfolk: BibleWorks, 2006.

Kaiser, Walter C. *The Messiah in the Old Testament*. Studies in Old Testament Biblical Theology. Grand Rapids: Zondervan, 1995.

Bibliography

Keener, Craig S. *The Gospel of John: A Commentary.* Vol. 1. Peabody, MA: Hendrickson, 2003.

———. *The Gospel of John: A Commentary.* Vol. 2. Peabody, MA: Hendrickson, 2003.

———. *Revelation.* NIVAC. Grand Rapids: Zondervan, 2000.

Keil, C. F., and F. Delitzsch. *Twelve Minor Prophets.* Translated by James Martin. Grand Rapids: Eerdmans, 1949.

Kennicott, Benjaminus. *Vetus Testamentum Hebraicum, Cum Variis Lectionibus.* Vol. 2. Oxonii: E. typographeo Clarendoniano, 1780.

Kim, Seyoon. "Jesus—Son of God, the Stone, the Son of Man, and the Servant: The Role of Zechariah in the Self-Identification of Jesus." In *Tradition and Interpretation in the New Testament: Essays in Honor of E. Earle Ellis for His 60th Birthday,* edited by Gerald F. Hawthorne, 134–45. Grand Rapids: Eerdmans, 1987.

Kimḥi, David, and Alexander M'Caul. *Rabbi David Kimchi's Commentary upon the Prophecies of Zechariah.* London: James Duncan, 1837.

Kistemaker, Simon J. *Exposition of the Book of Revelation.* NTC. Grand Rapids: Baker, 2001.

Klauck, H. J. "Geschrieben, Erfüllt, Vollendet: Die Schriftzitate in der Johannespassion." In *Israel und seine Heilstraditionen im Johannesevangelium: Festgabe für Johannes Beutler SJ zum 70 Geburtstag,* edited by Michael Labahn et al., 140–57. Paderborn: Ferdinand Schöningh, 2004.

Klein, George L. *Zechariah.* NAC 21b. Nashville: Broadman & Holman, 2008.

Klink III, Edward W., ed. *The Sheep of the Fold: The Audience and Origin of the Gospel of John.* SNTSMS 141. Cambridge: Cambridge University Press, 2007.

Koester, Craig R. *Revelation: A New Translation with Introduction and Commentary.* AB 38a. New Haven: Yale University Press, 2014.

Kohler, August. *Die nachexilischen Propheten.* Erlangen: A. Deichert, 1862.

Köstenberger, Andreas J. "The Challenge of a Systematized Biblical Theology of Mission: Missiological Insights from the Gospel of John." *Missiology* 23 (1995) 445–64.

———. "Jesus the Good Shepherd Who Will Also Bring Other Sheep (John 10:16): The Old Testament Background of a Familiar Metaphor." *BBR* 12 (2002) 67–96.

———. *John.* BECNT. Grand Rapids: Baker, 2004.

———. "John." In *Commentary on the New Testament Use of the Old Testament,* edited by G. K. Beale and D. A. Carson, 415–512. Grand Rapids: Baker, 2007.

Bibliography

———. *The Missions of Jesus and the Disciples according to the Fourth Gospel: With Implications for the Fourth Gospel's Purpose and the Mission of the Contemporary Church*. Grand Rapids: Eerdmans, 1998.

———. "The Seventh Johannine Sign: A Study in John's Christology." *BBR* 5 (1995) 87–103.

———. *A Theology of John's Gospel and Letters*. Biblical Theology of the New Testament. Grand Rapids: Zondervan, 2009.

Köstenberger, Andreas, and Peter T. O'Brien. *Salvation to the Ends of the Earth: A Biblical Theology of Mission*. NSBT 11. Downers Grove, IL: IVP, 2001.

Köstenberger, Andreas J., and Richard D. Patterson. *Invitation to Biblical Interpretation: Exploring the Hermeneutical Triad of History, Literature, and Theology*. Invitation to Theological Studies. Grand Rapids: Kregel, 2011.

Köstenberger, Andreas J., and Stephen O. Stout. "'The Disciple Jesus Loved': Witness, Author, Apostle—A Response to Richard Bauckham's Jesus and the Eyewitnesses." *BBR* 18 (2008) 209–31.

Köstenberger, Andreas J., and Scott R. Swain. *Father, Son and Spirit: The Trinity and John's Gospel*. NSBT 24. Downers Grove, IL: InterVarsity, 2008.

Kraus, Wolfgang. "Johannes und das alte Testament: Überlegungen zum Umgang mit der Schrift im Johannesevangelium im horizont biblischer Theologie." *ZNW* 88 (1997) 1–23.

Kruse, Colin G. "John." In *Commentary on the New Testament Use of the Old Testament*, edited by G. K. Beale and D. A. Carson, 415–512. Grand Rapids: Baker, 2007.

———. *The Letters of John*. PNTC. Grand Rapids: Eerdmans, 2000.

Kubiś, Adam. *The Book of Zechariah in the Gospel of John*. Études Bibliques 64. Paris: J. Gabalda et Cie, 2012.

———. "Zechariah 6:12–13 as the Referent of Γραφή in John 2:22 and 20:9: A Contribution to Johannine Temple-Christology." *BibAn* 2 (2012) 153–194.

La Potterie, I. de. "Il Costato Trafitto Di Gesú (Gv 19, 34). Senso Rivelatorio E Senso Sacrificale Del Suo Sangue." In *Sangue E Antropologia Nella Liturgia, II*, edited by F. Vattioni, 625–49. CSSC 4. Roma: Pia Unione Preziosissimo Sangue, 1984.

Lacocque, André. *Zacharie 9–14*. CAT. Neuchatel: Delachaux & Niestlé, 1981.

Ladd, George Eldon. *A Commentary on the Revelation of John*. Grand Rapids: Eerdmans, 1972.

———. *A Theology of the New Testament*. Grand Rapids: Eerdmans, 1974.

———. "Why Not Prophetic-Apocalyptic?" *JBL* 76 (1957) 192–200.

Bibliography

Lagrange, Marie Joseph. *Évangile Selon Saint Jean*. 5th ed. Ebib. Paris: J. Gabalda, 1936.

Lamarche, Paul. *Zacharie IX–XIV: Structure Littéraire et Messianisme*. Études Bibliques. Paris: Gabalda, 1961.

Leim, Joshua E. "In the Glory of His Father: Intertextuality and the Apocalyptic Son of Man in the Gospel of Mark." *JTI* 7 (2013) 213–232.

Lenski, R. C. H. *The Interpretation of St. John's Gospel 11–21*. Minneapolis: Augsburg, 1942.

———. *The Interpretation of St. John's Revelation*. Minneapolis: Augsburg, 1943.

Leupold, H. C. *Exposition of Zechariah*. Grand Rapids: Baker, 1971.

Lévy, Emil Natan. "Sacharja 12,10." *MGWJ* 81 (1937) 293–96.

Lincoln, Andrew T. "The Beloved Disciple as Eyewitness and the Fourth Gospel as Witness." *JSNT* 85 (2002) 3–26.

———. *The Gospel according to Saint John*. BNTC. Peabody, MA: Hendrickson, 2005.

Lindars, Barnabas. *The Gospel of John*. NCB. Grand Rapids: Eerdmans, 1981.

———. *Jesus Son of Man: A Fresh Examination of the Son of Man Sayings in the Gospels*. Grand Rapids: Eerdmans, 1984.

———. *New Testament Apologetic: The Doctrinal Significance of the Old Testament Quotations*. London: SCM, 1961.

———. "The Place of the Old Testament in the Formation of New Testament Theology: Prolegomena." In *The Right Doctrine from the Wrong Text? Essays on the Use of the Old Testament in the New*, edited by G. K. Beale, 137–45. Grand Rapids: Baker, 1994.

Linnemann, Eta. *Historical Criticism of the Bible: Methodology or Ideology?* Translated by Robert W. Yarbrough. Grand Rapids: Kregel, 1990.

Litwak, Kenneth D. "Echoes of Scripture? A Critical Survey of Recent Works on Paul's Use of the Old Testament." *CurBS* 6 (1998) 260–88.

Long, Gary Allen. "דקר." In *NIDOTTE* 1:983.

Longenecker, Richard N. *Biblical Exegesis in the Apostolic Period*. 2nd ed. Grand Rapids: Eerdmans, 1999.

———. "'Who Is the Prophet Talking About?' Some Reflections on the New Testament's Use of the Old." *Themelios* 13 (1987) 4–8.

Longman III, Tremper. *Daniel*. NIVAC. Grand Rapids: Zondervan, 1999.

———. "The Glory of God in the Old Testament." In *The Glory of God*, edited by Christopher W. Morgan and Robert A. Peterson, 47–78. Theology in Community. Wheaton: Crossway, 2010.

Lövestamm, Evald. *Jesus and "This Generation": A New Testament Study*. Translated by Moira Linnarud. ConBNT 25. Stockholm: Almqvist & Wiksell International, 1995.

Bibliography

Luter, A. Boyd. "The 'Preaching Texts' of the Apocalypse (Dan 7:13 and Zech 12:10): Fulfillment and Theological Significance." *CTR* 12 (2014) 23–47.

MacArthur, John. *Revelation 1–11*. Chicago: Moody, 1999.

———. *The Second Coming: Signs of Christ's Return and the End of the Age*. Wheaton: Crossway, 1999.

MacDonald, John. "The Particle את in Classical Hebrew: Some New Data on Its Use with the Nominative." *VT* 14 (1964) 264–275.

Malina, Bruce J., and Richard L. Rohrbaugh. *Social-Science Commentary on the Gospel of John*. Minneapolis: Fortress, 1998.

Maloney, Francis J. *The Gospel of John*. SP 4. Collegeville: Liturgical, 1998.

Manns, Frédéric. "Zacharie 12,10 Relu En Jean 19,37." *Liber annuus* 56 (2006) 301–10.

Marshall, I. Howard. "Acts." In *Commentary on the New Testament Use of the Old Testament*, edited by G. K. Beale and D. A. Carson, 513–606. Grand Rapids: Baker, 2007.

———. *Acts*. TNTC 5. Grand Rapids: Eerdmans, 1980.

———. "An Assessment of Recent Developments." In *It Is Written: Scripture Citing Scripture, Essays in Honor of Barnabas Lindars*, edited by D. A. Carson and H. G. M. Williamson, 1–21. New York: Cambridge University Press, 1988.

———. *The Epistles of John*. New International Commentary on the New Testament. Grand Rapids: Eerdmans, 1978.

———. *New Testament Theology: Many Witnesses, One Gospel*. Downers Grove, IL: IVP, 2004.

Marti, Karl. *Das Dodekapropheton*. KHC 13. Tübingen: J. C. B. Mohr, 1904.

Mason, Rex. "The Use of Earlier Biblical Material in Zechariah 9–14: A Study in Inner Biblical Exegesis." In *Bringing Out the Treasure: Inner Biblical Allusion in Zechariah 9–14*, edited by Mark J. Boda and Michael H. Floyd, 234–40. JSOT 370. London: Sheffield Academic, 2003.

McComiskey, T. E. "Zechariah." In *The Minor Prophets: An Exegetical and Expositional Commentary*, edited by T. E. McComiskey, 3:1003–1244. Grand Rapids: Baker, 1998.

McDonough, Sean M. *YHWH at Patmos: Rev 1:4 in Its Hellenistic and Early Jewish Setting*. WUNT 107. Tübingen: Mohr Siebeck, 1999.

McKnight, Edgar V. "Presuppositions in New Testament Studies." In *Hearing the New Testament: Strategies for Interpretation*, edited by Joel B. Green, 278–300. Grand Rapids: Eerdmans, 1995.

Menken, Maarten J. J. "Not a Bone of Him Shall Be Broken (John 19:36)." In *Old Testament Quotations in the Fourth Gospel: Studies in Textual Form*, edited by Maarten J. J. Menken, 147–66. Kampen: Kok Pharos, 1996.

Bibliography

———. "The Quotations from Zech 9,9 in Mt 21,5 and in Jn 12,15." In *John and the Synoptics*, edited by Adelbert Denaux, 570–578. BETL 101. Leuven: University Press, 1992.

———. "The Textual Form and the Meaning of the Quotation from Zechariah 12:10 in John 19:37." *CBQ* 55 (1993) 494–511.

Menken, Maarten J. J., ed. *Old Testament Quotations in the Fourth Gospel: Studies in Textual Form*. CBET 15. Kampen: Kok Pharos, 1996.

Merkle, Benjamin L. "Could Jesus Return at Any Moment? Rethinking the Imminence of the Second Coming." *TrinJ* 26 (2005) 279–92.

———. "Romans 11 and the Future of Ethnic Israel." *JETS* 43 (2000) 709–21.

Merrill, Eugene. *Haggai, Zechariah, Malachi: An Exegetical Commentary*. Chicago: Moody, 1994.

Metzger, Bruce M. *A Textual Commentary on the Greek New Testament*. 2nd ed. Stuttgart: Deutsche Bibelgesellschaft, 1994.

Metzner, Rainer. *Das Verständnis der Sünde im Johannesevangelium*. WUNT 122. Tübingen: Mohr Siebeck, 2000.

Meyer, Rudolf. *Hebräische Grammatik*. Berlin: de Gruyter, 1992.

Meyer, Lester V. "The Messianic Metaphors in Deutero-Zechariah." PhD diss., University of Chicago, 1972.

Meyer, Rudolf. "Bemerkungen zur syntaktischen Funktion der sogenannten Nota Accusativi." In *Beiträge zur Geschichte von Text und Sprache des alten Testaments*, edited by Waltraut Bernhardt, 206–14. BZAW 209. Berlin: de Gruyter, 1993.

Meyers, Alicia D. *Characterizing Jesus: A Rhetorical Analysis on the Fourth Gospel's Use of Scripture in Its Presentation of Jesus*. LNTS 458. London: T. & T. Clark, 2012.

Meyers, Carol L., and Eric M. Meyers. "The Fortunes of the House of David: The Evidence of Second Zechariah." In *Fortunate the Eyes That See: Essays in Honor of David Noel Freedman in Celebration of His Seventh Birthday*, edited by Astrid B. Beck, 207–23. Grand Rapids: Eerdmans, 1995.

———. *Zechariah 9–14*. AB 25. New York: Doubleday, 1993.

Michaels, J. Ramsey. "The Centurion's Confession and the Spear Thrust." *CBQ* 29 (1967) 102–9.

———. *The Gospel of John*. NICNT. Grand Rapids: Eerdmans, 2010.

Miller, Paul. "'They Saw His Glory and Spoke of Him': The Gospel of John and the Old Testament." In *Hearing the Old Testament in the New Testament*, edited by Stanley E. Porter, 127–51. Grand Rapids: Eerdmans, 2006.

Milne, Bruce. *The Message of John*. BST. Downers Grove, IL: IVP, 1993.

Minear, Paul S. *John: The Martyr's Gospel*. Eugene, OR: Wipf & Stock, 2003.

Mitchell, David C. *The Message of the Psalter: An Eschatological Programme in the Book of Psalms*. Sheffield: Sheffield Academic, 1997.

Bibliography

———. "Messiah Bar Ephraim in the Targums." *Aramaic Studies* 4 (2006) 221–41.

Mitchell, Hinckley G. T. *A Critical and Exegetical Commentary on Haggai, Zechariah, Malachi, and Jonah*. ICC. New York: Scribner, 1912.

Mlakuzhyil, George. *Christocentric Literary-Dramatic Structure of John's Gospel*. 2nd ed. AnBib 117. Roma: Gregorian & Biblical, 2011.

Mollat, Donatien. "L'Évangile Selon Saint Jean." In *L'Evangile et Les Épitres de Saint Jean*, edited by Donatien Mollat and F.-M. Braun. 3rd ed. Paris: Editions du Cerf, 1973.

Moo, Douglas J. *The Old Testament in the Gospel Passion Narratives*. Sheffield: Almond, 1983.

———. "The Problem of Sensus Plenior." In *Hermeneutics, Authority, and Canon*, edited by D. A. Carson and John D. Woodbridge, 179–211. Eugene, OR: Wipf & Stock, 2005.

Morris, Leon. *The Apostolic Preaching of the Cross*. 3rd ed. Grand Rapids: Eerdmans, 1965.

———. "The Atonement in John's Gospel." *CTR* 3 (1988) 49–64.

———. *The Book of Revelation: An Introduction and Commentary*. TNTC 20. Grand Rapids: Eerdmans, 1987.

———. *The Gospel according to John*. NICNT. Grand Rapids: Eerdmans, 1971.

Morton, Russell. "Glory to God and to the Lamb: John's Use of Jewish and Hellenistic/Roman Themes in Formatting His Theology in Revelation 4–5." *JSNT* 83 (2001) 89–109.

Moseman, R. David. "Interpreting the Dissonance and Unity of Zechariah: A Holistic Reading with Special Attention to Chapter 9." PhD diss., Baylor University, 2000.

Motyer, J. Alec. *Isaiah: An Introduction and Commentary*. TOTC 18. Downers Grove, IL: IVP, 1999.

Moule, C. F. D. "Fulfillment-Words in the New Testament: Use and Abuse." *NTS* 14 (1968) 293–320.

Mounce, Robert H. *The Book of Revelation*. NICNT. Grand Rapids: Eerdmans, 1998.

Moyise, Steve. "Authorial Intention and the Book of Revelation." *AUSS* 39 (2001) 35–40.

———. "Does the Author of Revelation Misappropriate the Scriptures?" *AUSS* 40 (2002) 3–21.

———. "Does the NT Quote the OT Out of Context?" *Anvil* 11 (1994) 133–43.

———. "Intertextuality and Biblical Studies." *Verbum et Ecclesia* 23 (2002) 418–31.

———. "Intertextuality and Historical Approaches to the Use of Scripture in the New Testament." *Verbum et Ecclesia* 26 (2005) 447–58.

———. "The Language of the Old Testament in the Apocalypse." *JSNT* 76 (1999) 97–113.

———. "Scripture in the New Testament: Literary and Theological Perspectives." *Neot* 42 (2008) 305–26.

———. "Word Frequencies in the Book of Revelation." *AUSS* 43 (2005) 285–99.

Muñoz León, Domingo. "La Estructura Del Apocalipsis de Juan: Una Aproximación a La Luz de La Composición Del 4 de Esdras Y Del 2 de Baruc." *Estudios bíblicos* 43 (1985) 125–72.

Muraoka, Takamitsu. *Emphatic Words and Structures in Biblical Hebrew*. Leiden: Brill, 1985.

———. "A New Index to Hatch and Redpath." *ETL* 73 (1997) 257–76.

Nelson, Neil D. "'This Generation' in Matt 24:34: A Literary Critical Perspective." *JETS* 38 (1996) 369–85.

Nicholson, Godfrey C. *Death as Departure: The Johannine Descent-Ascent Schema*. SBLDS 63. Chicago: Scholars, 1983.

O'Brien, Peter T. *The Letter to the Ephesians*. PNTC. Grand Rapids: Eerdmans, 1999.

O'Rourke, John. "John's Fulfillment Texts." *ScEccl* 19 (1967) 433–43.

Obermann, Andreas. *Die christologische Erfüllung der Schrift im Johannesevangelium: Eine Untersuchung zur johanneischen Hermeneutik anhand der Schriftzitate*. WUNT 2/83. Tübingen: Mohr, 1996.

Oesterley, W. O. E. *A History of Israel: From the Fall of Jerusalem, 586 B.C. to the Bar-Kokhba Revolt, A.D. 135*. Oxford: Clarendon, 1939.

Orelli, C. Von. *The Twelve Minor Prophets*. Translated by J. S. Banks. Minneapolis: Klock & Klock, 1897.

Orlinsky, Harry Meyer. "The Treatment of Anthropomorphisms and Anthropopathisms in the Septuagint of Isaiah." *HUCA* 27 (1956) 193–200.

Osborne, Grant R. *Revelation*. BECNT. Grand Rapids: Baker, 2002.

Oswalt, John N. *The Book of Isaiah: Chapters 40–66*. NICOT. Grand Rapids: Eerdmans, 1998.

Otzen, Benedikt. *Studien über Deuterosacharja*. ATDan. Copenhagen: Prostant apud Munksgaard, 1964.

Ozanne, C. G. "The Language of the Apocalypse." *TynBul* 16 (1965) 3–9.

Packer, J. I. "An Evangelical View of Progressive Revelation." In *Evangelical Roots*, edited by Kenneth S. Kantzer, 143–58. Nashville: Nelson, 1978.

———. "Infallible Scripture and the Role of Hermeneutics." In *Scripture and Truth*, edited by D. A. Carson and John D. Woodbridge, 325–56. Grand Rapids: Baker, 1992.

Bibliography

Patterson, Paige. *Revelation*. NAC 39. Nashville: Broadman & Holman, 2012.

Paul, Ian. "The Use of the Old Testament in Revelation 12." In *The Old Testament in the New Testament: Essays in Honor of J. L. North*, edited by Steve Moyise, 256–76. Sheffield: Sheffield Academic, 2000.

Paulien, Jon. "Allusions, Exegetical Method, and the Interpretation of Revelation 8:7–12." PhD diss., Andrews University, 1987.

———. "Dreading the Whirlwind: Intertextuality and the Use of the Old Testament in Revelation." *AUSS* 39 (2001) 5–22.

———. "Elusive Allusions: The Problematic Use of the Old Testament in Revelation." *BR* 33 (1988) 37–53.

Pentecost, J. Dwight. *Things to Come: A Study in Biblical Eschatology*. Grand Rapids: Zondervan, 1958.

Peterson, David G. *The Acts of the Apostles*. PNTC. Grand Rapids: Eerdmans, 2009.

Peterson, David L. *Zechariah 9–14 and Malachi: A Commentary*, edited by James L. Mays et al. OTL. Louisville: Westminster John Knox, 1995.

Petterson, Anthony R. *Behold Your King: The Hope for the House of David in the Book of Zechariah*. LHBOTS 513. New York: T. & T. Clark, 2009.

———. *Haggai, Zechariah, & Malachi*. AOTC 25. Nottingham: Apollos, 2015.

Piper, John. *Desiring God: Meditations of a Christian Hedonist*. 2nd ed. Sisters: Multnomah, 1986.

———. *God Is the Gospel: Meditations on God's Love as the Gift of Himself*. Wheaton: Crossway, 2005.

Plöger, Otto. *Theokratie und Eschatologie*. WMANT. Neukirchen: Neukirchener, 1959.

Porter, Stanley E. "Allusions and Echoes." In *As It Is Written: Studying Paul's Use of Scripture*, edited by Stanley E. Porter and Christopher D. Stanley, 29–40. SBLSymS 50. Atlanta: Society of Biblical Literature, 2008.

Poythress, Vern S. "Divine Meaning of Scripture." *WTJ* 48 (1986) 241–79.

———. "Johannine Authorship and the Use of Intersentence Conjunctions in the Book of Revelation." *WTJ* 47 (1985) 329–36.

———. "Review of Beale on Revelation." *WTJ* 62 (2000) 143–46.

———. "Testing for Johannine Authorship by Examining the Use of Conjunctions." *WTJ* 46 (1984) 350–69.

Prigent, Pierre. *Commentary on the Apocalypse of St. John*. Translated by Wendy Pradels. Tübingen: Mohr Siebeck, 2001.

Prior, David. *The Message of Joel, Micah & Habakkuk: Listening to the Voice of God*. BST. Downers Grove, IL: InterVarsity, 1998.

Pryor, John W. "Covenant and Community in John's Gospel." *RTR* 47 (1988) 44–51.

———. "Jesus and Israel in the Fourth Gospel—John 1:11." *NovT* 32 (1990) 201–18.

———. *John: Evangelist of the Covenant People*. Downers Grove, IL: InterVarsity, 1992.

———. "The Use of the Son of Man Idiom in the Gospel of John." In *"Who Is This Son of Man?" The Latest Scholarship on a Puzzling Expression of the Historical Jesus*, edited by Larry W. Hurtado and Paul L. Owen, 101–29. LNTS 390. New York: T. & T. Clark, 2011.

Rainbow, Paul A. *Johannine Theology: The Gospel, the Epistles, and the Apocalypse*. Downers Grove, IL: IVP Academic, 2014.

Räisänen, Heikki. *Beyond New Testament Theology*. 2nd ed. London: SCM, 2000.

Reim, Günter. *Studien zum alttestamentlichen Hintergrund des Johannesevangeliums*. SNTSMS 22. Cambridge: Cambridge University Press, 1974.

Reynolds, Benjamin E. *The Apocalyptic Son of Man in the Gospel of John*. WUNT 249. Tübingen: Mohr Siebeck, 2008.

Ridderbos, Herman N. *The Coming of the Kingdom*, edited by Raymond O. Zorn. Translated by H. de Jongste. St. Catharines: Paideia, 1978.

———. *The Gospel of John: A Theological Commentary*. Translated by John Vriend. Grand Rapids: Eerdmans, 1997.

———. *Redemptive History and the New Testament Scriptures*. Translated by H. De Jongste. Biblical & Theological Studies. Phillipsburg: P & R, 1963.

Robertson, O. Palmer. "Is There a Distinctive Future for Ethnic Israel in Romans 11?" In *Perspectives on Evangelical Theology: Papers from the Thirtieth Annual Meeting of the Evangelical Theological Society*, edited by Kenneth S. Kantzer and Stanley N. Gundry, 209–227. Grand Rapids: Baker, 1979.

Rogers, Randolph R. "An Exegetical Analysis of John's Use of Zechariah in the Book of Revelation: The Impact and Transformation of Zechariah's Text and Themes in the Apocalypse." PhD diss., Southwestern Baptist Theological Seminary, 2002.

Rosenberg, Roy A. "The Slain Messiah in the Old Testament." *ZAW* 99 (1987) 259–61.

Rosner, Brian S. "Biblical Theology." In *NDBT* 3–11.

Rossi, Geovanni Bernardo de. *Variae Lectiones Veteris Testamenti*. Vol. 3. Parmae: Ex Regio typographeo, 1786.

Rubin, Aaron David. "Studies in Semitic Grammaticalization." PhD diss., Harvard University, 2004.

Ruffin, M. L. "Symbolism in Zechariah: A Study in Functional Unity." PhD diss., Southern Baptist Theological Seminary, 1986.

Bibliography

Russell, Elbert. "Possible Influence of the Mysteries on the Form and Interrelation of the Johannine Writings." *JBL* 51 (1932) 336–51.

Sæbø, Magne. *Sacharja 9–14: Untersuchungen von Text und Form*. WMANT 34. Neukirchen-Vluyn: Neukirchener, 1969.

Sanchez, Jr., Juan Ramon. "The People of God: Toward an Evangelical Ecclesiology." PhD diss., Southern Baptist Theological Seminary, 2015.

Sanders, J. N., and B. A. Mastin. *The Gospel According to St. John*. HNTC. Peabody, MA: Hendrickson, 1968.

Saydon, P. P. "Meanings and Uses of the Particle את." *VT* 14 (1964) 192–210.

Schlatter, Adolf. "The Theology of the New Testament and Dogmatics." In *The Nature of New Testament Theology: The Contributions of William Wrede and Adolf Schlatter*, edited by Robert Morgan, 117–66. Naperville, IL: A. R. Allenson, 1973.

Schmidt, Jr., Donald Lee. "An Examination of Selected Uses of the Psalms of David in John and Acts in Light of Traditional Typology." PhD diss., Southwestern Baptist Theological Seminary, 2014.

Schnabel, Eckhard J. *Acts*. ECNT 5. Grand Rapids: Zondervan, 2012.

———. "John and the Future of the Nations." *BBR* 12 (2002) 243–71.

Schnackenburg, Rudolf. *The Gospel according to St. John*. Translated by K. Smyth and C. Hastings. New York: Crossroad, 1990.

———. *The Gospel according to St. John: Commentary on Chapters 13–21*. Translated by D. Smith and G. A. Kon. Vol. 3. HTKNT 4. New York: Crossroad, 1982.

Schreiner, Thomas R. *The King in His Beauty: A Biblical Theology of the Old and New Testaments*. Grand Rapids: Baker, 2013.

———. *New Testament Theology: Magnifying God in Christ*. Grand Rapids: Baker, 2008.

Schuchard, Bruce G. *Scripture within Scripture: The Interrelationship of Form and Function in the Explicit Old Testament Citations in the Gospel of John*. SBLDS 133. Atlanta: Scholars, 1992.

Schüssler Fiorenza, Elisabeth. "Composition and Structure of the Book of Revelation." *CBQ* 39 (1977) 344–66.

———. "The Quest for the Johannine School." *NTS* 23 (1977) 402–27.

———. "Redemption as Liberation: Apoc 1:5f and 5:9f." *CBQ* 36 (1974) 220–32.

Schwarz, Günther. "Gen 1:1, 2:2a und John 1:1a, 3a—Ein Vergleich." *ZNW* 73 (1982) 136–37.

Selman, Martin J. "Messianic Mysteries." In *The Lord's Anointed: Interpretation of Old Testament Messianic Texts*, edited by P. E. Satterthwaite et al., 281–302. Grand Rapids: Baker, 1995.

Shepherd, Michael B. "Daniel 7:13 and the New Testament Son of Man." *WTJ* 68 (2006) 99–111.

Bibliography

Silva, Moisés. "The New Testament Use of the Old Testament: Text Form and Authority." In *Scripture and Truth*, edited by D. A. Carson and John D. Woodbridge, 147–65. Grand Rapids: Baker, 1992.

———. *Biblical Words and Their Meaning: An Introduction to Lexical Semantics*. Grand Rapids: Zondervan, 1994.

Skarsaune, Oskar. *The Proof from Prophecy: A Study in Justin Martyr's Proof-Text Tradition: Text-Type, Provenance, Theological Profile*. SNTSMS 56. Leiden: Brill, 1987.

Smalley, Stephen S. *John: Evangelist and Interpreter*. Nashville: Nelson, 1978.

———. "John's Revelation and John's Community." *BJRL* 69 (1987) 549–71.

———. *The Revelation to John: A Commentary on the Greek Text of the Apocalypse*. Downers Grove, IL: InterVarsity, 2005.

Smidt, Kobus de. "A Meta-Theology of 'Ο ΘΕΟΣ in Revelations 1:1–2." *Neot* 38 (2004) 183–208.

Smith, Christopher R. "The Structure of the Book of Revelation in Light of Apocalyptic Literary Conventions." *NovT* 36 (1994) 373–93.

Smith, Jr., D. Moody. *The Composition and Order of the Fourth Gospel: Bultmann's Literary Theory*. Yale Publications in Religion 10. New Haven: Yale University Press, 1965.

Smith, Ralph. *Micah–Malachi*. WBC 32. Waco, TX: Word, 1984.

Snyder, Barbara Wootten. "Combat Myth in the Apocalypse: The Liturgy of the Day of the Lord and the Dedication of the Heavenly Temple." PhD diss., Graduate Theological Union and University of California, 1991.

Spellman, Ched. *Toward a Canon-Conscious Reading of the Bible: Exploring the History and Hermeneutics of the Canon*. New Testament Monographs 34. Sheffield: Sheffield Phoenix, 2014.

Sperber, Alexander, ed. *The Bible in Aramaic: Based on Old Manuscripts and Printed Texts*. Vol. 3. Leiden: E. J. Brill, 1962.

Steinmann, Andrew E. *Daniel*. CC. St. Louis: Concordia, 2008.

Stevens, George B. *The Johannine Theology: A Study of the Doctrinal Contents of the Gospel and Epistles of the Apostle John*. New York: Scribner, 1899.

Stibbe, Mark. "Telling the Father's Story: The Gospel of John as Narrative Theology." In *Challenging Perspectives on the Gospel of John*, edited by John Lierman, 170–93. WUNT 2.219. Tübingen: Mohr Siebeck, 2006.

Stiver, Dan R. "Method." In *Dictionary for Theological Interpretation of the Bible*, edited by Kevin J. Vanhoozer, 510–12. Grand Rapids: Baker, 2005.

Stott, John R. W. *The Cross of Christ*. Downers Grove, IL: InterVarsity, 2006.

———. *The Letters of John*. TNTC 19. Downers Grove, IL: InterVarsity, 1988.

Stuckenbruck, Loren T. "Revelation 4–5: Divided Worship or One Vision?" *SCJ* 14 (2011) 235–48.

Bibliography

Stuhlmacher, Peter. *Historical Criticism and Theological Interpretation of Scripture: Toward a Hermeneutics of Consent.* Translated by Roy A. Harrisville. Philadelphia: Fortress, 1977.

———. *How to Do Biblical Theology.* Eugene, OR: Wipf & Stock, 1995.

Stuhlmueller, Carroll. "'First and Last' and 'Yahweh-Creator' in Deutero-Isaiah." *CBQ* 29 (1967) 495–511.

Swain, Scott R., and Michael Allen. "The Obedience of the Eternal Son." *IJST* 15 (2013) 113–34.

Swete, Henry Barclay. *The Apocalypse of St. John: The Greek Text with Introduction, Notes, and Indices.* New York: Macmillan, 1909.

Tasker, R. V. G. *The Gospel according to St. John: An Introduction and Commentary.* TNTC 4. Grand Rapids: Eerdmans, 1960.

Thielman, Frank. *Theology of the New Testament: A Canonical and Synthetic Approach.* Grand Rapids: Zondervan, 2005.

Thiselton, Anthony C. *New Horizons in Hermeneutics.* Grand Rapids: Zondervan, 1992.

Thomas, John Christopher, and Frank D. Macchia. *Revelation.* THNTC. Grand Rapids: Eerdmans, 2016.

Thompson, Alan J. *The Acts of the Risen Lord Jesus: Luke's Account of God's Unfolding Plan.* NSBT 27. Downers Grove, IL: IVP, 2011.

Thompson, Marianne Meye. *John: A Commentary.* NTL. Louisville: Westminster John Knox, 2015.

———. "Signs and Faith in the Fourth Gospel." *BBR* 1 (1991) 89–108.

Thompson, Steven. *The Apocalypse and Semitic Syntax.* SNTSMS 52. New York: Cambridge University Press, 1985.

Thyen, H. "Johannes und die synoptiker: auf der suche nach einem neuen Paradigma zur Beschriebung ihrer Beziehungen anhand von Beobachtungen an Passions- und Ostererzählungen." In *John and the Synoptics*, edited by Adelbert Denaux, 81–107. BETL 101. Leuven: Peeters, 1992.

Tov, Emanuel. "The History and Significance of a Standard Text of the Hebrew Bible." In *Hebrew Bible/Old Testament: The History of Its Interpretation*, edited by Magne Sæbø, 1:49–66. Göttingen: Vandenhoeck & Ruprecht, 1996.

———. *The Text-Critical Use of the Septuagint in Biblical Research.* 2nd ed. Jerusalem Biblical Studies 8. Jerusalem: Simor, 1997.

———. *Textual Criticism of the Hebrew Bible.* Minneapolis: Fortress, 1992.

———. *Textual Criticism of the Hebrew Bible.* 3rd ed. Minneapolis: Fortress, 2012.

———. "Theologically Motivated Exegesis Embedded in the Septuagint." In *The Greek & Hebrew Bible: Collected Essays on the Septuagint*, 257–69. VTSup 72. Leiden: Brill, 1999.

Bibliography

Troki, Isaac ben Abraham. *Faith Strengthened*. Translated by Moses Mocatta. New York: Ktav, 1970.

Trudinger, L. Paul. "Some Observations Concerning the Text of the Old Testament in the Book of Revelation." *JTS* 17 (1966) 82–88.

Tuckett, Christopher M. "Zechariah 12:10 and the New Testament." In *The Book of Zechariah and Its Influence*, edited by Christopher M. Tuckett, 111–121. Burlington, VT: Ashgate, 2003.

Tuckett, Christopher M., ed. *The Book of Zechariah and Its Influence*. Burlington, VT: Ashgate, 2003.

Turner, Max. "Atonement and the Death of Jesus in John—Some Questions to Bultmann and Forestell." *EQ* 62 (1990) 99–122.

Turretin, Francis. *Institutes of Elenctic Theology*, edited by James T. Dennison, Jr. Translated by George Musgrave Giger. Vol. 2. Phillipsburg: P&R, 1994.

Ulrich, Dean R. "Two Offices, Four Officers, or One Sordid Event in Zechariah 12:10–14." *WTJ* 72 (2010) 251–65.

Unger, Merrill F. *Zechariah: Prophet of Messiah's Glory*. Eugene, OR: Wipf & Stock, 2014.

Van Hoonacker, A. *Les Douze Petits Prophètes: Traduits et Commentés*. Études Bibliques. Paris: J. Gabalda, 1908.

VanderKam, James, and Peter Flint. *The Meaning of the Dead Sea Scrolls: Their Significance for Understanding the Bible, Judaism, Jesus, and Christianity*. London: T. & T. Clark, 2002.

VanGemeren, Willem A. *Psalms*. EBC 5. Grand Rapids: Zondervan, 2008.

Vanhoozer, Kevin J. "Body Piercing, the Natural Sense and the Task of Theological Interpretation: A Hermeneutical Homily on John 19:34." In *First Theology: God, Scripture and Hermeneutics*, 275–308. Downers Grove, IL: InterVarsity, 2002.

———. "Does the Trinity Belong in a Theology of Religions? On Angling in the Rubicon and the 'Identity' of God." In *The Trinity in a Pluralistic Age: Theological Essays on Culture and Religion*, edited by Kevin J. Vanhoozer, 41–71. Grand Rapids: Eerdmans, 1997.

———. *Is There a Meaning in This Text? The Bible, the Reader, and the Morality of Literary Knowledge*. Grand Rapids: Zondervan, 1998.

Vanhoye, Albert. "L'utilisation Du Livre d'Ézéchiel Dans l'Apocalypse." *Bib* 43 (1962) 436–76.

Vanni, Ugo. "Un Esempio Di Dialogo Liturgico in Ap 1:4–8." *Bib* 57 (1976) 453–67.

Wallace, Daniel B. *Greek Grammar: Beyond the Basics*. Grand Rapids: Zondervan, 1996.

Bibliography

Waltke, Bruce K. "A Canonical Approach to the Psalms." In *Tradition and Testament: Essays in Honor of Charles Lee Feinberg*, edited by John S. Feinberg and Paul D. Feinberg, 3–18. Chicago: Moody, 1981.

———. *An Old Testament Theology: An Exegetical, Canonical, and Thematic Approach*. Grand Rapids: Zondervan, 2007.

Wead, David W. "The Johannine Double Meaning." *ResQ* 13 (1970) 106–20.

Webb, Barry G. *The Message of Zechariah: Your Kingdom Come*, edited by J. A. Motyer. Bible Speaks Today. Downers Grove, IL: InterVarsity, 2003.

Wellum, Stephen J. *God the Son Incarnate: The Doctrine of Christ*. Foundations of Evangelical Theology. Wheaton: Crossway, 2016.

———. "Jesus as Lord and Son: Two Complementary Truths of Biblical Christology." *CTR* 13 (2015) 23–45.

Wengst, Klaus. *Das Johannesevangelium*. ThKNT 4. Stuttgart: W. Kohlhammer, 2000.

Wenzel, Heiko. *Reading Zechariah with Zechariah 1:1–6 as the Introduction to the Entire Book*. CBET 59. Leuven: Peeters, 2011.

Westcott, B. F. *The Gospel according to St. John*. Grand Rapids: Eerdmans, 1971.

Whitacre, Rodney A. *John*. IVPNTC. Downers Grove, IL: IVP, 1999.

Williams, Joshua E. "The Message of the Pentateuch." *SWJT* 51 (2009) 2–16.

Williamson, H. G. M. "First and Last in Isaiah." In *Of Prophets' Visions and the Wisdom of Sages: Essays in Honour of R. Norman Whybray on His Seventieth Birthday*, edited by Heather A. McKay and David J. A. Clines, 95–108. LHBOTS 162. Sheffield: JSOT, 1993.

Willi-Plein, Ina. *Haggai, Sacharja, Maleachi*. ZBK. Zürich: Theologischer Verlag, 2007.

Wilson, Alfred M. "The Particle את in Hebrew, I." *Hebraica* 6 (1890) 139–50.

Wilson, Alfred M. "The Particle את in Hebrew, II." *Hebraica* 6 (1890) 212–224.

Witt, Douglas Allan. "Zechariah 12–14: Its Origins, Growth and Theological Significance." PhD diss., Vanderbilt University, 1991.

Wittstruck, Thorne. "So-Called Anti-Anthropomorphisms in the Greek Text of Deuteronomy." *CBQ* 38 (1976) 29–34.

Woude, A. S. van der. "Pluriformity and Uniformity: Reflections on the Transmission of the Text of the Old Testament." In *Sacred History and Sacred Texts in Early Judaism: A Symposium in Honor of A. A. van Der Woude*, edited by J. N. Bremmer and García Martínez, 151–69. Kampen: Kok Pharos, 1992.

———. *Zacharia*. POuT. Nijkerk: Uitgeverij G. H. Callenbach, 1984.

Wright, Brian J. "Jesus as ΘΕΟΣ: A Textual Examination." In *Revisiting the Corruption of the New Testament: Manuscript, Patristic, and Apocryphal*

Evidence, edited by Daniel B. Wallace, 229–66. Text and Canon of the New Testament. Grand Rapids: Kregel, 2011.

Wright, Christopher J. H. *The Message of Ezekiel*. BST. Downers Grove, IL: IVP, 2001.

———. *The Mission of God: Unlocking the Bible's Grand Narrative*. Downers Grove, IL: InterVarsity, 2006.

Wright, D. P. "Unclean and Clean." In *ABD* 6:729–41.

Wright, N. T. *Jesus and the Victory of God*. Christian Origins and the Question of God 2. Minneapolis: Fortress, 1996.

———. *The New Testament and the People of God*. Christian Origins and the Question of God 1. Minneapolis: Fortress, 1992.

———. *The Resurrection of the Son of God*. Christian Origins and the Question of God 3. Minneapolis: Fortress, 2003.

Yarbrough, Robert W. "Divine Election in the Gospel of John." In *The Grace of God, the Bondage of the Will*, edited by Thomas R. Schreiner and Bruce A. Ware, 1:47–62. Grand Rapids: Baker, 1995.

———. *1–3 John*. BECNT. Grand Rapids: Baker, 2008.

Yeago, David S. "The New Testament and Nicene Dogma." *Pro Ecclesia* 3 (1994) 152–64.

Zehnder, Markus. "Why the Danielic 'Son of Man' is a Divine Being." *BBR* 24 (2014) 331–47.

Zeigler, Joseph. *Duodecium Prophetae*. Vol. 8. Septuaginta: Vetus Testamentum Graecum. Göttingen: Vandenhoeck & Ruprecht, 1967.

Index of Modern Authors

Abbott, E. A., 197
Achtemeier, E. R., 6, 102
Adams, E., 137
Allen, M., 92
Archer, G., 224
Aune, D. E., 12, 125, 134, 144, 147

Baker, D. L., 1
Baldwin, J. G., 6, 7, 30, 32, 52, 54, 64, 72, 74, 75, 151, 160, 193
Ball, D. M., 100
Balla, P., 19
Bandy, A., 164
Barnett, P., 216
Baron, D., 224
Barrett, C. K., 8, 114, 180
Barthélemy, D., 33
Bauckham, R., 12, 14–17, 58, 62, 78, 92, 100, 104, 108, 124, 125, 129, 130, 134, 135, 142–44, 155, 156, 158, 160, 161, 164, 204, 206, 208, 209, 215, 223
Beale, G. K., 1, 12–15, 19–24, 27, 87, 122, 123, 125–27, 129, 130, 132–34, 140, 141, 143, 145, 151–53, 155, 157, 160, 163, 164, 168, 171, 178, 199, 206, 208, 221
Beasley-Murray, G. R., 9, 116, 137, 158, 175, 193, 200
Beauchamp, P., 84
Beckwith, I. T., 17
Beckwith, R. T., 18
Bekins, P. J., 38, 43
Belle, G., 97
Belleville, L., 195

Bilić, N., 1, 6, 7, 37, 40, 45, 51
Black, M., 86
Black, M. C., 1, 3
Blomberg, C. L., 136, 137
Blount, B. K., 12, 143, 208
Bock, D. L., 87, 118, 160, 161
Bockmuehl, M., 16, 26
Boda, M. J., 6, 7, 19, 22–24, 48, 53, 56, 74
Boer, M. C. D., 186, 189
Boismard, M. É., 181, 192
Borchert, G. L., 8
Boxall, I., 12, 144
Brandenburg, H., 6, 54, 74
Brendsel, D. J., 103, 104, 110
Brodie, T. L., 81
Brooke, G. J., 59
Brown, R. E., 9, 17, 105, 114, 179, 185, 192, 199, 209
Bruce, F. F., 75, 123, 199
Brunner, F. D., 8
Brütsch, C., 133
Bultmann, R., 8, 113, 173
Burge, G. M., 9
Burkett, D., 159
Burridge, R. A., 82
Butterworth, M., 58
Bynum, W. R., 60, 61, 64, 79, 84, 86, 100, 105, 106, 116, 117, 139, 179, 182, 186, 189, 191, 192, 197, 206, 215

Caird, G. B., 12, 143, 204, 208
Calvin, J., 54, 56
Campbell, W. T., 96

259

Index of Modern Authors

Caragounis, C. C., 158, 159, 161
Carnazzo, S. A., 114
Carson, D. A., 1, 9, 10, 17, 19, 23, 51, 52, 75, 82, 83, 85, 86, 89–93, 95, 96, 100, 102, 114, 136, 137, 169, 174, 175, 179, 180, 193, 194, 200, 201, 212, 213, 215
Casey, M., 159
Cathcart, K., 40–42
Chary, T., 5, 6, 37, 51, 55, 69, 74
Childs, B. S., 25
Chilton, D., 132
Choi, B. K., 154, 156
Cirafesi, W. V., 17
Clark, D. J., 51
Cohen, A., 5, 49, 50, 70
Collins, A. Y., 133
Collins, J. J., 124
Condamin, A., 1, 6, 39, 49, 51, 72, 74
Conrad, E. W., 6, 71
Cook, S., 75
Cook, W. R., 14, 119, 168, 173
Cooke, G. A., 6, 55
Cullmann, O., 99
Culpepper, R. A., 96

Dahms, J. V., 91
Dahood, M., 39
Davies, G. I., 43
Deissler, A., 1, 32, 48, 74
Delcor, M., 7, 36, 44, 53, 54, 60, 61, 65, 66, 81
Delitzsch, F., 6, 32, 45, 52, 74
Dempster, S. G., 19
Dennis, J., 113
DeSilva, D. A., 127, 208
Devillers, L., 1, 3, 28, 114, 139, 179, 181, 187, 192
Di Lella, A. A., 123
Dodd, C. H., 1, 22, 23, 68, 89, 103, 119, 173
Dogniez, C., 42
Dolezal, J. E., 48
Driver, S. R., 45, 66
Duguid, I., 1, 3, 6, 55, 74
Duhm, D. B., 72
Dunn, J. D. G., 156

Ellis, E. E., 18
Erdmann, M., 14
Evans, C. A., 4, 82, 85, 86

Fee, G. D., 215
Feuillet, A., 17
Fishbane, M., 43
Flemming, D., 206, 208, 210
Flint, P., 63
Floyd, M. H., 5, 44, 45, 49, 50, 70–72
Ford, J. M., 12
France, R. T., 136, 137
Freed, E. D., 79
Fritsch, C. T., 65
Fuller, R. E., 61, 64

Gentry, K. L., 132
Gentry, P. J., 143, 160, 161, 224
Geza, V., 159
Giesen, H., 125, 127, 133, 134, 142, 157
Glasson, T. F., 138
Goldsworthy, G., 87
Gordon, R. P., 40–42
Goshen-Gottstein, M. H., 33
Gradl, H. G., 14, 124, 128, 135, 157
Gren, C. R., 63
Günther, H. W., 125

Haenchen, E., 8, 184
Haily, H., 52
Ham, C. A., 1, 3, 20, 52, 75, 136
Hamilton, J. M., 98, 100, 125, 126, 133, 134, 137, 144, 152, 159–61, 196, 208
Hanson, A. T., 183
Hanson, P. D., 5, 70
Harris, M. J., 209
Hatton, H. A., 51
Haukaas, M. A., 127, 147, 158
Hays, R. B., 12, 21, 68
Hendriksen, W., 8
Hengel, M., 74, 86, 90
Herghelegiu, M. E., 147
Hill, A. E., 25, 72
Hirsch, E. D., 11, 23
Hofius, O., 91

Index of Modern Authors

Hoftijzer, J., 43
Hoonacker, A., 5, 49, 50, 69
Hoskins, P. M., 17, 35, 73, 84, 98, 99, 102, 103, 110, 111, 113, 114, 134, 136, 139, 141, 145, 177, 183, 184, 188, 189, 191, 193, 199, 206, 208, 222, 223
Hoskyns, E. C., 9, 114, 119
Hübenthal, S., 1-3, 11, 12, 41, 79, 125, 162, 179, 181, 197
Hultberg, A. D., 3, 12-14, 55, 75, 134, 144, 152, 157, 164
Hurtado, L. W., 150, 155, 156, 159, 162, 209, 223

Isbell, B. A., 130

Jacobs, A., 16
Jansma, T., 33, 39, 41
Jauhiainen, M., 79, 126, 133, 134, 143, 147, 148, 154, 164
Jobes, K. H., 36, 41, 60
Johnson, D. E., 134
Jones, L. P., 114
Jonge, M., 17
Joosten, J., 60, 61, 65

Kaiser, W. C., 6, 37
Keener, C. S., 9, 17, 87, 91, 103, 134, 144, 174, 176, 188, 189, 199, 200-202, 208, 215
Keil, C. F., 6, 32, 45, 52, 74
Kennicott, B., 33, 34
Kim, S., 55
Kimḥi, D., 5, 40, 70
Kistemaker, S. J., 12, 134, 140, 144
Klauck, H. J., 41, 181, 182, 192
Klein, G. L., 25, 28, 30, 32, 38, 51, 54, 57, 64-66, 71, 75, 112, 193
Klink, E. W., 17
Koester, C. R., 134, 142
Kohler, A., 6, 37, 52, 74, 1
Köstenberger, A. J., 10, 11, 14, 16, 17, 51, 78, 81, 82, 85, 88, 90-93, 95-97, 99, 100, 102, 103, 119, 168, 173, 174, 177, 185, 194-97, 200, 202, 204, 206, 207, 211, 213, 215

Kraus, W., 84
Kruse, C. G., 116
Kubiś, A., 1-3, 6-8, 11, 32, 36, 39, 43, 47, 48, 51-53, 59, 60, 61, 66, 74-76, 79, 80, 86, 105-7, 113, 114, 139, 145, 179-84, 188, 189, 192, 197

La Potterie, I., 113, 145
Lacocque, A., 1, 5, 32, 37, 44, 48, 51, 70
Ladd, G. E., 12, 119, 124, 125, 134, 140, 144, 147, 168, 173, 189, 196, 213
Lagrange, M. J., 184
Lamarche, P., 6, 36, 37, 51, 74, 75
Lamouille, A., 181, 192
Leim, J. E., 161
Lenski, R. C. H., 9, 144, 180, 185
Leupold, H. C., 54, 56
Lévy, E. N., 6, 71
Lincoln, A. T., 9, 194
Lindars, B., 1, 9, 22, 159, 179-81, 186, 192
Linnemann, E., 87
Litwak, K. D., 12
Long, G. A., 56
Longenecker, R. N., 1, 19, 22
Longman, T., 98, 151
Lövestamm, E., 137
Luter, A. B., 143, 147

M'Caul, A., 5, 40, 70
MacArthur, J., 224
Macchia, F. D., 134
MacDonald, J., 42, 43
Malina, B. J., 114
Maloney, F. J., 26, 181, 182, 192
Manns, F., 84, 116, 192
Marshall, I. H., 16, 68, 116, 118, 168, 191, 198
Marti, K., 6, 72
Mason, R., 1, 5, 51, 70, 74
Mastin, B. A., 8, 184, 185
McComiskey, T. E., 6, 7, 29, 30, 46, 48, 51, 52, 74, 193
McDonough, S. M., 13-15, 123, 128, 135, 141, 153, 157, 163
McKnight, E. V., 16

Index of Modern Authors

Menken, M. J. J., 1, 3, 4, 9, 36, 40, 41, 45, 59, 79, 81, 86, 106, 146, 179–86, 188, 192
Merkle, B. L., 134, 143, 224
Merrill, E., 6, 7, 37, 51, 53, 54, 56, 74
Metzger, B., 201
Metzner, R., 113, 200
Meyer, L. V., 74
Meyer, R., 43
Meyers, A. D., 116
Meyers, C. L., 5, 6, 46, 47, 51, 70–72
Meyers, E. M., 5, 6, 46, 47, 51, 70–72
Michaels, J. R., 8, 79, 180, 194
Miller, P., 89
Milne, B., 8
Minear, P. S., 114
Mitchell, D. C., 6, 36, 41, 42, 74
Mitchell, H. G. T., 10, 49, 66, 71
Mlakuzhyil, G., 81
Mollat, D., 81
Moo, D. J., 1, 3, 18, 19, 34, 68, 79, 80, 84, 87, 88, 93, 101, 185, 202, 221
Morris, L., 8, 12, 79, 93, 113, 116, 125, 130, 134, 140, 144, 160, 194–95, 199, 200, 213
Morton, R., 156
Moseman, R. D., 25
Motyer, J. A., 136
Moule, C. F. D., 84
Mounce, R. H., 12, 125, 134, 140, 144, 189, 208, 222
Moyise, S., 12, 22, 23, 122, 164
Muñoz León, D., 125
Muraoka, T., 42, 43, 46, 59

Nelson, N. D., 137
Nicholson, G. C., 99

O'Brien, P. T., 106, 213
O'Rourke, J., 9, 10, 105
Obermann, A., 86, 182
Oesterley, W. O. E., 6, 39, 72
Orelli, C., 34, 51, 52
Orlinsky, H. M., 65
Osborne, G. R., 125, 134, 140, 141, 143, 144, 152, 153, 199
Oswalt, J. N., 136, 151
Otzen, B., 6, 26, 49, 71

Ozanne, C. G., 17

Packer, J. I., 19, 169
Patterson, P., 12
Patterson, R. D., 16
Paul, I., 20, 22
Paulien, J., 20, 21, 23, 122, 123
Pentecost, J. D., 224
Peterson, D. G., 118
Peterson, D. L., 47
Petterson, A. R., 6, 27–30, 51, 52, 62, 74, 75, 115, 138, 154, 172, 193, 205, 206
Piper, J., 98, 216
Plöger, O., 6, 71
Porter, S. E., 21
Poythress, V. S., 17, 126, 169
Prigent, P., 12, 134
Prior, D., 27
Pryor, J. W., 75, 190, 194

Rainbow, P. A., 14, 17, 84, 85, 90, 91, 93, 116, 149, 171, 189, 223
Räisänen, H., 17, 168
Reim, G., 80
Reynolds, B. E., 134, 160
Ridderbos, H. N., 9, 16, 82, 91, 95, 101, 114, 137, 174, 194, 199, 202
Robertson, O. P., 224
Rogers, R. R., 13, 14, 144
Rohrbaugh, R. L., 114
Rosenberg, R. A., 42, 50, 74
Rosner, B. S., 16, 168
Rossi, G. B., 33, 34
Rubin, A. D., 43
Ruffin, M. L., 25
Russell, E., 17

Sæbø, M., 1, 33, 34, 36, 39, 42
Sanchez, J. R., 130
Sanders, J. N., 8, 184, 85
Saydon, P. P., 43
Schlatter, A., 16
Schmidt, D. L., 84, 86, 101
Schnabel, E. J., 118, 143, 204, 208
Schnackenburg, R., 9, 105, 114, 179, 181, 192
Schreiner, T. R., 82, 98

Index of Modern Authors

Schuchard, B. G., 4, 61, 79, 86, 106, 139, 179, 186, 187, 189, 191
Schüssler Fiorenza, E., 17, 125, 157
Schwarz, G., 102
Selman, M. J., 6, 74
Shepherd, M. B., 160
Silva, M., 19, 36, 41, 55, 60, 87
Skarsaune, O., 3, 134, 172, 202, 203
Smalley, S. S., 12, 17, 119, 144, 168
Smidt, K., 149
Smith, C. R., 125
Smith, D. M., 81
Smith, R., 56
Snyder, B. W., 125
Spellman, C., 18, 138
Sperber, A., 40
Steinmann, A. E., 152
Stevens, G. B., 14
Stibbe, M., 92
Stiver, D. R., 16
Stott, J. R. W., 99, 116, 198
Stout, S. O., 194, 196
Stuckenbruck, L. T., 156
Stuhlmacher, P., 16, 168
Stuhlmueller, C., 136
Swain, S. R., 78, 88, 90–92, 96, 100
Swete, H. B., 12, 140, 158

Tasker, R. V. G., 8
Thielman, F., 113, 213
Thiselton, A. C., 16
Thomas, J. C., 134
Thompson, A. J., 214
Thompson, M. M., 8, 180, 214
Thompson, S., 135
Thyen, H., 194
Tov, E., 33, 34, 36, 39, 41, 59, 60, 65
Troki, I. A., 5, 40, 70
Trudinger, L. P., 122
Tuckett, C. M., 1, 3, 9, 106, 179, 187

Turner, M., 113, 116
Turretin, F., 109

Ulrich, D. R., 64, 74, 75
Unger, M. F., 32

VanderKam, J., 63
VanGemeren, W. A., 63
Vanhoozer, K. J., 11, 16, 20, 23, 78, 114
Vanhoye, A., 123, 140, 141
Vanni, U., 147, 157

Wallace, D. B., 90, 91, 129, 132, 139, 149, 194, 213
Waltke, B. K., 19, 26, 47, 68, 118, 179
Wead, D. W., 99
Webb, B. G., 74
Wellum, S. J., 78, 109, 143, 170, 224
Wengst, K., 9
Wenzel, H., 25
Westcott, B. F., 189
Whitacre, R. A., 9
Williams, J. E., 179
Williamson, H. G. M., 1, 136
Willi-Plein, I. 49, 55
Wilson, A. M., 38, 42, 43, 46, 47
Witt, D. A., 42, 43
Wittstruck, T., 65
Woude, A. S., 39, 40, 48
Wright, B. J., 90
Wright, C. J. H., 151, 204, 206
Wright, D. P., 57
Wright, N. T., 16, 129, 136

Yarbrough, R. W., 116, 198, 213
Yeago, D. S., 105, 209, 223

Zehnder, M., 158, 161
Zeigler, J., 39

Index of Ancient Sources

OLD TESTAMENT

Genesis

1	160
1:1	28, 102
1:24–27	205
1:28	160
2:1–3	82
2:7	28, 104
3:24	205
9:24	47
12:3	137, 142
12:7	69
17:11	47
22:2	143
22:9	60, 61
22:12	143
22:16	143
23:32	57
28:14	137, 142
49:1	44
49:10–11	76, 82
49:10	31
50:10	57

Exodus

1:14	47
3:6	38, 47, 65
3:14	95, 157
4:22–23	69, 89
4:22	143, 149
4:23	143
4:24	65
6:7	28
6:17	143
11:5	143
12–14	130
12:10	110
12:12	143
12:29–30	143
12:46	34, 35, 110
13:21–22	160
13:21	75, 102, 205
14:24	205
15:13	130
16–17	82
16:7	98
16:10	98
19:6	130
19:16	152
20:8–11	82
20:18	152
24:8	58
24:10	65
24:11	65
24:12	31, 112
28	112
28:36	112
29:33	40
31:18	31, 112
33:12	46
33:18—34:7	98
34:1	31, 112
34:4	31, 112
40:34–38	160
40:34–35	98, 103
40:38	205

265

Index of Ancient Sources

Leviticus

4:3	57
4:14	57
4:32–33	57
5:21	64
12:6–8	57
16:2	160
16:3	57
16:5–6	57
18:20	64
26:12	28

Numbers

3:21	143
6:11	57
6:14	57
9:12	34, 35, 110
9:15	103
12:8	65, 91
14:22	98
16:26	99
21:9	38, 47, 146
25:1–9	141
25:8	41, 56
31:16	141

Deuteronomy

1:22	47
4:13	31, 112
4:37	130
5:12–15	82
8:3	94
10:17	153
13:1–12	57
13:1–5	150
21:23	85
28:49	205
29:2–4	195
32:47	94
33:26	160

Joshua

1:15	40
2:10	47
9:14	65

Judges

6:31	40
9:54	41, 56, 63
20–21	69
20:45–47	5, 69
21:2	69
21:22	47

Ruth

2:11	47
2:18	44
3:4	44

1 Samuel

2:8	138
10:8	44
12:7	47
15:16	44
16:3	7, 44
16:7	38
17:47	138
21:3	47
21:9	47
25:1	57
28:8	7, 44
31:3	62
31:4	41, 56, 63

2 Samuel

1:12	57
5:14	143
7	160
7:5	149
7:6	103
7:13–14	90
7:13	160
7:14	62
10:1	154
11:26	57
14:17–20	75
16:17	47
19:38	44
22:12	103, 160
22:28	31, 112

Index of Ancient Sources

1 Kings

4:9	56
4:25	31, 76
8:10–11	160
8:15	47
8:41	205
11:34	40
13:30	57
16:31–32	141
21:25–26	141

2 Kings

3:14	38, 47
9:22	141
23:29	123
24:20–22	6
25:25–26	73
25:25	5, 71

2 Chronicles

24:20–22	6
35:22–25	5

Ezra

2:36	30
2:60	30
8:29–30	30

Nehemiah

9:15	82

Job

3:22	39
5:26	39
15:22	39
21:11	60
29:19	39

Psalms

2	76, 115, 191
2:1–9	62
2:1–4	140
2:1–2	191
2:1	191
2:7	52, 64, 90
8	160
8:2	160
8:4–5	160
8:4	160
8:5	160
11:6	28, 99
17:10 LXX	160
18:9	160
18:40	61
21:17 LXX	62
22	10, 62
22:1–2	62
22:16	61, 62, 89
22:17	62, 63
22:18	35, 88, 89
22:28	138
27:1	102
27:2	71
28:2	30, 37
28:6	37
31:22	30, 37
31:23 LXX	30, 37
34:5	38, 47
34:20	34, 35, 110
35:19	34, 88, 101
36:9	102
41:9	35, 88, 101
45:6	52, 62
68:18	105
69	101
69:4	34, 35, 88, 101
69:6–8	62
69:9	88
69:10 LXX	101
69:21	35
69:22 LXX	101
71:17	142
72	76
72:8–11	62
72:15	62
72:17–19	62
72:17	137
75:8	28
78:8	47
86:6	30, 37

267

Psalms (continued)

88:28 LXX	123, 124
89	129
89:15	102
89:18	138
89:27	123, 129
89:44	31
95:7–11	82
95:13 LXX	157
96:2	160
97:2 LXX	160
104:2	102
107:25–32	82, 104
110	154, 161
110:1–7	62
110:1	31, 154, 159–61
110:5	31, 154
114:4	60
114:6	60
116:1	30, 37
118:10–27	62
118:22	112
119:6	38
119:25	94
119:107	94
130:1–4	30, 58
130:2	37
132:17	31, 64, 154
140:6	30, 37
143:1–2	30
143:1	37, 58
148:14	205

Ecclesiastes

3:4	60

Isaiah

1–39	136
1:24	149
2:2–4	31
2:2	62, 99
2:11	26, 62, 99
2:17	26, 62, 99
4:2	31, 154
5:16	62, 99
5:26	205
6	103, 127
6:1	65, 104, 108
6:3	104, 128
6:5	91
6:10	34, 103, 104, 198
7:14	34
8:18	30
8:23	136
9:6–7	76
9:6	52, 62, 90
10:17	102
10:33–34	154
11:1	31, 76, 154
12:4	62, 99
13:9–11	137
13:10–13	153
13:15	41, 56, 63
13:21	60
19:1	160
22:11	38
22:19	7, 53
22:22	129
24–27	124
25:6–8	31, 82
25:7	82
26:18	112
26:19	129
28:16	34
30:18	62, 99
32:15	27
35:4	157
35:5–6	82
37:21–22	7, 53
40–55	62
40	102
40:1–5	98
40:3	103
40:5	103, 138
40:9	103
40:10–11	103
40:10	135, 157, 163
40:11	104
41:4	135, 151
41:22	44
41:22–24	135
42:7	198
42:9	135
42:18–20	198

Index of Ancient Sources

42:25	29	66:14	47
43:9	135	66:15	135, 157
43:10	95	66:18–24	155
44:3	27	66:18	138
44:6–28	151		
44:6	135		
44:7–9	135	## Jeremiah	
44:18–19	135	2:2	149
45	223	3:16–18	31
45:14	22	5:15	205
45:21	135	6:11	29
45:23	105	7:20	205
45:24	7, 53	7:23	28
46:4	95	8:23	62
46:9	95	10:25	29
46:10	151	14:12	141
47:5–11	205	16:4	57
48:3	135	16:17	31, 112
48:6–8	135	21:6	205
48:11–16	135, 151	23	31
48:12	135	23:1–6	88
49:3	103	23:3	213
49:5	103	23:5–6	52, 62, 75
50:6	103	23:5	31, 73, 76, 154
51:1	38, 47	24:6	31, 112
51:2	38, 47	24:7	28
51:6	38, 47	25:15	28, 99
51:16	28	26:19	70
51:17	28, 99	26:20–23	73
52:8	138	26:20	6, 71
52:10	138	30:22	28
52:13	62, 63, 99, 103, 108	31:9	58
53	9, 10, 35, 74	31:10–14	82
53:1	88, 89, 103, 104	31:10–12	31
53:2–12	103	31:18–21	58
53:5–12	62	31:27	205
53:5	35, 52, 61, 62, 89	31:33	28
53:11	63	31:34	31, 58, 112
55:1	207	32:38	28
55:4–5	207	32:43	205
56:3–8	213	33:6–16	205
57:19	205	33:15	31, 76, 154
59:20–21	224	33:16	52
60:14	22	36:39	205
60:20	102	37:10	41, 56
61:1	27	38:6–7	46
62:11	164	38:8	45
66:2	38	38:9	7, 45, 46, 50

Jeremiah (continued)

41:1–18	73
41:1–2	5
41:1	71
41:2	71
41:12	40
49:12	28, 99
51:4	41, 56, 62, 65
51:7	28, 99

Lamentations

3:1	7, 53
4:9	41, 56, 62

Ezekiel

1	127
1:1—2:10	127
1:4	112, 160
1:7	112
1:15–29	151
1:16	112
1:24	151
1:26–28	125
1:26	159
1:28	95
2:4	149
3:18	99
5:5–7	141
7:8	29
10:5	151
11:19	27
14:12–23	141
14:13	205
17:16	40
18:18	99
18:24	99
18:26	99
20:11	40
20:21	40
20:23	142
22:31	29
23:22	7, 44
25:13	205
26:26–28	27
28:23	62
29:8	205
30:4	62
32:28	62
34	31, 88
34:11–16	52, 62
34:13	104, 213
34:23–24	52, 62
34:23	73, 76
35:8	62
36	44
36:11	205
36:25–27	27, 102
36:25–26	57
36:26–28	112
36:23	65
36:24	213
36:26	58
36:27	44
36:28	28
36:33	57
37–48	124
37:1–10	129
37:3–14	94
37:4	104
37:23	28
37:24–28	52, 73
37:24–25	62
37:24	76
39:21	98
39:29	27
40–48	31
43:1–12	153
43:2	151
43:19–20	57
43:22	57
47:1–12	103, 153

Daniel

2	126
2:22	102
2:28–45	131
2:28–29	126, 137, 144, 177
2:34–45	28
2:44–45	28
2:45	137
2:46	95
3:20	61
3:22	61

Index of Ancient Sources

3:26	161
3:28	161
3:32	161
4:14	161
4:37 LXX	153, 163
5:18	161
6:17	161
6:21	161
7	126, 127, 134, 152, 158, 160
7:1–14	161
7:9	151, 160, 161
7:10	160
7:11–12	133, 158
7:12	126
7:13–14	35, 124, 133, 136, 160
7:13	19, 88, 123, 124, 127, 131–34, 136–37, 147, 148, 152, 158–62, 165
7:14	158, 160, 161
7:15–27	159, 161
7:15–21	158
7:18	161
7:19–27	132, 134
7:22	133, 158, 161, 162
7:25	161
7:26	158, 160
7:27	133, 161
8:16	161
9	126
9:3	37
9:17	37
9:18	37
9:21	161
9:24	159
9:26	159
10–12	126
10:1—12:4	127
10:5–6	152
10:6	152
10:9–17	152
10:9	152
10:10	152
10:15	152
11:27	137
11:29	137
11:35	137
11:40	137
12:2	88, 129, 174

Hosea

2:18	26
2:23	26
5:10	29
6:3 LXX	157
11:1	21–22, 69, 89
11:3	61
13:14	82, 145

Joel

2:5	60
2:28–32	27, 118
2:28	29
2:29	29
2:30–31	118, 153
2:31	137
3:1–2	27
3:15–16	153

Amos

1:6	149
1:9	149
1:11	149
1:13	149
9:11–14	31, 82
9:11	26

Obadiah

1	149

Jonah

2:5	38, 47

Micah

2:3	149
3:5	149
4:1–4	31
5:2	52

Habakkuk

1:13	38, 47
2:3–4 LXX	135

Habakkuk (continued)

2:3 LXX	157
2:16	28
3:4	102
3:6–11	153

Zephaniah

1:3	205
3:8	29
3:16	26

Haggai

1:1	26
2:7–9	31
2:23	72

Zechariah

1–6	126
1:1–6	26
1:1	18
1:3	111, 149
1:4–5	26
1:4	149
1:7	18
1:14	111, 149
1:15	40, 112, 205
1:16–17	111
1:16	18, 111, 112, 149
1:17	18, 149
2	205
2:1–12	31
2:1–4	112
2:4	205
2:5–9	111
2:5	205
2:8–9	205
2:8	111, 205
2:9	112
2:10–15	111
2:10–12	153
2:10	31, 164, 205, 206
2:12–13	112
2:12	18
2:14–16	111
2:14	163
2:15–16	112
2:15	26, 205
2:16	112
2:17	160
3:1–9	112
3:6–9	30
3:7	18
3:8–9	154
3:8	30, 31, 72, 76
3:9	31, 58, 112
3:10	26, 31, 76, 112
4:6–10	72
4:6–7	27, 112
4:7	29, 111
4:8	18
4:10	31, 112
4:14	162
5:5–11	112
5:10–11	30
5:14	30
6:1–8	112, 205
6:9	18
6:9–14	31
6:12–15	111
6:12	18, 30, 72
6:13–14	31
6:13	31, 75, 112, 154
6:15	18
7:1	18
7:4	18
7:7	26
7:8	18
7:9	18
7:13	7, 54
8:1	18
8:2	18
8:3–5	111
8:3	111, 112
8:6–8	111
8:7	32, 54
8:8	112
8:11–13	111
8:12	32, 75, 112
8:13	32, 205
8:15	111
8:18–19	112
8:18	18
8:20–23	111, 206

Index of Ancient Sources

8:22	205	12:1–4	115
9–14	37, 72, 75, 117, 139	12:1	18, 27, 28, 139, 140
9–12	117	12:2—13:1	196
9–11	88	12:2–9	28–30, 115, 163, 171
9:1–17	29	12:2	28, 37, 115
9:1–6	112, 205	12:3	26, 28, 37, 66, 170
9:1	18, 28, 138, 144	12:4	26, 29, 37, 115, 170
9:4–8	28	12:6–7	115
9:7–8	205, 206	12:6	26, 37, 115, 170
9:7	111, 112	12:7–8	75, 115
9:8	28, 111, 112	12:7	76
9:9–13	28	12:8	26, 66, 75, 76, 132, 170
9:9–11	30	12:9	26, 29, 37, 59, 64, 66, 70, 115, 170
9:9–10	7	12:10—13:1	29, 158, 211
9:9	31, 32, 37, 52, 54, 58, 76, 88, 117, 206	12:10–14	29, 30, 35, 122, 131, 132, 136, 137, 143, 145–48, 163, 165, 171, 182, 186, 187
9:10	32, 54, 75, 76	12:10–12	134, 202
9:11	28, 58, 112	12:10–11	53, 141, 185
9:12	111	12:10	1–15, 17–19, 23, 24–30, 32–40, 42–61, 64–70, 73–85, 87–89, 104–14, 117–24, 130–34, 139–43, 145–48, 153, 156–59, 162, 164, 165, 167–73, 179, 182–89, 191–94, 196, 197, 199, 201, 202, 204, 207–12, 214, 216, 218–20, 222–25
9:13–15	112		
9:14–17	28		
9:14–15	28, 32, 54, 75		
9:15	31		
9:16–17	28, 112		
9:16	26, 31, 32, 52, 54, 111		
10:2	31		
10:3–5	112		
10:3	31, 52		
10:7	29, 53, 65	12:11–14	123
10:8–12	28	12:11	26, 30, 69, 115, 123, 143, 170, 189
10:8–10	111		
10:8	31, 52, 104, 213	12:12–14	12, 30, 142, 143, 171, 212
10:9	37, 205	12:12—13:1	193
10:10	213	12:12	143
10:11	28, 54, 65, 112	12:13	143
10:12	28, 29	12:14	143
11:1–3	112	13:1–7	82
11:4–17	31	13:1–6	112
11:4	18	13:1–2	112
11:12–13	54	13:1	26, 27, 29, 30, 57, 58, 62, 72, 73, 113, 114, 145, 170, 171, 189, 201, 212
11:17	28		
12–14	27, 141, 146, 165		
12–13	61, 66, 70, 73, 169	13:2–6	58
12:1—13:1	74, 76, 170	13:2	26, 66
12	37, 115, 132, 139, 146, 191, 192	13:3	41, 49, 50, 51, 56–61, 64
12:1–9	28, 29, 48, 70, 71, 112, 115, 132, 141, 147, 158, 170, 203	13:4	26, 40
12:1–8	6, 72	13:7	9, 29, 30, 32, 49, 52, 61, 63, 74–76, 88, 194

Index of Ancient Sources

Zechariah (continued)

13:9	28, 37, 111
14	164
14:1–21	28, 32, 54, 75
14:1–9	203
14:1–5	28
14:2–5	29, 141, 158
14:2	111
14:3–5	112, 163
14:3	163
14:5	135, 157, 170
14:6–11	163
14:6–9	28, 29, 112
14:6–7	164
14:4	26
14:6	26
14:7	142
14:8–9	153
14:8	26, 103, 164
14:9	26, 28
14:10–11	28
14:10	111
14:11	29, 164
14:12–15	28, 112, 163
13:13	26
14:16	29, 111, 112, 142, 155, 163, 206
14:17–19	163
14:17	142, 143
14:18–19	112
14:20–22	163
14:20–21	111, 112
14:20	26, 28
14:21	26, 28, 82

Malachi

1:1	28
1:14	28
3:1	82
3:3	82
3:7	28
4:1	28
4:12–13	28

APOCRYPHA

Sirach

1:1–4	18

1 Maccabees

9:17	72
16:11–17	6, 72

2 Maccabees

4:34	6, 72

NEW TESTAMENT

Matthew

1:21	34
1:23	34
2:6	52
2:15	21, 69, 90
4:21	93
13:41	137
13:49	137
16:18	115
16:19	129
16:27	137
20:18	160
20:28	160
21:5	58
21:16	160
24	137
24:6	137
24:13	137
24:14	137, 144
24:26–28	183
24:29	118, 137
24:30–31	136, 137, 144, 159, 183
24:30	75, 183–85, 202
24:33	137
24:34	137
25:31–32	174
26:15	75
26:28	58, 75, 112
26:31	52, 75
26:56	194
26:64	159, 160

27:9–10	75	1:9	198
27:55–56	182	1:10–13	195
28:18	160	1:10–11	212
		1:10	97, 200
		1:11	190
		1:12–13	212

Mark

1:14	93	1:12	190
1:15	126, 158, 168	1:13	94, 206
1:20	93	1:14	52, 83, 90, 91, 94, 97, 102, 103, 108, 109, 113, 119, 170, 195, 198, 209, 215
13	137		
13:24–25	118		
13:26	133	1:16	90
14:24	58, 113	1:17	90, 94
14:27	194	1:18	90, 91, 117, 170, 198, 203, 209
14:50	194	1:19—12:50	8
15:40–41	182	1:19—10:42	82
		1:23	80, 102, 103
		1:29	99, 113, 171, 190, 196, 200, 202

Luke

		1:32–34	202
1:31–33	161	1:36	202
1:32–33	90	1:37	202
3:31	143	1:39	97
3:38	89	1:41	90
17:22–37	137	1:45	80
21:25–28	118	1:49	88
21:25	118	1:50–51	96
22:19	113	2:1—12:50	82, 84
22:20	58	2:1–11	82, 96
23:27	182, 193	2:2	194
23:44–45	118	2:4	83, 98, 174
23:47–49	182	2:6	190
24:13–35	68	2:11	96, 97, 194–96, 213
24:44–49	68	2:12–22	82
24:44–47	160	2:13	190
24:44	18	2:17	18, 82, 88, 100, 101
24:49	196	2:18–22	206
		2:19–22	113

John

		2:22	18, 100, 195, 213
		2:23	96
1:1–18	51, 81, 92	3:1–10	68, 102
1:1–4	52	3:1–8	206
1:1–3	97, 170	3:3–10	27
1:1	90, 91, 96, 102, 108, 109	3:2	96
1:3	102	3:3–6	195
1:5	102	3:3	96, 171
1:6	95	3:5	114, 171
1:7–8	102	3:11–13	18
1:9–10	190	3:11–12	94

275

Index of Ancient Sources

John (continued)

Reference	Pages
3:11	128
3:13–14	88
3:14–16	174, 203
3:14–15	146
3:14	99, 215
3:15–16	203
3:15	206
3:16–17	90, 192, 200, 201, 203, 212
3:16	90, 99, 110, 116, 171, 197, 206
3:17	91
3:18	90, 175
3:19	102, 190, 200
3:20	102, 190
3:21	102
3:31	94
3:32–34	18
3:32	94
3:33	94
3:34	93, 94
3:36	94, 98, 116, 175, 201, 203
4:1	194
4:2	102
4:6	97
4:8	194
4:10	103, 114, 116
4:13–14	215
4:14	114, 116, 174, 215
4:19	95
4:21	98, 174, 176
4:22	190
4:23	83, 97, 115, 177
4:27	194
4:34	82
4:35	197
4:38	93, 207
4:42	192, 200, 201
4:46—5:17	82
4:46–54	96
4:50	94
4:52	97
4:53	97
4:54	96, 97
5:1–9	96
5:1	190
5:8–9	94
5:16	188
5:17–19	82
5:17–18	96, 97
5:18	92, 188
5:19–20	93, 94, 96
5:20	82, 96
5:23–24	93
5:23	155, 156, 210
5:24–30	176
5:24	94, 98, 99, 116, 146, 175
5:25–29	118, 173
5:25	94, 97, 104, 171, 174, 175
5:26	91
5:27–29	88, 115, 119
5:27	146
5:28–29	94, 174
5:28	97, 171, 174, 175
5:29	146, 175, 201
5:30	90
5:35	97
5:36–38	93
5:36	82, 96
5:37–46	68, 102
5:37–38	94
5:39	18
5:46	18, 80
5:47	95
6:1–59	82
6:1–15	96
6:14	96, 97, 200
6:16–21	104
6:20	95, 100
6:22	194
6:24	194
6:26	96, 199
6:29	93
6:31	82
6:36	146, 195, 199
6:37	176, 206, 213, 215
6:38–39	93, 176
6:38	176
6:39–40	119
6:39	99, 174, 200, 206, 213
6:40	146, 176, 198, 199, 203, 213–15, 225
6:44	93, 176, 206
6:45	82
6:46	91
6:51–58	99
6:51–56	114

Index of Ancient Sources

6:51	113, 174, 200	8:44	190
6:54	176, 215	8:47	18, 94, 102, 206
6:56	215	8:51	94
6:57	93	8:54	97
6:60	194, 196	8:58	95, 100
6:61	194	9	96
6:63	94	9:1–41	82
6:66	195	9:2	194
6:68–69	195	9:3	82, 96
6:68	94	9:4	93
6:69	195	9:5	102, 200
7:1	189, 190	9:16	97
7:2	190	9:24	129
7:3	194	9:27	194
7:7	190, 200	9:28	194
7:15	95	9:30	91
7:16	93, 94	9:32–33	82
7:18	93, 97	9:37–38	146
7:21	96, 97	9:39–41	146, 195
7:28–29	93	9:39	198
7:29	91	9:41	195, 198
7:30	83, 98, 174	10:10–18	104
7:31	96	10:10	192
7:37	215	10:11–18	52, 88
7:38–39	27, 100, 114, 116, 174, 195	10:11	113
7:38	83, 103, 203	10:15–16	200
7:39	18, 97, 100, 145, 171, 196	10:15	113
7:46	95	10:16–18	206, 212
8:12	102, 190, 198	10:16	113, 115, 197, 200, 201, 203, 206, 213
8:14	128		
8:16	93	10:18	212
8:18	93, 128	10:25–29	88
8:20	83, 98, 174	10:25	82, 96
8:21	99, 190	10:26–27	206
8:23	190	10:28–30	104
8:24	95, 99, 100, 113, 114, 190	10:29	99, 206
8:26	18, 93, 94	10:30	92
8:28	18, 88, 94, 95, 99, 100, 110, 206	10:31	189
8:29	93	10:32–33	82
8:31–32	94	10:32	96
8:31	189, 190, 195, 215	10:33	95
8:32–34	94	10:34	82
8:34	190	10:36	93
8:36	114	10:37–38	82
8:38	18, 94, 190	10:38	95, 96
8:40	94, 189	11:1—12:50	81, 82
8:41	102	11:1–53	82
8:42	93	11:1–44	97

277

John (continued)

Reference	Pages
11:7	194
11:8	194
11:9	97, 102
11:10	102
11:12	194
11:23	176
11:24	174, 176
11:25–26	176
11:27	177
11:31	176
11:40–42	82
11:40	96, 195, 196
11:42	93
11:43–44	104
11:43	94
11:45–46	195
11:45	190
11:47	96
11:50	113
11:51–52	200
11:52	103, 113, 200, 201, 203, 206, 213
12:4	194
12:11	190
12:13–15	88
12:14	82
12:15–16	58
12:15	75, 116, 206
12:16	18, 97, 100, 194, 195
12:18	96, 97
12:23–24	97, 98
12:23	83, 88, 98, 103, 174, 201
12:24–26	207
12:24	197
12:27–28	98
12:27	83, 98, 174, 212
12:28	97, 98, 196, 201
12:29	84
12:31–32	196
12:31	114–16, 171, 190, 201
12:32–33	110
12:32	99, 113, 201, 206, 213
12:33	201, 206
12:34	88
12:35	102
12:36	102
12:37–50	83
12:37–40	89, 111
12:37	103, 190, 199, 213
12:38–41	80, 103, 108, 110, 111
12:38–40	85, 116
12:38–39	86, 185
12:38	84, 88, 89, 95
12:40	34, 195, 198
12:41	103
12:44–45	93, 146
12:45	96, 198
12:46	102, 203
12:47	200
12:49–50	18, 94
12:49	93
13:1—20:31	83, 84
13:1—20:29	81, 82
13:1–3	83
13:1	83, 98, 174
13:5	194
13:18–19	83, 212
13:18	18, 35, 84, 88, 95, 101
13:19	95, 100
13:20	93
13:21	83
13:22	194
13:23	93, 194
13:31–32	97, 98, 196
13:31	88, 103
13:38	83
14–16	27, 83, 193, 196
14:1–3	172
14:2–3	119
14:6–11	94
14:6–7	94
14:9	92, 96, 198, 203
14:10–11	95
14:10	93, 94, 96
14:11	82
14:15–26	116
14:16	196
14:17	195, 196, 200
14:19	200
14:22	200
14:24	93, 94
14:26	18, 100, 101, 145, 195, 196, 202
14:27	200
14:29	83

Index of Ancient Sources

14:30–31	83, 201	17:2	99, 115, 206
14:30	114, 115, 190	17:3	90, 93, 116, 174, 215
15:2	207	17:4–5	97
15:4–5	207	17:4	96
15:4	215	17:5	90, 200
15:6	215	17:6	195
15:8–12	207	17:8	93, 94, 195
15:8	207	17:12	35, 83, 84
15:12–13	83	17:14	195, 210
15:13	113	17:18	93, 207
15:16	197, 207	17:19	113
15:18–27	115	17:20–24	206
15:18–19	210	17:20–21	113
15:18	190, 200	17:20	197, 206, 207
15:19	195, 200	17:21	93
15:20	83, 214	17:22	195, 196
15:21	93	17:24	90, 97, 213
15:23–25	190	17:25	93
15:24	95, 146	17:26	95
15:25	18, 34, 83, 84, 88, 95, 101, 190	18–19	188
		18:1	194
15:26–27	18, 101, 116, 196	18:3	115, 139
15:26	91, 100, 145, 196	18:5–6	95
15:27	101, 206, 207	18:6	100
16:2	98, 174	18:9	83, 95
16:4	18, 97	18:11	99
16:5	93	18:12	181, 188
16:7–15	116	18:14	113, 139, 188
16:7–14	145	18:15–16	93, 194
16:7	100, 196	18:17	194
16:8	190, 200	18:19	194
16:11	99, 114, 190, 191, 201	18:20	190
16:12–14	202	18:22	103
16:13–15	18	18:25	194
16:13	100, 101, 195, 196	18:28–32	115
16:14	101, 195	18:31	139, 188
16:16	83	18:32	83, 95
16:17	194	18:36	188
16:20	83, 146, 190, 193, 194, 200	18:37	94, 128
16:21	97, 174, 200	19–20	180
16:22	83, 146, 193	19	188
16:25	98, 174	19:1–16	115
16:27	91, 213	19:6–7	139
16:28	91, 94	19:7	181, 188
16:32	88, 98, 174, 194	19:11	83
16:33	83, 115, 201	19:12–14	181
17:1–5	83, 213	19:12	188
17:1	83, 98, 174	19:14	97

279

John (continued)

19:16	188, 189
19:20	180–82
19:24	35, 84, 88, 89, 101
19:25	180–82
19:26–27	194
19:26	93, 194
19:27	93, 97, 174, 194
19:28	35, 83, 84, 101
19:29	101
19:31	85, 139, 188
19:32–33	85
19:33	180, 181, 192
19:34	85, 113, 114, 139, 145, 170, 171, 180–82, 188, 214
19:35	16, 85, 101, 106, 107, 119, 146, 180, 181, 186, 193, 194, 196–98, 202, 213
19:36–37	34, 86, 87, 101, 110, 111, 116, 185, 196, 198, 210
19:36	34, 35, 84, 99, 110, 200
19:37	1–4, 8–11, 14, 15, 19, 24, 33, 34, 39, 51, 55, 58, 73, 75, 77, 79, 80, 85–88, 103, 105–7, 115, 116, 119, 120, 122, 131, 139, 142, 146, 148, 162, 164, 167–73, 179–89, 192, 193, 197, 199, 201–3, 208, 210, 212, 215, 216, 218–22, 225
19:38	86, 194
20:2–4	93
20:8	93, 194, 213
20:9	100, 176
20:17	97, 115
20:18	194
20:19	194
20:21–23	207, 213
20:21–22	115
20:21	93, 197, 225
20:22–23	145
20:22	100, 104, 146, 195
20:23	113, 171, 197
20:24–29	146
20:25	194
20:26	194
20:27–28	110, 180
20:28	146, 162, 210
20:29–31	198
20:29	197, 198
20:30–31	16, 83, 96, 102, 168, 197, 217
20:30	97
20:31	85, 89, 92, 97, 102, 171, 177, 180–82, 197, 203, 214, 215
21:1–25	82
21:19	97
21:20	194
21:23	119
21:24	101, 196
21:25	16, 96, 200

Acts

1:4	196
1:6	93
1:8	196
1:9–11	133
1:13	93
1:20	22
2:1–21	27
2:16–37	214
2:16–21	118
2:22	118
2:23	189, 212, 214
2:33	196
2:36	162, 189
2:41	214
2:43	118
3:15	189
4:10	189
4:19–21	191
4:19	115
4:21	115
4:23–30	140
4:23	115, 191
4:25–28	115
4:27–28	212
4:27	191
5:30	189
6:7	214
7:56	160
8:23–39	214
13:33	90
13:48	214
16:14	214
20:28	130
24:15	174

Index of Ancient Sources

Romans

1:5	144
1:7	124
3:25	130
5:6	113
5:8	113
5:9	130
8:32	113
9:5	209
10:9	162
10:11	34
10:14	225
11	143
11:26–27	224
11:26	224
11:36	147
14:15	113
15:8–9	115
15:11	105
16:20	124
16:27	144, 147

1 Corinthians

1:3	124
1:13	113
2:8	142
8:5–6	162
10:16	130
11:24	113
11:25	58
15:3–4	217
15:3	113, 210, 225
15:20	129
15:52	174
15:55	145
16:22	162
16:23	124

2 Corinthians

3:18	216
4:4	216
4:5	216
4:6	216
5:14	113

Galatians

1:5	147
2:9	93
2:20	113
3:13	113
3:16	69
4:26	115

Ephesians

1:7	130
2:11–13	205
2:19–22	205
4:8	105, 106
5:25	113
6:10–18	115

Philippians

2:5–11	209
2:9–11	162
2:10–11	208, 223

Colossians

1:6	207
1:15–19	91
1:16–17	201
1:18	129
2:14–15	142

1 Thessalonians

4:14–17	138, 144
4:16–17	183, 208
5:10	113

2 Thessalonians

1:7–10	138, 140, 144

1 Timothy

1:17	147
2:6	113
6:16	102, 147, 156

Titus

2:13	209
2:14	113

Hebrews

1:2–3	91
1:5	90
1:8–9	209
2:6–9	160
2:9	113
3:7—4:10	82
5:5	90
6:20	113
8:7–13	112
9:18	58
9:20	58
10:37	135, 157
12:19	152
12:22	115
12:24	58
13:20	52

James

1:13	212

1 Peter

2:5–9	130
2:5	130
2:6	34
2:9	130
2:21	113
3:15	162
3:18	113
4:11	156
5:4	52
5:11	156

2 Peter

1:1	209
1:16	163
3:12	163

1 John

1:1–4	198
1:1–3	16, 197, 198
1:9	171, 202
2:2	200, 202
2:15–16	200
2:18–19	200
2:20	116
2:23	156
2:27	200
3:1	200
3:2	216
3:6	198–200, 212, 214, 215
3:8	89, 114, 201
3:12	190
3:13	200
3:16	99, 113
3:24	196, 200
4:1–6	196
4:1	200
4:2	200
4:3	200
4:6	18
4:9–10	99
4:9	91
4:10	116, 212
4:13–14	196
4:17	146
5:4–5	115, 200, 201
5:6	196
5:18	115, 201
5:19	190, 199, 200
5:20	196, 209

3 John

7	225
11	198, 199, 200

Jude

25	147, 156

Revelation

1:1–20	124, 125
1:1–8	125
1:1–3	125, 127, 131, 177

Index of Ancient Sources

1:1–2	125, 149	2:13	128, 207, 210
1:1	18, 124, 149, 177	2:14	141
1:2	16, 125, 131, 144, 149	2:16	133, 141, 144, 146, 150, 178
1:3	124–26, 131, 147, 157, 168, 177, 207	2:17	150
1:4—22:21	128	2:18	124, 149, 150
1:4–8	125, 127, 157	2:19	207
1:4–5	157	2:20	141
1:4	13, 14, 127, 128, 130, 131, 135, 144, 157, 158, 162, 216	2:21	141, 146, 178
		2:22–23	150
1:5–7	161, 213	2:22	144
1:5–6	124, 127, 130, 131, 147, 154, 155, 157, 207, 214, 215	2:23	178
		2:26–27	115, 150
1:5	123, 124, 127, 129, 130, 132	2:28	150
1:6	124, 129–31, 150, 155, 225	3:1	124, 149
1:7–8	127, 162	3:3	144, 146, 150, 178
1:7	1–4, 8, 12–15, 19, 24, 33, 35, 55, 73, 77, 80, 107, 115, 119–25, 127, 130–32, 134–36, 138–44, 146–48, 157, 160, 162, 164, 165, 167–69, 172, 173, 179, 180, 182–89, 191–93, 199, 201–4, 208, 210, 212, 216–18, 220–22, 224	3:5	150
		3:7	124, 129, 149
		3:9	22, 191
		3:11	133
		3:12	150
		3:14	124, 149
		3:16	150
		3:18	150, 199
		3:19	144, 146, 178
		3:21	150, 153
1:8	131, 135, 144, 151, 157, 158, 162	4–5	156
1:9–20	125, 127, 128, 150, 151	4	156
1:9–11	131	4:1	125, 152
1:9–10	125	4:2	18
1:9	127, 130, 149, 207, 214	4:8	128, 135, 162
1:10	18, 152	4:9	154
1:11	124, 127, 216	4:11	154, 162, 210
1:12–19	125	5	156
1:13	124, 127, 134, 160, 161	5:2	152
1:14	151, 152	5:5–6	129
1:15	152	5:5	155
1:17–18	152	5:6–10	127
1:17	151, 152	5:6	129
1:18	127, 129, 131, 132, 161	5:9–14	155, 210
1:19	125, 127, 131, 152	5:9–10	130, 155, 207, 213, 215, 225
1:20	127	5:9	130, 143, 155, 201, 225
2–3	149, 150	5:10	130
2:1	124, 127, 149	5:11	153
2:5	144, 146, 150, 178	5:12–13	156
2:7	150	5:12	154, 155, 225
2:8	124, 149, 150	5:13–14	154
2:9	191	5:13	153, 155
2:10–11	150	6:1	152
2:12	124, 149		

Revelation *(continued)*

6:8	141
6:9–11	207
6:9	149
6:12–17	137, 153, 171, 193
6:12–16	201
6:12	118
6:15–17	129
6:16–17	144, 146
6:17	208
7:2	152
7:9–12	210
7:9	201
7:10–12	156
7:12	154
7:15	102
7:17	52, 154
9:20–21	141, 144, 146, 210
9:20	212
10:1	160
11–20	140
11	126
11:2	207
11:3–7	207, 208, 213
11:3	207, 225
11:4	162
11:7–10	140, 214
11:7	149
11:8	191
11:9	143, 201
11:10	191
11:11–12	208
11:13	154, 208
11:15–18	135
11:15	162
11:17	162, 163
12	208
12:1–17	201
12:5	115
12:6	207
12:7–12	215
12:7	140
12:9	191
12:10–11	129
12:11	130, 149, 207
12:12	102
12:14	207
12:17	149, 207
13	126
13:4	210
13:5	207
13:6	102
13:7	143, 201
13:8	210
14:1–3	156
14:4	144
14:6	143
14:7	146, 155
14:10	146
14:10–11	204
14:11	210
14:14–20	183
14:14–16	144
14:14	134, 160
14:17–20	144
15	144
15:2–4	144, 201
15:3	162
15:4	154, 162
15:8	154
16:2	141
16:6	140
16:7	162
16:9–11	141
16:9	144, 146, 155, 212
16:11	146
16:15	134
16:16	141
17	140
17:3	18
17:12–14	129
18:1	155
18:7	155
18:8	162
19–20	126, 133, 134, 203
19:1–3	144, 201
19:1	154
19:6–8	144, 201
19:6	162
19:7	154
19:10	155
19:11–21	171, 193
19:11–16	138, 164
19:14	144
19:15–21	144
19:15–19	115

19:15	146, 178
19:16–18	129
19:16	163
19:17—20:3	164
19:19–21	153
19:19–20	210
19:21	178
20:4–6	129
20:4–5	174
20:4	149, 153, 207
20:6	130
20:10	204
20:11–15	174
21:1—22:5	164
21:3	213
21:6	135, 151
21:10	18
21:11	154
21:22–26	210
21:22	162
21:23–25	164
21:23	102, 154
21:24	154, 155
21:26	154, 155
22:1	153, 164, 213
22:2	213
22:3	154, 156, 164
22:5	162
22:6–21	125
22:6	16, 18, 162
22:7	133, 134, 217
22:8–9	18
22:8	16, 155
22:9	155
22:10	18
22:11	144
22:12	133, 134, 163, 178, 217
22:13	135, 151
22:14	213
22:16	149, 163, 216
22:17	178, 207
22:18–19	18
22:20	133, 134, 162, 178, 217
22:21	124, 128, 154

DEAD SEA SCROLLS

4QXIIe	24, 61, 64
5/6HevPsalms	63, 89

RABBINIC WRITINGS

Targum Jonathan

Zechariah

12:10	39–42

Targum Tosefta

Zechariah

12:10	42, 49, 50, 74

Talmud

b. Sukkah

52a	76, 186

GRECO-ROMAN WRITINGS

Josephus

Ag. Ap.

1:38–42	18

Ant.

11.7.1	71, 73

EARLY CHRISTIAN WRITINGS

Irenaeus

Haer.

5.30.3	133

Justin Martyr

1 Apol.

52.11–12	3, 74, 134

Index of Ancient Sources

Dial.

14.8   134

32.2   3, 74, 134, 172
81.4   134

www.ingramcontent.com/pod-product-compliance
Lightning Source LLC
Chambersburg PA
CBHW071235230426
43668CB00011B/1450